teach yourself...
Excel 5.0

for the Macintosh

by John Weingarten

MIS:
PRESS

A Subsidiary of
Henry Holt and Co., Inc.

Copyright © 1994   MIS:Press
a subsidiary of Henry Holt and Company, Inc.
115 West 18 Street
New York, NY 10011

ISBN 1-55828-370-6

Printed in the United States of America.

10 9 8 7 6 5 4 3 2 1

Library of Congress Cataloging-in-Publication Data

Weingarten, John
     Teach yourself-- Excel 5.0 for the Macintosh / John Weingarten.
          p. cm.
     Includes index.
     ISBN 1-55828-370-6 : $21.95
          1. Microsoft Excel (Computer file) 2. Business--Computer programs.
     3. Electronic spreadsheets I. Title
     HF 5548.4.M523W45   1994   94-18591
     650'.0285'5369--dc20   CIP

MIS:Press books are available at special discounts for bulk purchases for sales promotions, premiums, fund raising, or educational use. Special editions or book excerpts can also be created to specification.

For details contact: Special Sales Director
MIS:Press
a subsidiary of Henry Holt and Company, Inc.
115 West 18 Street
New York, NY 10011

Acknowledgments

This book was a team effort and I want to thank everyone who helped make it possible. If I've left anyone out of the following list, please know that you are appreciated

Matt Wagner, of Waterside Productions, is more than just a great agent. I can't thank him enough for his encouragement and guidance.

Ron Varela, who spent countless hours pouring over the manuscript to make sure I didn't say anything too stupid, helped with many suggestions and endless encouragement. He's a great guy and I'm honored that he is my friend.

Judy Brief, of MIS:Press, shepherded this project from beginning to end. Her wonderful sense of humor made working with her a joy. Her hard work and genuine concern for the quality of the product have been inspiring.

Janey Brand of Solstice Communications, Inc., and Cari Geffner of MIS:Press did great jobs making this book look as good as it does, and for doing so in so short a time.

John Wiemann helped to ensure the technical accuracy of this book. His help and suggestions were greatly appreciated.

Gwynne Jackson, copyeditor, helped to ensure the consistency and coherence throughout the book, a particularly difficult feat amidst the hundreds of numbered lists.

Steve Berkowitz, of MIS:Press, had the immense wisdom and good taste to have me write this book. But seriously, as the publisher, he provided the leadership necessary to ensure that this book is consistent with all the other top-notch MIS books.

Thanks also go to my Mom, Cyrille, and her Mac-loving friends. They know who they are.

Finally, my wife Pam, and children, Sarah and Joshua, provided love and encouragement. For their support and patience, they deserve the most thanks of all.

Contents

v

Introduction

This book is for people who want to learn the essentials of Excel 5.0 quickly. You won't find detailed discussions of arcane and seldom-used features here. What you will find are step-by-step procedures for putting Excel to work for you.

The examples in the book are based on real world situations and should provide you with enough practical insight to tailor the procedures to your own requirements. Tasks and concepts are presented in a logical order, progressing from simple navigation and data entry to more complex tasks, such as charting, database manipulation, and linking multiple worksheets. Don't be intimidated if some of these terms seem foreign to you. They are all clearly defined and explained in the appropriate part of the book.

I hope you'll find the writing style clear, concise and friendly, with even a bit of humor thrown in. You shouldn't have to be bored to tears to learn the basics of Excel. It should be fun!

Who Should Read This Book

No previous knowledge of spreadsheets is required. If you've never even seen a spreadsheet before, you'll easily be able to follow the procedures. You'll be amazed at how quickly you become comfortable working with Excel.

If you've worked with a previous version of Excel or another spreadsheet program without mastering its ins and outs, this book will help you learn version 5.0 while providing a refresher on general spreadsheet basics.

The Highlights of Version 5.0

This version of Excel offers many powerful new features, as well as refinements to make working with the program easier and more intuitive. Following are some of the more interesting new features which are covered in this book.

Improved Help Facilities

The help Excel provides is more extensive and helpful than in previous versions. Help has even acquired some intelligence. With the new TipWizard feature, Excel can tell you a better way to do what you just did.

More and Better Wizards

Excel 4.0 introduced Wizards for stepping you through the completion of several tasks. Version 5.0 enhances the Wizards' capabilities and now includes Wizards for applying functions, applying formats to charts, and creating PivotTables.

In-Cell Editing

Editing the contents of a cell has become easier now that you can edit in the cell itself, instead of having to use the formula bar.

Enhanced List Management

Working with lists and databases is easier now that you can work in an automatically-created form dialog box. The form dialog box even lets you find, edit, and delete records in the database. The new AutoFilter feature makes it a snap to display just the records you want.

PivotTables

The new PivotTable feature, with its own Wizard for creating them, replaces the Crosstab feature in version 4.0. PivotTables make analyzing and summarizing list data easier than ever.

Conventions Used in This Book

Keyboard combinations are separated by commas and/or plus signs (+). A combination separated by commas means press and release the first key and then press and release the second key. A combination separated by a plus sign means press and hold down the first key, then press the second key, and then release both keys. For example, if you are instructed to press **Ctrl+X**, press and hold down the **Ctrl** key and then, while still pressing the Ctrl key, tap the **X** key. **Ctrl+X**, **Y** means press and hold the **Ctrl** key while pressing the **X** key, then release them and then tap the **Y** key.

The first time an important term is used in the book, it appears in italics. The term is defined and explained in the chapter and in the glossary at the end of the book.

A Final Thought

If you take the time to work through all the chapters in this book, you'll be rewarded with a new skill that allows you to perform many of your business and personal tasks in much less time than you currently spend. You'll have more time for the things you really enjoy. And don't let this book be the last of your Excel explorations. Excel is a rich program with vast capabilities. You'll have plenty to explore when you finish. Enjoy the journey.

John Weingarten
Spokane, Washington

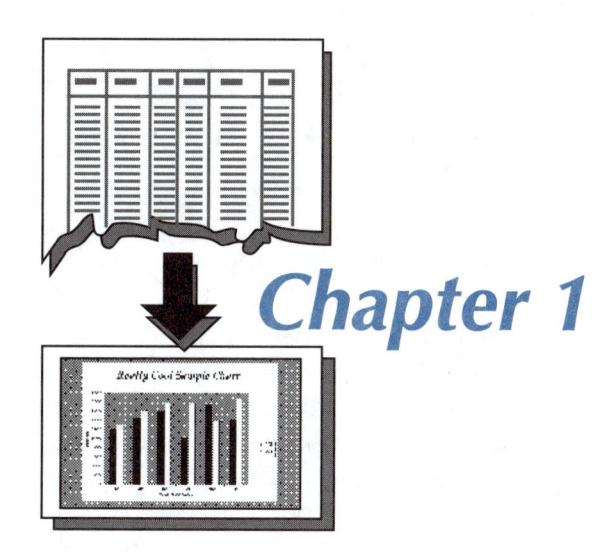

Chapter 1

Excel—The Big Picture (A Little Perspective)

- Spreadsheets—How the Computer Revolution Started
- What Spreadsheets Are (And Aren't) Good For
- What Sets Excel Apart From the Competition
- What's New In Excel 5
- A Final Thought

Spreadsheets—How the Computer Revolution Started

The spreadsheet is a formidable computer tool that lets you record the past, analyze the present, and predict the future. Spreadsheets allow for easy preparation of accounting records and financial statements, as well as budgets and forecasts.

Because of their ability to use mathematical formulas and functions to calculate results when numbers are changed, spreadsheets are marvelous facilities for playing *what if*. In a business, you might want to know the answer to "what if our supplies costs increase by 10% next year?" or "what if we increased our selling price by three percent?"

Before the development of the first spreadsheet program about 15 years ago, few people thought of computers as *personal*. Large corporations used huge mainframe computers, often costing millions of dollars, for very specific accounting applications such as accounts receivable and inventory control. The only contact most corporate workers had with these computers was by way of printed reports or, perhaps, entering data through terminals.

When the first spreadsheet program, *Visicalc*, appeared on the scene shortly after the introduction of the first Apple personal computers, small and medium-sized businesses quickly realized that they now had the ability to have greater control over their business. They could do budgeting and forecasting on their own desktop computers.

Computers and software have come a long way since those early Visicalc days. Other categories of software, such as word processing, database, and desktop publishing programs now share spots on the software best seller lists along with spreadsheets. But spreadsheets remain one of the primary reasons for the tremendous proliferation of personal computers.

What Spreadsheets Are (And Aren't) Good For

Almost any task that requires numeric calculations is a good candidate for spreadsheet consideration. Budgeting and forecasting are the tasks that come to mind first when thinking about what spreadsheets are good for, but virtually anything requiring the storage and manipulation of data can be done with a spreadsheet. This doesn't mean that spreadsheets are the *best* tools for any of these tasks.

It has become increasingly difficult in recent years to choose the most appropriate software category for a particular task. Many word processing programs offer spreadsheet-like features, and database programs include the ability to work with data in rows and columns, which makes them look like spreadsheets.

If the work you need to perform is heavily text-oriented, where reporting on certain aspects of the document's contents isn't required, a word processing program is likely your best bet.

If you need to share your information with many other people but don't want two people updating the same data at the same time, *and* you want to be able to restrict the types of data being entered (as in an inventory control system), then a database program would make more sense.

As we explore Excel, you'll see that you can accomplish most word processing and database tasks with this powerful spreadsheet program, but the fact that you *can* do it doesn't mean you *should* do it.

What Sets Excel Apart From the Competition

Excel 5 includes virtually every feature and refinement you could imagine a spreadsheet containing. You'll find a wide variety of powerful functions for almost any type of business, financial, or scientific calculation. Charting and database facilities, as well as proofing tools such as spell checking and spreadsheet analysis, round out Excel's impressive capabilities.

However, none of these features truly sets Excel apart from the competition. There are several other products that include practically the same feature set. So what *does* set Excel apart? Ease of use and integration.

Excel 5 introduces a number of features that make the program easier to use, and to troubleshoot when you run into problems.

Shortcut Menus

Holding down the **Ctrl** key while pressing the mouse button on almost any object on the Excel screen displays a shortcut menu of options for manipulating that object. This can be a tremendous time saver. Rather than a variety of menus to find the appropriate options, they are right there in one place.

Wizards

Wizards present you with a series of dialog boxes to aid you in performing a variety of tasks. Wizards can step you through the creation of charts, pivot tables, and functions. With Wizards, you can create sophisticated documents, even if you don't know how to use most of the features involved in their creation. For example, the Function Wizard really cuts function creation down to size.

Using functions, especially the more complex ones, has always been one of the more confusing spreadsheet tasks. The Function Wizard guides you through the process of filling in the required information for the function you are using. This is one of Excel's greatest contributions to spreadsheet usability.

The TipWizard

Excel has added a piece of help wizardry that may make you think the program is smarter than you are. The TipWizard watches as you perform your work and suggests a better way to do what you just did.

Workbooks

All sheets, whether worksheets, chart sheets, or macro sheets, are stored in workbooks. When you save your work, all the sheets in the active workbook are saved. This makes organizing related sheets easier and more logical. You can even name the individual sheets and have their names appear on Sheet Tabs at the bottom of the workbook window.

In-Cell Editing

You don't have to edit a cell's contents on the formula bar anymore. By double clicking on a cell (or pressing **⌘+U**), you can edit the cell's contents right in the cell. This can really make editing more efficient.

Drag and Plot

Adding a new data series to a chart used to require some thought and several mouse actions or keystrokes. To add a new data series in Excel 5, just drag it onto the chart. It's that simple.

Improved List Management

The data management capabilities (including easy creation of lists and almost automatic sorting) let you do more with your normal worksheet data, and may prove powerful enough to save you the dollar and time investment of a stand-alone database program. Working with database lists in Excel is vastly improved in this version. The AutoFilter feature lets you display records in your list that meet certain criteria by clicking on drop-down arrows on each column in the list.

Sorting the list is easier now that Excel automatically recognizes the parts of the list to sort. There's even a feature to subtotal groups within the list.

Don't worry if some of these concepts seem a bit foreign to you now. As we progress through the book, you'll learn to use these and many other new features. Also, if you are familiar with the previous version of Excel, you'll find you can do almost everything just as you did it before. However, I promise it will be worth your time to learn to use the new features and shortcuts.

An additional issue for those seeking ease of use is the ability to switch easily to other types of computers without having to spend a great deal of time learning a new program. Excel is practically identical on both Macintosh and IBM-compatible computers. If your business uses both types of machines, you'll be able to use Excel on either without giving a thought to which machine you're using.

Integration is how smoothly Excel works with other Windows applications, especially other Microsoft applications. Microsoft, the company that makes Excel, has gone to great lengths to make Excel work like its other Windows programs. An example of this is the similarity of menu structure between Excel and Microsoft's word processing program called Word. In addition, Excel is one of the first applications to support the new standard for sharing data with other Windows programs, OLE 2.0. OLE will be discussed later.

A Final Thought

This chapter sets the stage for a better understanding of Excel's place in the computing world. While you can certainly use Excel productively without this information, this background should help to shed some light on the big picture.

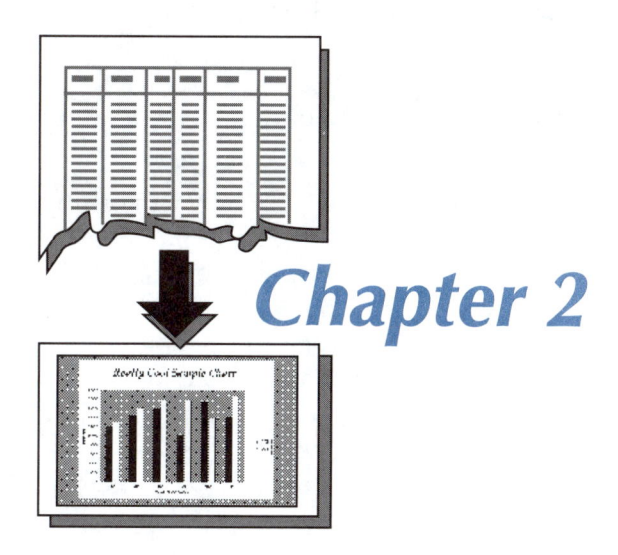

Chapter 2

Getting Started—Excel Basics

- Using the Mouse and the Keyboard
- Starting Excel
- Touring the Excel Screen
- Using Menus and Dialog Boxes
- Using Toolbars
- Navigating the Worksheet
- Using Excel's Help Facility
- Exiting Excel
- A Final Thought

Telling Your Mac What To Do

You communicate with your Macintosh by using either the keyboard, the mouse, or both. In this book, the mouse method is emphasized, but that doesn't mean it is always the most efficient way to carry out an operation. Where there is a keyboard method that is clearly a shortcut, I'll point it out. However, most people who are new to Macintosh computers find the mouse action more intuitive and easier to remember.

The mouse pointer, or *cursor*, on the screen moves as you move the mouse across the surface of your desk. In addition to moving the mouse to reposition the pointer, there are several basic mouse operations you need to master: *dragging*, *clicking*, and *double-clicking*.

Dragging means moving the mouse while holding down the mouse button. Clicking is pressing and releasing the mouse button. Double-clicking means clicking the mouse button twice in rapid succession.

N O T E   I'm assuming you're using System 7 or 7.1. If you're using System 6, most of the operations are exactly the same. I'll point out the few differences when we get to them.

Starting Excel

The big moment has arrived. It's time to start Excel and get this show on the road. To start a program, you can click on its program icon, then pull down the File menu and select **Open**, or you can simply double-click on the program icon. Double-clicking is always faster than using the menu access method.

1. Double-click on the folder that contains the Excel program (usually called Microsoft Excel).
2. Double-click on the **Microsoft Excel** icon.

After a few seconds, the main Excel screen will appear on your screen, as depicted in Figure 2.1.

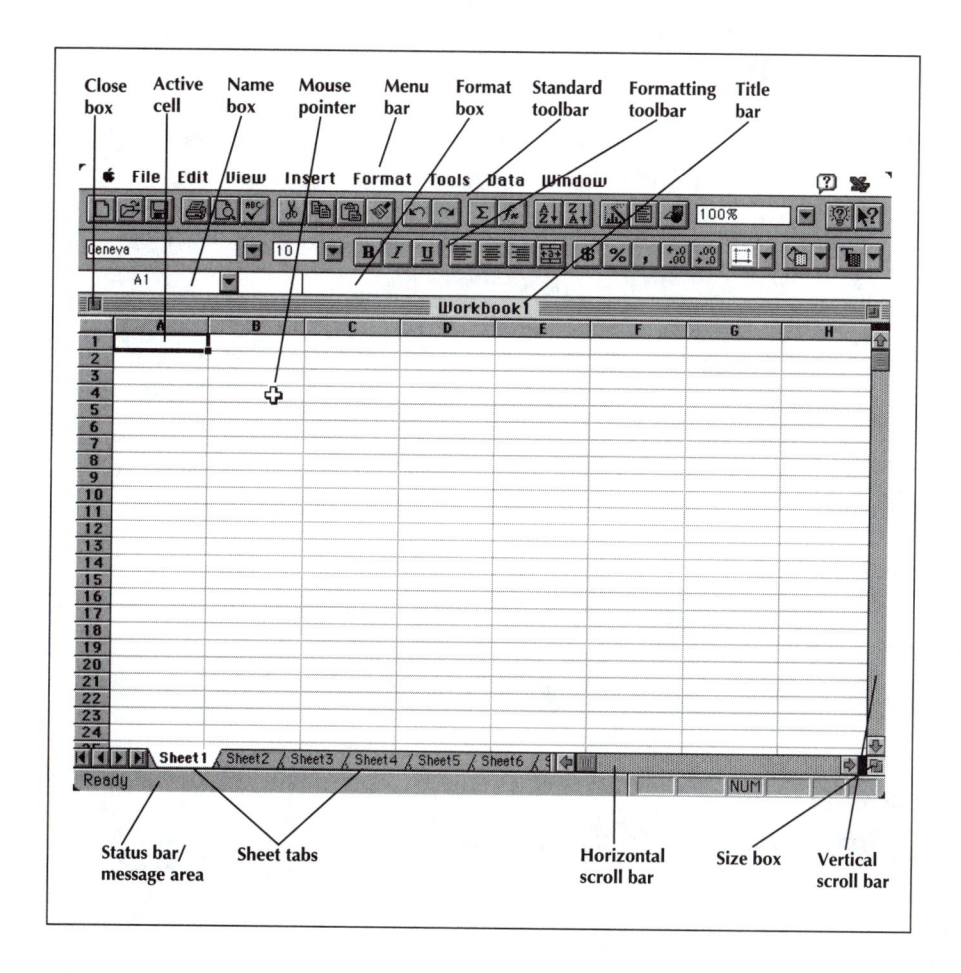

Figure 2.1 *The opening Excel screen.*

Because you may have a different type of display monitor or your monitor may be set up differently than mine, the number of rows and columns that appear on your screen may differ from what you see in Figure 2.1.

A Quick Tour Of the Excel Screen

If you're familiar with other Macintosh applications, many of the elements in the opening Excel screen should seem familiar to you. The title bar, menu bar, close box, zoom box, size box, and scroll bars all work the same way as they do in other Mac programs. There are also a few new screen elements that we'll be discussing shortly.

The worksheet consists of lettered columns and numbered rows. The intersection of a column and a row is called a *cell* and its name is the column letter followed by the row number. The *active cell* is surrounded by a border, and its name is displayed in the cell reference area.

The hollow cross on the worksheet is the mouse pointer and it changes shapes as it is moved to different parts of the worksheet.

Using Dialog Boxes

Many Macintosh applications, including Excel, use dialog boxes to allow more detailed or efficient communication with the program than menus alone can provide. There are many types of dialog boxes providing various kinds of input.

Some dialog boxes will appear automatically if you make some sort of mistake or ask Excel to do something that requires confirmation. Many dialog boxes appear as a result of choosing a menu command that requires additional input. You can tell which menu commands will produce dialog boxes because they are followed by an ellipsis (...). Let's examine one of the more complex dialog boxes to see how they work.

1. Pull down the Tools drop-down menu. (Point to Tools on the Menu bar and press and hold down the mouse button.)

   Notice that several of the menu commands have triangles next to them. These commands have sub-menus with additional commands. You'll use sub-menus later. Other menu commands are followed by an ellipsis, indicating that choosing that command will produce a dialog box.

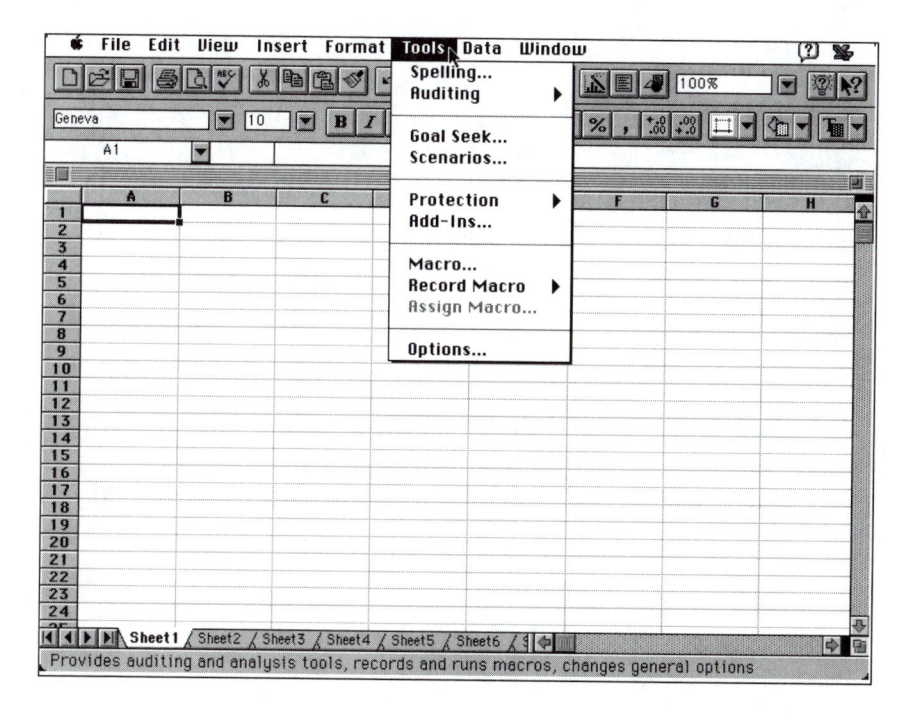

Figure 2.2 *The Tools drop-down menu.*

2. Select **Options** (drag the mouse down the menu commands until Options is highlighted and release the mouse button) to produce the Options dialog box shown in Figure 2.3.

Most dialog boxes don't have as many options as the Options dialog box. However, this is a good example of what you will encounter in various Excel dialog boxes. *Radio buttons* (sometimes called option buttons) allow you to choose only one of the options in a category. Check-box categories can have multiple boxes checked. List boxes let you select a choice from a list.

Tabbed dialog boxes let you switch among various sets of options by clicking on the tab. In Figure 2.3, notice that the View tab is highlighted. Let's take a look at another set of options in the same dialog box.

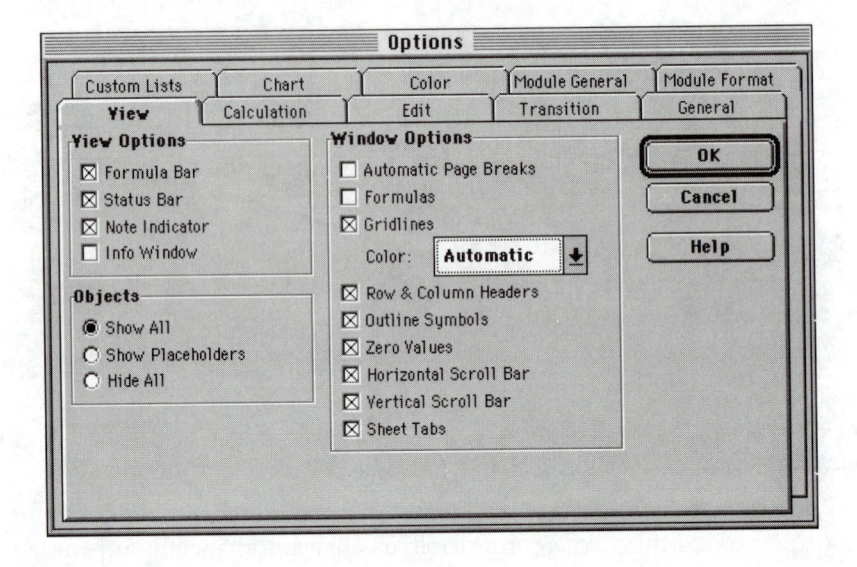

Figure 2.3 *The Options dialog box.*

3. Click on the **General** tab.

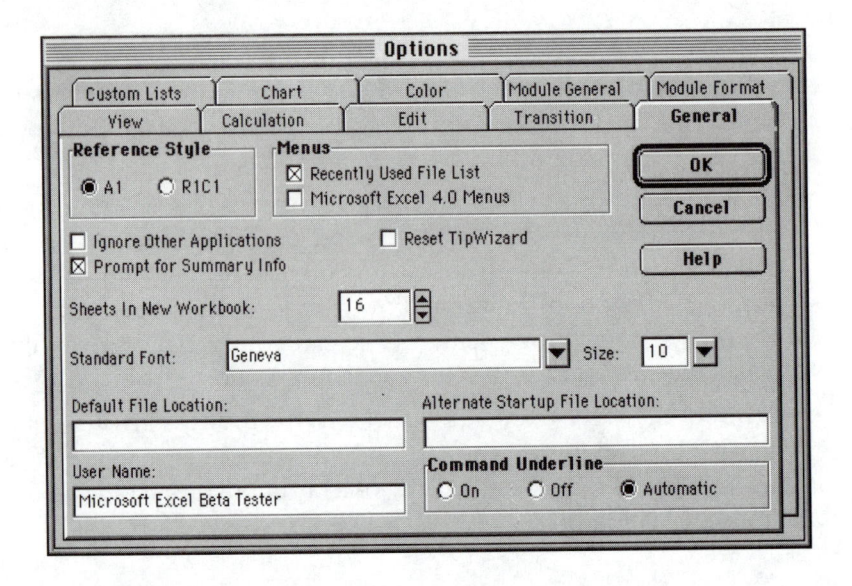

Figure 2.4 *The Options dialog with the General tab highlighted.*

This set of options includes one more input method—a text box into which you can type information.

4. Click on the **Cancel** button on the right side of the dialog box, or press the **Esc** key to clear the dialog box.

Using the Toolbars

You've learned that there are often keyboard shortcuts for accomplishing certain tasks. Excel's toolbars are like shortcut keys that are accessible by clicking on them with the mouse. Another advantage of the toolbars is that they keep the shortcuts visible so they are easier to remember than keyboard shortcuts.

Excel supplies predefined toolbars for a variety of situations. Refer to Figure 2.1 to see the two *default* toolbars that automatically appear when you start Excel. The term *default* means the way things are set automatically. The one on the top is called the *Standard toolbar* and the one below it is the *Formatting toolbar.*

Each toolbar button is an icon (picture) that represents a command, or series of commands. Some of the icons are fairly self-explanatory, but you may be wondering how you'll be able to figure out what the rest of those cryptic little pictures mean. Never fear. Excel provides an easy way to determine what each of the toolbar buttons does. By simply moving the mouse pointer over one of the buttons, the status bar displays a description of what the button does, and a *tool tip* pops up just below the mouse pointer with the button's name. Let's try this out.

1. Without clicking, position the mouse pointer over the Print toolbar button. It's the fourth button from the left on the Standard toolbar.

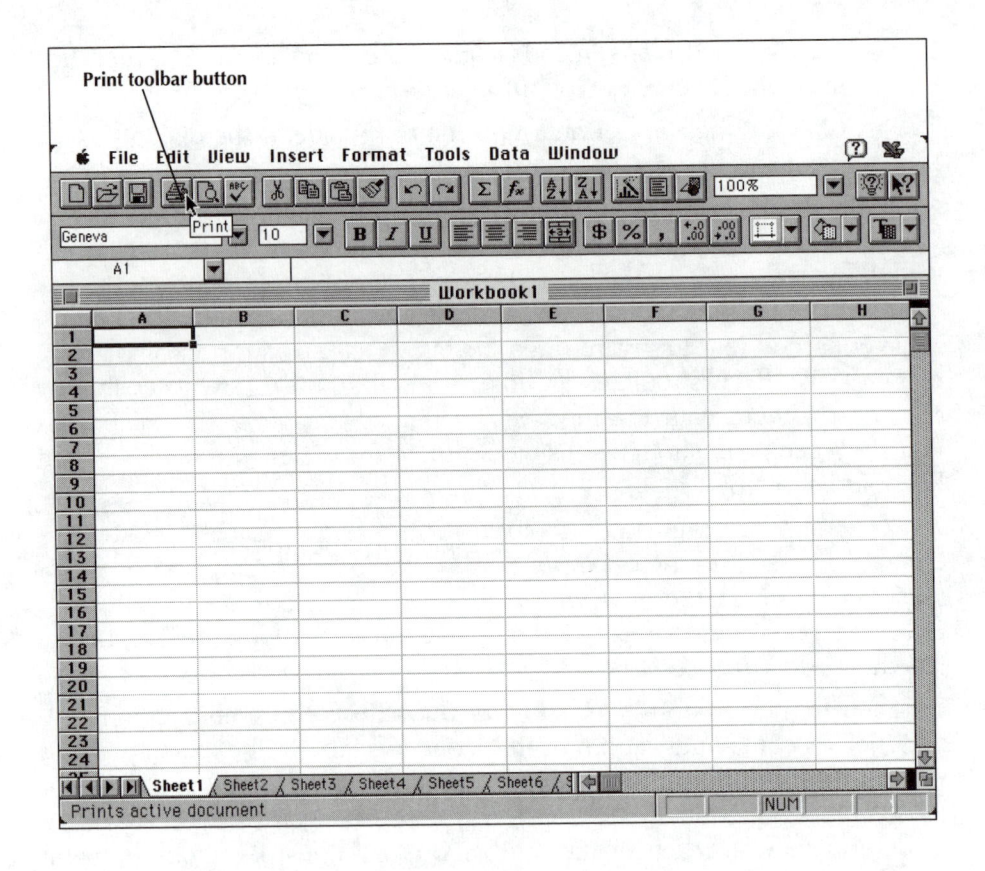

Figure 2.5 *The mouse pointer on the Print toolbar button.*

Notice the tool tip that says Print, and the status bar that tells you that clicking this would cause the active document to print.

2. Move the pointer over some of the other toolbar buttons and check out the tool tip and the status bar to get an idea of what some of the other buttons can accomplish.

Throughout the book, we'll be working with various toolbars and toolbar buttons. You'll learn later how to choose which of the many toolbars you want to appear on screen, how to change their position, and even how to customize them to create special toolbars to meet your own requirements.

Navigating the Worksheet

As you start entering and editing data in worksheets, you'll need to know how to move about. There are quite a few ways to navigate the worksheet using either the keyboard or the mouse. The simplest method is simply clicking the mouse pointer on the cell you want to move to, or using the arrow keys to move to the cell you want to be active.

1. Use the arrow keys to move to several different cells. Notice the cell reference area tells you what the active cell is.

2. Use the mouse to click on several different cells.

   While this method works well for moving short distances, it's inefficient for moving long distances. For those long-distance journeys, the scroll bars are a good form of rapid transit.

   * You can click on the scroll bar buttons to move a row at a time.

   * Drag the scroll box to move to a distant location

   * Click in the scroll bar above or below the scroll box to move one screen up or down.

   Using the scroll bars doesn't change the active cell; it only changes the portion of the worksheet you are looking at. Once you've moved to the desired location using the scroll bars, click in the cell you want to become active.

   One of the most useful ways to get to where you want to go is to use the Go To dialog box. With the Go To dialog box, you can enter the cell address you want to move to and, zap! You're there. Let's try it.

3. Choose **Edit**, **Go To** (or press **Ctrl+G**)

   As we work through the book, we'll cover a number of ways to use the Go To dialog box. For now, let's just move to a new cell. Notice the vertical line in the Reference text box. This is called the *insertion point* and indicates that this is where you can start typing. If the insertion point isn't in the Reference text box, just click in the Reference text box and the insertion point will be there.

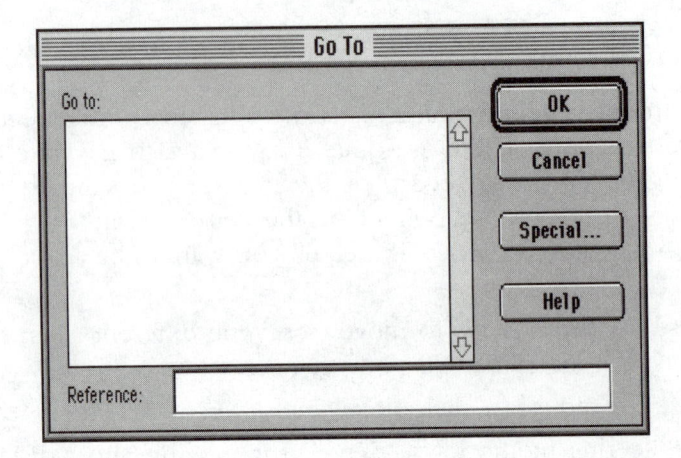

Figure 2.6 The Go To dialog box.

4. Type: **Z45** and click on the **OK** button to make Z45 the active cell.

Another quick way to zip to a cell is by clicking in the **Name** box (the area just to the left of the Formula bar), then typing the cell reference, and then pressing the **Return** key.

SHORTCUT

In addition to the scroll bars and Go To dialog box, there are many keyboard combinations for navigating and performing other activities in Excel. I'll mention some of these when they are clearly more efficient than other alternatives. You can also find lists of keyboard alternatives in the Excel help facility's Reference Information. The next section explains how to use Excel's Help facility.

NOTE

Using Excel's Help Facilities

One of the most important skills you can learn is how to get yourself unstuck when you run into difficulty. Fortunately, Excel provides some very useful tools for getting help. It even includes electronic demonstrations of many aspects of the program.

Let's use the Excel's help facility to see what's available.

1. Pull down the Help menu (it looks like a comic book thought balloon with a question mark in it) to produce the Help pull-down menu.

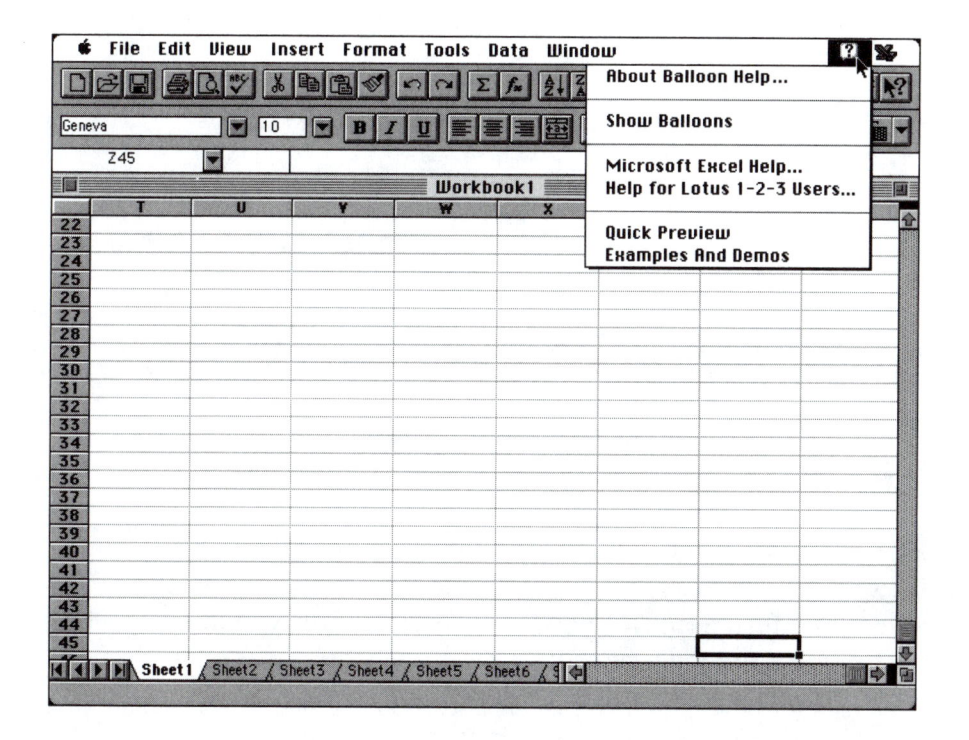

Figure 2.7 *The Help pull-down menu.*

2. Select **Microsoft Excel Help** to show the MS Excel Help window, as shown in Figure 2.8.

SHORTCUT

A quick keyboard shortcut for opening the MS Excel Help screen is ⌘+/ (the forward slash below the question mark symbol).

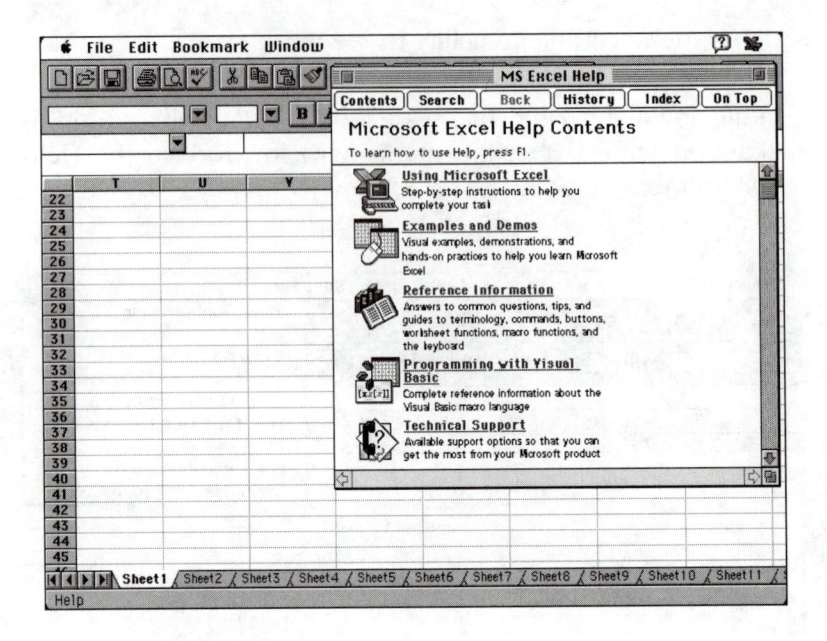

Figure 2.8 *The MS Excel Help window.*

Help is segmented into the following logical groups.

* The first group, *Using Microsoft Excel*, leads you to more sections about using the program.

* *Examples and Demos* provides illustrated mini-tutorials on various aspects of the program.

* *Reference Information* provides lists and explanations you might need, such as keyboard shortcut guides, installation information, specifications, etc.

* *Programming with Visual Basic* gives you information you'll need when you start delving into the more technical aspects of Excel programming.

* *Technical Support* leads you to the many options for obtaining answers to your technical questions.

    You can move to any of these sections by moving the mouse pointer over one of the underlined headings (also in green on color screens) and clicking. You can tell when the mouse pointer is positioned over a topic you can move to, because the pointer takes the shape of a hand with a pointing finger.

Let's try moving to one of the help sections now.

3. Position the mouse pointer over the Reference Information heading (the pointer becomes a hand with a pointing finger) and click to display the first Reference Information help window, as shown in Figure 2.9.

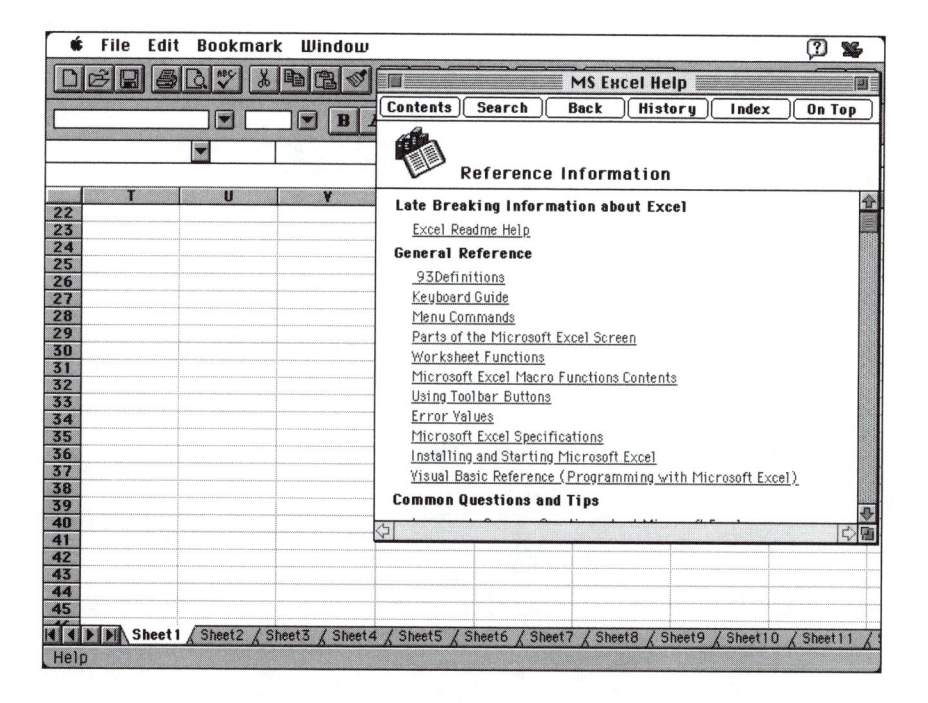

Figure 2.9 *The Reference Information help window.*

We can now choose from a whole new set of categories. Let's move to the Definitions category.

4. Move the mouse pointer over the underlined Definitions category, and click to display a list of items for which we can obtain definitions, as shown in Figure 2.10.

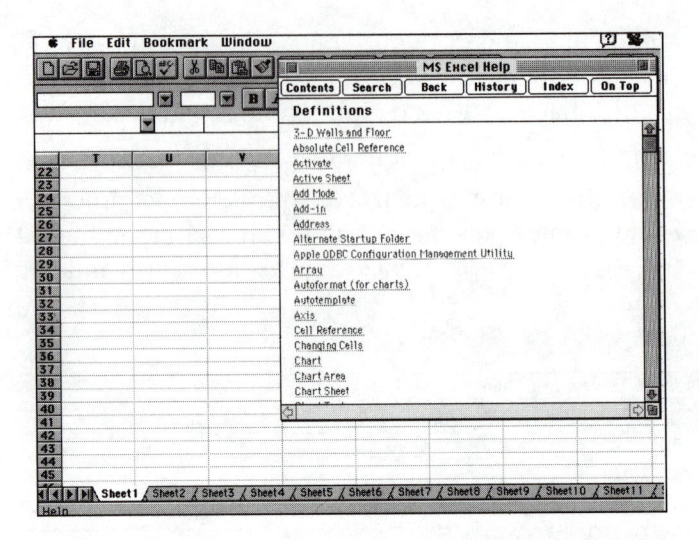

Figure 2.10 *The Definitions help window.*

Notice that these items are underlined with dashed underlines. A dashed underline means that you can click on that item to display a definition of the item.

5. Click on **Chart** to display a definition of a chart, as shown in Figure 2.11.

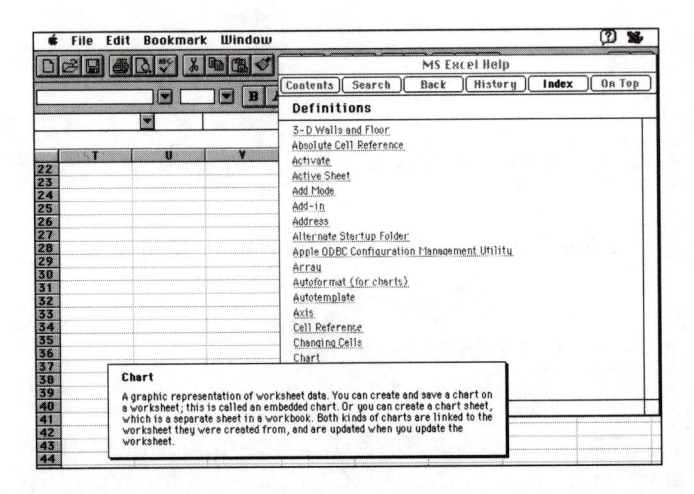

Figure 2.11 *The definition of a chart.*

When you have read the definition, you can clear it by clicking the mouse anywhere.

6. Click the mouse to clear the definition.

   You can use the buttons just below the MS Excel Help title bar to move to other portions of Help. For example, you can use the **Back** button to retrace your steps, one screen at a time. The **History** button displays a dialog box listing all the help screens you've used in the current help session so you can jump back to one directly by double-clicking on it.

7. Click on the **History** button to display the Help History dialog box, as shown in Figure 2.12.

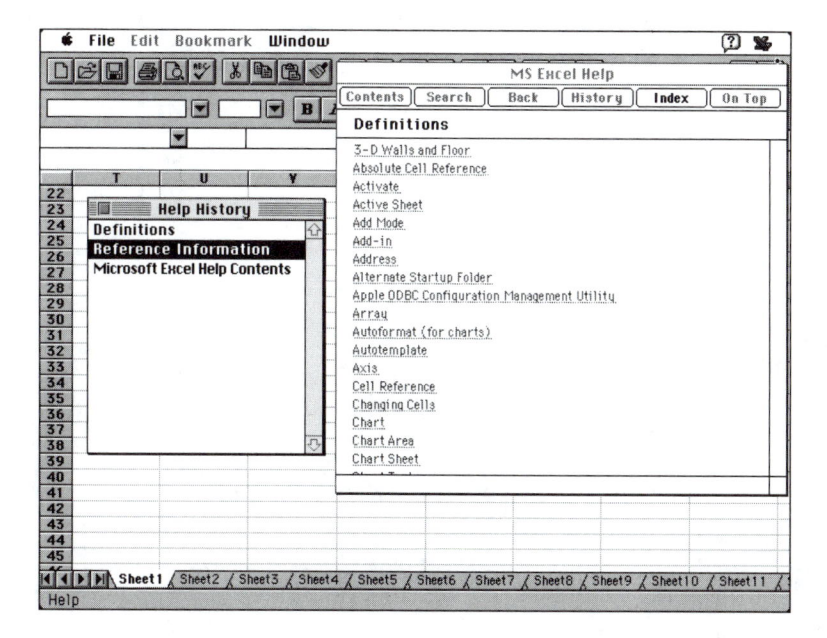

Figure 2.12 *The Help History dialog box.*

The last screen you used is highlighted. Let's jump back to the Reference Information screen.

8. Double-click **on Reference Information** in the Help History dialog box.

The Help History dialog box remains on screen next to the main help window so you can move to previous help screens whenever you want to. The Help History dialog box will close when you close MS Excel Help.

Now that you know how to move around in Help, let's take a look at how you can search for a help screen for a particular topic.

9. Click on the **Search** button to display the Search dialog box, as shown in Figure 2.13.

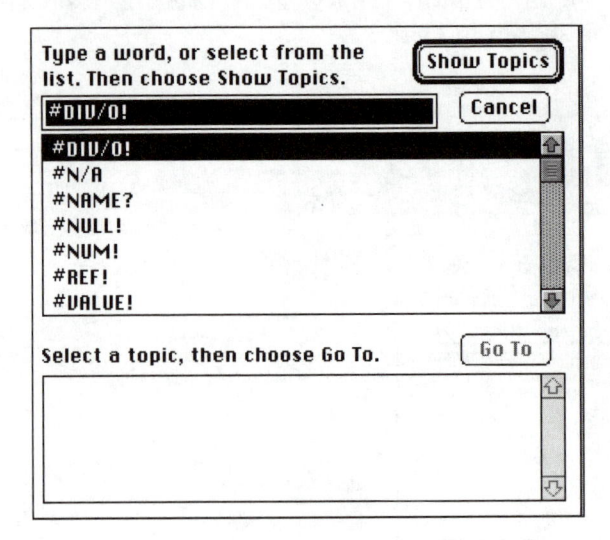

Figure 2.13 *The Search dialog box in Help.*

You can go directly to the Search dialog box without having to navigate through the main help window by double-clicking on the **Help** tool button.

You can either scroll to a category item in the list or just start typing the name of the feature you need help with in the text box above the list. As you type, the category items starting with those letters will appear in the list. When the category item you want is visible, you can click on the Show Topics button, or just double-click on the item.

Suppose you can't remember how to specify a print area for your worksheet. Let's try searching for help on print area now.

10. Type: **p** and notice that the list jumps to the first features that start with the letter p.

11. Type: **rin** and the print area category comes into view. Click on it and then click on the Show Topics button to display a list of related help screens you can jump to, as shown in Figure 2.14.

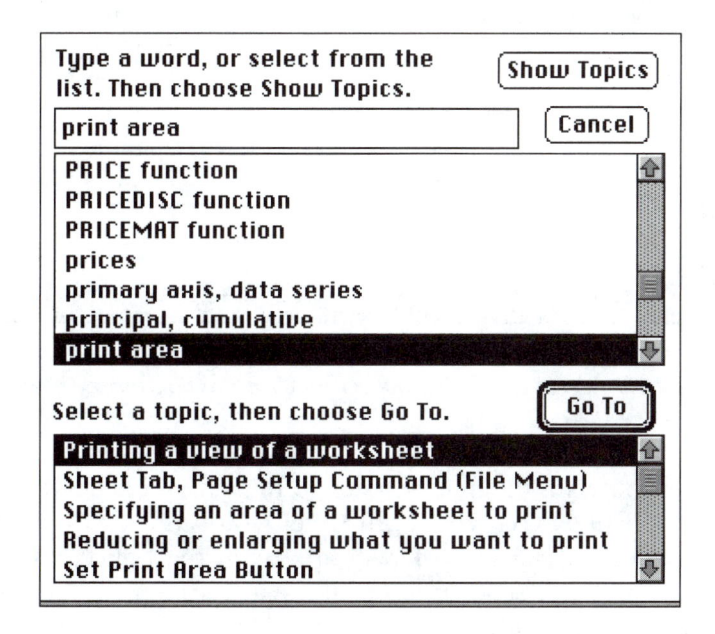

Figure 2.14 The Search dialog box with the print area topics displayed.

12. Click on **Specifying an area of a worksheet to print** in the list of topics in the lower portion of the dialog box, and then click on the **Go To** button to display the help window shown in Figure 2.15.

After you've found the help screen you're looking for and read the information, you can close the Help window by clicking on the MS Excel Help window's close box.

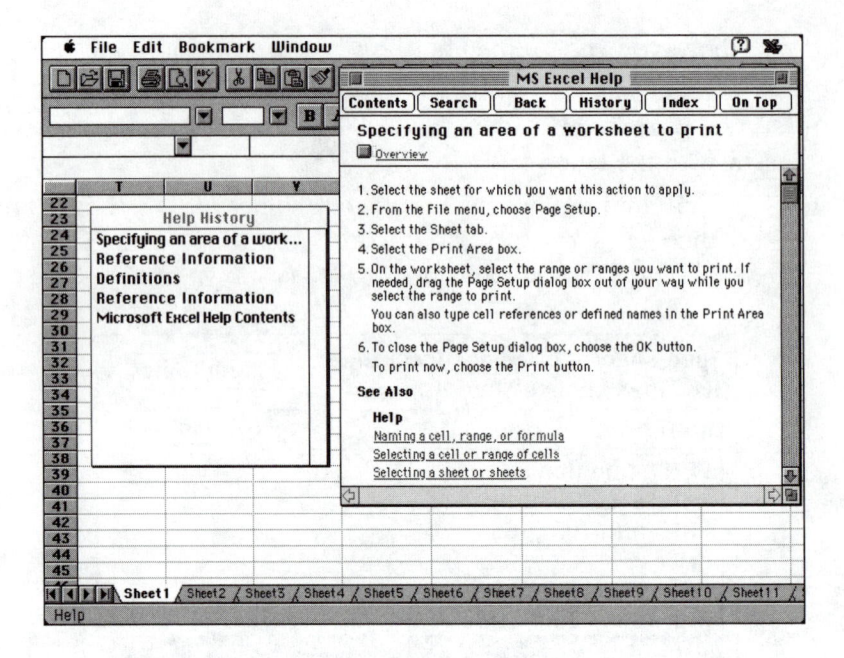

Figure 2.15 The help window for specifying an area of a worksheet to print.

NOTE

If you want the help screens to remain visible so you can refer to them as you work with Excel, you can click on the **On Top** button. A check mark will appear in the button and the help screens will stay *on top* of the Excel screen as you work until you close Help.

13. Click on the **close** box to exit Help.

    There may be times when you want help with some object you see on your screen. You could call up Help and search for the appropriate screen, but there's a faster way. By clicking on the **Help toolbar** button, you can simply click on the object for which you want more information. Let's say you want more information about the scroll bars.

14. Click on the **Help toolbar** button, as shown in Figure 2.16.

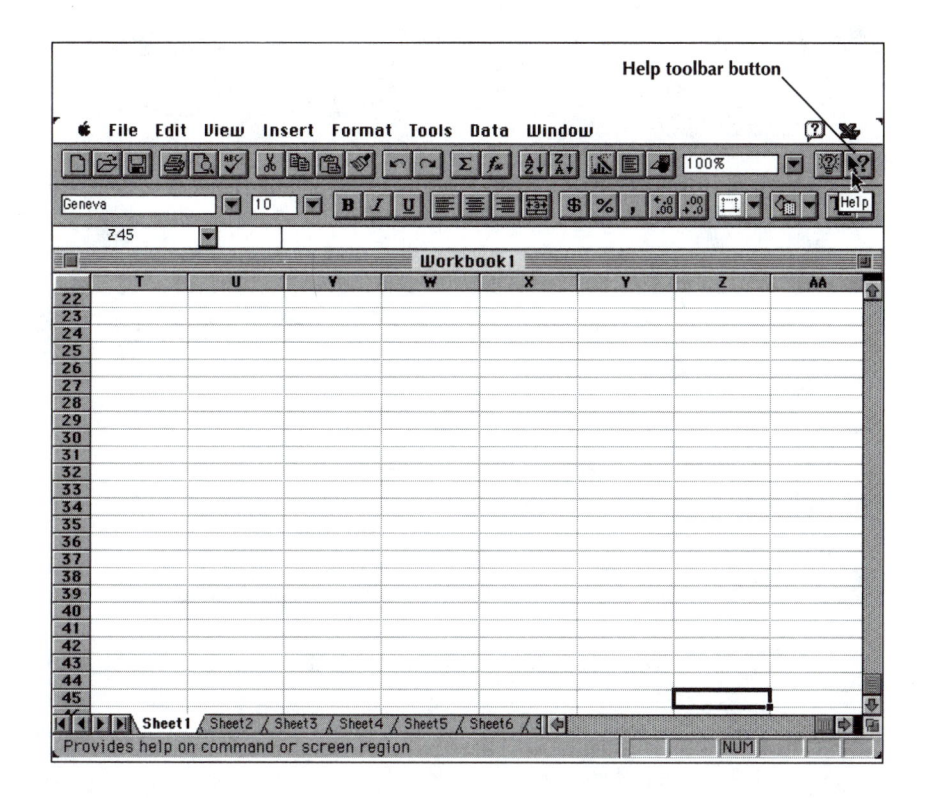

Figure 2.16 *The Help toolbar button.*

SHORTCUT

The keyboard alternative to clicking on the Help toolbar button is ⌘**+Shift+/.**

Notice that the mouse pointer turns into an arrow with a large question mark attached.

15. Position the tip of the pointer inside either the vertical or horizontal scroll bar, and click to summon the Scroll Bars help screen, as shown in Figure 2.17.

N O T E

Excel also lets you get help on almost any dialog box by clicking the **Help** button in the box.

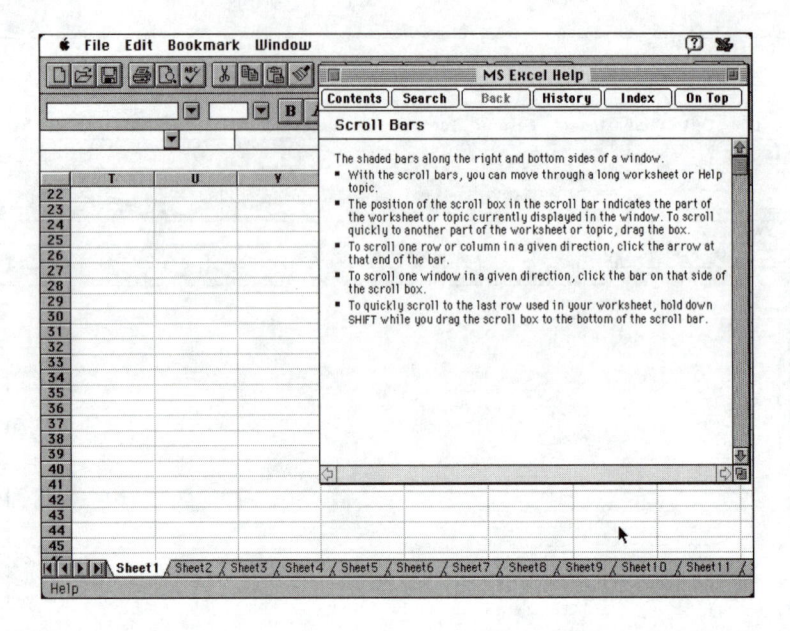

Figure 2.17 *The Scroll Bars help screen.*

16. Remove the Scroll bars help window by clicking on the **Close** box.

Using the TipWizard

Not only does Excel make it easy to find and use Help for the topics you're struggling with, the TipWizard can even make suggestions about better ways to perform tasks after you've done them. Talk about a smart program.

When the TipWizard has a suggestion for you, the TipWizard button *lights up*. Lighting up means turning yellow on a color screen or just highlighted if you don't have color.

NOTE When you start Excel, the TipWizard lights up before you've done anything. This lets you know that it is ready to give you the *tip of the day* which is a random hint or shortcut for performing some commonly-used Excel task.

To display the suggestion the TipWizard has for you, just click on the **TipWizard toolbar** button. To clear the suggestion, click on the **TipWizard** button again. The TipWizard button is lit because, aside from offering us a tip of the day, it has a suggestion for a more efficient way to move to a new cell than the Go To box we used to move to cell Z45 in the last section. Let's take a look at the suggestion, as well as the tip of the day.

1. Click on the **TipWizard toolbar** button to display the tip between the Formatting toolbar and the Formula bar, as shown in Figure 2.18.

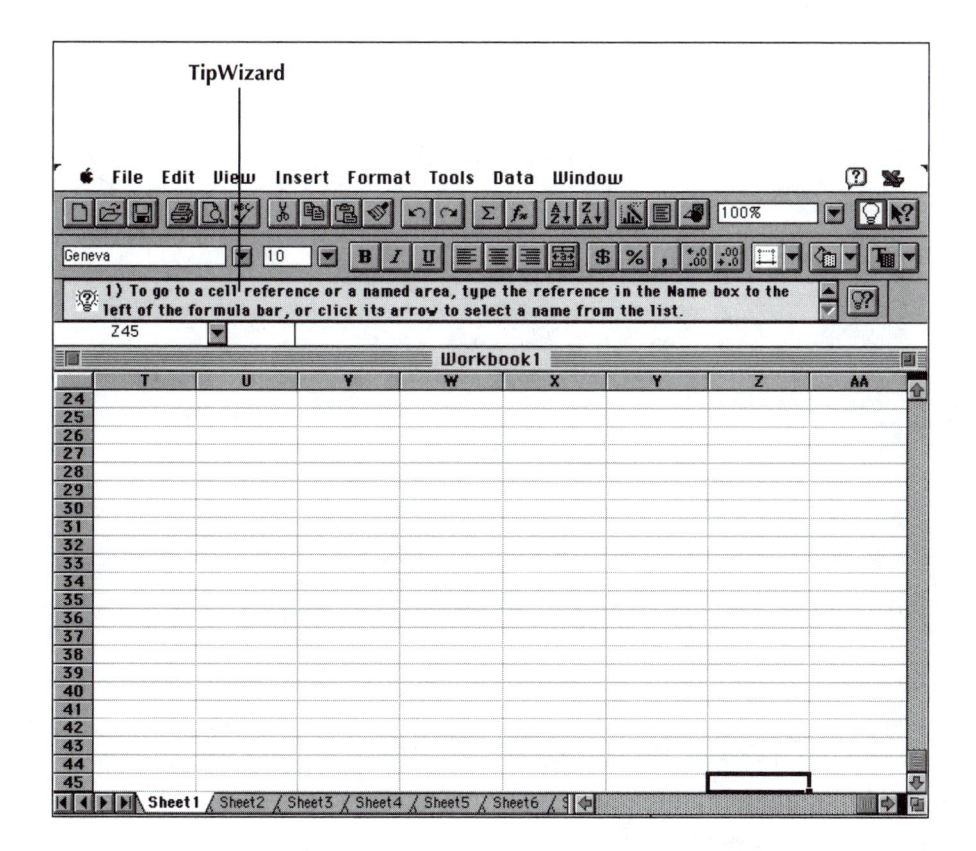

Figure 2.18 *The TipWizard's tip for moving to a different cell.*

Just to the right of the tip text are up and down arrows for moving to the previous or next tip. There is no next tip, so let's move to the previous tip.

2. Click on the **Up Arrow** to the right of the tip text to display the tip of the day.

You can leave the TipWizard open to display suggestions automatically, or you can close it and then just open it when you want to see a suggestion. For now, let's leave it open and perform a task in a less-than-optimally-efficient manner. Even though there is nothing in the active cell (Z45), we'll tell Excel that we want to cut (delete) the cell contents using the menu.

3. Pull down the Edit menu and select **Cut** to display a suggestion for cutting using a toolbar button, as displayed in Figure 2.19.

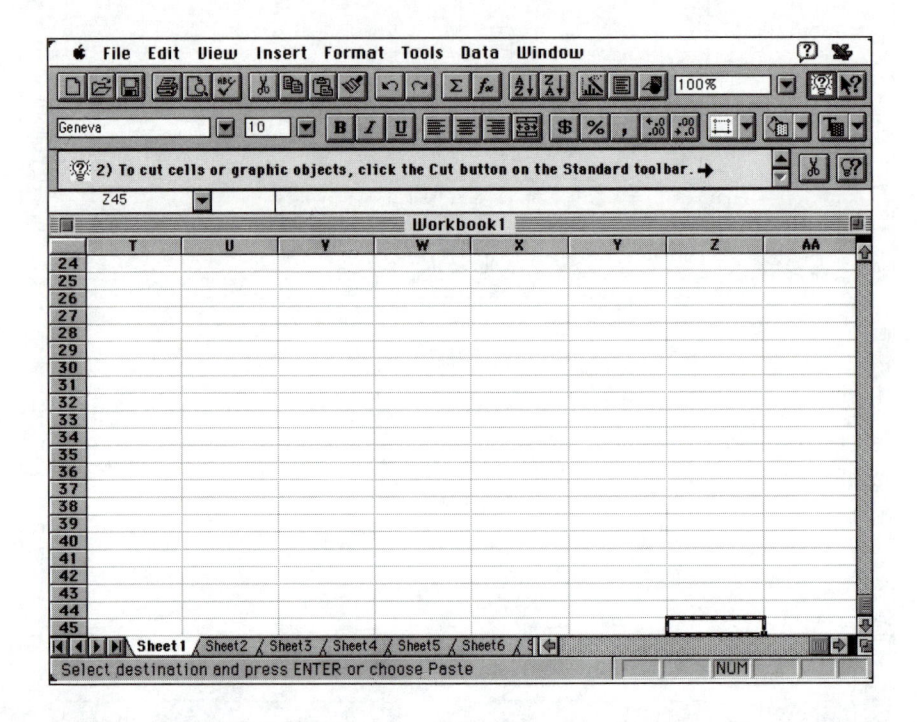

Figure 2.19 *The tip for using the Cut toolbar button.*

Because Excel uses a great deal of intelligence for providing tips, you may see a different tip. Don't worry, Excel is just trying to give you the best suggestion for your particular situation.

You'll also discover that Excel only provides a tip once in each Excel session, unless you perform the task inefficiently three more times.

> If the tip suggests that you use a toolbar button, the button will be displayed to the right of the up and down arrows, as you see for this tip. There is also a Tip Help displayed for tips so that you can jump directly to a help screen for more detailed information about the procedure.
>
> We won't keep the TipWizard displayed for the figures in the remainder of the book, since it does take up some valuable screen real estate. However, don't hesitate to display it as you work through the book to see if there are better ways of accomplishing what you are doing. Of course, just because the TipWizard suggests something, that doesn't mean it's the best approach. It's just giving you a suggestion. Use your own judgment.

4. Click on the **TipWizard toolbar** button to remove the TipWizard.

Using Balloon Help

If you're using System 7, you can take advantage of Balloon Help to see descriptions of various parts of the screen by just moving the mouse pointer over them.

Let's try it.

1. Pull down the Help menu and select **Show Balloons**.
2. Position the mouse pointer on the Help button on the Standard toolbar to see the information for the Help button shown in Figure 2.20.

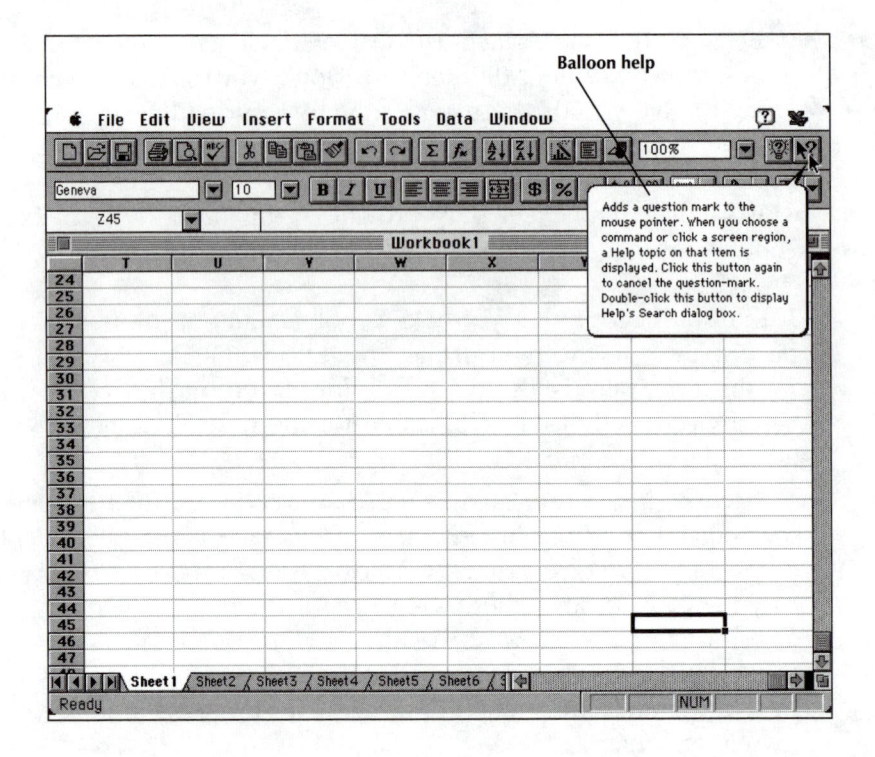

Figure 2.20 *The balloon help for the Help button.*

 **NOTE** Balloon help popping up all over the screen as you move the mouse pointer can be more irritating and distracting than helpful. You can get rid of those pesky balloons by pulling down the Help menu and selecting **Hide Balloons**.

Exiting Excel

When you're ready to leave Excel, you can do so in the same manner as closing any other window.

1. Pull down the File menu and select **Quit**, or press ⌘+**Q**.

Excel will close and return to the icon you started it from. If you've made changes to a worksheet, Excel is considerate enough to ask you if you want to save the changes. If you see such a message at this point, just click on the **No** button to finish exiting Excel.

A Final Thought

The information you've learned in this chapter gives you the tools to *get around* in Excel. In the next chapter, you'll finally get a chance to put Excel to work creating worksheets and entering data.

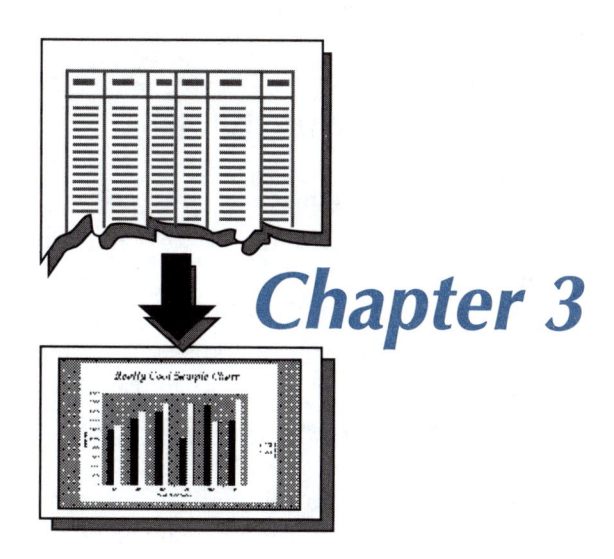

Chapter 3

Creating a Worksheet

Planning a Worksheet

The worksheet is where you'll enter the information you want to store and manipulate. Like almost anything you build, a worksheet will be more useful, efficient, and understandable if you take the time to plan before you dive in and start entering data willy-nilly.

The first step is to decide what the purpose of the worksheet is. For example, if the worksheet is to contain a monthly budget for the next year, then the purpose is to forecast and gain greater control over inflows and outflows for your business.

Second, give some thought to the level of detail you want to include in the worksheet. Too little detail may render the worksheet useless by omitting critical information required to make decisions based on the analysis of data entered into the worksheet. Too much detail can make the worksheet unwieldy and mask the results, not letting you see the *big picture.*

You may also find it useful to use paper and pencil to sketch out the overall design of your worksheet. This lets you see how the worksheet will look to the user (whether that user is you or someone else) before you take the time to enter a bunch of data.

One more planning tip to keep in mind: remember that the ultimate result of most worksheets is a printed report of some sort. Many things that seem obvious to you as you create or edit a worksheet can easily be obscured or invisible in the printout. For example, formulas you create to perform calculations can be revealed in the worksheet, but are generally not part of the printed output. Also, the printed report is often only a small portion of the entire worksheet, so the context that might make the worksheet understandable on screen might not be a part of the printout.

Building a Text Framework

The most common, and often the most practical way to start putting together a worksheet is to enter titles, column and row headings, and any other text elements that will provide a structure for your worksheet as you enter the data.

There are no hard-and-fast rules for the text framework but, tradition-ally, columns contain time periods such as hours, days and months, and row headings contain categories such as rent, insurance, cost of goods, etc.

We'll be creating a budget worksheet for a small locksmith business that also sells bagels. In order to get a better handle on projected income and expenses, the Spokane Locks and Bagel Corporation decided to use Excel to create a budget worksheet to let them compare budgeted amounts with actual figures down the road. Figure 3.1 depicts the initial text framework for this budget worksheet.

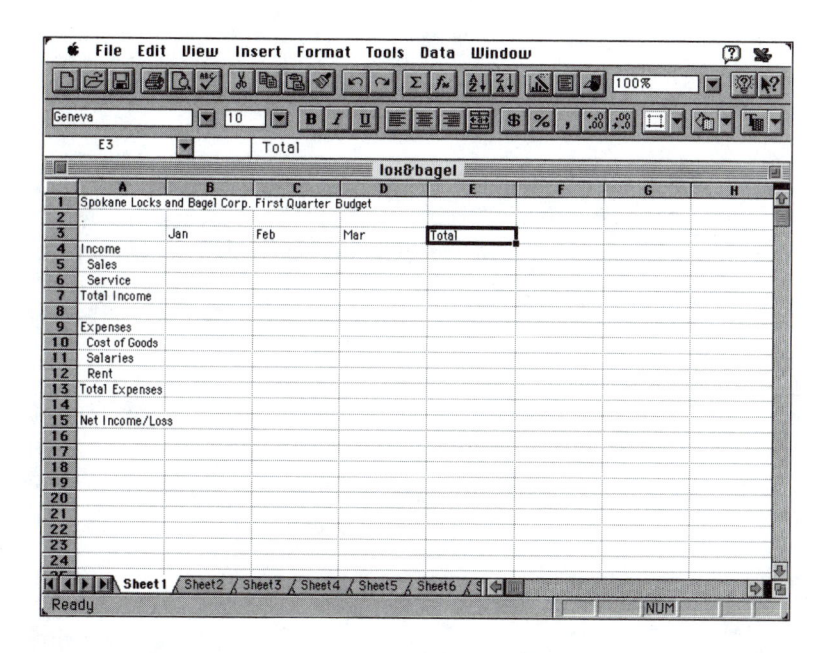

Figure 3.1 *The text framework for the Spokane Locks and Bagel Corporation.*

Entering and Editing Text

To enter text into an Excel worksheet, simply move to the cell in which you want to enter the text and start typing. As you type, the text will appear in both the cell and the formula bar. Let's start entering the text shown in Figure 3.1.

1. Start Excel if you don't have it on your screen. Refer to Chapter 2 if you don't remember the steps for starting Excel.

2. Be sure A1 is the active cell. Check the cell reference area to double-check that you are in the right place.

3. Type: **Spokane Locks and Bagel Corp. First Quarter Budget**

   As you start typing, notice that a flashing vertical line, called an *insertion point*, appears to the right of the text, as shown in Figure 3.2. The insertion point lets you know where text will be entered or deleted. You'll also notice that, as soon as you start a cell entry, three new icons appear on the left side of the formula bar. From left to right, these icons are the Cancel box, the Enter box and the Function Wizard box.

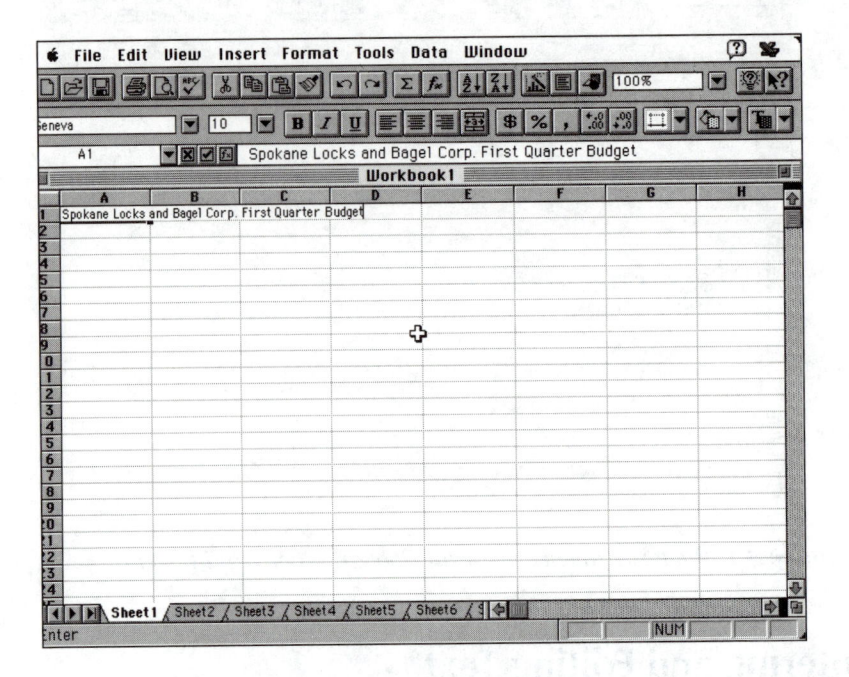

Figure 3.2 *The beginnings of a cell entry.*

If you make a mistake while typing, simply press the **Delete** key to erase the character to the left of the insertion point. If you've really messed up, you can click the **Cancel** box or press the **Esc** key.

N O T E   While you are entering text in a cell, you can't press the left or right arrow keys to reposition the insertion point for editing. Pressing an arrow key causes Excel to complete the cell entry with what you've typed so far and move in the arrow's direction to the next cell on the worksheet.

Notice that the text you typed in cell A1 has apparently spilled over into the adjacent cells in columns B, C, and D. But do those other cells really contain part of the information? No. The entire worksheet title is in A1. The cell reference area says you are in A1 and the formula bar displays the whole title. If you were to move to B1, for example, you'd see from the formula bar that B1 contains no data. In fact, it is because B1, C1, D1 and E1 are empty that the contents of A1 are allowed to spill over into them. If these cells contained data, even a space, the entry in A1 would be truncated.

To see how this works, let's enter something in B1. There are several ways to complete a cell entry, including clicking the **Enter box**, pressing the **Return** key, or moving to another cell. The last method is usually the fastest, since you'll often need to make entries in other cells.

4. Press the **Right Arrow** key to move to cell B1.

    Notice that cell B1 is empty.

5. Press the **Spacebar** and then click the **Enter** box.

    The text in A1 is limited to what will fit in the current column width. We'll get rid of the space in B1 to restore the title.

6. While B1 is still the active cell, press the **Delete** key and then click the **Enter** box to allow the title to flow across the columns.

N O T E   Column widths can be changed to allow for the amount of text entered in the column. Changing column widths, which will be covered in the next chapter, is usually the preferred method for accommodating long text entries.

7. Click on cell **B3** to make it the active cell and notice the entry in cell A1 is complete.

Now that the worksheet title is in place, let's enter the column headings.

8. In cell B3, type: **Jan**.

   Now, you could move to cell C3 and type **Feb** and then type **Mar** in D3, but there's an easier way. In the lower-right corner of the box surrounding the active cell is the *fill handle*. The fill handle allows you to perform several copying actions. for now we'll use the fill handle to take advantage of Excel's intelligence. By dragging the fill handle to the right so the outline extends through cell D3, Excel will automatically enter **Feb** and **Mar** for you, like magic!

9. Position the mouse over the fill handle until the mouse pointer turns into thin crosshairs, and drag to the right until the cell outline extends to cell D3, as depicted in Figure 3.3.

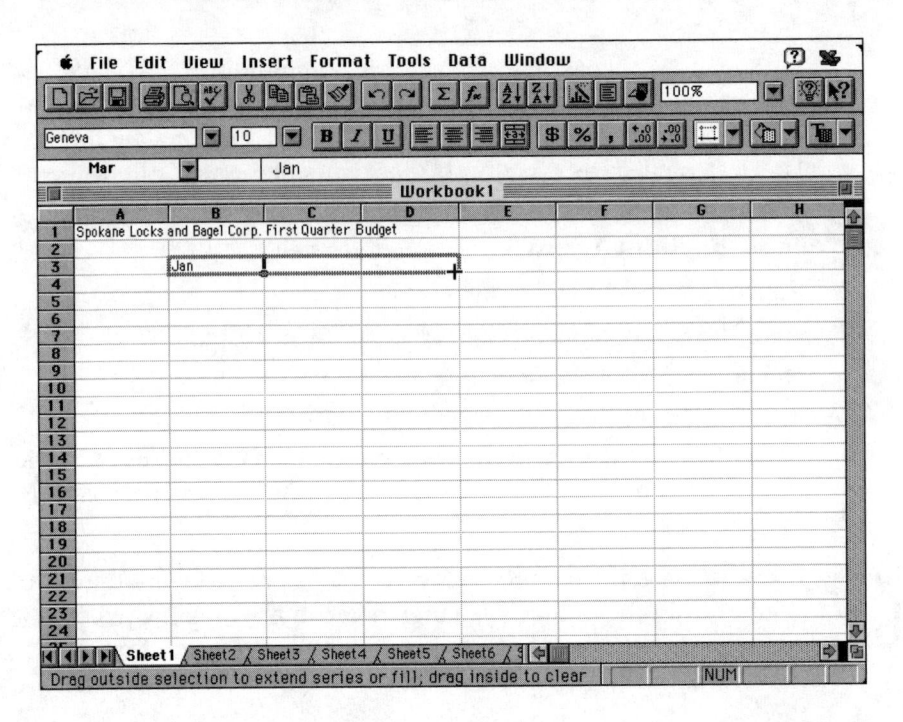

Figure 3.3 *The fill handle being dragged.*

10. Release the mouse button to complete the fill.

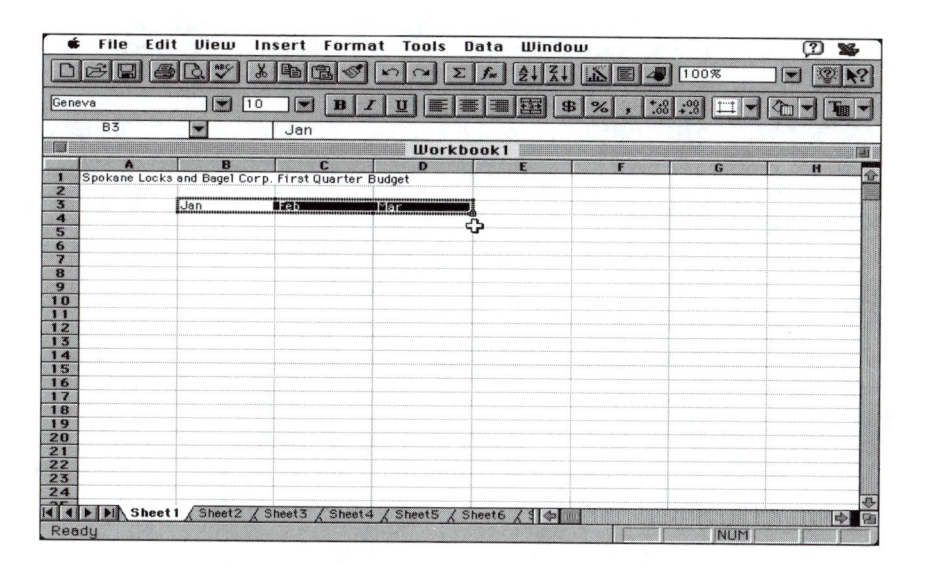

Figure 3.4 *The results of the fill after releasing the mouse button.*

NOTE

This type of fill operation works with many different kinds of series.For example, if a cell contains Mon or Monday, dragging with the fill handle will increment the days of the week as Tue, Wed, Thu (or Tuesday, Wednesday, Thursday), etc. Also, a cell containing text and a number, such as Qtr1 or 1st Period will fill as Qtr2, Qtr3, or 2nd Period, 3rd Period, etc.

You can use the fill handle to increment a series by dragging to the right or down. If you want to use the fill handle to decrement a series, drag to the left or up. If a cell contained Jan, dragging left or up would fill as Dec, Nov, Oct, etc.

11. Click in cell **E3** and type: **Total**.
12. Move to cell A4 and type: **Income**.

WARNING

If you're entering several contiguous cells in a row or column, there are several shortcuts for completing the cell entries.

* Press the **Return** key to confirm a cell entry and move to the next cell down in the column.

* Press **Shift+Return** to confirm a cell entry and move up one cell.

* Press **Tab** to confirm a cell entry and move to the next cell to the right.

* Press **Shift+Tab** to confirm a cell entry and move one cell to the left.

13. Press the **Return** key to complete the entry and move to the next cell in the column.

    Refer to Figure 3.1 and notice that the next two entries in the column are indented just a bit. This was accomplished by preceding the entries with two spaces.

14. Press the **Spacebar** twice and type: **Sales**, then press the **Return** key.

15. Enter the following text:

    A6Service

    A7Total Income

    A9Expenses

    A10Cost of Goods

    A11Salaries

    A12Rent

    A13Total Expenses

    A15Net Income/Loss

Refer to Figure 3.1 to be sure your screen matches the figure.

Entering Numbers

Entering numbers is done in the same way as entering text. What you see on screen, however, depends on what sort of number you enter. For example, if you enter **100**, the screen will display **100**. If you enter **100.43** the screen will display **100.43**. But if you enter **100.00**, **100** without the decimal point or trailing zeros will be displayed. Here's another example. Suppose you enter **100000000**. It will be displayed as **1E+08**. Hey, what the heck is going on here?

Let me reassure you that Excel isn't actually changing the *number* you enter, just the way it is displayed. The actual number you enter in the cell is used in any calculations Excel performs. Now, here's what's happening. Excel formats numbers using what it calls *General formatting*. General formatting doesn't display trailing zeros after a decimal point and converts very large numbers to scientific notation, which uses exponents.

The way numbers (or text, for that matter) are formatted can be changed to suit your taste and requirements. The techniques for changing cell formatting will be covered in the next chapter.

N O T E

Let's start entering the numbers for the budget worksheet that are displayed in Figure 3.5

	A	B	C	D	E	F	G	H
1	Spokane Locks and Bagel Corp. First Quarter Budget							
2								
3		Jan	Feb	Mar	Total			
4	Income							
5	Sales	228000	247000	310000				
6	Service	36000	39000	41000				
7	Total Income							
8								
9	Expenses							
10	Cost of Goods	137000	154000	183000				
11	Salaries	14000	14000	14000				
12	Rent	1300	1300	1300				
13	Total Expenses							
14								
15	Net Income/Loss							

Figure 3.5 *The budget worksheet with its initial numbers entered.*

1. Move to cell B5 and type: **228000** and press the **Return** key.

    The text entries you made earlier were aligned at the left side of the cell. Excel aligns numbers at the right side of the cell. Of course, just like most settings in Excel, these default settings can be changed, and you'll learn how in the next chapter.

2. Fill in the remaining numbers in the appropriate cells as shown in Figure 3.5.

Creating Formulas

Formulas are a spreadsheet's *raison d'etre*. If all we needed to do was to put text and numbers in rows and columns, just about any word processing program would fill the bill. Formulas allow us to perform calculations using values from any cells, and have the results appear in the formula cell.

You build formulas using the four mathematical operators:

*   The *plus sign* (+).
*   The *minus sign* (-).
*   The *asterisk* (*) for multiplication.
*   The *slash* (/) for division.

You always start a formula by moving to an empty cell where you want the results of the formula to appear and typing the equal sign (=), which tells Excel to get ready for a formula. For example, you could type the formula =2*2 in a cell and, after completing the cell entry, the cell would display the result of the formula, 4, but the formula bar displays the formula.

At this point, you know how to use your fancy spreadsheet program like a pocket calculator. Big deal, you say. Well, the real power of formulas comes into play when you use *cell referencing*. Instead of entering a formula using values, you can enter a formula using cell references, such as *=C12*D14*. If 2 is the value in both C12 and D14, the result will still be 4. However, if the values in C12 or D14 change, the result will automatically change as well.

Let's create the formula for January's Total Income in our budget worksheet. The formula will add the values in cells B5 and B6.

1. Move to cell B7 and type: **=B5+B6**, then click the **Enter** box to complete the cell entry while keeping B7 as the active cell.

   If you originally entered the values in B5 and B6 as specified (and I know that you did), cell B7 now displays the value **264000**, while the formula bar displays the formula, =B5+B6, as shown in Figure 3.6.

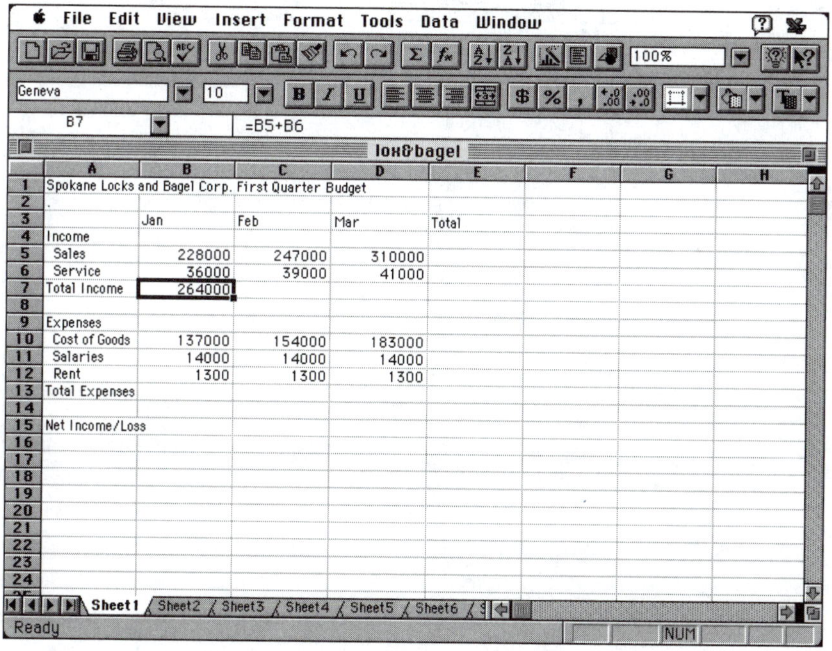

Figure 3.6 *A formula and its result.*

Now, let's try a different method of specifying the cells to be included in a formula. We'll use the pointing method to click on the cells we want to include, thus eliminating any possibility of entering an incorrect cell reference. We'll use the pointing method to create the formula for January's Total Expenses.

2. Move to cell B13 and start the formula by typing: **=**.

3. Click on **B10** to let Excel know that B10 is the first cell you want to include in the formula.

The beginning of the formula (=B10) followed by the insertion point appears in the formula cell and a dashed border appears around B10, as depicted in Figure 3.7.

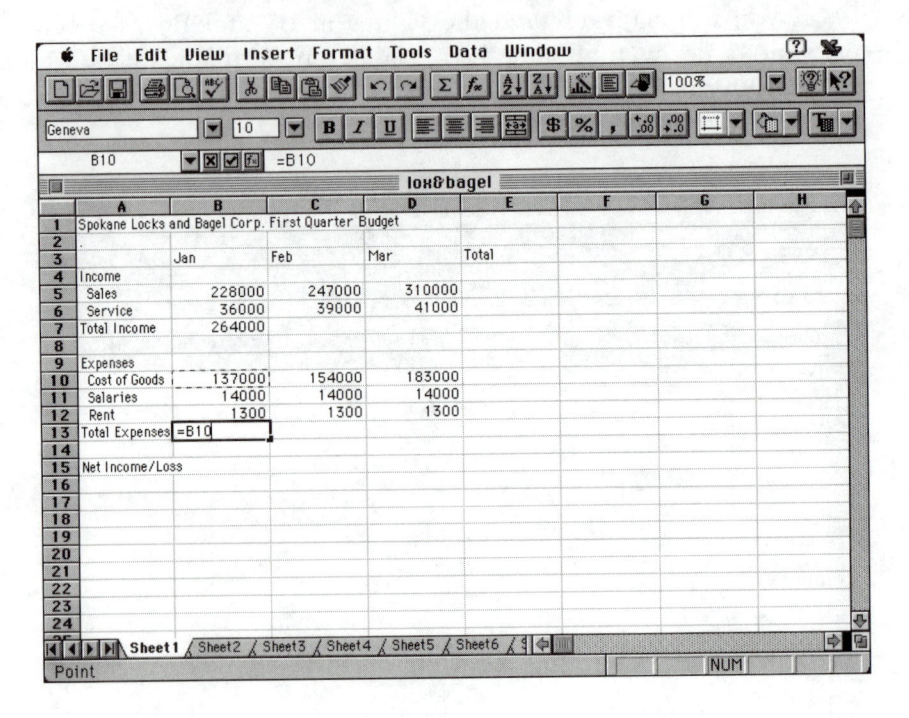

***Figure 3.7** The beginning of a formula using the pointing method.*

4. Type: **+** then click on cell B11, type: **+** again and click on **B12**.

5. Click on the **Enter** box or press the **Return** key to accept the formula.

In this example, pointing may not appear more advantageous than just typing in the cell references, but when dealing with more distant cell references or specifying ranges of cells, pointing can make a substantial difference. I think you'll start to see the advantage of pointing as we create the formula for January's Net Income/Loss.

6. Move to cell B15 and type: **=**

7. Click on cell **B7** (January's Total Income), then type: - (the minus sign). Now click on **B13** (January's Total Expenses) and press the **Return** key.

With the three formulas entered, your screen should now look like Figure 3.8.

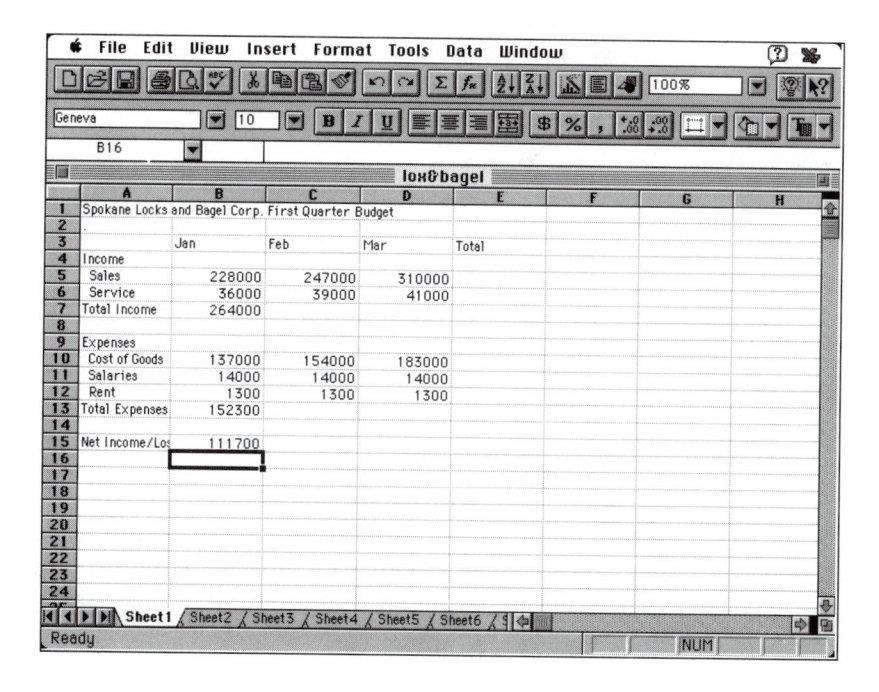

Figure 3.8 *The budget worksheet with the first three formulas entered.*

Understanding and Using Functions

Think of functions as predefined formulas. Using just the four mathematical operators, you could duplicate just about any of the supplied Excel functions. However, it might take a long while to recreate a function with the math operators, particularly for some of the more complicated functions. Just as importantly, you'd have to go through the same process every time you wanted to use the formula.

Perhaps the most common function is the **SUM** function, which adds the values in a range of cells. Most functions require *arguments*, contained within parentheses, which are just pieces of information the function needs to complete the calculation. Only one argument is required for the **SUM** function—the range of cells to be added.

One advantage of using the **SUM** function (versus specifying plus signs between each cell reference) is that it's just plain easier. Using the plus signs between each cell reference can become very unwieldy for a large range of cells. For example,

```
=C2+C3+C4+C5+C6+C7+C8+C9+C10+C11+C12
```

is much more cumbersome and error-prone than

```
=SUM(C2:C12)
```

don't you think?

The colon between the two cell references in the argument is the separator. It means *through*, as in C2 *through* C12.

Also, using the range argument makes it easier to insert or delete cells within the range without having to modify the function's argument. Let's say you needed to add a row for a new category within the range of C2 through C12. If you had used the SUM function, the new row would automatically be included in the range.

Let's use the **SUM** function to calculate February's Total Income.

1. Move to cell C7 and type: **=SUM(**.

   You are now ready to enter the range of cells to be summed. Of course we'll use the pointing method to enter the range, and we can do it in one fell swoop.

2. Point to cell C5, drag down to C6 and release the mouse button.

   A dashed border surrounds the range of cells, C5 through C6, and the cell references have been entered after the left parenthesis, as shown in Figure 3.9.

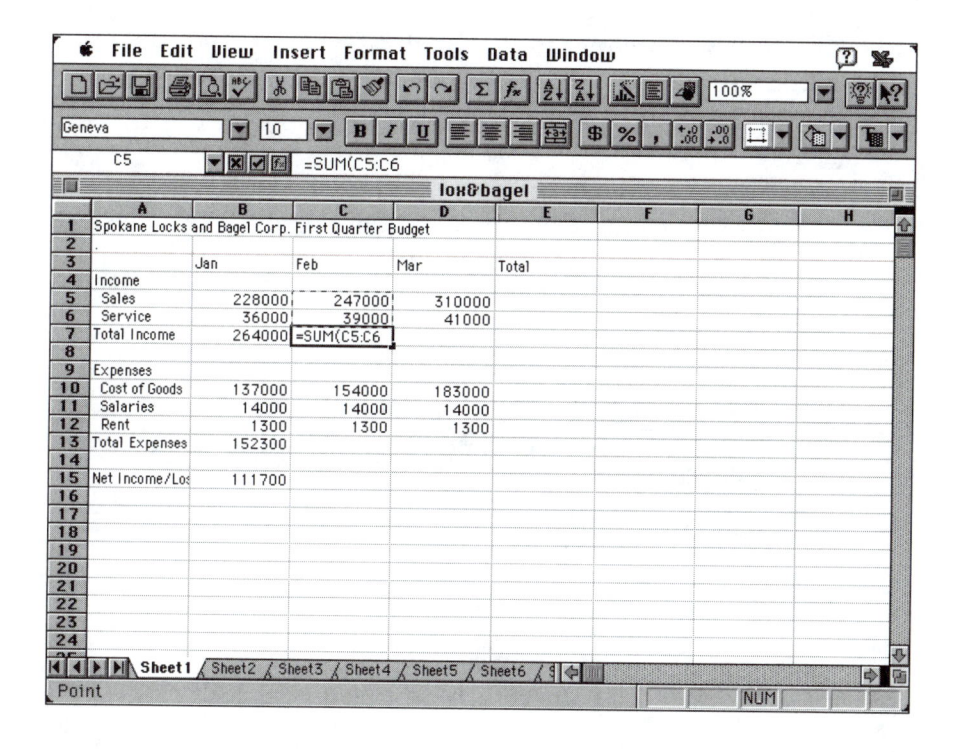

Figure 3.9 *The beginning of the SUM function with its argument.*

I know you think the next step is probably to enter the right parenthesis. Not so fast. Excel is so smart, it usually knows when a closing parenthesis is required and enters it for you when you complete the cell entry. Let's try it.

3. Click on the **Enter** box to complete the cell entry.

The result of the function's calculation appears in cell C7 (**286000**), and the function with its argument and both parentheses appears in the formula bar.

Now get ready for some Excel magic. Most of the time, when you want to **SUM** a range of numbers, you don't even need to enter the function or specify the range. You can put Excel's brains to work and usually figure out the proper range to sum. Let's try it to **SUM** the March Total Income.

4. Click in cell **D7**.

5. Click on the **AutoSum** button on the toolbar.

The **SUM** function is automatically entered and the closest contiguous range (D5 through D6) is specified as the argument as shown in Figure 3.10.

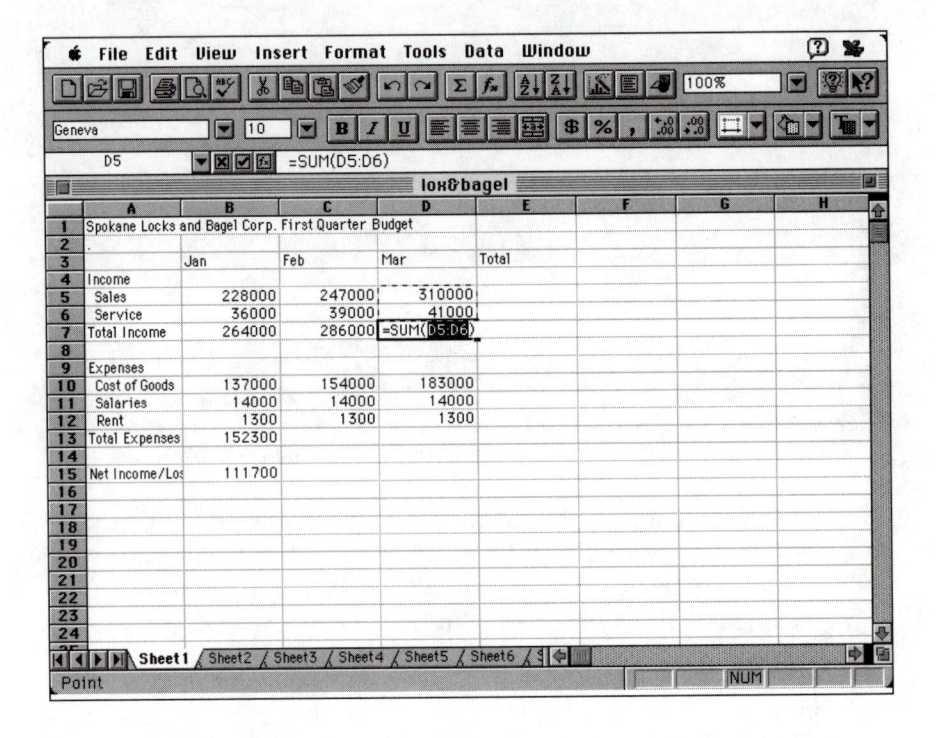

Figure 3.10 *Using the AutoSum button.*

6. Press the **Return** key to complete the entry.

SHORTCUT

If you are sure that Excel will select the correct range for the argument, you can double-click on the **AutoSum** button and the entry will be completed for you. This isn't too dangerous, even if the wrong range is selected. You can always undo or delete and start over.

Okay, that was pretty darned easy, but what about all those other functions that are hidden away somewhere in Excel? Don't worry, they aren't too hidden. In the following steps, I'll show you just how easy it is to find just the function you need.

Let's use one of the more complex functions—one that requires several arguments to see what the monthly payments would be for a new piece of equipment the Spokane Locks and Bagel Corporation is thinking of purchasing. It's one of those fancy new combination key-duplicator-and-cream-cheese-spreading machines.

The function we'll use is the **PMT** function, which will calculate the payments if we simply supply a few arguments. The information we need to supply is the interest rate per payment period, the number of payment periods, and the present value (the amount of the loan). We'll enter those three pieces of information onto the budget worksheet now.

7. Click in the vertical scroll bar just below the scroll box to move to a new screenful of rows, click in cell **A25** (which should be the top row on your screen) and type: **Interest Rate**.

8. In cell A26, type: **Term**.

9. In cell A27, type: **Loan Amount**.

10. In cell A28, type: **Payment.**

11. In cell B25, type: **10%** and click on the **Enter** box.

    Notice that **10%** is displayed in the cell. **0.1** (the actual value used in calculations) appears in the formula bar.

12. In cell B26, type: **5** to represent a five-year loan period.

13. In cell B27, type: **28500**, which is the amount the company wants to finance over the five-year period.

    We could move to the cell which is to contain the function (B28) and enter the function name and the appropriate arguments, but with three arguments required, it can be difficult to remember what goes where. Never fear! Excel Function Wizard to the rescue. Excel 5 includes several wizards—specialized help systems that take you by the hand and step you through some of the more mysterious procedures. We'll cover other wizards later in the book, but the Function Wizard is one of the most useful.

You can invoke the Function Wizard in a variety of ways. Pulling down the Insert menu and selecting **Function** will do it, or you can click on the **Function Wizard** toolbar button, which is what we'll do now.

14. Click in cell **B28** and then click on the **Function Wizard** button on the toolbar.

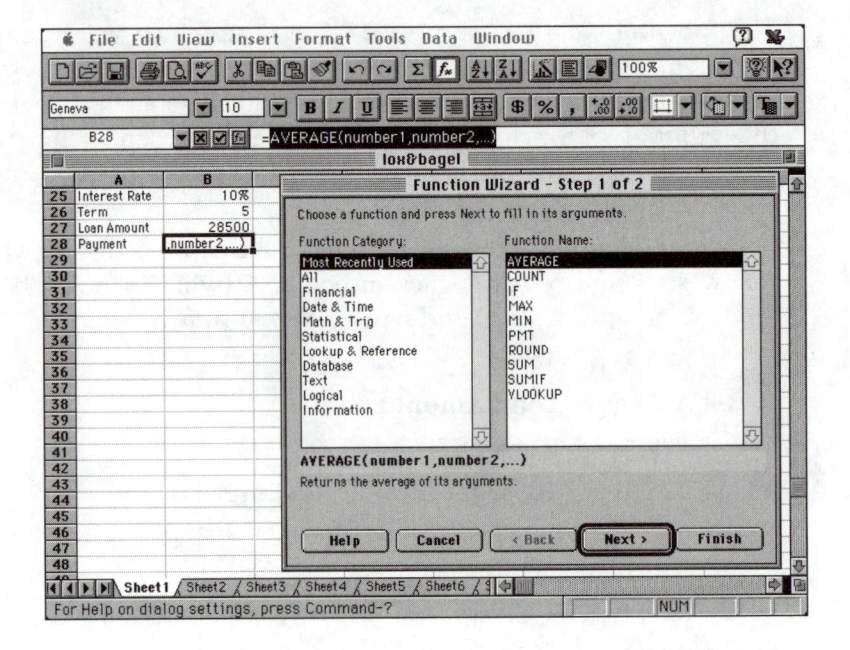

Figure 3.11 *The Function Wizard dialog box.*

If the dialog box obscures the values in column B, point to its title bar, drag to the right about an inch, and release the mouse button.

If the function you want is visible in the Function Name list on the right side of the dialog box, you can click on it. Otherwise, click on the category of functions you think your function might be in and then use the scroll bar to find it.

We'll go through the steps to find the **PMT** as though it weren't visible and we didn't know what category to choose.

15. Click on **All** in the Function Category list to list all the available functions in every category.

16. Use the Scrollbar in the Function Name list to scroll down until **PMT** is visible.

17. Click on **PMT**.

SHORTCUT

You can type the first letter of the function name and the highlighter jumps to it. Then you only have to search through the functions that start with that letter.

With **PMT** selected, the dialog box displays the proper syntax for the function and, below that, a brief explanation of what the function will do, as portrayed in Figure 3.12.

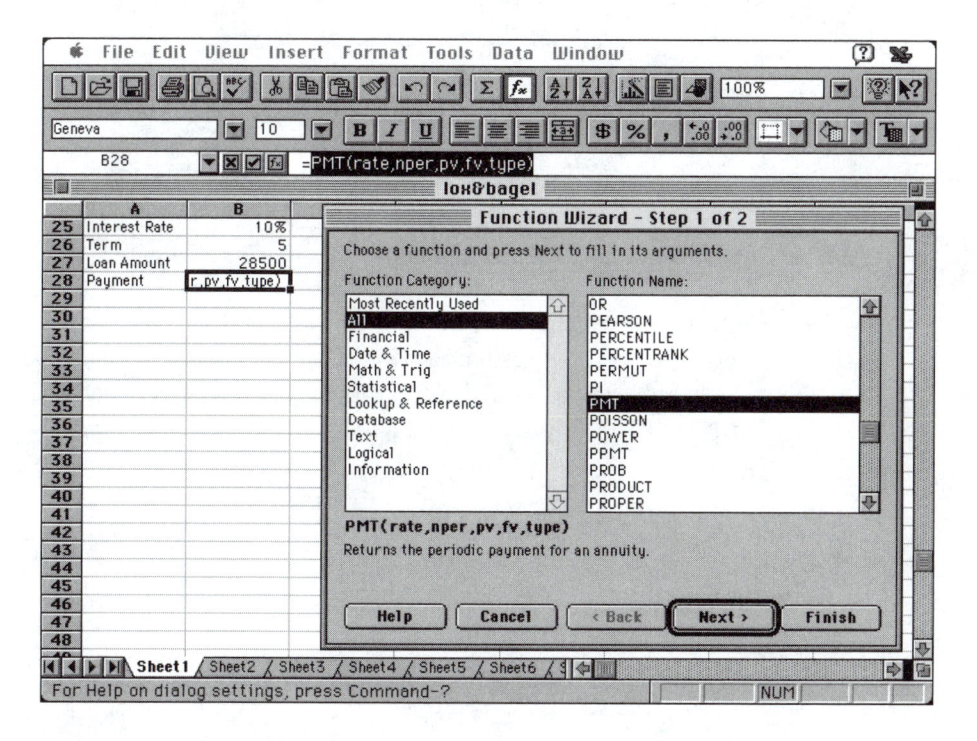

Figure 3.12 *The Function Wizard dialog box with the PMT function selected.*

If you want to enter the arguments manually, you can click on the **Finish** button, but it's much easier to let the Wizard step you through the argument entry process.

18. Click on the **Next** button to proceed to the Function Wizard dialog box that lets you enter the arguments, as shown in Figure 3.13.

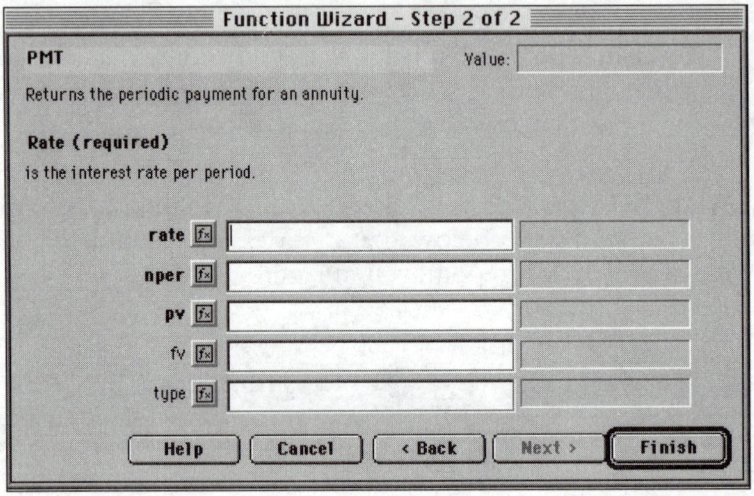

Function Wizard – Step 2 of 2

PMT   Value:

Returns the periodic payment for an annuity.

Rate (required)
is the interest rate per period.

rate
nper
pv
fv
type

Help   Cancel   < Back   Next >   Finish

Figure 3.13 *The Function Wizard dialog box for entering arguments.*

The insertion point is in the rate text box. Just above and to the left of the text box, the dialog box lets you know that you are ready to enter the rate per period and that this entry is a required argument.

You could type the cell reference for the rate, but it's easier to point and click.

19. Click on cell **B25** (the interest rate).

B25 is entered in the rate text box and **0.1** is entered in the box to the right of the text box. We need to make an adjustment here. Remember that the rate the function needs is the rate *per period*. Since we want to determine the monthly payment, and 10% is an annual rate, we need to divide it by 12.

20. Type: **/12**.

    Notice that the rate in the box to the right now displays the monthly interest rate, **0.0083333333**.

21. Press the **Tab** key to move to the NPER (number of payment periods) text box and click on cell **B26**.

    Again we need to modify the entry. Cell B26 contains the number of years for the loan, and we want the number of months, so we need to multiply by 12.

22. Type: ***12**.

    The value to the right of the text box now displays the value 60, which is the correct number of months.

23. Press the **Tab** key to move to the PV (present value) text box and click on cell **B27**.

    This entry doesn't need to be altered so the dialog box should now look like Figure 3.14. The **FV** (future value) and **TYPE** arguments are optional and we won't use them. With all the required arguments entered, the dialog box displays the value **-605.5407743** in the upper-right corner. This is the result of the calculation that will appear (formatted as a dollar figure) in cell B28 when we are finished.

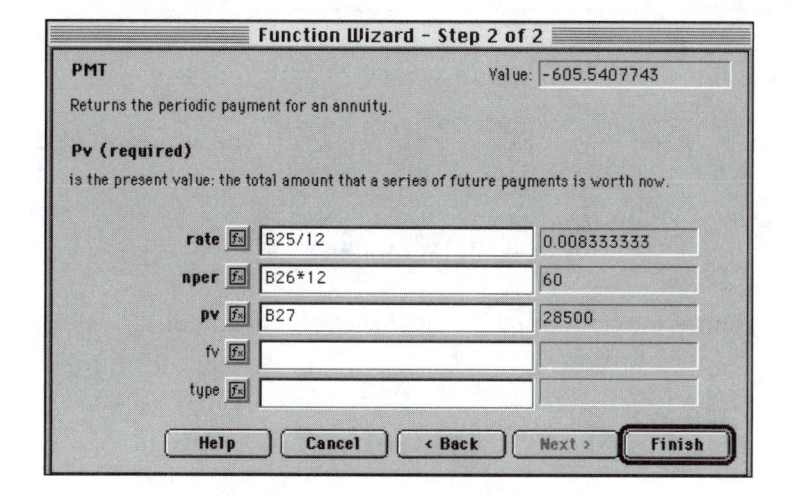

Figure 3.14 The filled-in dialog box.

24. Click on the **Finish** button to complete the Function Wizard procedure.

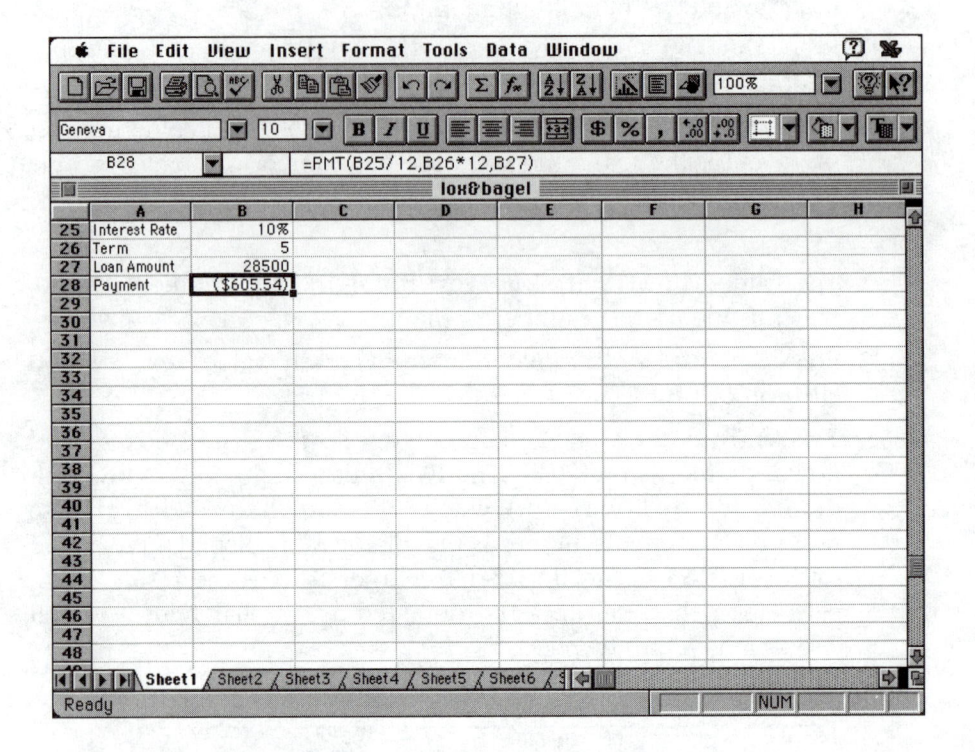

Figure 3.15 *The result of the PMT function.*

The value in cell B28 is in parentheses and in red (if you have a color monitor) to let you know that this is a negative value. The monthly payment is negative because it will result in an outflow from the business. If this were money being received, it would be positive.

Before moving on to the next section, let's return to cell A1.

25. Click in the **Name** box (displaying the active cell) on the left side of the formula bar.

26. Type: **A1** and press the **Return** key.

Naming a Worksheet

An Excel workbook can contain many sheets. For example, you might have one worksheet for budget calculations, one for a chart representing some of the data, and one for a customer list.

Each sheet in a workbook can have its own name, replacing the default Sheet1, Sheet2, Sheet3, etc. that appears on the sheet tabs. You don't have to rename the sheets but doing so can make it easier to work with a workbook that does contain several sheets.

1. Move the mouse pointer to the sheet tab for this worksheet and hold down the **Ctrl** key while pressing the mouse button.

   The sheet shortcut menu pops up, as shown in Figure 3.16.

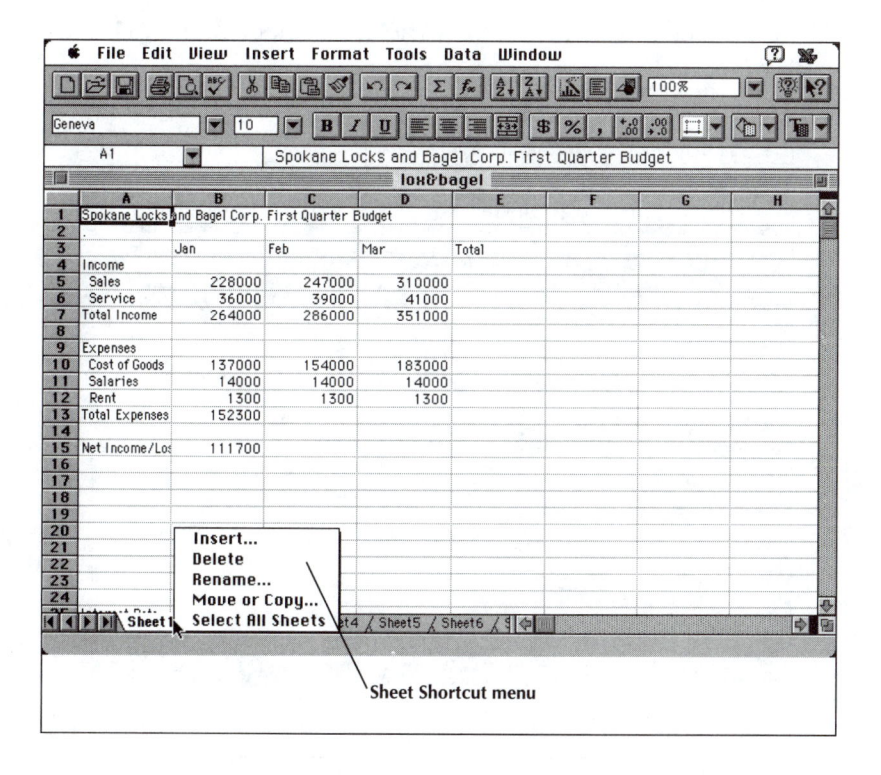

Figure 3.16 *The sheet shortcut menu.*

2. While still holding down the **Ctrl** key, drag the mouse to highlight the Rename command and release the mouse button.

   The **Rename** Sheet dialog box appears, as shown in Figure 3.17.

Figure 3.17 *The Rename Sheet dialog box.*

3. Type: **Q1 Budget**, then click on the **OK** button.

   The sheet tab now displays the new sheet name, as shown in Figure 3.18.

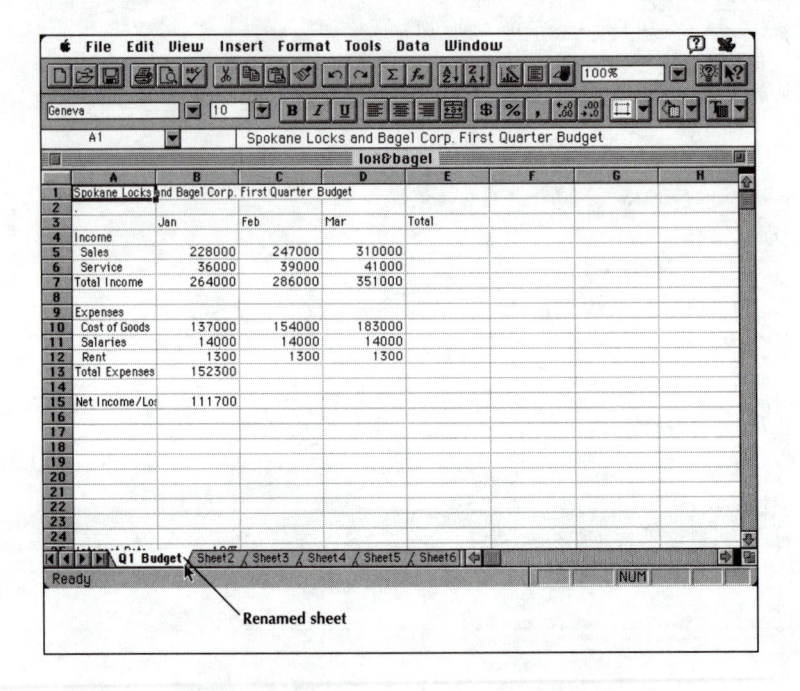

Figure 3.18 *The renamed sheet tab.*

Saving Your Work

Perhaps the most important habit to learn and use is to save your work on a regular basis. Until you save, the data you enter or edit is in your computer's temporary memory called RAM (*Random Access Memory*). Okay, so what's the definition of *regular basis?* Often enough that, if you lost all the work you had done since the last time you saved, you wouldn't be too upset.

Excel stores worksheets in files called *workbooks*. Within a single workbook, you can have many worksheets, all of which are saved to your computer's disk when you save. You don't need to specify which sheet or which portions of a sheet you want to save.

The first time you save a workbook, you'll be presented with several questions. You'll need to assign a filename and, if you like, fill in a summary dialog box with more detailed information about the workbook. Filenames can be up to 31 characters long, including spaces.

Let's save the workbook that contains the worksheet we've been working on with the name **lox&bagel**. Excel automatically assigns the name Workbook 1 to its first blank, unnamed workbook, so that's likely the name you see on your title bar now.

1. Pull down the File menu and select **Save As**.

   Figure 3.19 shows the dialog box used for naming and saving workbooks.

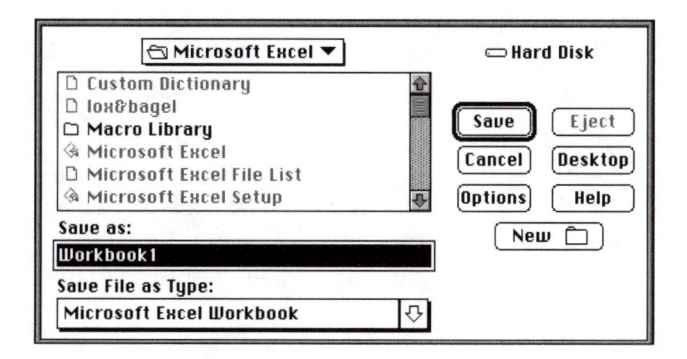

Figure 3.19 *The dialog box for saving workbooks.*

2. In the Save As text box, type: **lox&bagel**.

   If you want to save to a another location, as would be the case if you wanted to save to a floppy disk, click on the **Desktop** button, then click on the desired destination.

3. Click on the **Save** button.

   The Summary Info dialog box appears, as shown in Figure 3.20, with the author's name already filled in. The author is the name of the registered user of the program.

Summary Info	
File Name:	loxbagel
Directory:	Hard Disk:Microsoft Excel
Title:	
Subject:	
Author:	John Weingarten
Keywords:	
Comments:	

OK Cancel Help

Figure 3.20 *The Summary Info dialog box.*

You can fill in addit]ional information that might help you locate the workbook when you're looking for it later. You can enter any combination of title, subject or comments.

4. Click on the **OK** button to finish saving your workbook.

   As you work in Excel entering and editing data, you'll want tosave often, perhaps every ten or twenty minutes. The fastest way to do this is to click on the **Save** toolbar button. The saved file on your disk will automatically be replaced with the updated version and you won't even have to confirm that you want to replace it.

5. If you aren't continuing on to the next chapter now, pull down the File menu and select **Quit**.

A Final Thought

With what you've learned in this chapter, you already know as much as 80% of the spreadsheet users out there and you are ready to put Excel to productive use. Give yourself a pat on the back.

In the next chapter, you'll learn to work with some additional functions and learn about Excel's date and time handling.

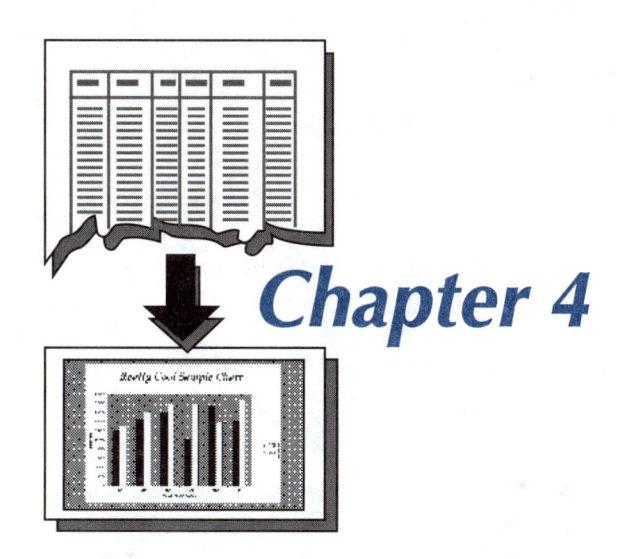

Chapter 4

Exploring More Excel Functions

- Finding the Functions You Need
- Exploring Additional Functions
- Working with Dates and Times
- A Final Thought

To become truly adept at building and managing Excel worksheets, you'll require a more through understanding of how to put Excel's vast array of functions to work. This chapter can't explain everything you'll want to know about functions–entire books have been written on the subject–but it will explore a few common functions and cover enough ground so you'll understand the concepts for putting more complex functions to work, and where to turn for help when you're lost. Notice that the function category is in parentheses after each function name heading.

Each of the functions will be presented in the context of our example business, the Spokane Locks and Bagel Corporation. However, each will be used in a separate worksheet, rather than using them to build one huge sheet. You'll be instructed to move to a new worksheet in a workbook for each function.

Although you can recreate the capabilities of most of the functions by using the operators discussed in the previous chapter, you'll save time and reduce errors if you track down the function that will do the job for you. If you're not sure which function to use for a particular task, do some browsing. Click on the **Function Wizard** button and look through the functions in the category that seem to match your needs. You'll see a brief description of the function at the bottom of the Function Wizard dialog box.

Using the NPER function (Financial)

The **NPER** function lets you calculate how many payment periods will be required to amortize a loan. Suppose the Spokane Locks and Bagel Corporation is thinking about purchasing that nifty piece of equipment discussed in the previous chapter, but they determine that they can only afford monthly payments of, say, $575.00. They can figure out how long they'll be in hock for this purchase by using the **NPER** function.

1. Start Excel if it isn't running.

2. If a workbook containing data is on the screen, click on the **NewWorkbook** button on the Standard toolbar to display a blank workbook.

   The title bar of a new workbook displays the name **Workbook** followed by the number of the workbook. If you were working on the BUDGET workbook, and that was the first workbook you used in the current Excel session, clicking on the **New Workbook** button will cause the title bar to display **Workbook 2**.

3. In cell A1, type: **Interest Rate**.

4. Move to cell A2 and type: **Payment**.

5. Move to cell A3 and type: **Loan Amount**.

6. Move to cell A4 and type: **Number of Payments**.

NOTE
I've increased the width of column A to accommodate the longest entries. It's not necessary to do this for your practice sheets. However, if you can't wait to learn how to change column widths, it's covered in the next chapter.

7. In cell B1, type: **10%**.

8. In cell B2, type: **-575**.

   The minus sign is important because this is an expense (money going out) rather than income.

9. In cell B3, type: **28500**.

10. Move to cell B4, where the result of the function's calculation will appear, and click on the **Function Wizard** button on the Standard toolbar.

    The first Function Wizard dialog box appears.

11. In the Function Category list of the Function Wizard dialog box, click on **Financial**.

12. In the Function Name list, click on **NPER**, then click on the **Next** button.

The second Function Wizard dialog box appears, with the argument text boxes for the **NPER** function, as shown in Figure 4.1. If the dialog box obscures the entries you made on the worksheet, move it out of the way by dragging it by its title bar.

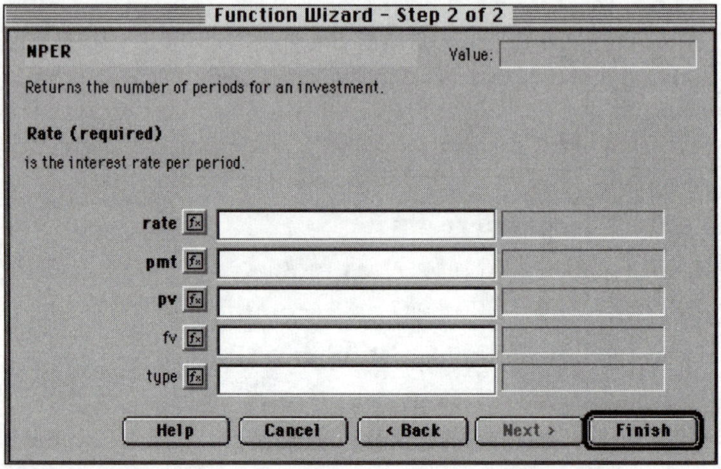

Function Wizard - Step 2 of 2

NPER   Value:

Returns the number of periods for an investment.

Rate (required)
is the interest rate per period.

rate

pmt

pv

fv

type

[Help] [Cancel] [< Back] [Next >] [Finish]

Figure 4.1 *The Function Wizard dialog box for the NPER function.*

You can get more detailed information about the use and proper syntax for a function by clicking on the **Help** button in the Function Wizard.

13. Click on the **Help** button.

The help screen appears, as shown in Figure 4.2. Remember, you can click on the **Zoom** button on the far right side of the help screen's title bar to enlarge it.

14. After you finish perusing the help screen, click on the **Close** box on the left side of the help screen's title bar.

15. Click in the Function Wizard's **Rate** text box.

You may have to drag the Function Wizard dialog box down or to the right so you can see cells B1 through B4.

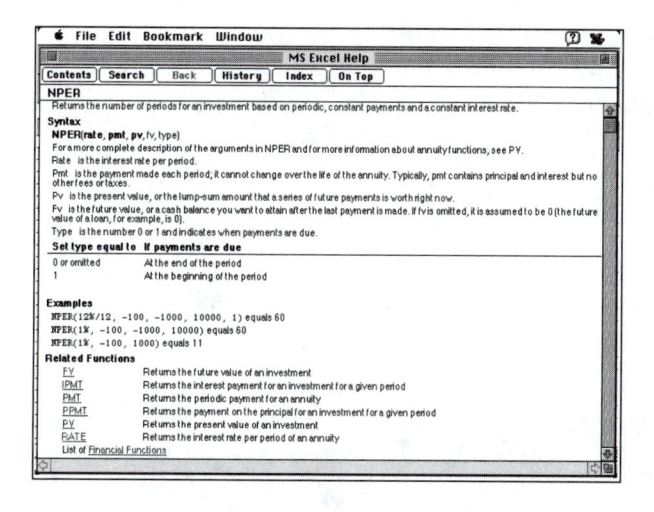

Figure 4.2 *The help screen for the NPER function.*

16. Click on cell **B1**, then type: **/12** to convert the annual interest rate to a monthly rate.

17. Press the **Tab** key to move the insertion point to the *pmt* text box, then click on cell **B2**.

18. Press the **Tab** key, then click on cell **B3**.

Now that the three required values are entered, the answer appears in the Value portion of the Function Wizard dialog box. It's going to take a little more than 64 months to amortize this piece of equipment.

NOTE

We're not using the two optional parameters–*future value* and *type*. You can use future value to enter a dollar amount you want to reach at the end of the amortization period. The type parameter determines whether the payments are made at the beginning or end of each payment period.

19. Click on the **Finish** button to accept the entries you've made in the Function Wizard.

Before moving to the next worksheet to explore another function, let's name the sheet.

20. Move the mouse pointer to the sheet tab for this worksheet, and hold down the **Ctrl** key and press the mouse button to display the sheet shortcut menu.

21. Select the **Rename** command in the shortcut menu.

22. Type: **Loan Length**, then click on the **OK** button.

The results of the **NPER** function and the renamed sheet tab are shown in Figure 4.3. The number of payment periods displays too many decimal places. Don't worry. You'll learn to format numbers in the next chapter.

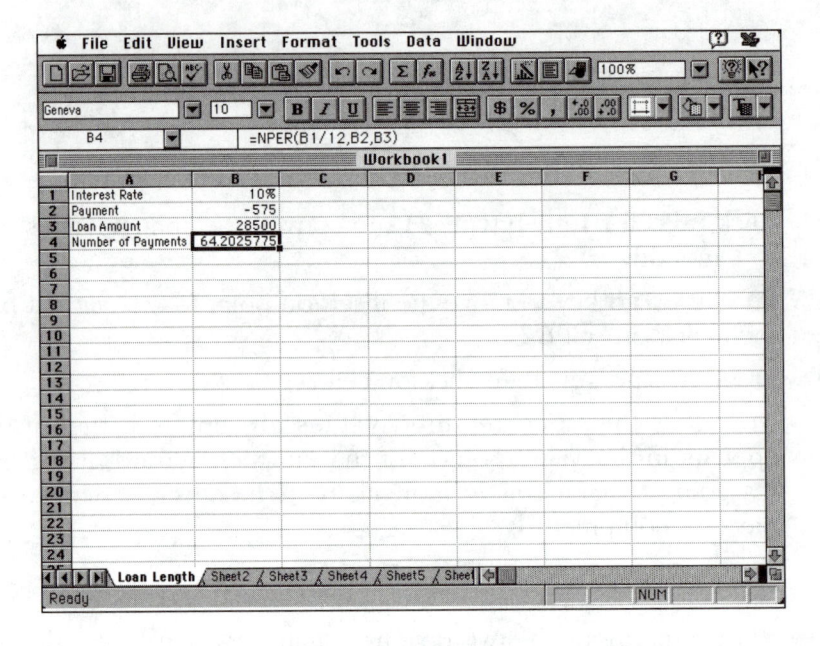

Figure 4.3 *The results of the NPER function.*

Using the PV function (Financial)

The **PV** (Present Value) function helps you determine what future cash flows are worth in today's dollars. Suppose Spokane Locks and Bagels is considering investing $10,000 of its cash reserves in a fixed-rate annuity that will return three annual payments of $4,000.

Sounds good. After all, $4,000 times 3 is $12,000. That's a two-thousand dollar profit. However, there's an opportunity cost. If you figure that Spokane Locks and Bagel could get 8% by just parking the money in CDs, then how do the two investments compare? The **PV** function will tell us.

1. Click on the **Sheet2 tab** to bring a blank worksheet into view.
2. In cell A1, type: **Initial Investment**.

   The initial investment isn't used as one of the arguments in the PV function. We're just putting it on the worksheet for reference.
3. In cell A2, type: **Interest Rate**.
4. In cell A3, type: **Number of Payments**.
5. In cell A4, type: **Payment**.
6. In cell A5, type: **Present Value**.
7. In cell B1, type: **$10,000**.
8. In cell B2, type: **8%**.
9. In cell B3, type: **3**.
10. In cell B4, type: **4000**.
11. Move to cell B5, where the result of the function's calculation will appear, and click on the **Function Wizard** button on the Standard toolbar.
12. Be sure Financial is highlighted in the Function Category list, then click on **PV** in the Function Name list.
13. Click on the **Next** button.
14. Click in cell **B2**, the cell containing the interest rate.
15. Press the **Tab** key, then click in cell **B3**, the cell containing the number of payments.

    Notice that the name of the argument for the number of payments is nper (for number of periods), just like the **NPER** function discussed in the previous section.
16. Press the **Tab** key again and click in cell **B4**, the cell containing the annual payment amount.
17. Click on the **Finish** button.

NOTE

As in the previous examples, if you use the default column widths, some of the text in column A will be truncated. Even worse, the result of the formula in cell B5 is too wide to fit and is therefore represented by number signs (#####). You can adjust the column width by positioning the mouse pointer on the right column-heading border and then dragging. For more information about adjusting column widths, take a look at the next chapter.

Ah ha! The investment appears to be a good one, as you can see in Figure 4.4.

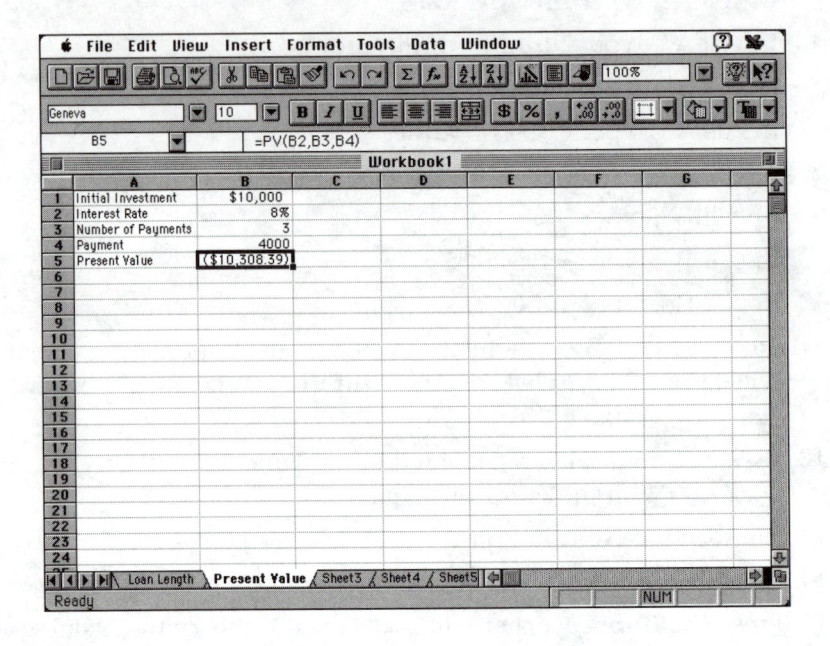

Figure 4.4 The Present Value worksheet.

18. Name the worksheet **Present Value**.

19. Save the workbook by clicking on the **Save** button on the Standard toolbar. Enter **function practice** in the Save As text box and then click on the **Save** button.

   If the Summary Info dialog box appears, just click on the **OK** button to complete the save operation.

Using the MIN and MAX functions (Statistical)

In the group of statistical functions, two of the more common functions are MIN and **MAX**. These functions return the smallest or largest number in a range. The only argument for these functions is the range (or ranges).

Spokane Locks and Bagels could use these functions to determine which is the lowest- or highest-priced item in a list of products, or which customer spent the least or the most.

1. Click on the **Sheet3 tab** to bring another blank worksheet into view.

2. Name the worksheet **MinMax**.

3. Enter the data in columns A and B on the new worksheet, as shown in Figure 4.5.

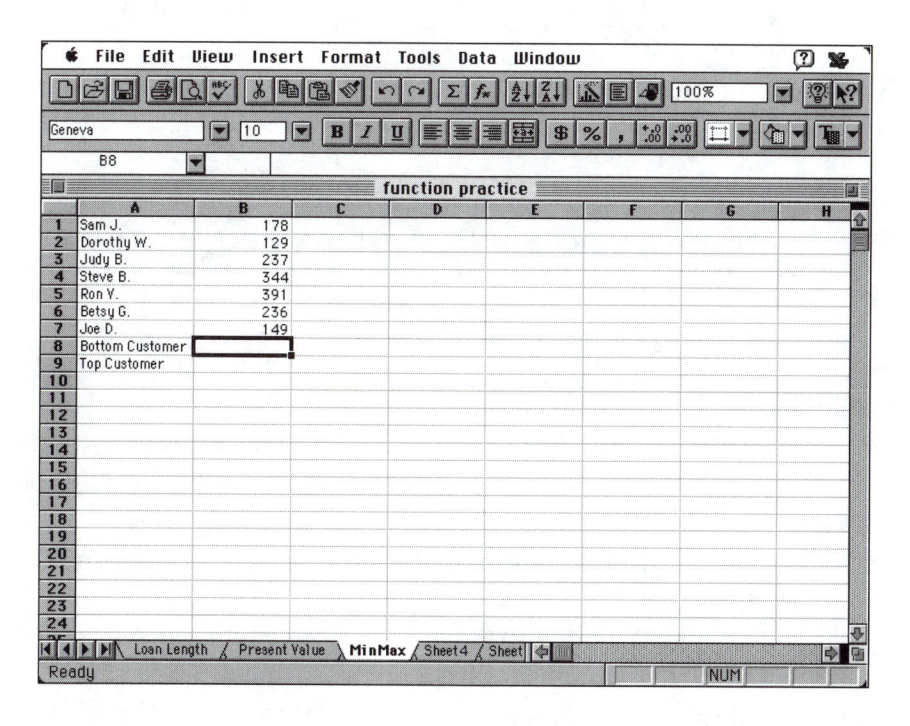

Figure 4.5 *The data for the MinMax worksheet.*

4. Click in cell **B8**, where the result of the **MIN** function will appear.

5. Click on the **Function Wizard** button.

6. In the Function Wizard dialog box, click on **Statistical** in the Function Category list.

7. Scroll down the Function Name list until **MIN** is visible.

8. Click on **MIN** and then click on the **Next** button.

    Drag the Function Wizard dialog box out of the way of cells B1 through B7, if necessary.

9. Drag over cells B1 through B7 to include those cells in the function's argument.

    A dashed line appears around B1 through B7, as shown in Figure 4.6.

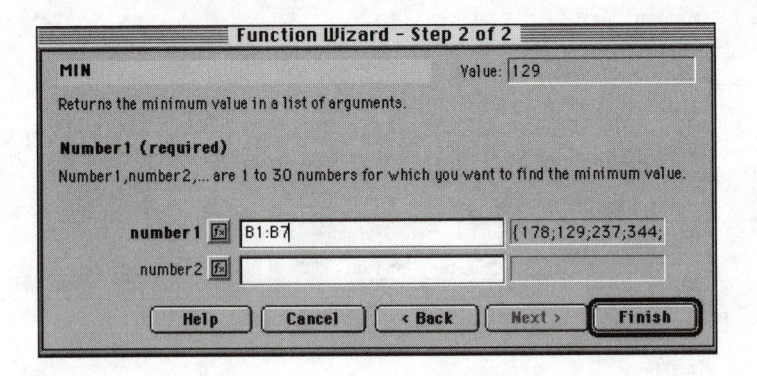

Figure 4.6 Using the MIN function with the argument range selected.

10. Click on the **Finish** button.

    The smallest number in the list is displayed in cell B8. Obviously this would be a more useful function with a much larger list, but you can see how it works.

11. Move to cell B9, where the result of the **MAX** function will appear.

12. Click on the **Function Wizard** button and be sure Statistical is highlighted in the Function Category list.

13. Scroll down the Function Name list until **MAX** is visible.

14. Click on **MAX**, then click on the **Next** button.

15. Drag over cells B1 through B7 to include those cells in the function's argument.

16. Click on the **Finish** button.

The largest number in the list appears in cell B9, as shown in Figure 4.7.

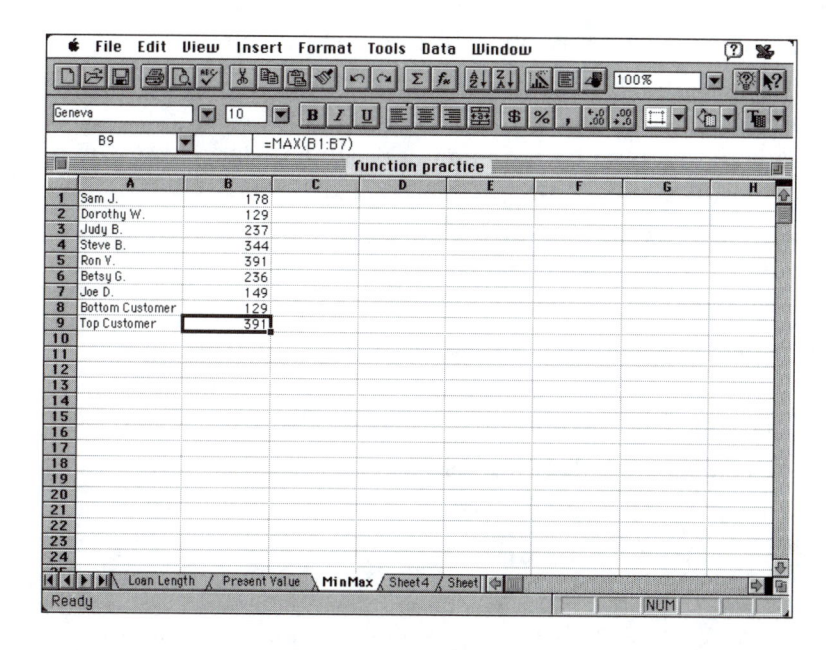

Figure 4.7 *The MinMax worksheet with the results of both the MIN and the MAX functions.*

17. Save the function practice workbook by clicking on the **Save** button on the Standard toolbar.

Using Date and Time functions

Excel employs a variety of functions to facilitate date and time calculations. One of the common uses for date calculations is for aging an accounts-receivable report. For example, Spokane Locks and Bagels might use an aged receivable report to determine how long its credit customers are taking to pay their bills. This can be important information, because it is generally true that the longer an account remains past due, the less likely it is to be collected. Calculating the length of time an account is past due could also allow Spokane Locks and Bagel to tack on late fees.

When you enter dates and times in Excel, they are displayed as dates and times. Makes sense. In fact, you will learn to change the way they are displayed in. Chapter 6, which covers cell formatting.

Excel keeps track of dates and times using a systems of numbers. Dates are tracked as serial numbers based on the year 1904. So January 1st, 1904 is represented by the number 0. January 2nd, 1904 is number 1. April 15, 1994 is 32977. Times are stored as decimal fractions.

1. Click on the **Sheet4 tab** to bring another blank worksheet into view.

2. Name the sheet **Dates-Times**.

   We'll try a few date and time entries. As you enter these dates and times, notice the way Excel displays them.

3. In cell A1, type: **July 15, 1994**.

4. In cell A2, type: **2:30 pm**.

5. In cell A3, type: **12 am**.

6. In cell A4, type: **=now()**.

   You may have to adjust the column width to see the results of the NOW function.

   The NOW function uses the date from your computer's clock/calendar. The parentheses are required, although no argument is entered between them. Of course, you could use the Function Wizard to apply the **NOW** function, as well as numerous other date and time functions. However, since **NOW** doesn't require any arguments, it's just as easy to enter it manually.

NOTE   If the incorrect date appears when you move to the next cell, you'll need to reset your computer's time and date. To do this, pull down the Apple menu and select Control Panels. Double click on the **Date & Time** icon in the Control Panels window to open the Date & Time dialog box. Adjust the date and time and then click on the close box.

Now we'll let Excel calculate what the date will be 45 days from now.

7. In cell A5, type: **=now()+45** and press the **Return** key.

The date displayed in A5 is 45 days later than the date displayed in A4. Figure 4.8 displays the date and time entries as they should appear on your worksheet. Of course, some of your dates and times may differ, depending on the time and date set on your computer.

If you want to see the actual numbers Excel is using to keep track of dates and times, you can format the cells to General format instead of the default date format. Chapter 6 covers formatting cells.

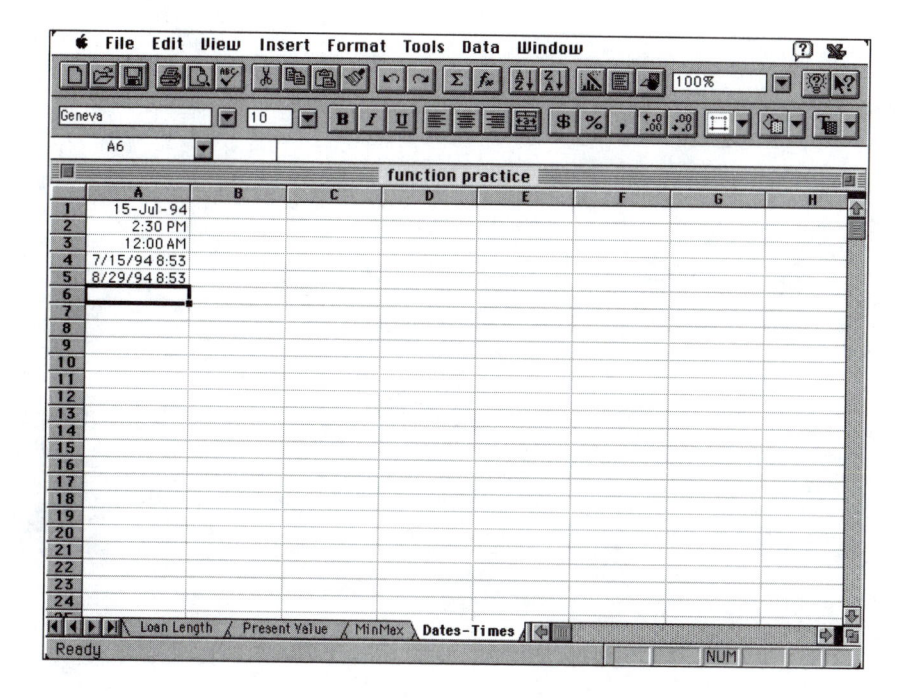

Figure 4.8 *The Dates-Times worksheet.*

8. Save your work by clicking on the **Save** button.

9. Exit Excel if you're not continuing to the next chapter now.

A Final Thought

In this chapter you learned to put several of the more common functions to work and how Excel handles dates and times.

In the next chapter, you'll learn to make some modifications to your worksheet, including inserting and deleting data, copying formulas, and formatting cells.

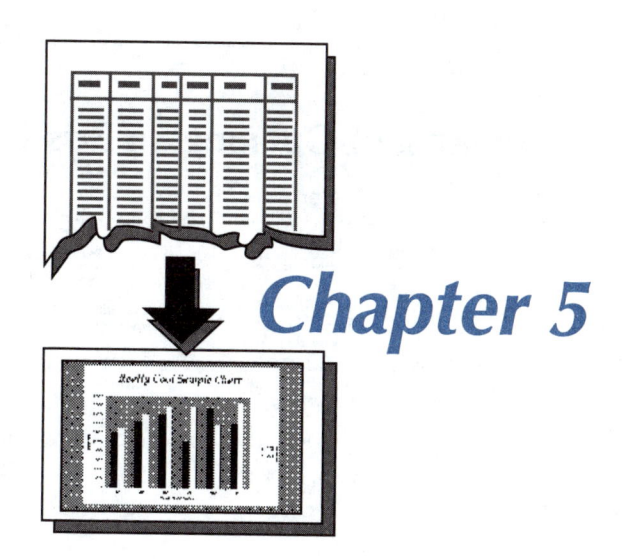

Chapter 5

Modifying a Worksheet

- Finding and Opening an Existing Document
- Copying Formulas
- Selecting Ranges
- Defining and Using Names
- Inserting and Deleting Rows and Columns
- Changing Columns Widths
- A Final Thought

Finding and Opening an Existing Worksheet

One of the biggest fears of new computer users is that they'll put a lot of time and energy into creating a document, dutifully save it to the disk, close the document, and never be able to find it again. It will be lost forever, as though sucked into a black hole.

Relax! Your document is there and Excel makes it easy to find it. You *did* save it, didn't you?

Shortly, we'll open the **lox&bagel** workbook, but first let's explore some of the ways to open a document.

1. Start Excel, if it isn't running.

   Unless you've been doing some work with Excel behind my back, the last two workbooks you had on your screen were **function practice** and **lox&bagel**. Even if you were working on a couple of other documents since working with the function practice and lox&bagel workbooks, Excel will display **function practice** and **lox&bagel** along with the two other recently opened files at the bottom of the File menu.

2. Pull down the File menu.

   Notice the group of four file names at the bottom of the menu, just above the Exit command, in Figure 5.1. Your File menu may only display one or two file names, if those are the only files you've worked with.

   You could open the lox&bagel workbook by clicking on it or pressing the number in front of its name. Instead, let's examine some other methods for finding and opening the file.

3. Release the mouse button without selecting a command to clear the menu.

4. Click on the **Open** toolbar button.

Pressing the **Open** toolbar button is the same as pulling down the File menu and selecting **Open**, and calls up the Open dialog box illustrated in Figure 5.2.

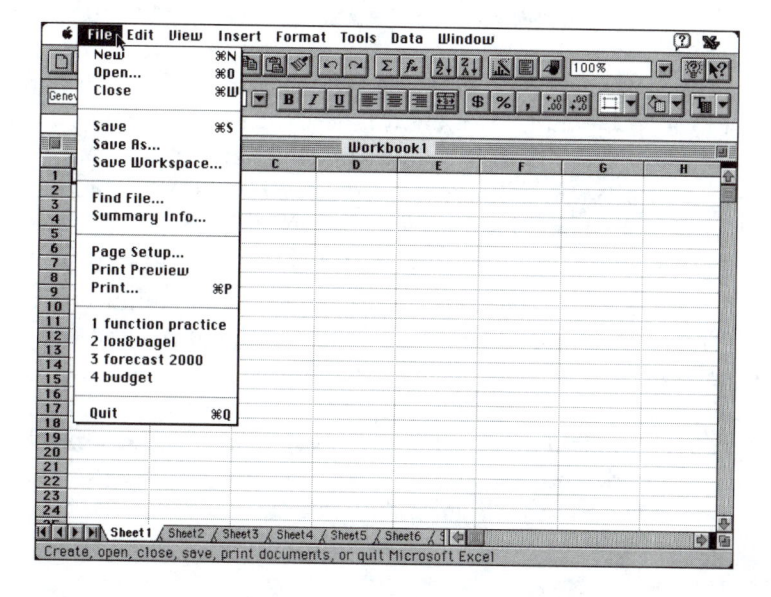

Figure 5.1 *The File menu with the four most recently opened files displayed.*

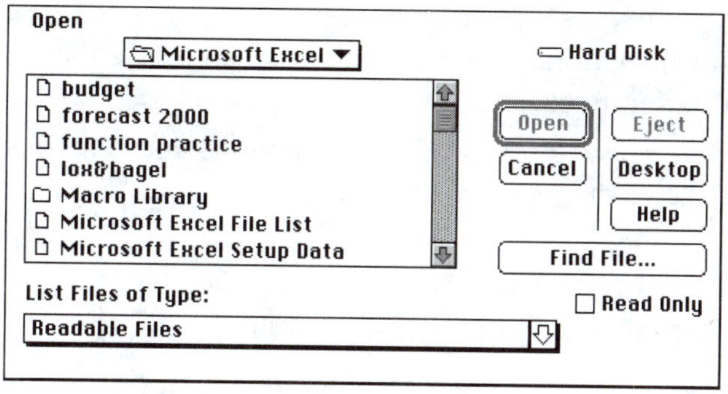

Figure 5.2 *The Open dialog box.*

You can open a workbook by double-clicking on its name in the list of files.

5. If **lox&bagel** isn't displayed in the list of files, use the scroll bar to scroll down the list to bring it into view. If it still isn't visible, click on the folder name button above the list of files and switch to the folder containing the workbook.

6. Click on **lox&bagel**, the click on the **Open** button to open the **lox&bagel** workbook.

The first two methods we discussed for opening a file are fine if the file you want to open was one of the last four you worked with, or if you know its name and the name of the folder where it is located. But suppose you haven't worked on the file recently. In fact, it's been so long that you've forgotten its name and even the folder where you saved it. Hey, it happens to the best of us.

It's *still* easy to find the file using Excel's magnificent Find File facilities. As long as you know *something* about the file, such as the approximate date when it was saved last, or some information you entered into the Summary Info dialog box, or even just some unique text that is contained anywhere in the file, Excel will do the legwork and find the long lost file for you. For more information about how to use Find File, refer to Excel's Help system.

Copying Formulas and Functions

In the last chapter, you learned how to create formulas and use functions to perform calculations. Often, you'll need to apply the same formula or function to several cells.

Before we copy any formulas or functions, let's use the AutoSum button to add the calculations for February and March Total Expenses.

1. Make C13 the active cell.

2. Double-click on the **AutoSum** toolbar button.

3. Move to D13 and, once again, double-click on the **AutoSum** button.

With all the Total Income and Total Expenses calculations in place, we're ready to add the formulas for calculating the Net Income/Loss for February and March. Instead of creating separate formulas, we'll copy the formula for January's Net Income/Loss to February and March.

4. Move to cell B15.

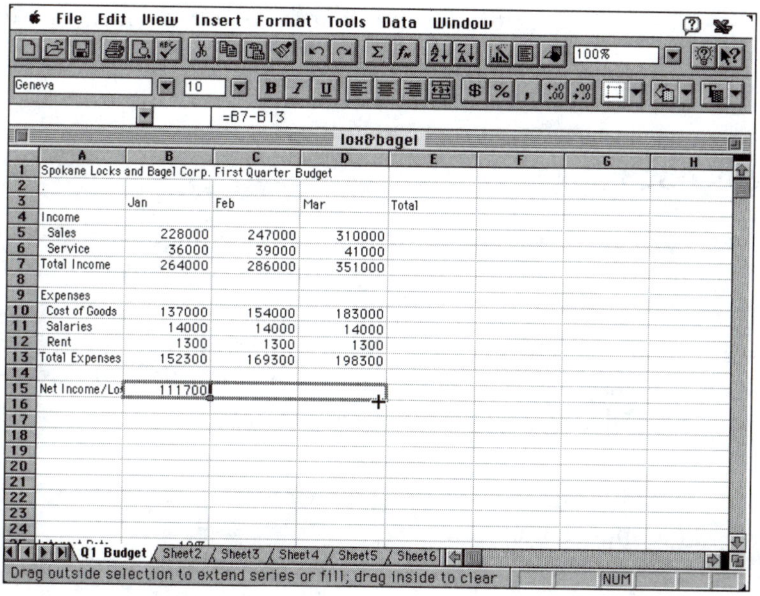

Figure 5.3 *Copying a formula with the fill handle.*

If you look in the formula bar, the formula *appears* to be =B7-B13. Well, appearances can be deceiving. Excel and other spreadsheets employ a type of cell referencing called *relative reference*. By using relative references, cells containing text, values, or even formulas or functions can be copied, and they will be automatically adjusted to perform properly in their new location.

Relative reference logic sees the formula in B15 as "subtract the value in the cell that is two rows up from the value in the cell that is eight rows up." When you copy a formula, the *logic* of the formula (not the actual formula) is copied, so the formula will work in its new location.

Let's use the fill handle that we used in the last chapter to create a series, to copy the formula to cells C15 and D15.

5. Position the mouse pointer over the fill handle and drag two cells to the right, as shown in Figure 5.3.

6. Release the mouse button and then press the **Right Arrow** key to make C15 the active cell.

    Take a look at the formula bar to assure yourself that the logic of the formula was correctly copied. You can check out cell D15 for further proof.

Selecting Ranges

So far, other than copying formulas to several cells, we've been manipulating one cell at a time. Excel lets you select a range of cells on which you want to perform some action.

The easiest way to select cells is to simply drag the mouse over the cells you want to select. Let's select E5 through E7 and use the AutoSum function to calculate the quarter total income.

1. Position the mouse pointer in E5, drag down to E7, and release the mouse button.

    The selected range is highlighted and the cell you started with is the active cell, as shown in Figure 5.4.

2. Double-click on the **AutoSum** button to add the function to all the selected cells at once.

    There will be times when you want to select non-contiguous ranges of cells. For example, suppose you wanted to sum the quarter totals for the expenses and the net income/loss at the same time. No problem. Just use the ⌘ key to add to a selection.

3. Position the mouse pointer in cell E10, drag down to E13 and release the mouse button.

4. Hold down the ⌘ key and click on cell **E15**.

    E10 through E13 and cell E15 are selected, as depicted in Figure 5.5. The last cell, E15, is the active cell.

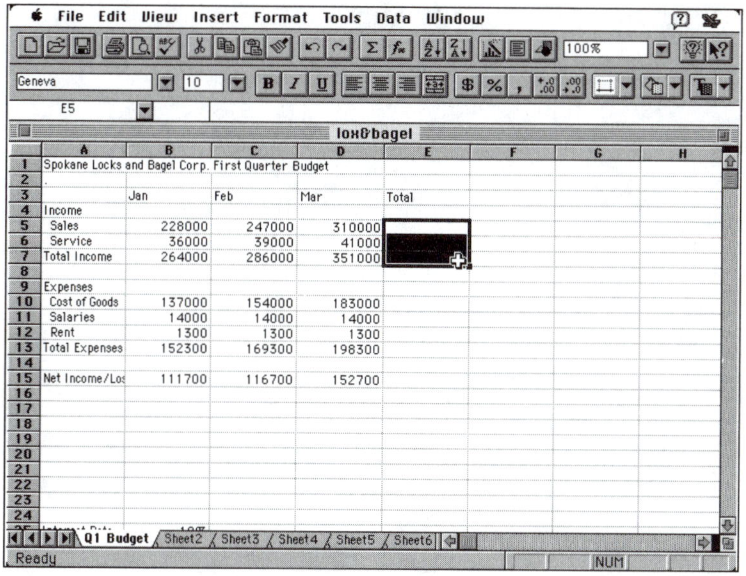

Figure 5.4 *A selected range.*

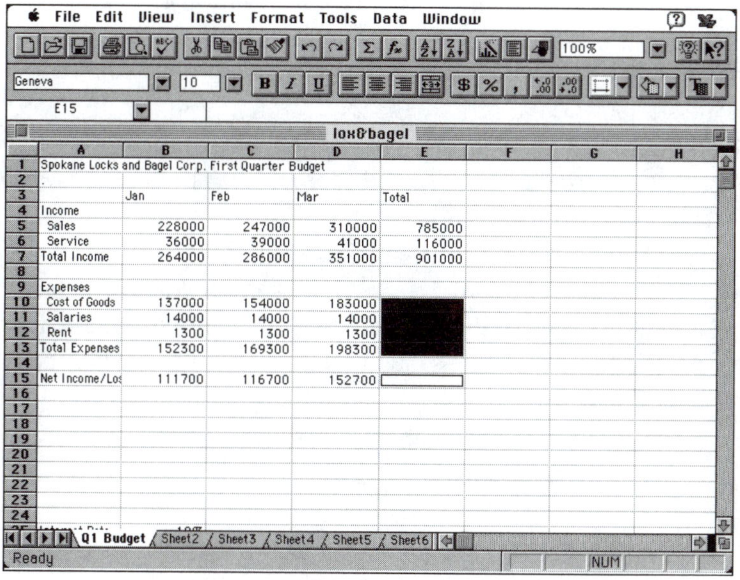

Figure 5.5 *Two non-contiguous selected ranges.*

5. Double-click on the **AutoSum** button again to add the function to the selected cells.

 If you need to select a rectangular range, the **Shift** key can make the task more efficient. Just click on one corner of the range you want to select, then hold down the **Shift** key and click on the opposite corner of the range.

You can also use the Name box just to the left of the formula bar or the Go To dialog box to select a range. Instead of typing a single cell address in the Reference text box, you can enter two cell addresses separated by a colon. When you press the **Return** key or click on the Go To dialog box **OK** button, the range will be selected.

Defining Names

So far, we've only referred to cells by their addresses. Naming ranges can make your worksheets much easier to understand. Using names in formulas instead of ranges of cell addresses can make it instantly clear what the formula does. For example, "B7-B13" is meaningless until you look at the worksheet and determine what these cell addresses represent. However, if the formula read "Total Income-Total Expenses", you'd know exactly what was going on.

You can name individual cells or ranges of cells. You can also specify the name you want to assign, or let Excel do it for you. Generally, an appropriate name is already adjacent to the cell or range of cells you want to name. If this is the case, you can include the name with the range and let Excel use it.

Let's create names for the income and expense categories, including total income and total expenses.

1. Select the ranges **A5** through **D7** and **A10** through **D13**, as shown in Figure 5.6.

Remember to use the **Ctrl** key to select non-contiguous ranges.

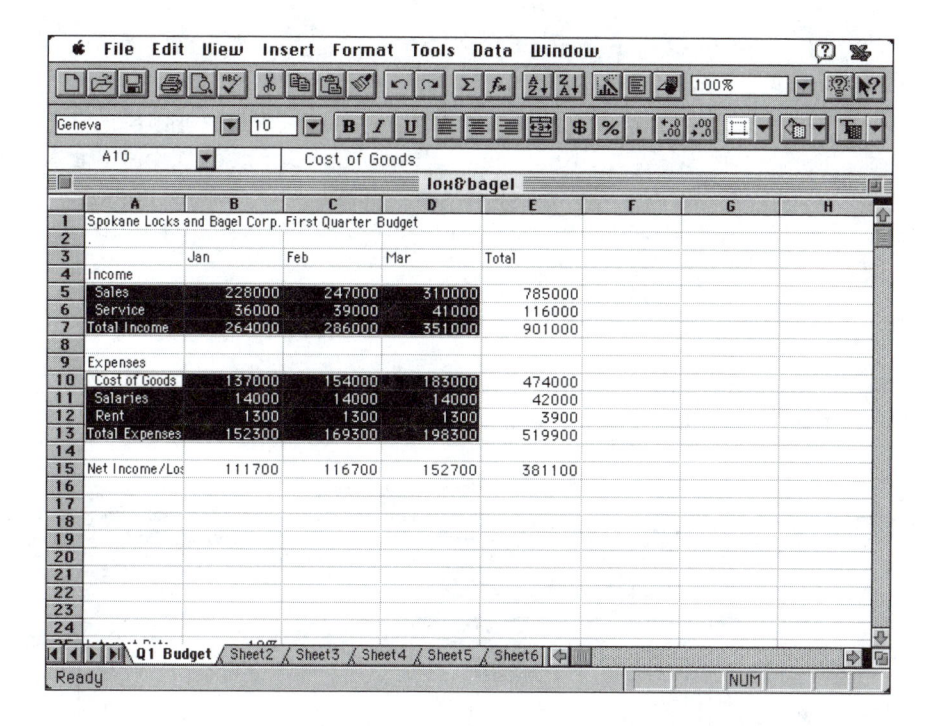

Figure 5.6 *The selected ranges to be named.*

2. Pull down the Insert menu and select **Name**, **Create**.

   The Create Names dialog box appears, as depicted in Figure 5.7, with the Create Names in Left Column check box checked.

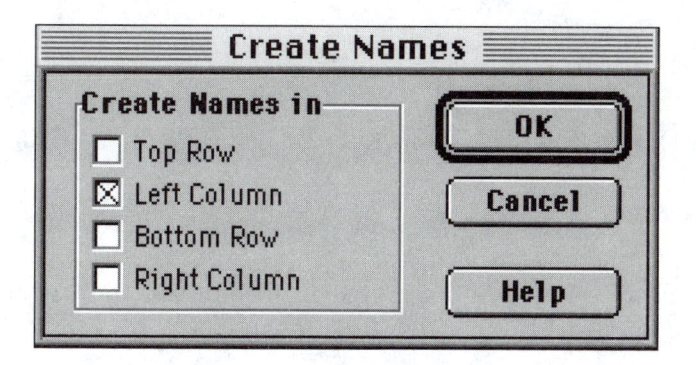

Figure 5.7 *the Create Names dialog box.*

3. Click on the **OK** button.

   Although Excel uses the names in the left column, they aren't included as part of the range. You can use the Define Name dialog box to see which ranges each name is applied to, but the easiest way–and a good shortcut for selecting a named range–is the *Name box* in the cell reference area. Let's use this method to select the Service range.

4. Click on the **Arrow** for the Name box, just to the right of the cell reference area.

   The drop-down list, pictured in Figure 5.8, displays the names that are contained in the worksheet.

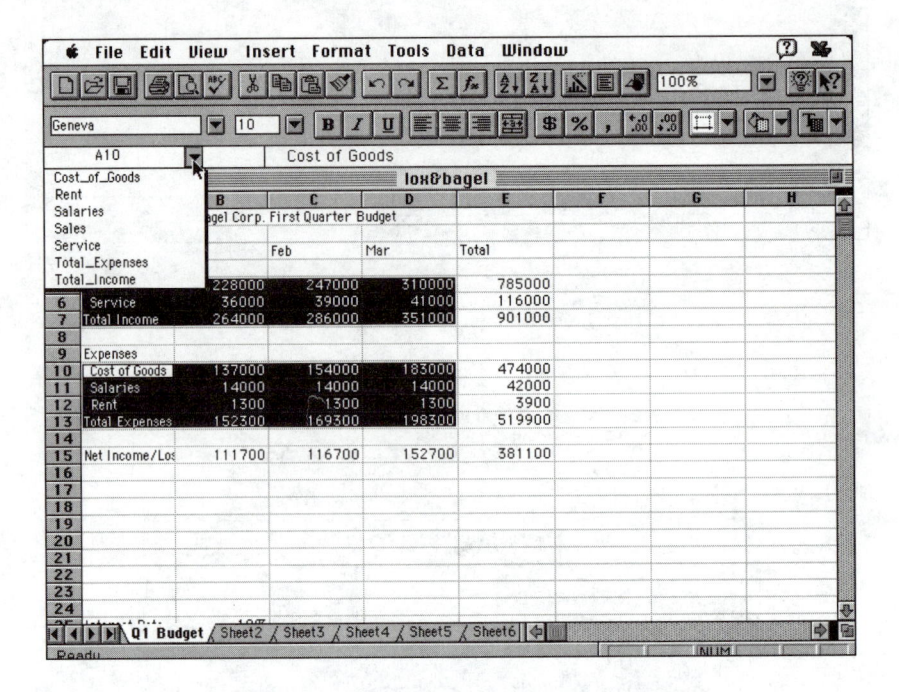

Figure 5.8 The worksheet's named ranges.

5. Drag down to select **Service** in the list and release the mouse button to select the range B6 through D6.

   Now let's make the formulas in the worksheet more understandable by substituting the range addresses with the range names.

To have Excel automatically apply range names, we first need to select the cells that contain formulas or functions. To make sure we don't miss any, we'll select the whole worksheet. A shortcut for selecting the entire worksheet is to click on the **Select All** box (the rectangle below the close box in the upper-left corner of the worksheet where the row and column heading intersect).

6. Click on the **Select All** box.

7. Pull down the Insert menu and select **Name**, **Apply**.

   The Apply Names dialog box, with all the range names listed, appears as shown in Figure 5.9.

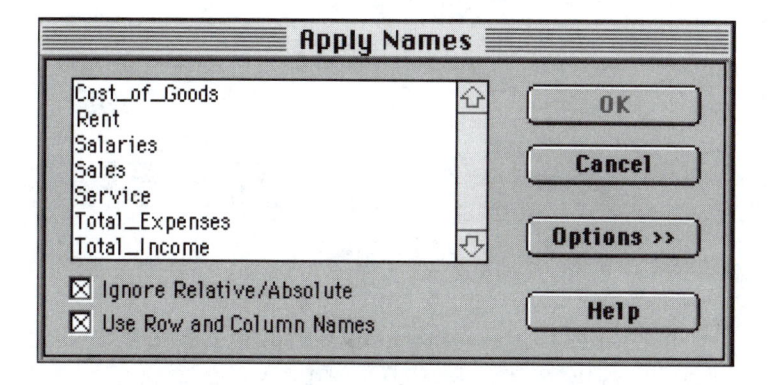

Figure 5.9 *The Apply Names dialog box.*

8. Click on each of the names in the list to highlight them.

9. Click on the **OK** button to apply the names to all the formulas and functions that refer to those ranges.

   The formula in B7 used to read =B5+B6. Let's take a look at how it's changed.

10. Click on cell **B7** and look at the formula bar.

    The new formula is =Sales+Service, as shown in Figure 5.10.

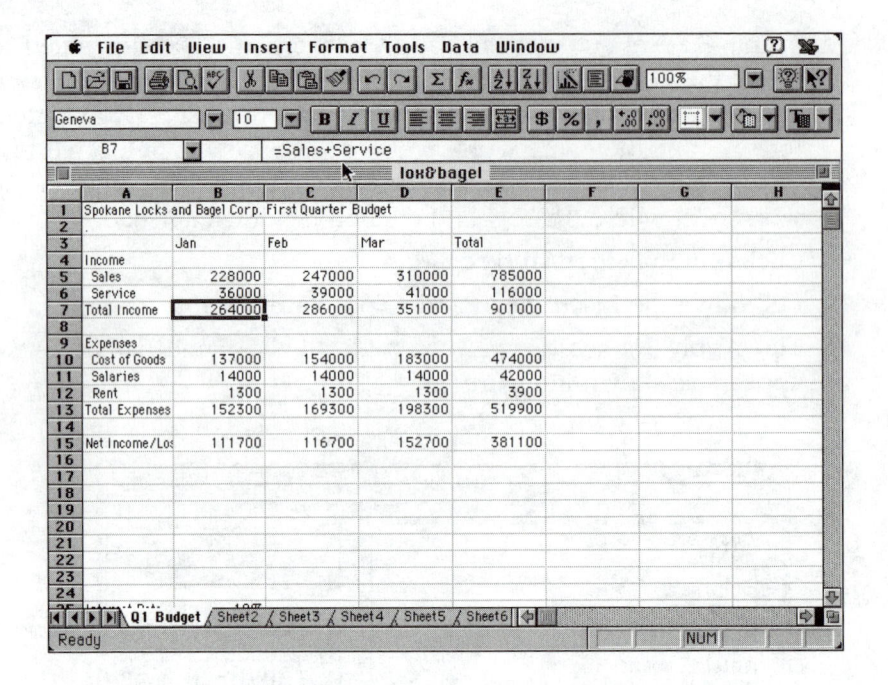

Figure 5.10 *The formula in cell B7 using range names.*

Click on some of the other cells containing formulas or functions to see how the names have been applied.

Inserting and Deleting Rows and Columns

As you create and edit worksheets, you'll frequently need to insert or delete rows and columns. Perhaps you want to add or remove categories or time periods.

Let's insert a row to add a new category, Income, to our budget worksheet, showing interest income for the company's investments.

WARNING

Inserting or deleting rows or columns can be very dangerous. You could inadvertently interfere with some data that you can't see on the screen. You could have data off to the side, or above or below the portion of the worksheet that is currently visible.

When inserting or deleting rows or columns, be sure to take into account the effect these actions could have on all portions of your worksheet.

N O T E

Also, even though Excel provides an undo feature to get you out of sticky situations, it's always a good idea to save your work just before making any sort of change that could wreak havoc on your worksheet.

1. Move to cell A6. Actually, any cell in row 6 will do.
2. Pull down the Insert menu and select **Rows**.

   A new row has been inserted and named ranges have been adjusted to reflect their new locations, as have cells containing formulas and functions.
3. Enter the data for the new row, pictured in Figure 5.11.

	A	B	C	D	E	F	G	H
1	Spokane Locks and Bagel Corp. First Quarter Budget							
2								
3		Jan	Feb	Mar	Total			
4	Income							
5	Sales	228000	247000	310000	785000			
6	Interest	1200	1400	1600				
7	Service	36000	39000	41000	116000			
8	Total Income	264000	287400	352600	904000			
9								
10	Expenses							
11	Cost of Goods	137000	154000	183000	474000			
12	Salaries	14000	14000	14000	42000			
13	Rent	1300	1300	1300	3900			
14	Total Expenses	152300	169300	198300	519900			
15								
16	Net Income/Los	111700	118100	154300	384100			
17								
18								
19								
20								
21								
22								
23								
24								

Q1 Budget / Sheet2 / Sheet3 / Sheet4 / Sheet5 / Sheet6

Ready — NUM

Figure 5.11 *The budget worksheet with the data entered for the newly inserted row.*

Notice that the January Total Income calculation didn't adjust to accommodate the new cell, but February and March did. What happened? January used a formula that added two specific cells, while February and March used the **SUM** function to add a range of cells. When we inserted a row, the new row is included in the **SUM** function's range, but isn't automatically added to the formula.

We'll fix this by replacing the formula with the **SUM** function. We'll also use AutoSum to add the calculation for the quarter total interest.

4. Move to cell B8 and double-click on the **AutoSum** toolbar button.

5. Move to cell E6 and double-click on the **AutoSum** button.

One way to reduce expenses would be to get rid of the rent. Let's delete row 13 to improve the company's profit picture.

6. Move to any cell in row 13.

7. Pull down the Edit menu and select **Delete**.

The Delete dialog box appears, as pictured in Figure 5.12.

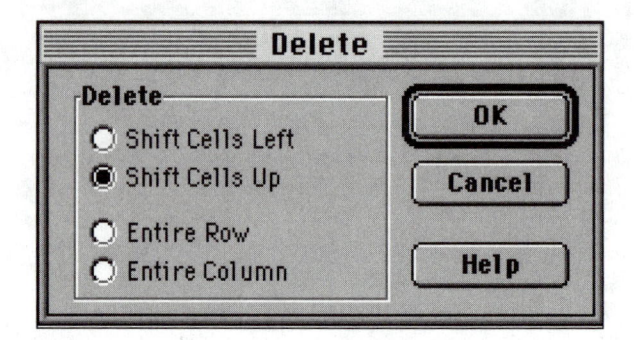

Figure 5.12 *The Delete dialog box.*

Because only a single cell is selected, Excel suggests shifting the cells below the active cell up. This is not what we had in mind. We want to get rid of the entire row.

8. Click the **Entire Row** radio button and click on **OK**.

N O T E If you see a dialog box telling you that Excel can't resolve the circular reference, click the **OK** button. A circular reference usually means that the formula in the formula cell refers to itself. For example, the formula =B4+B5+B6 in cell B6 would be a circular reference.

Also, don't worry about **REF**! in some of the cells that contain formulas. This is just another of Excel's methods for letting you know there is a reference problem in a formula.

Okay, that got rid of our rent, but wait a minute. Maybe we need to pay rent after all, so we'll have a place to operate our business. We'll use the Excel's Undo feature to reverse the deletion.

8. Pull down the Edit menu and select **Undo** or click on the **Undo** button on the Standard toolbar to restore the rent row.

Changing Column Widths

Finally, what you've been waiting for. When text entries are too long and they are truncated or numbers show up as pound signs (#), your column is probably too narrow and needs to be adjusted.

I'll bet you've been anxiously looking at column A since we first entered the numbers and lost part of the text. Well, the time has come to fix the problem and adjust the column.

You can change the column width by entering a new value in the Column Width dialog box when you pull down the Format menu and select **Column**, **Width**. But there's an even easier, more visual way. You can position the mouse pointer over the right border of the column heading and drag it to the left to reduce the width, or to the right to increase the width. Let's use the dragging method to increase the width of column A.

1. Position the mouse pointer over the right border of the column heading, and drag to the right about 1/2", as shown in Figure 5.13.

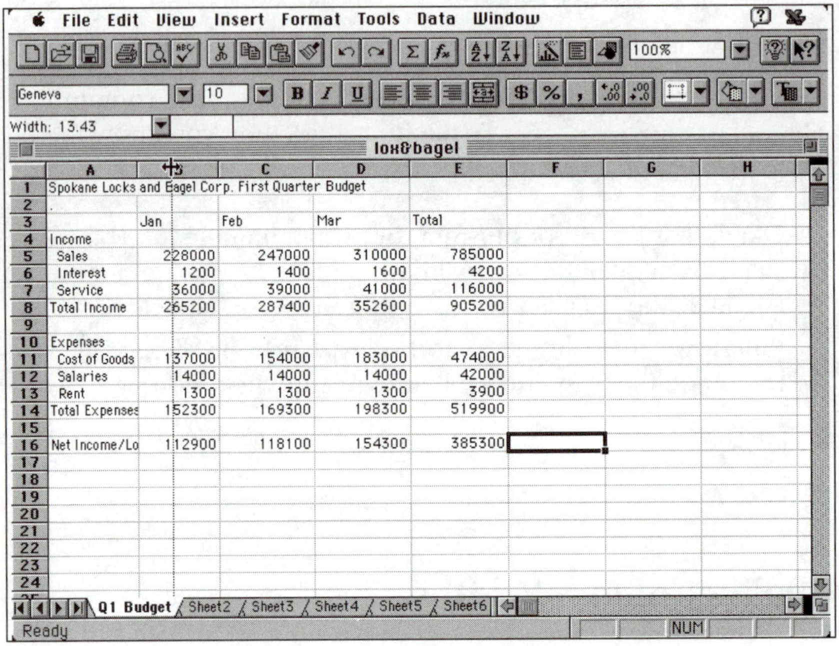

Figure 5.13 *The column width being adjusted.*

2. Release the mouse button to complete the adjustment.

    The column is now wide enough to display all the text in *most* of the cells. The disadvantage of the dragging method is that you may need to make several stabs at the proper adjustment before you get it right. Also, if there are long cell entries below what you can see, you won't know if you have it right until you scroll down or print the worksheet, and then it's too late.

    Of course, there's an even better way. When you double-click on the right border of the column heading, Excel will adjust the column so it is wide enough to accommodate the longest cell entry.

But wait a minute. If the column is adjusted for the longest entry, it will be wide enough for the title in cell A1, which would make the column much too wide for the remaining entries. So, we'll select the portion of the column we want Excel to accommodate, and pull down the Format menu and select Column, AutoFit Selection.

3. Select the range **A4** through **A16**.

4. Pull down the Format menu and select **Column**, **AutoFit Selection**.

Now the column width is adjusted properly.

5. Save your work and exit Excel if you're not continuing on to the next chapter now.

A Final Thought

Now you know that you will always be able to find your worksheets, and this worksheet is starting to shape up nicely. The columns are finally adjusted to accommodate the cell entries, and the range names make the worksheet clearer.

In the next chapter, you'll learn some ways to make the worksheet look snazzier. You'll also learn how to add notes to further clarify the worksheet, and how to protect portions of the worksheet.

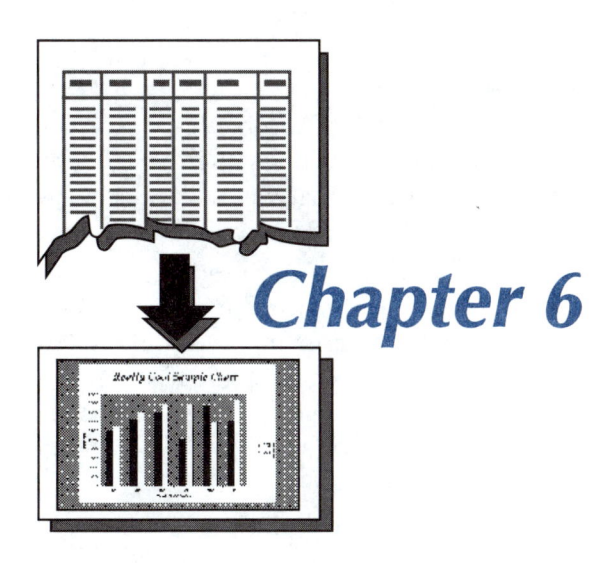

Chapter 6

Enhancing and Annotating Your Worksheet

- Aligning Cell Contents
- Formatting Cells
- Formatting Numbers
- Changing Fonts
- Adding Borders and Shading
- Using AutoFormat
- Adding Notes
- Protecting Data
- A Final Thought

The first chapters of this book focused on getting raw material (data) into your worksheet. This chapter concentrates on aesthetics, adding those nice little touches that will make the worksheet more attractive, readable, and perhaps most importantly, persuasive.

Most worksheets are prepared to persuade someone else to come to a particular conclusion. In the case of a budget or forecast, perhaps you're trying to convince your boss, or the board of directors, to go along with your assumptions. If you're preparing a business plan, maybe you need to sell your plan so a banker or venture capitalist will provide the needed funds for your new startup, or to expand your existing business.

Whatever your worksheet's purpose, the way it looks and how well it's documented *does* matter and should be given as much consideration as the underlying data. Don't worry if you think you don't have an eye for good design. Excel even has the ability to format your worksheet for you.

Aligning Cell Contents

Choosing the appropriate alignment for the contents of your cells can have an immediate impact on the look of the worksheet. You've seen that, by default, numbers are right-aligned and text is aligned on the left. A variety of alignment options can be applied to a single cell or to a range of cells.

Let's align the column headings so they are centered over the numbers. Aligning cells falls into the general category of *cell formatting*. You can reach the cell formatting options through the Format menu, but there is a shortcut.

1. Start Excel if it isn't running.
2. Open the lox&bagel workbook if it isn't on your screen.
3. Select cells **B3** through **E3**.

    Remember, there are several ways to select a range. You can simply drag the mouse over the range. You can pull down the Edit menu, select **Go To**, and enter the range separated by a colon in the Go To dialog box. Or you can enter the range separated by a colon in the Name box.

4. Move to the mouse pointer into the selected range and press the **Ctrl** key while holding down the mouse button to display the *Shortcut menu,* as portrayed in Figure 6.1.

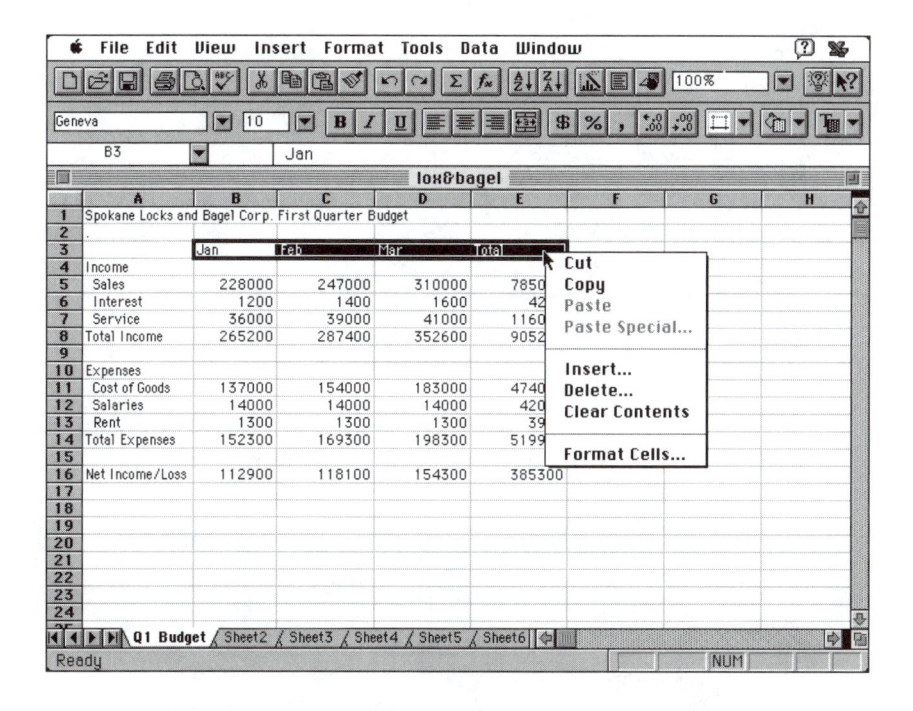

Figure 6.1 *The Shortcut menu for the selected cells.*

There are Shortcut menus for almost every screen or worksheet element. You can display any Shortcut menu by pointing to the object you want to manipulate and holding down the **Ctrl** key while pressing the mouse button. If you aren't sure what sort of manipulation you can perform on an object, the Shortcut menu will let you know. We'll be using Shortcut menus for many tasks as the book proceeds.

5. Drag the mouse down to select **Format Cells** from the Shortcut menu and then release the mouse button.

The Format Cells dialog box appears, as pictured in Figure 6.2.

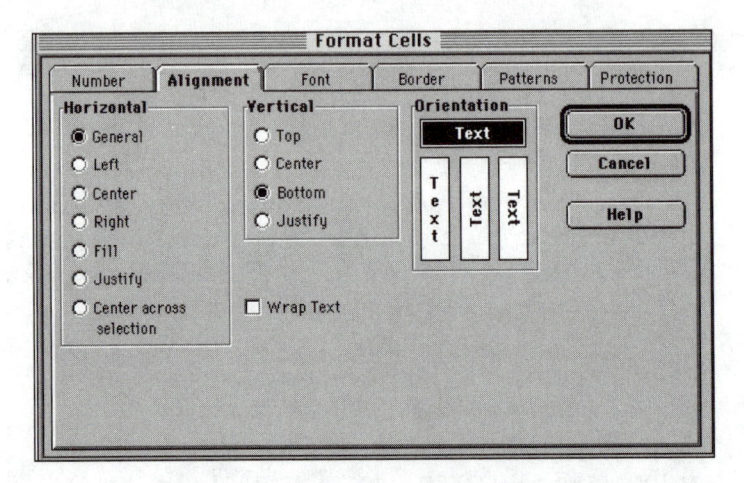

Figure 6.2 *The Number portion of the Format Cells dialog box.*

The tabs in the dialog box let you specify what sort of formatting you want to do. We want to get to the Alignment portion of the dialog box.

6. If it isn't already highlighted, click on the **Alignment** tab to display the Alignment portion of the dialog box.

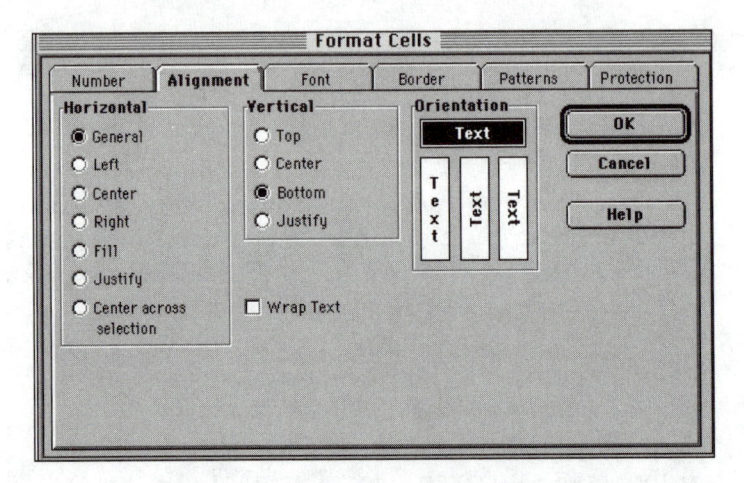

Figure 6.3 *The Alignment portion of the Format Cells dialog box.*

This dialog box lets you specify the type of horizontal and vertical alignment you want, the orientation of the text in the cells, and if you want long text entries *wrapped* (split into several lines).

The two alignment types that might need a bit of explanation are Justify and Fill. If the Wrap check box is checked, the **Justify** option will force the cell entry to spread out so the left and right edges are even, like the text in this book. The Fill option repeats the cell entry until the cell is filled.

7. Click on the **Center** option button in the Horizontal portion of the dialog box and click **OK**.

SHORTCUT

The toolbar has buttons for some of the more common cell formatting options, including some alignment options. Instead of using the dialog box, you can simply click on the appropriate toolbar button. In the previous step, you would click on the **Center** button on the Formatting toolbar.

Each column heading is now centered over its column, as shown in Figure 6.4.

The title in cell A1 would look better if it were centered over all the columns in use on the worksheet. We can't just center it in the cell. It's already longer than the column width of column A. What can we do? One of the alignment options is to center across a selection. That's the option we'll use for the title.

8. Select cells **A1** through **E1**.

You could choose the **Center Across Selection** option in the Format Cells dialog box. Instead, let's do it the easy way.

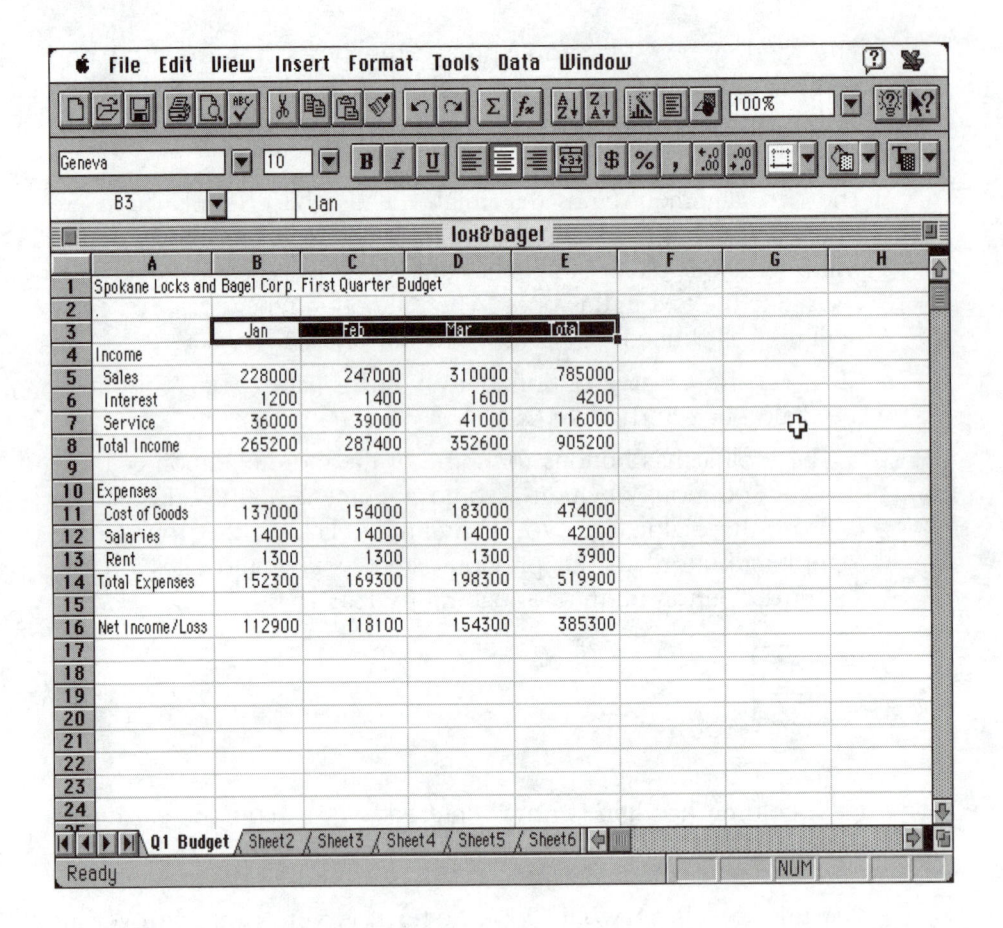

Figure 6.4 The center-aligned column headings.

9. Click on the **Center Across Columns** button on the Formatting toolbar.

The title is now centered between columns A and E, as shown in Figure 6.5.

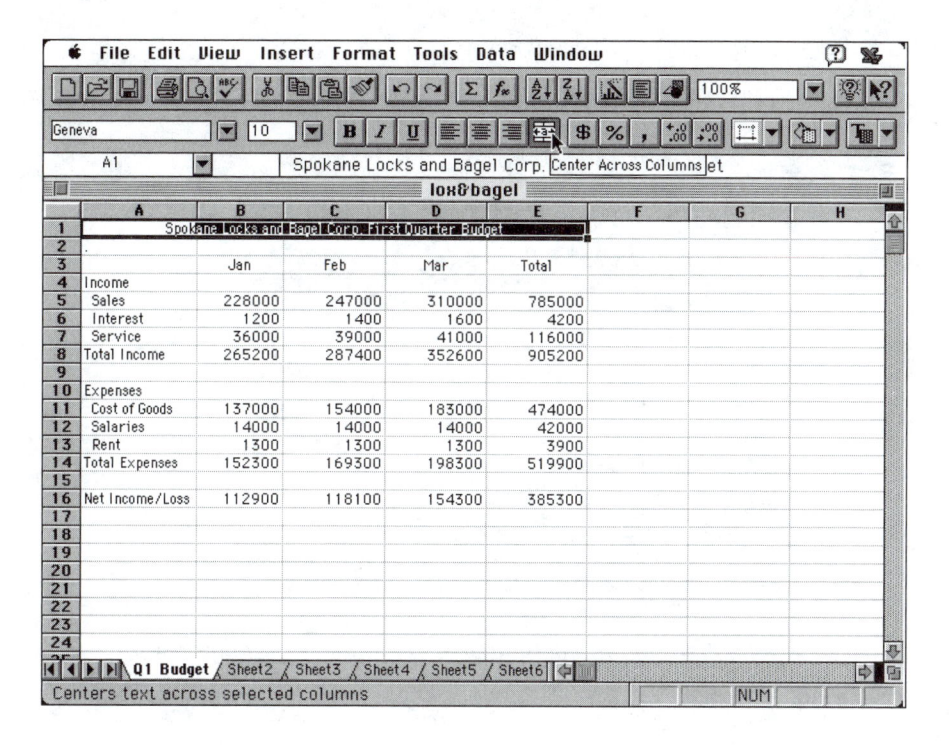

Figure 6.5 *The title centered over columns A through E.*

Formatting Numbers

In addition to changing cell alignment, you may also choose to alter the format of the numbers in your worksheet. All of the numbers have been entered using Excel's default formatting. The numbers would look better if they were formatted with commas separating thousands, and a decimal point with two decimal places.

1. Select **B5** through **E16**.
2. Position the mouse pointer inside the selected range and hold down the **Ctrl** key while pressing the mouse button to display the Shortcut menu.
3. With the Shortcut menu displayed, drag the mouse to highlight **Format Cells** and release the mouse button.

The Format Cells dialog box appears.

4. Click on the **Number** tab of the Format Cells dialog box to display the formatting options, as shown in Figure 6.6.

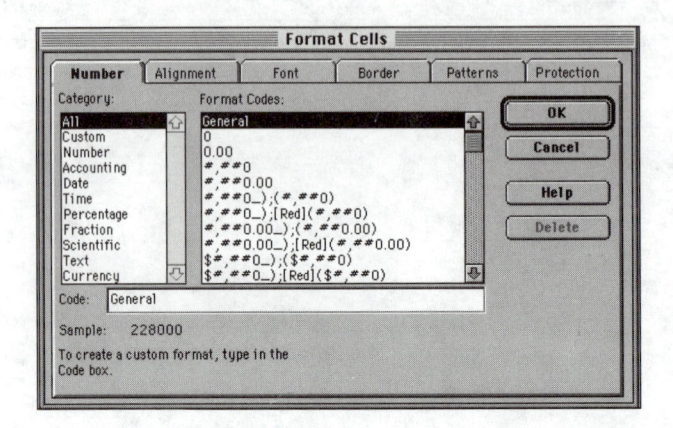

Figure 6.6 *The Number tab of the Format Cells dialog box.*

5. In the Category list, click on **Number**.

6. In the Format Codes list, click on the last (bottom) code to highlight it, as shown in Figure 6.7.

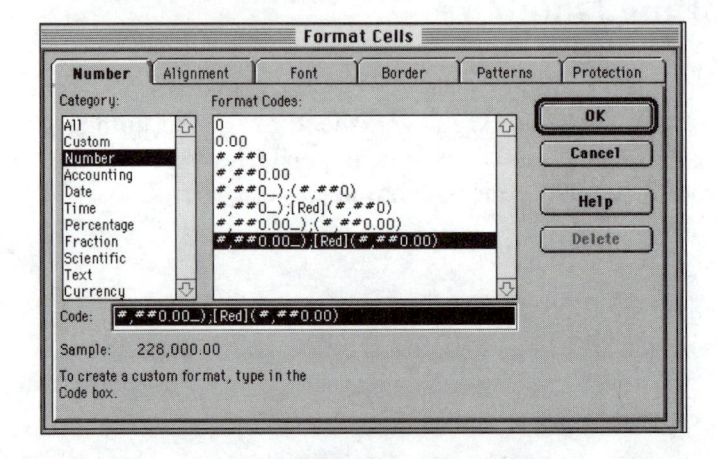

Figure 6.7 *The highlighted number format code.*

7. Click on the **OK** button to complete the number format change. The number format has been changed as depicted in Figure 6.8.

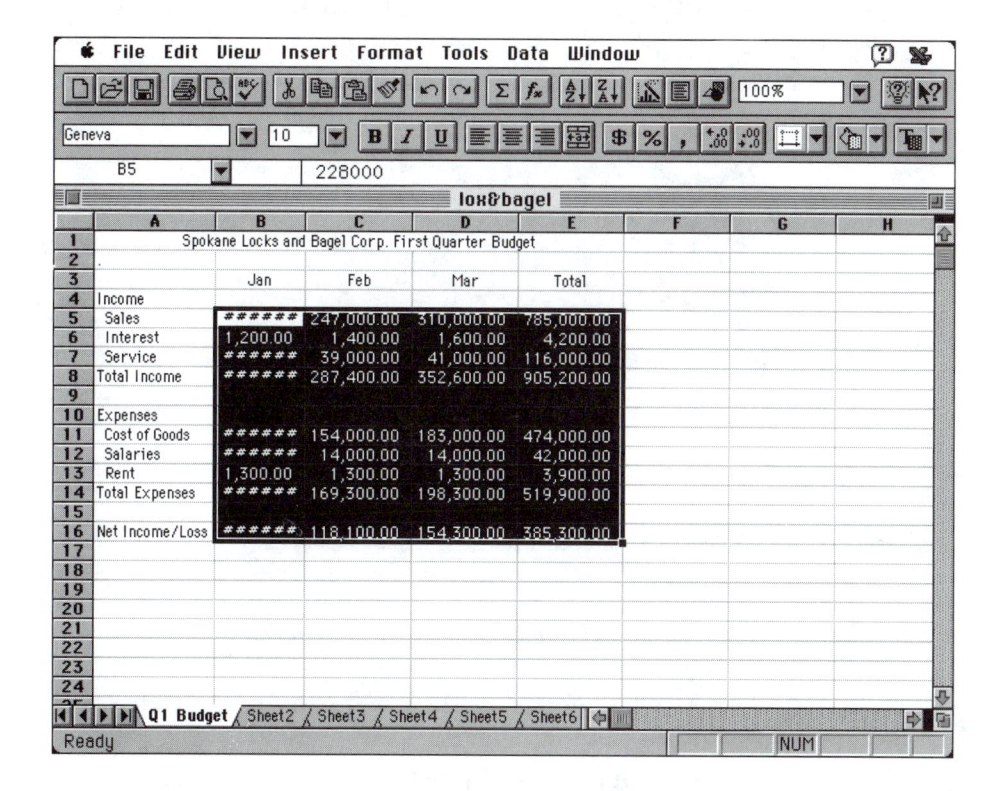

Figure 6.8 *The reformatted numbers.*

Unfortunately, some of the numbers have been replaced by pound signs. Uh oh! What does this mean? It means some of the numbers, with their commas and decimal places, are now too wide for the column width. Don't worry, we can fix that.

8. Pull down the Format menu and select **Column**, **AutoFit Selection**.

The column widths have been adjusted to accommodate the new number format, as shown in Figure 6.9.

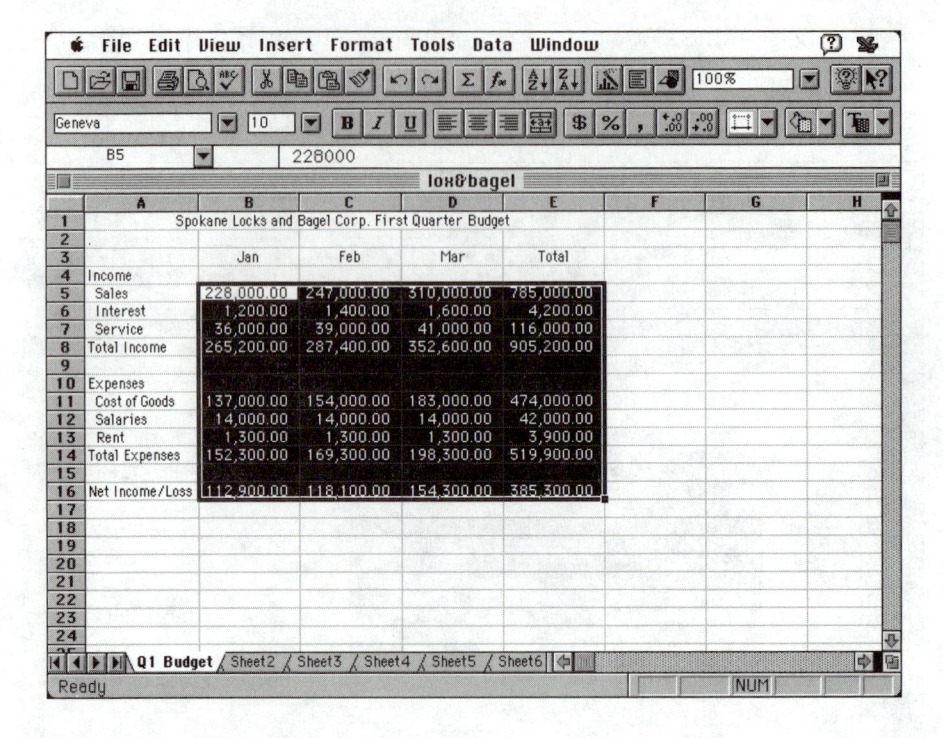

Figure 6.9 The reformatted number with the adjusted column widths.

The totals might look better if they were formatted with dollar signs, so let's take care of that little detail now.

9. Select the ranges **B8** through **E8**, **E5** through **E7**, **B16** through **E16**, and **E11** through **E14**. Remember to hold down the ⌘ key while dragging to select non-contiguous ranges.

10. Click on the **Currency Style** button on the Formatting toolbar.

The numbers have been reformatted. Again, the column widths must be adjusted.

11. Pull down the Format menu and select **Column**, **AutoFit Selection** to adjust the column widths for the currency style, as shown in Figure 6.10.

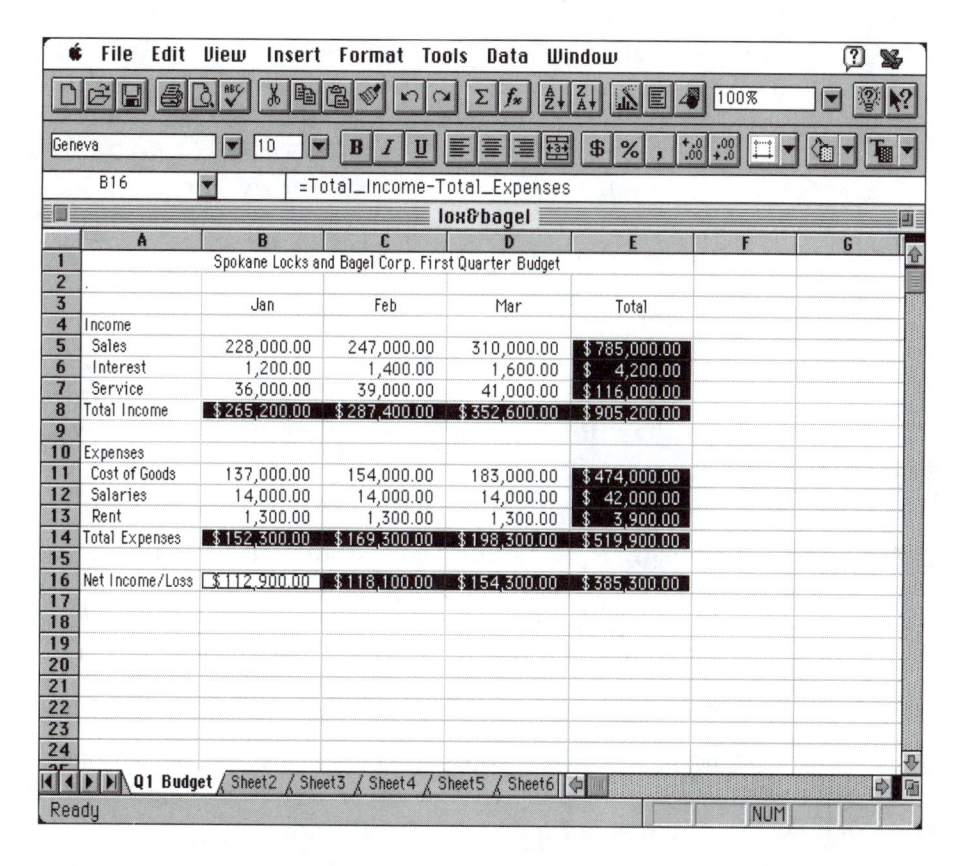

Figure 6.10 *The reformatted numbers and adjusted column widths.*

Before proceeding, this would be a good time to save your work.

12. Click on the **Save** button on the Standard toolbar.

Changing Fonts

Macintosh computers and Excel define *fonts* as typefaces. A variety of fonts are included with your computer and others are included with Macintosh-compatible printers, or can be purchased separately. Choosing the correct font for the situation can do more to help or hinder your cause than just about any other type of formatting you can do to your worksheet, so choose carefully.

Unless you want your document to look like a ransom note, don't use too many fonts in a single document. One of the surest ways to signal your novice font status is over-using the fonts you have available. I think this happens to new users because, when they first encounter the variety of fonts at their disposal, there is a great temptation to use them all just because they're there. Resist the temptation.

If in doubt, use only one font. Your documents will look more pro-fessional with one nice font, perhaps in a couple of sizes and styles, than two or more that don't go well together or are otherwise used improperly.

There are many good books available to help you choose and use fonts well. If one of your goals is to produce the most professional-looking and persuasive worksheets possible, learning more about fonts will be a worthwhile investment of your time and money.

In addition to changing the font, you can change the style (bold, italic, underline, etc.) and the size of the font. Font sizes are specified in *points* because most fonts these days are *proportional fonts*.

The fonts used on a typewriter (and even some that are still used on computers) a fixed-width or monospaced, where each character takes up the same amount of horizontal space. In proportional fonts, some characters are wider or narrower than others. For this reason, using the old method of measurement, based on the number of characters per inch (pitch) no longer works. Points measure the font's height. One point is roughly 1/72 of an inch.

Typical font sizes for the main body of the worksheet are between 9 and 12 points. Anything smaller than 9-point type is considered fine print; larger than 12-point is considered large type.

Let's change the font, style and size of the title so that it really stands out.

1. Click on cell **A1**.

   I know it looks like A1 is empty. It's not. Look in the formula bar to see that A1 really does contain the title.

2. Click on the **Arrow** for the font drop-down list on the Formatting toolbar to display the list of available fonts, as pictured in Figure 6.11.

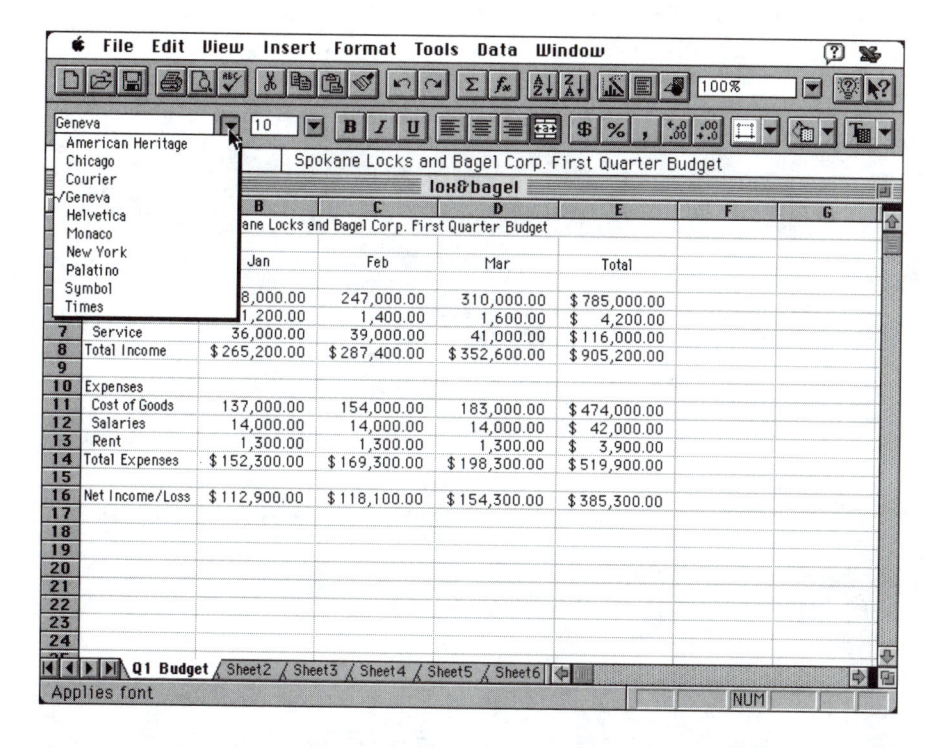

Figure 6.11 *The Formatting toolbar's drop-down font list.*

The fonts in your list may differ from those in the figure. Only those fonts that are installed and available on your system appear on the list.

The default font for Excel is Geneva. Let's use a slightly more ornate font called Times, which is at the bottom of the list in Figure 6.11. In the event that you don't have Times available, choose another font from your list so you can step through the process of changing fonts.

3. Drag down the list of fonts to highlight **Times** and release the mouse button.

   Notice that the typeface of the title has changed. Since this is a title, it should also be larger, so we'll change the size. The current size, as you can see from the Font Size box on the Formatting toolbar, is 10 points. Let's change it to 24 points.

4. Click on the **Font Size Arrow** on the Formatting toolbar to reveal the list of font sizes, as depicted in Figure 6.12.

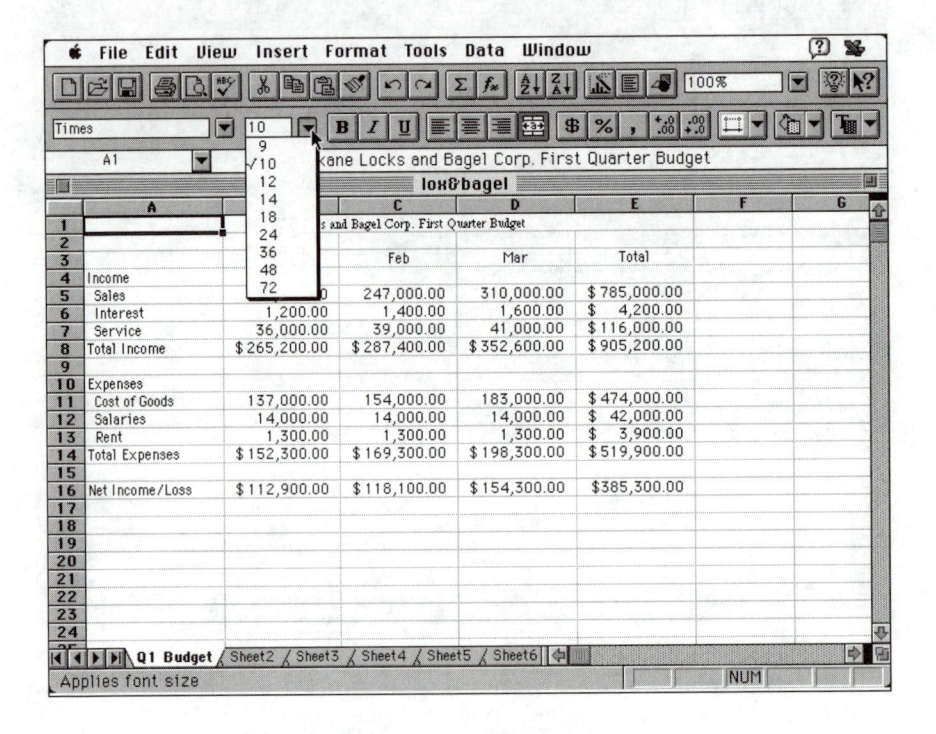

Figure 6.12 The Font Size drop down list.

Unlike the list of fonts, the Font Size list only lists the more common sizes. However, you aren't limited to these sizes. You can click in the **Font Size** box to highlight the current size and type in the size you wanted, say 19 points, and press the **Return** key.

5. Drag down to highlight **24** and release the mouse button to enlarge the title, as displayed in Figure 6.13.

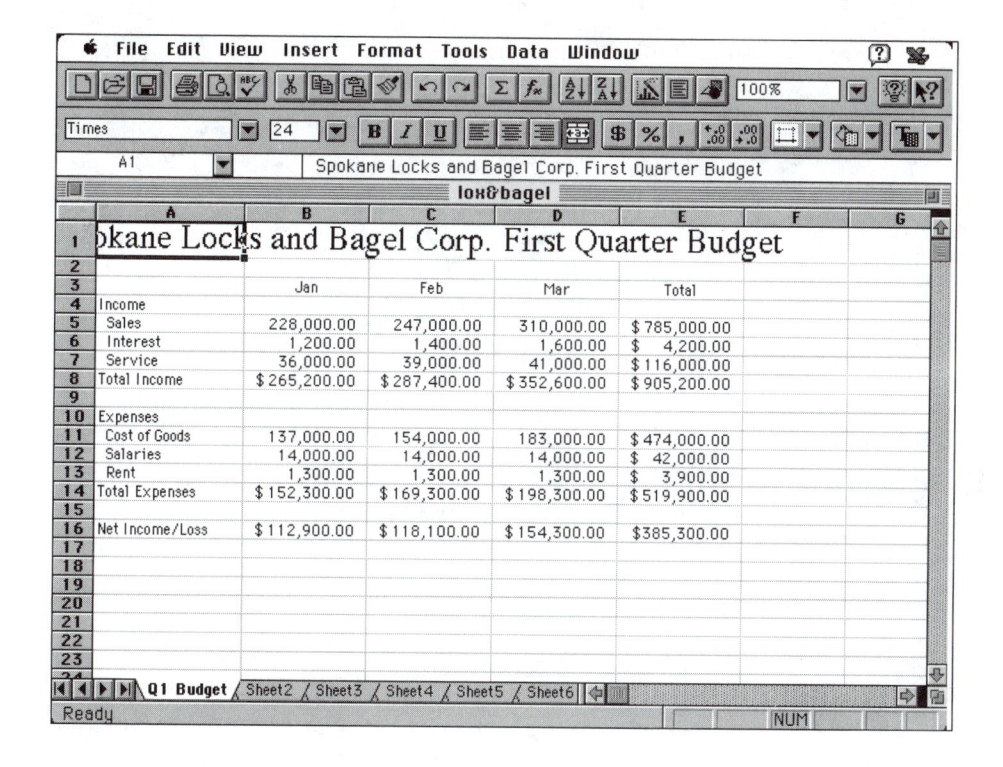

Figure 6.13 *The 18-point title.*

Notice that the row height automatically adjusted for the larger size. We do have one small problem here. Because the title is centered over columns A through E, the left portion of the text is cut off. We'll change the title back to left alignment to fix that problem.

6. Click on the **Align Left** button on the Formatting toolbar.

Now you can see the entire title again. We'll add one more embellishment before we're done. Let's make the title bold.

7. Click on the **Bold** toolbar button or press **Ctrl+B**.

Your worksheet should look like the one in Figure 6.14.

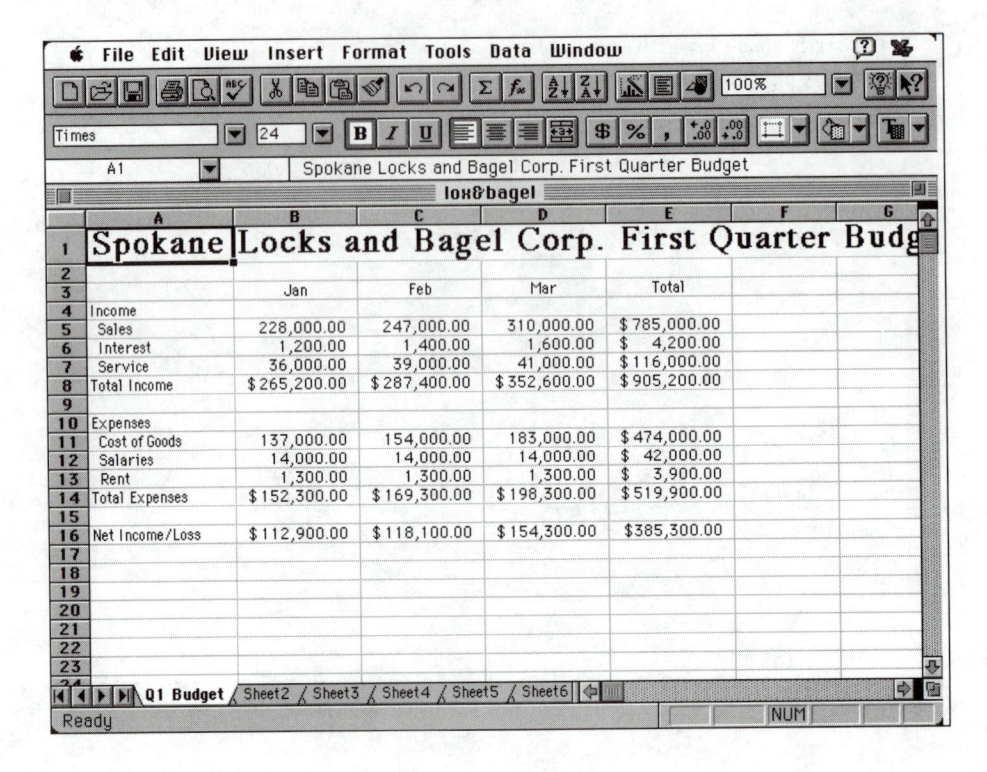

Figure 6.14 *The title is now bold and completely visible.*

8. Use the **Font** and **Font size** buttons to change cell A1 to Geneva 18 point. The worksheet should now look like Figure 6.15

N O T E

Although the fastest way to change fonts is from the toolbar, you may find an advantage to using the Font portion of the Format Cells dialog box, particularly if you aren't familiar with the way the different fonts look. The dialog box provides a preview of the font, including size and style, so you can see what the font will look like before you apply it.

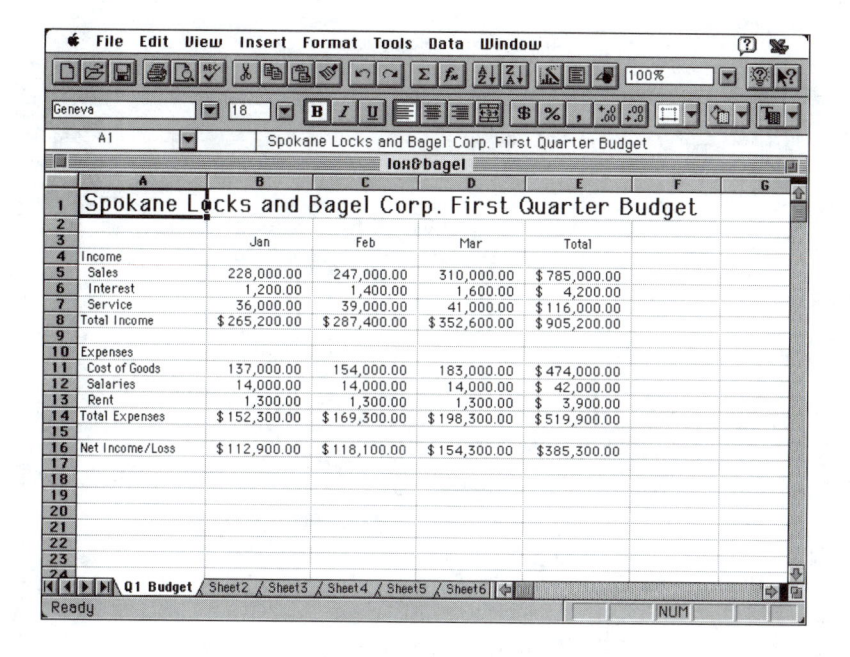

Figure 6.15 *The new worksheet.*

Adding Borders and Shading

To further embellish your worksheet, you can surround cells with borders and fill them with shading. Just like fonts, you need to use appropriate borders and shading or these elements can detract from the look of the worksheet.

Let's add a border and some shading to the column headings.

1. Select **B3** through **E3**.

2. Click on the **Arrow** for the Border drop-down box on the Formatting toolbar.

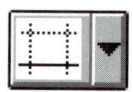

The Border drop-down box is displayed, as shown in Figure 6.16.

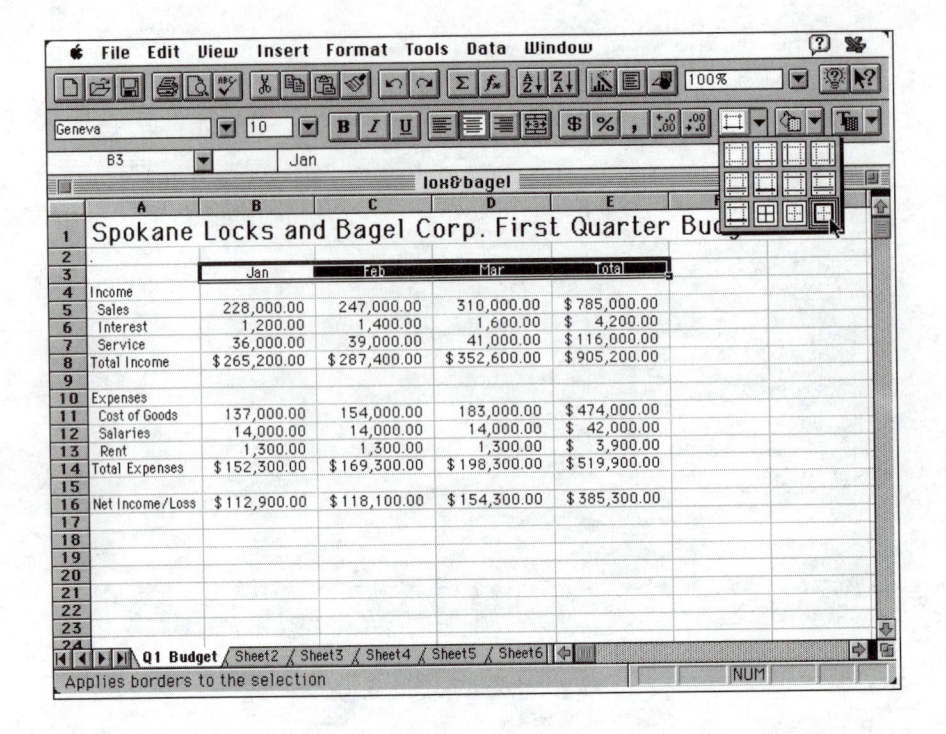

Figure 6.16 *The Border drop-down list.*

3. Drag down to highlight the **border style** in the lower-right corner on the drop-down box. (It's the one the mouse pointer is pointing to in the figure.)

4. Click outside the selection so you can see the border surrounding the column headings, as shown in Figure 6.17.

Now let's add some shading to the titles.

5. Select **B3** through **E3** again.

6. Position the mouse pointer inside the selection and hold down the **Ctrl** key while pressing the mouse button to display the shortcut menu.

7. Drag down to **Format Cells** and release the mouse button to display the Format Cells dialog box. Then click on the **Patterns** tab to see the Patterns portion of the dialog box, as portrayed in Figure 6.18.

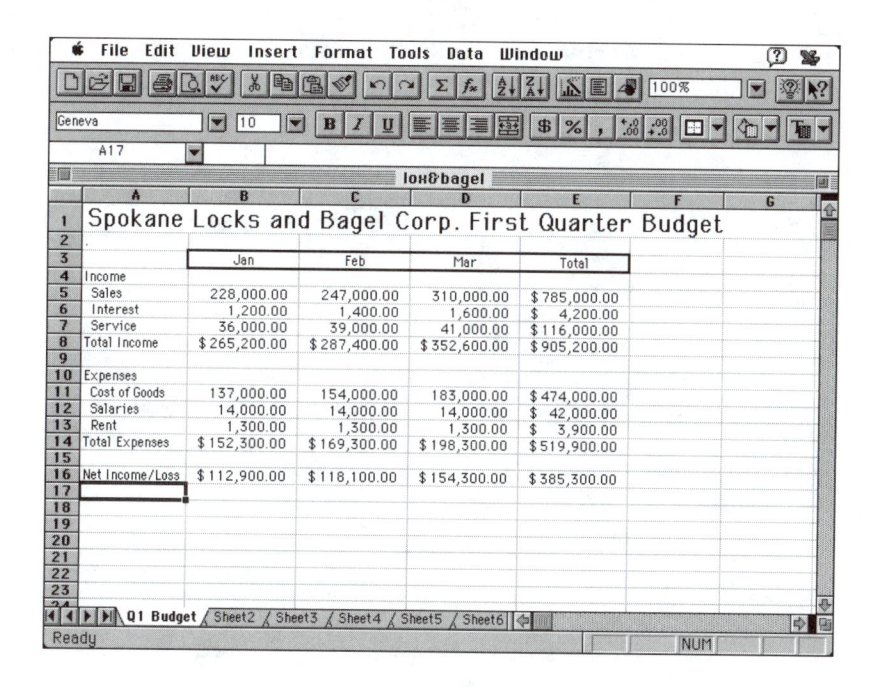

Figure 6.17 *The column headings surrounded by a border.*

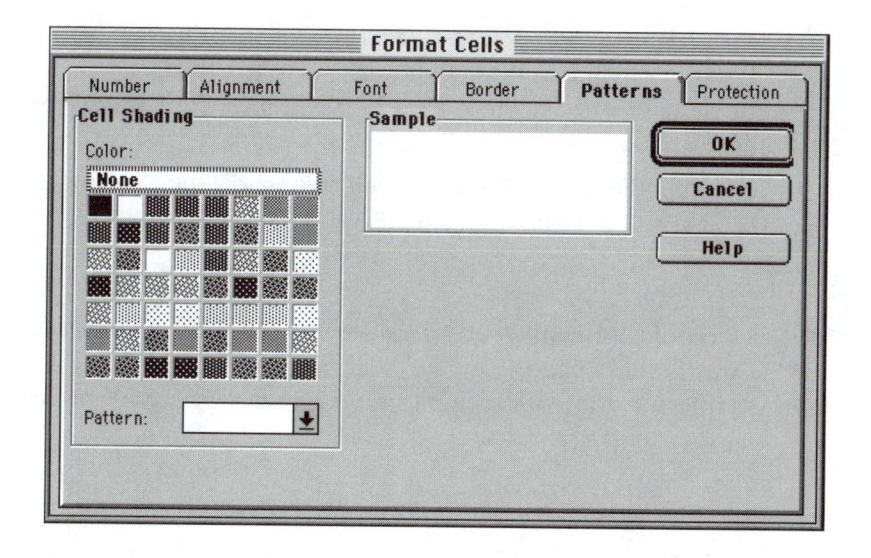

Figure 6.18 *The Patterns portion of the Format Cells dialog box.*

8. Click on the **Arrow** next to the Patterns box to display the available shading patterns.

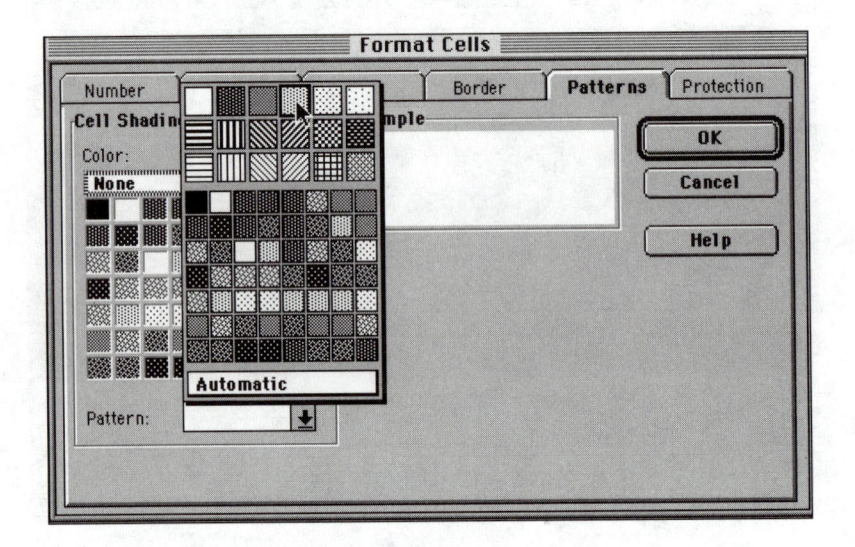

Figure 6.19 *The available patterns.*

9. Click on the fourth pattern from the left on the top row (it's the one the mouse pointer is pointing at in the figure).

The sample area in the dialog box displays the pattern you have chosen.

10. Click the **OK** button and then click outside the selected area so you can see the pattern's effect.

Graphic elements, such as shading, can look very different on the printed page than they do on screen. Don't decide that a pattern is too dark or light until you print your worksheet.

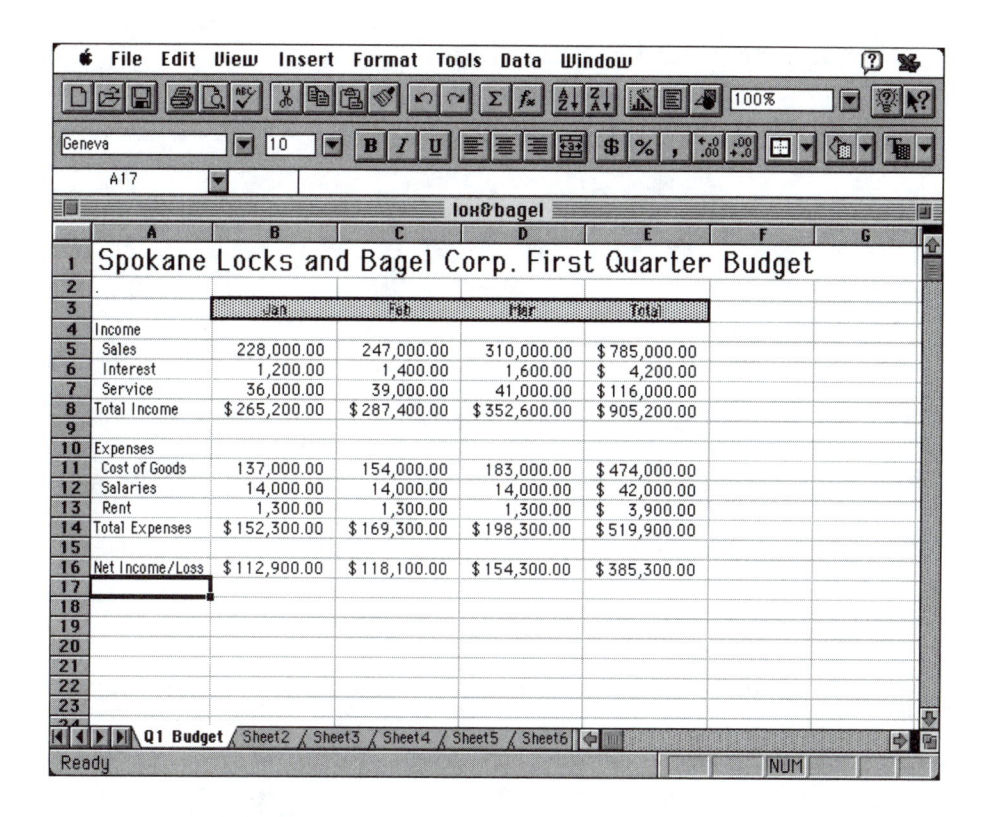

Figure 6.20 *The column headings with a border and shading.*

Using AutoFormat

Suppose you have as little design sense as I have–which is very little. Excel's AutoFormat feature will automatically turn your shabby old unformatted worksheet into a work of art.

All you have to do is select the portion of the worksheet you want automatically formatted and choose the most pleasing format style from the list in the AutoFormat dialog box. Let's try it out.

1. Select the range **A3** through **E16**.

2. Pull down the Format menu and select **AutoFormat** to display the AutoFormat dialog box, as shown in Figure 6.21.

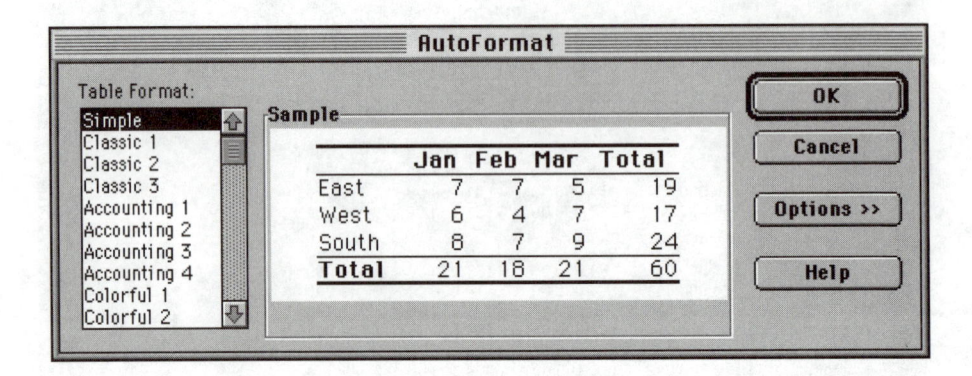

Figure 6.21 *The AutoFormat dialog box.*

The **Simple Table Format** is highlighted and you can see what that style looks like in the Sample area. The easiest way to check out the various options is by using the down arrow key. Each time you press the **Down Arrow** key, you'll see another format style in the sample area.

We'll use the Classic 1 style. It's simple, yet elegant. We don't want to use anything too overpowering, do we?

3. Click on **Classic 1**, then click the **OK** button. Click outside the selected area so you can behold the beauty of the newly formatted worksheet, displayed in Figure 6.22.

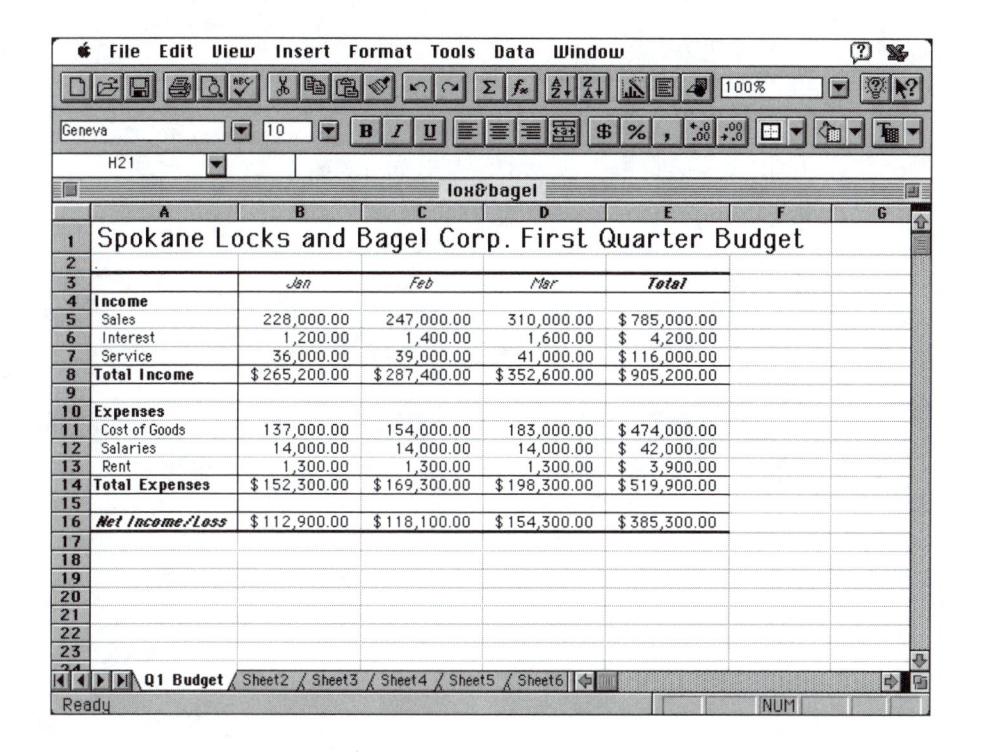

Figure 6.22 *The worksheet formatted with the Classic 1 style.*

Adding Notes

As hard as you try to make your worksheet understandable and self-explanatory to anyone who reads it, some entries just need more detailed explanations than the surrounding cells provide. Wouldn't it be great if you could write some explanatory text on one of those yellow sticky notes and attach it to a cell so your readers could see exactly what you had in mind?

Excel actually has a better system for attaching notes to cells than yellow stickies. To attach a cell note, just move to the cell where you want to attach the note, pull down the Insert menu, and select **Note**.

Let's attach a note to cell A12 to explain our assumptions for the salaries figures.

1. Click in cell **A12**.

2. Pull down the Insert menu and select **Note**, or press ⌘+**Shift**+**N**.

   The Cell Note dialog box appears, as displayed in Figure 6.23, with the insertion point in the Text Note area.

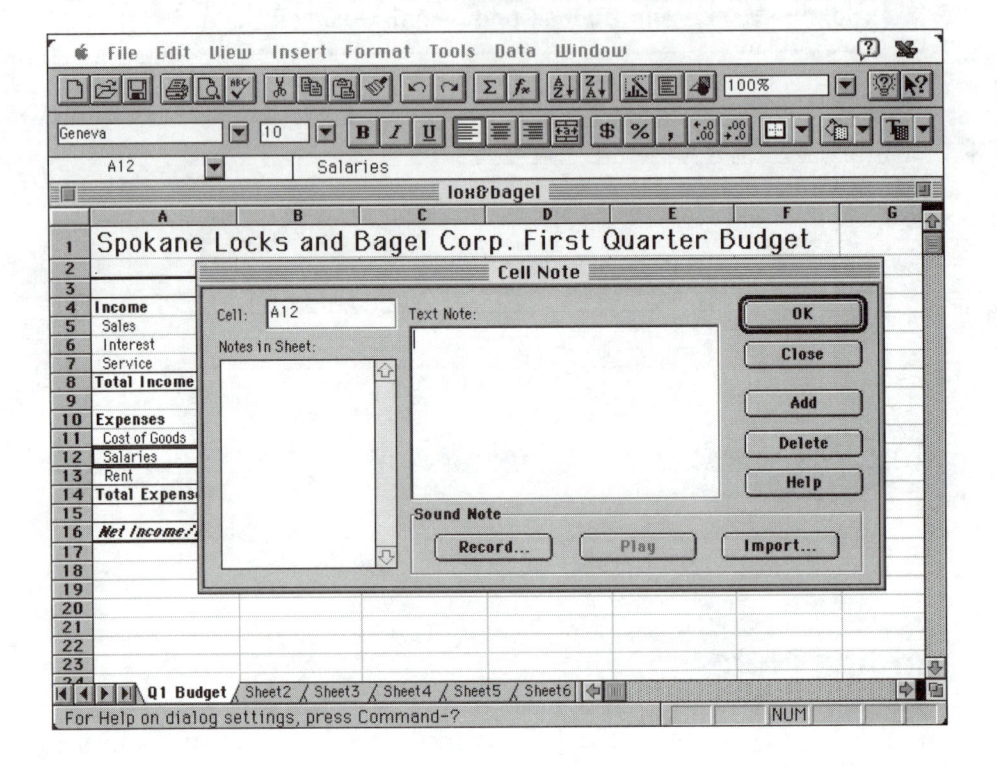

Figure 6.23 *The Cell Note dialog box.*

3. Type the following text: **The salary figures assume a 6% raise for Sally and Joe, and an 8% increase for Mary.**

4. Click on the **OK** button to attach the note to the cell.

5. Click on another cell in the worksheet so you can see the result of the note insertion.

   A dot appears in the upper-right corner of the cell indicating that there is a note attached. The dots don't print when you print the worksheet, although you can print the notes if you wish.

When you want to display a note that is attached to a cell, you follow pretty much the same procedures as for attaching a note. Let's display the note in cell A12.

6. Click on **A12** and pull down the Insert menu, and then select **Note**.

The note appears in the Cell Note dialog box, as shown in Figure 6.24. Any other notes will be listed in the Notes in Sheet list, and you can display those by clicking on them.

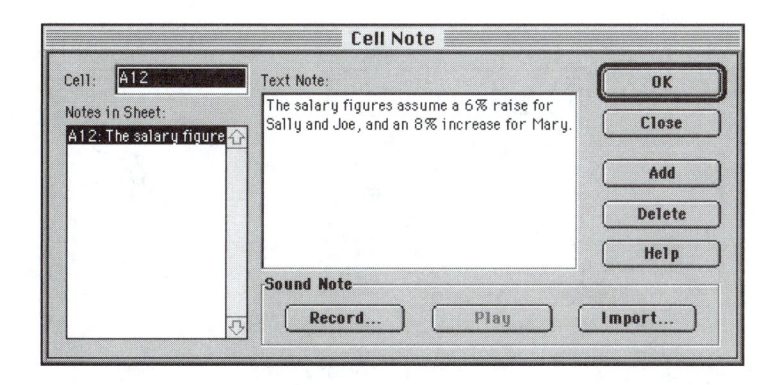

Figure 6.24 *The Cell Note dialog box with the note displayed.*

Protecting Data

If you want to ensure that certain cells in the worksheet can't be accidentally altered (or even seen at all), you can lock or hide them. It's often a good idea to lock cells containing formulas so someone can't accidentally delete them or enter something over them.

If your worksheet contains confidential information, you may want to hide portions of it. You can also require that a password be used to remove the protection you've specified.

Protecting cells may seem counter-intuitive because, to protect certain cells in a worksheet, you must first unprotect the cells you don't want protected. By default, when you turn on Excel's sheet protection, all cells are protected except those cells whose default protection you've turned off. Got that?

Let's protect our entries in column E.

1. Select cells **A1** through **D16**.

2. Position the mouse pointer inside the selection and hold down the **Ctrl** key while pressing the mouse button to display the shortcut menu.

3. Select **Format Cells** to display the Format Cells dialog box, and then click on the **Protection** tab.

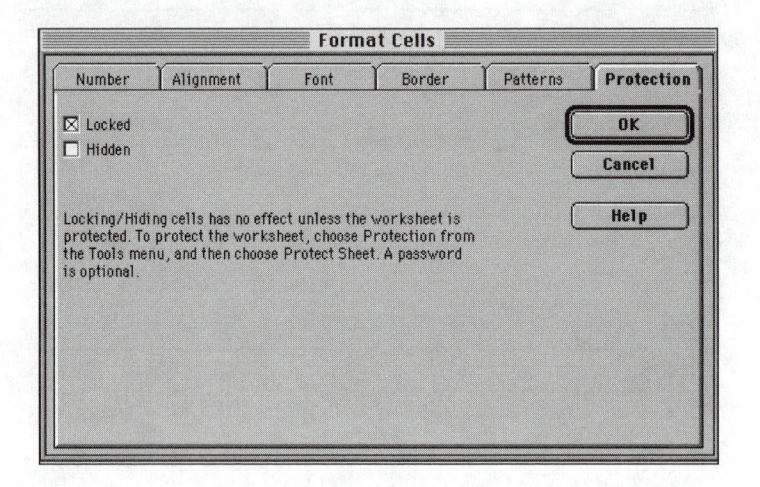

Figure 6.25 *The Protection portion of the Format Cells dialog box.*

4. Click in the **Locked** check box to remove the check mark, and then click on the **OK** button.

   Before the protection for the unselected portion of the worksheet will take effect, you must turn on the protection facility.

5. Pull down the Tools menu and select **Protection**, **Protect Sheet** to display the Protect Sheet dialog box displayed in Figure 6.26.

6. After making sure all three check boxes are checked, click on the **OK** button (we won't add a password).

   Now, let's see if the protection is really working.

7. Click on any cell in column E and press the **Delete** key to try to delete the contents of a locked cell.

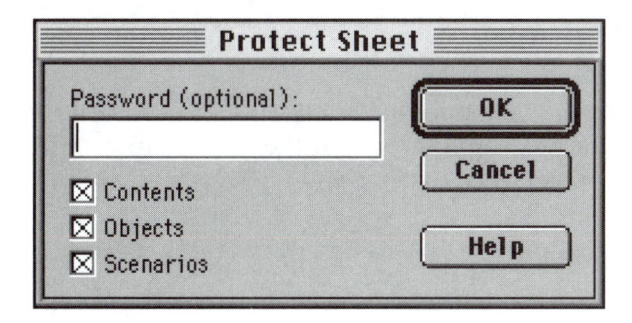

Figure 6.26 *The Protect Sheet dialog box.*

The message dialog box, as shown in Figure 6.27, lets you know that you can't mess with locked cells. It works!

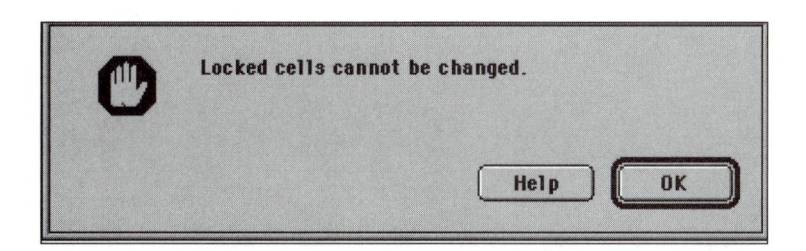

Figure 6.27 *The message dialog box showing that a cell is locked.*

8. Click on **OK** to clear the dialog box.

   Before proceeding, let's unprotect the worksheet so we won't run into problems when we try to modify it later.

9. Pull down the Tools menu and select **Protection**, **Unprotect Sheet**.

10. Save your work and exit Excel if you're not continuing on to the next chapter now.

Any additional worksheets you create within a workbook can each have their own formatting. However, once you have formatted the first sheet in the workbook, additional sheets will use that formatting by default.

A Final Thought

You now know how to put together a worksheet so that it is presentable, fully documented, and protected. In the next chapter, you learn how to transfer your masterpiece to the printed page.

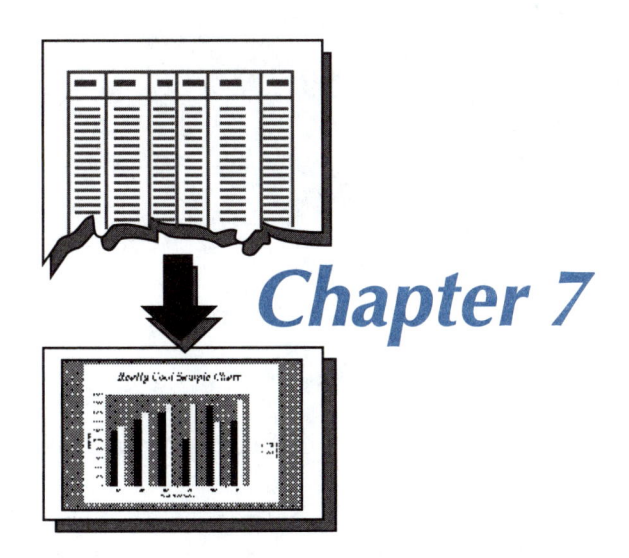

Chapter 7

Printing Worksheets

- Setting Up the Page
- Creating Headers and Footers
- Previewing Pages
- Printing Your Worksheet
- A Final Thought

Because the printed page is ultimately how the information in most worksheets is communicated, printing may be the most important task you can learn in Excel. The options for what portion of your workbook (or worksheets) you want to print, and how you want them printed, are almost limitless.

Setting Up Pages

Excel needs some information about how you want your pages printed before you start printing. If you don't provide this information, Excel will print using its current settings, which may not be what you want to use.

Let's explore the available options in the Page Setup dialog box.

1. Pull down the File menu and select **Page Setup**. If the **Page** tab isn't highlighted, click on it.

   The Page Setup dialog box appears, as shown in Figure 7.1.

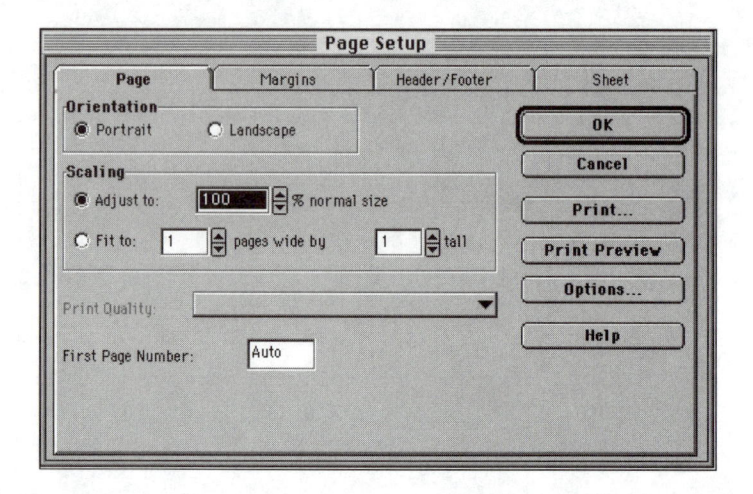

Figure 7.1 *The Page tab of the Page Setup dialog box.*

- The Orientation section of the dialog box lets you determine whether you want the information printed on the page in the normal upright (Portrait) orientation, or sideways

(Landscape). Portrait orientation allows you to print more rows but fewer columns on a page. Landscape will accommodate more columns but fewer rows. We'll keep Portrait as our orientation option.

Some printers, such as Apple's Stylewriter, don't allow you to change orientation in the Page Setup dialog box. You must click on the **Options** button and specify orientation in a separate dialog box.

- The Scaling area lets you adjust the size of the document you're about to print. The **Adjust to** option button lets you print at 100% (normal size) or at a smaller or larger percentage. For example, if you adjust to 200%, all the data, including text, numbers, and graphics, will print at twice their normal size. Of course, this means that each page will only hold half as much data. You can scale pages up to 400% and down to 10%.

  The **Fit to** option lets you force the information you want to print to fit on a specified number of pages. This can be useful for shoehorning your data into fewer pages than it might otherwise require. This option will not, however, enlarge the data on the worksheet to fit on the specified pages.

Be careful with this option. You could end up with such small print that you can't read it. Actually, come to think of it, for some worksheets, that might be an advantage!

- The Print Quality drop down list lets you choose the quality of print for your document. The tradeoff here is that choosing a higher quality will generally result in slower print speeds. You may want to print with a lower print quality for drafts and a higher quality for final prints.

NOTE

Some printers, such as some laser printers, don't allow a change in print quality. Instead, you can alter the *print density*–how dark or light the print appears–by clicking the **Options** button in the Page Setup dialog box, and then the **Options** button in the next dialog box. You can then adjust print density by dragging a slider.

• The First Page Number text box lets you specify the starting number that is printed on the first page of a worksheet. For example, if you enter **3** as the First Page Number for a three-page worksheet you are about to print, the pages will be numbered 3, 4 and 5. This option has no effect if you choose not to have page numbers printed on your pages.

We won't be changing any of the options on the Page portion of the dialog box, so let's take a look at the Margins portion of the dialog box.

2. Click on the **Margins** tab of the Page Setup dialog box to display the Margins portion of the dialog box, as displayed in Figure 7.2.

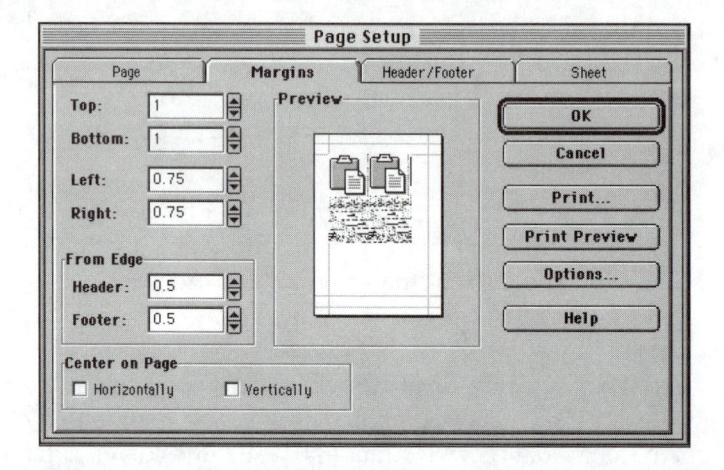

Figure 7.2 *The Margins portion of the Page Setup dialog box.*

Changing the margin setting lets you determine where your document will appear on the printed page. The default top, bottom, left and right margins are generally adequate, but you may wish to reduce the margins so you can fit more data on a page, or you may want to increase the margins so you'll have more breathing room (white space) around your data.

You can also specify how far from the edge of the page your headers and footers will appear. You'll learn more about headers and footers in just a bit.

We will use a couple of the options on this dialog box to center the data both vertically and horizontally on the printed page.

3. Click in both the **Horizontally** and **Vertically** check boxes in the Center on Page area of the dialog box.

    Notice that the Preview area now shows a representation of the data as centered on the page.

    Next, let's move to the Sheet tab. Don't worry. We'll get back to the Header/Footer tab later.

4. Click on the **Sheet** tab to display the Sheet portion of the Page Setup dialog box, as shown in Figure 7.3.

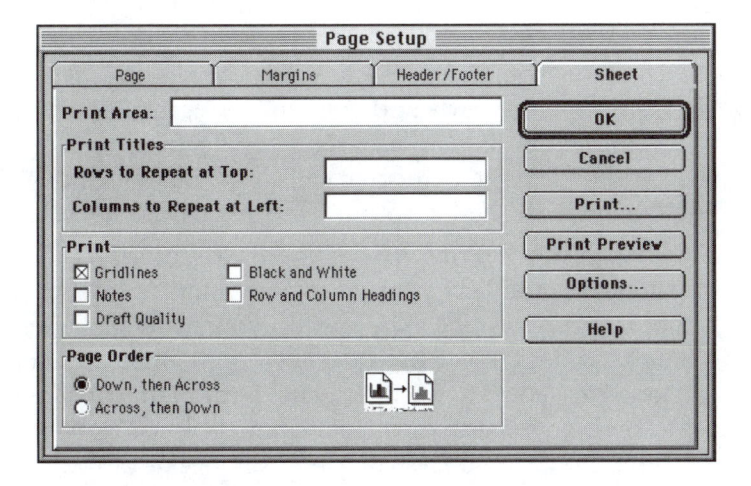

Figure 7.3 *The Sheet portion of the Page Setup dialog box.*

In the Print Area text box, you can specify a range of cells to print. Let's specify the range A1 through F16.

5. Click in the **Print Area** text box and type: **A1:F16**.

The reason we need to go all the way over to column F is to make sure the entire title is printed. Even though the title is actually in cell A1, the print area specifies an actual rectangular area on the worksheet. If we only printed over to column E, for example, we'd end up cutting off the last word of the title.

SHORTCUT

You can use the pointing method to specify a print area. Simply point to one corner of the rectangular area you want to print and then drag to the opposite corner and release the mouse button. The range will automatically be entered in the Print Area text box.

This method can be a little tricky because the Page Setup dialog box usually obscures the range you want to print. You can drag over the dialog box, but that's kind of like flying blind. Whether typing the range or pointing and dragging, it's a good idea to know what range you want to print *before* you display the Page Setup dialog box.

The Rows to Repeat at Top and the Columns to Repeat at Left text boxes let you specify one or more rows and columns to repeat on each page of multiple-page printouts. This can be useful for keeping track of which column and row headings a particular cell entry belongs to. We don't have a multiple-page worksheet to print, so we won't use these options.

The check boxes in the Print area of the dialog box provide several options for customizing the way your pages will print. **Gridlines** lets you choose whether to print the lines you see on your worksheet separating rows and columns. Check the **Notes** check box to print any cell notes you have attached to your worksheet. The **Draft Quality** check box causes Excel to omit any charts or other graphic objects, as well as gridlines, from your printout. Draft Quality will often cause your pages to print faster.

You'll want to choose the **Black and White** check box if you have used any colors for text or graphics on your worksheet and are printing on a black and white printer. This option may also cause your pages to print faster on a color printer, since color printers often print slower in color than in black and white.

The **Row and Column Heading** will cause the row numbers and the column letters to print. This can make it easier to determine which cell a particular entry is in, but it can also detract from the look of the page.

The **Print Order** area of the dialog box lets you specify how multiple pages will print. This won't affect our single-page printout.

Creating Headers and Footers

Before we finish setting up the pages, let's take a look at headers and footers.

1. Click on the **Header/Footer** tab to display the Header/Footer portion of the Page Setup dialog box, as shown in Figure 7.4.

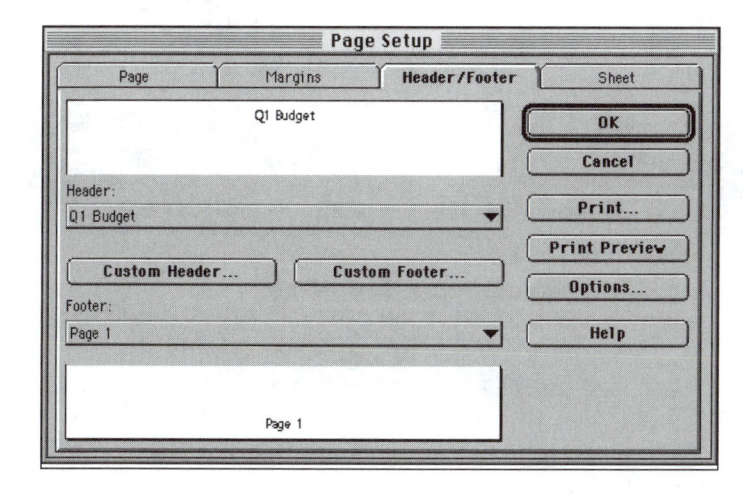

Figure 7.4 *The Header/Footer portion of the Page Setup dialog box.*

Headers and *footers* are text elements that will appear at the top and bottom of your printed documents. There is no difference between a header and a footer, except that a header appears at the top of the printed page and a footer appears at the bottom.

Excel will print default headers and footers, unless you specify different ones, or specify none at all. The default header simply prints the sheet name, in this case, Q1 Budget. The default footer is Page 1 for the first page, Page 2 for the second page, and so on.

Excel also provides a variety of predefined headers and footers that you can use. Figure 7.5 displays some of the predefined headers (the predefined footers are the same) that can be seen by clicking on the arrow for the Header drop-down list.

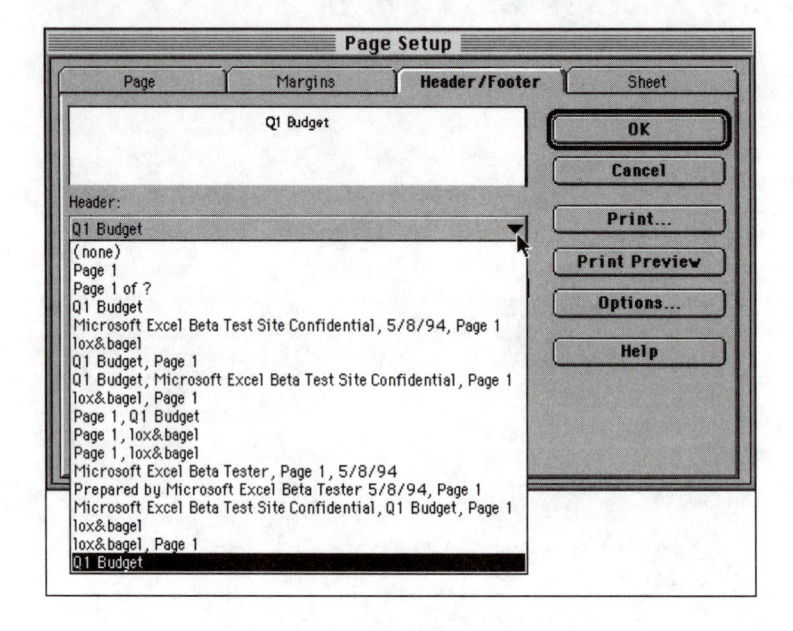

Figure 7.5 *The Header drop-down list.*

Instead of using one of the predefined headers, let's create a custom header.

2. Click on the **Custom Header** button to display the Header dialog box portrayed in Figure 7.6.

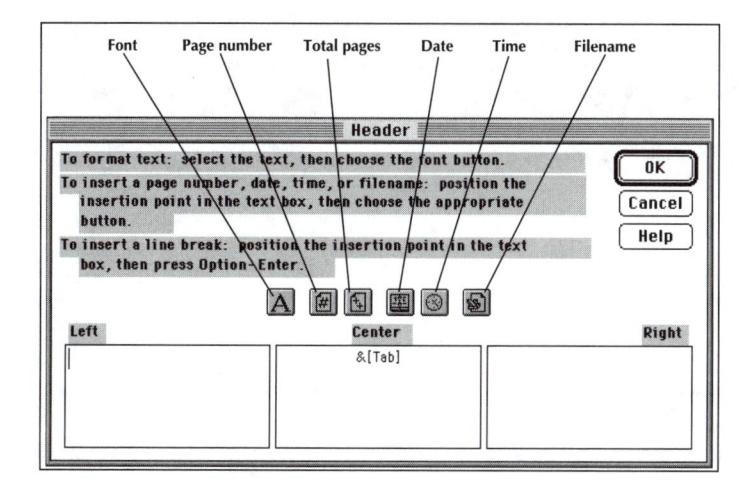

Figure 7.6 *The Header dialog box.*

The dialog box displays the current header. But wait a minute–that thing in the middle box doesn't look like the header we saw in the previous dialog box. The default header is the sheet name centered between the left and right margins. What you see in the Header dialog box is the *code* for the sheet name. In addition to the sheet name, when creating a custom header (or footer), you can insert codes for the page number, the total number of pages, the date and time, and the filename by clicking on the appropriate icon. There's even an icon to allow you to change the font you're using for the header or footer.

Let's type some text in the Left Section.

3. Click in the Left section box and type: **Prepared by Saul Salmon**.

4. Drag over the text in the Center section box and press the **Delete** key to erase it.

5. Click on the **Date** icon to insert the date code in the Center section. (See Figure 7.6)

6. Click in the Right Section box and then click on the **Filename** icon.

Your screen should now look like Figure 7.7.

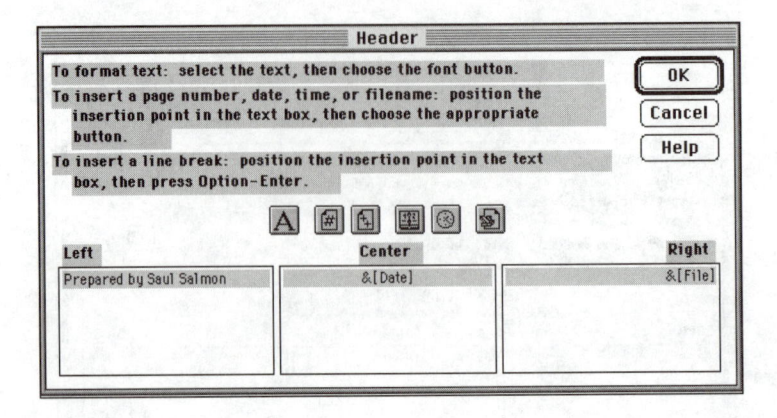

Figure 7.7 The Header dialog box with the custom header filled in.

7. Click on the **OK** button to accept the custom header and return to the Header/Footer section of the Page Setup dialog box, where you'll see what your new header will actually look like, as shown in Figure 7.8.

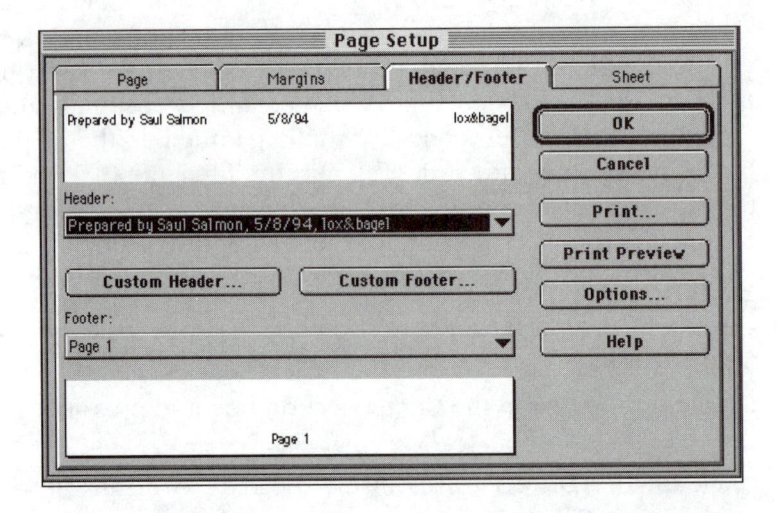

Figure 7.8 The completed custom header.

8. Click on the **OK** button to accept the header and footer and return to the worksheet.

Previewing Pages

We're just about ready to print, but first we'll preview the page. It's almost always a good idea to preview before sending a document to the printer. It can save time and paper by letting you ensure that everything is just the way you want it.

NOTE Except for some differences in quality between your screen image and the printed page, and colors you may have on your screen that your black and white printer won't reproduce, the Print Preview screen is an excellent facsimile of the actual printed page. In fact, Print Preview *is* a printed page. It's just printed on the screen instead of on paper.

1. Click on the **Print Preview** button to have Excel print your document to the screen, as shown in Figure 7.9.

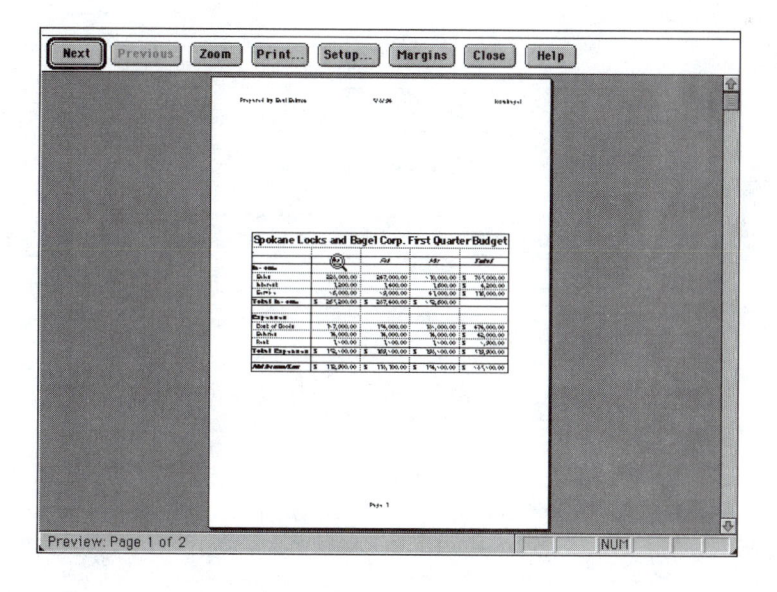

Figure 7.9 *The Print Preview screen.*

Because you're looking at a full page, it's hard to see the details of the worksheet (unless you have a very large screen). Notice that as you move the mouse pointer over the representation of the page, the pointer turns into a magnifying glass. By clicking on a portion of the page, you can zoom in on that portion.

Let's zoom in on the January column heading (where the mouse pointer is in Figure 7.9).

2. Click on **Jan**.

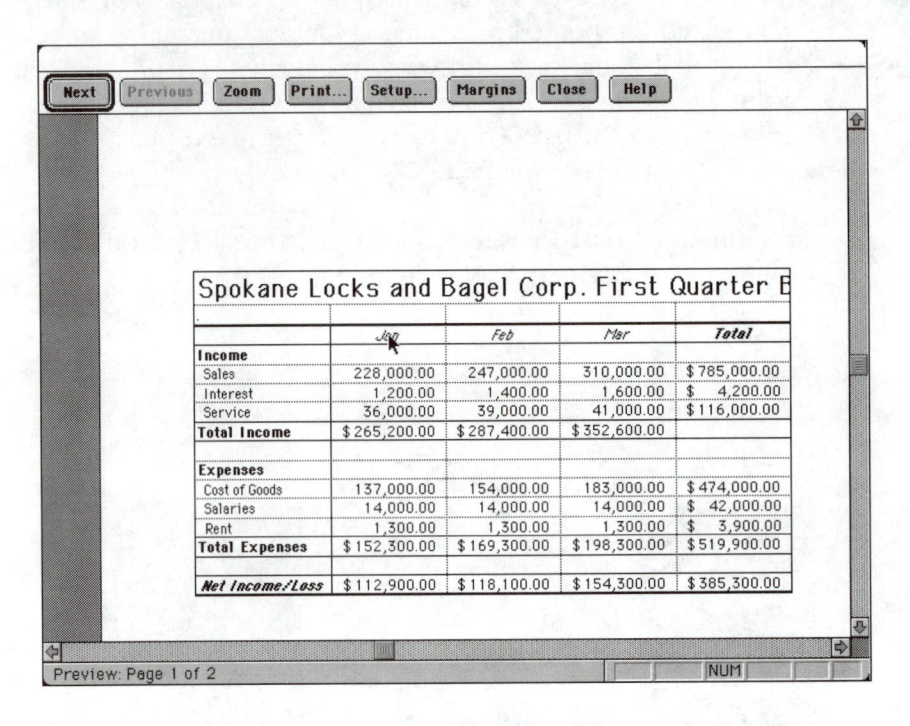

Figure 7.10 The zoomed preview.

You can zoom out by clicking anywhere on the page, or clicking on the **Zoom** button at the top of the Preview screen.

3. Click anywhere on the Print Preview to zoom back out.

The Next and Previous buttons let you preview the next and previous pages in multi-page documents. The Setup button takes you back to the Page Setup dialog box.

The one button in preview that does something a bit unique is the Margins button. I know, we already looked at the Margins portion of the Page Setup dialog box. But clicking on the **Margins** button in Print Preview lets you change margins by dragging margin and column markers so you can see the result prior to printing.

4. Click on the **Margins** button to display the margin handles, as shown in Figure 7.11.

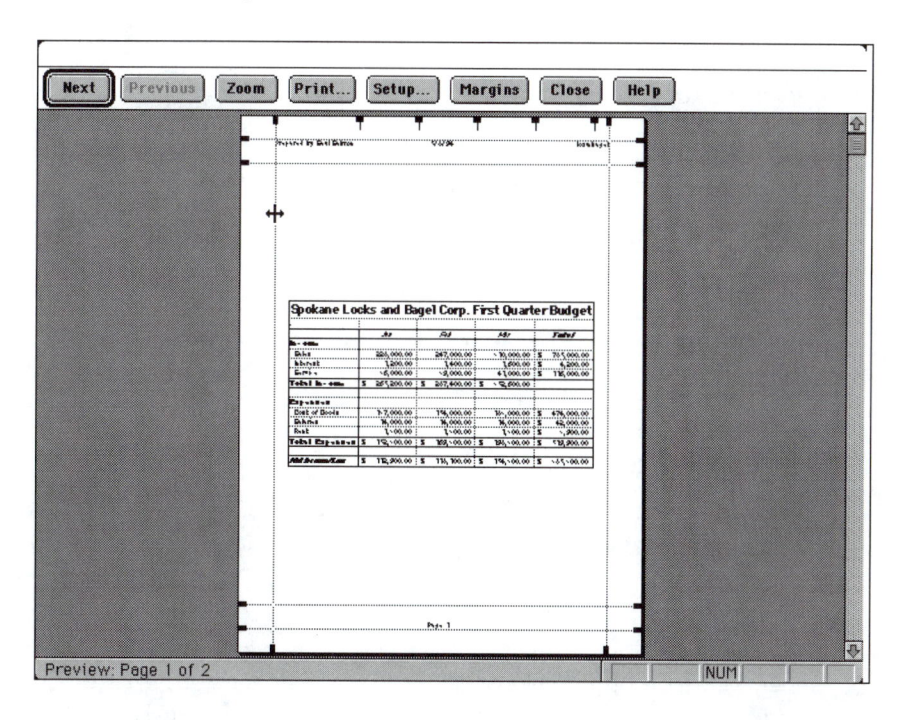

Figure 7.11 *The margin markers displayed in Print Preview.*

By moving the mouse pointer over one of the markers or guidelines until it turns into crosshairs as shown in Figure 7.11, you can reposition any of the margins or columns by dragging. The status bar will display information about which margin you are changing and its position as you drag.

We won't change any of the margins here.

Printing Your Work

It's time to print. Be sure your printer is properly connected, has paper, is turned on and on line, and ready to print.

1. Click on the **Print** button to display the print dialog box, as shown in Figure 7.12.

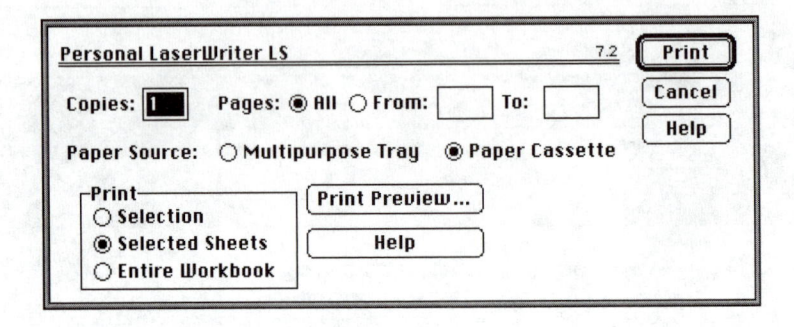

Figure 7.12 The Print dialog box.

This dialog box lets you specify how many copies of your document you want to print. You can choose whether to print all the pages or just the specified pages. If your printer has multiple paper sources, you can specify which source to use. If you've selected a portion of the worksheet before displaying this dialog box, you can specify whether to print the selection, the selected sheet, or the entire workbook. You can also return to the Print Preview screen from here by clicking on the dialog box's **Print Preview** button.

You can also reach this dialog box by pulling down the File menu and selecting **Print** or by pressing **⌘+P**.

We won't make any changes in this dialog box, so let's proceed.

2. Click on the **Print** button to send the worksheet to the printer.

You'll see a message dialog box informing you that you are printing to the printer you've selected, as shown in Figure 7.13. In a few seconds, your printed worksheet should appear.

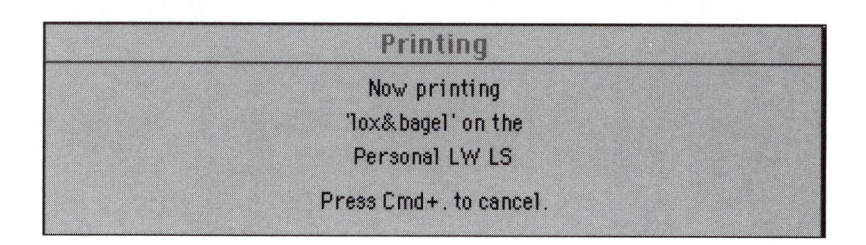

Figure 7.13 *The Print message box.*

The next time you want to print using the same settings, simply click on the **Print** button on the Standard toolbar.

3. Save your work so the print setting will be retained for the next time you want to print.
4. Exit Excel if you aren't moving on to the next chapter now.

A Final Thought

The process of setting up your pages for printing and sending them to your printer should be a piece of cake by now. In the next chapter, you'll learn how to turn your worksheet's text and numbers into beautiful charts and graphs.

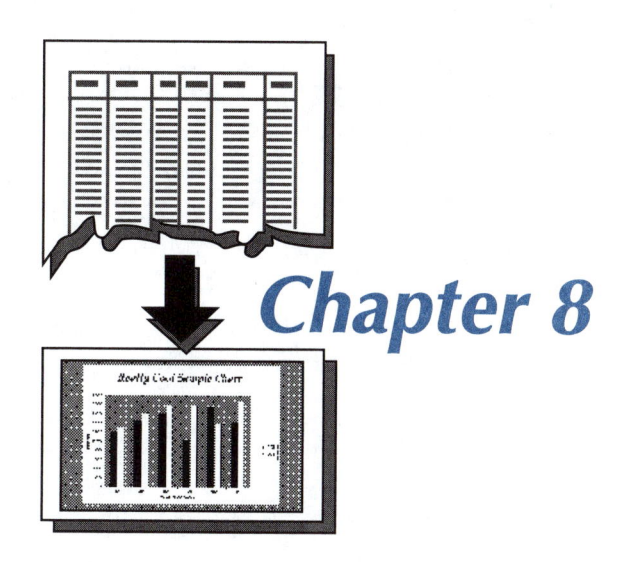

Chapter 8

Creating a Chart

- Chart Fundamentals
- Choosing a Chart Type
- Creating Embedded Charts
- Adding a Data Series
- Using Excel's Drawing Tools
- Creating Charts in Chart Sheets
- Printing Charts
- A Final Thought

As the saying goes, a picture is worth a thousand words. If you've ever thought of a chart as a *nice little extra*, or even a *waste of time and energy,* think again!

If the purpose of your worksheet is to increase your readers' understanding of the numerical data and to persuade them to accept your point of view, then adding a chart is much more than a frill. It's an integral part of the information package. A chart can enhance clarity and add strength to your message.

Until now we've been working strictly with numerical data. I won't deny the importance of numbers–just try sending a bunch of pictures to the IRS and see how far you get! But often, numeric data is just a means to an end. A chart can enable you to direct your reader's focus and make your points with pizzazz.

Chart Fundamentals

Before we start creating charts, we need to understand some fundamental chart concepts and terminology. After all, the world of charts is very different from the worksheet world we've been working with until now. We are really charting new territory here. Sorry about that. I just couldn't help myself.

If some of the terminology we are about to cover seems a bit murky and arcane, don't worry. As we progress through the steps in this chapter, the fog will lift. Excel makes preparing charts automatic enough that you don't need to master all the details of charting to be able to create good looking charts. However, a basic understanding of charting basics will increase your comfort level and allow you to prepare even more powerful charts.

A chart is a graphical representation of the numeric data in a worksheet. Each cell (piece of data) represented in the chart is called a *data point.* Data points are represented on the chart by bars, columns, lines or some other graphical device. A group of related data points is called a *data series.* For example, if we were charting the quarter's monthly income compared with expenses, each month's income or expense figure would be a data point. The Jan, Feb and Mar income figures are one data series, and the Jan, Feb and Mar expense figures are another data series.

Typically, values are plotted along the vertical plane (*y-axis*) and categories are plotted along the horizontal plane (*x-axis*). Labels that run horizontally under the various data series and display the categories represented are *x-axis labels*. Labels running vertically and listing the value increments are the *y-axis labels*.

Figure 8.1 shows a typical chart with the data series represented by columns. This is called a column chart.

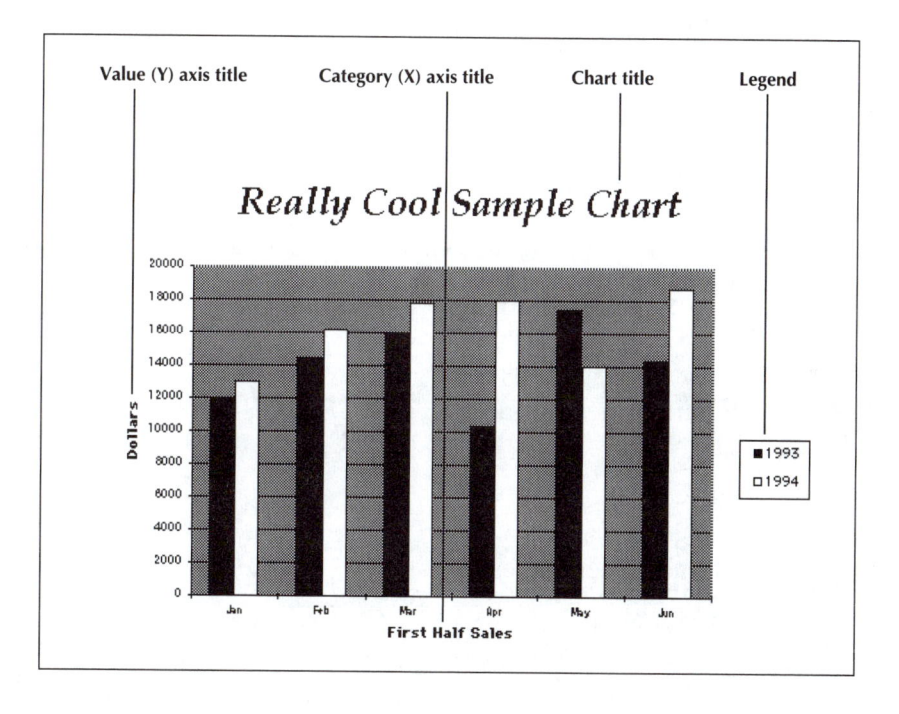

Figure 8.1 *A typical column chart with the basic chart elements.*

Most charts will include a title, a legend to help clarify what each data series represents, a y-axis title and an x-axis title. Many other elements can be added to a chart and all of the chart elements can be customized to suit your requirements, but these are the most common elements you'll find in a chart.

You'll use Excel's ChartWizard to step you through the chart creation process. You can create charts that are embedded in the worksheet or place charts on their own chart sheets. It makes sense to place charts on their own chart sheets if you'll want to print charts on separate pages from the worksheet data so you can use them for handouts. You might want to incorporate chart files in a presentation graphics program, such as Microsoft PowerPoint. *Embedded charts* are placed on the same worksheet as the data they represent. Using an embedded chart, you can see the chart and numerical data at the same time.

Whether a chart is embedded or on a chart sheet, it is linked to the data it represents. This means that, if the numbers change, the chart changes to reflect the new numbers.

Choosing a Chart Type

Excel lets you choose from a dizzying array of chart types. To add to your decision-making burden, you can also choose from a variety of formats for each of the chart types. So how do you decide which chart type to use for a particular situation? There are no hard-and-fast rules. However, if you understand the primary intended uses for each of Excel's chart types, the choice will be easier.

Column Charts

Excel's default chart type is the *column chart*. Column charts are made up of vertical columns that represent data series, and are often used for comparing two or more related data series at a specific point in time, or a small amount of data over time. Excel provides options for several column chart formats, including side-by-side columns, overlapping columns, and stacked columns, as shown in Figure 8.2.

The stacked column chart formats (options 3, 5, 9, and 10) are useful for displaying how much a piece of data contributes to the aggregate. Option 2 is the best choice for column charts representing only one data series, since each column in the series will use a different color or pattern.

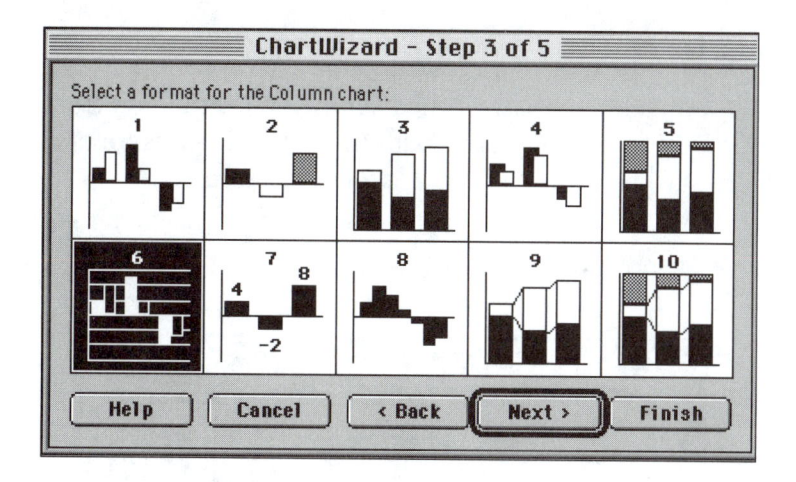

Figure 8.2 *The various Column chart formats.*

In addition to the array of two-dimensional column charts, there are also several three-dimensional (3-D) column chart formats. Choosing a three-dimensional versus a two-dimensional chart is mostly a matter of aesthetics. However, the third dimension gives three-dimensional column charts an additional axis–the Z (value) axis.

Figure 8.3 shows the 3-D column chart formats.

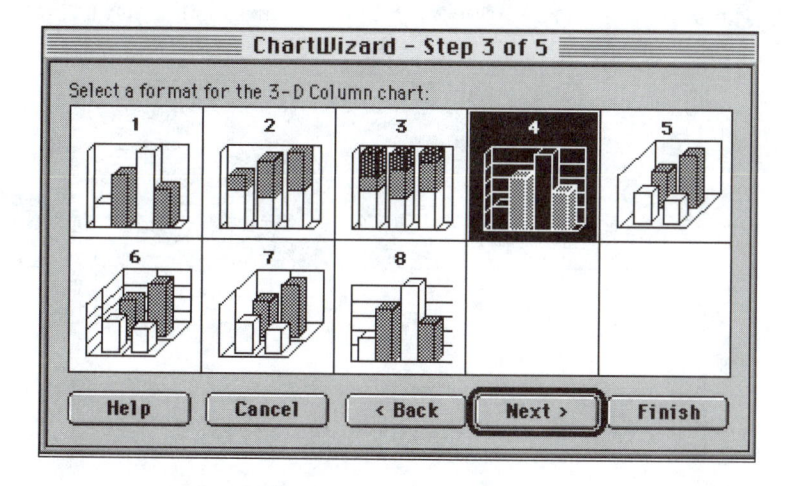

Figure 8.3 *The 3-D Column chart formats.*

Bar Charts

Bar charts are column charts turned on their side–the columns are horizontal instead of vertical. Just as with the column charts, options 3, 5, 9, and 10 are stacked bars. Option 2 is the choice for charts with a single data series.

Figure 8.4 shows the bar chart formats.

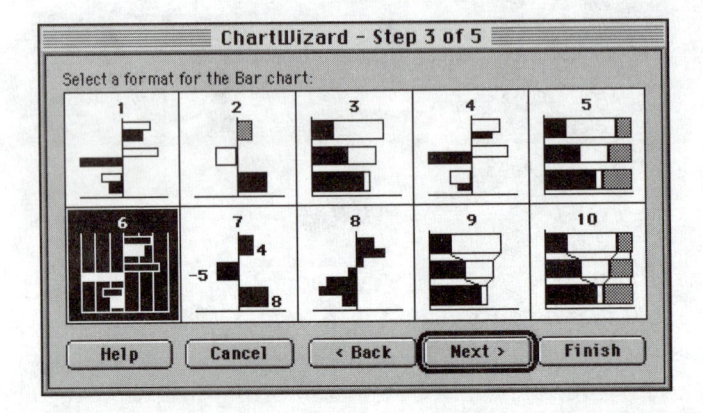

Figure 8.4 *The Bar chart formats.*

You can also select from a variety of 3-D bar charts, as shown in Figure 8.5.

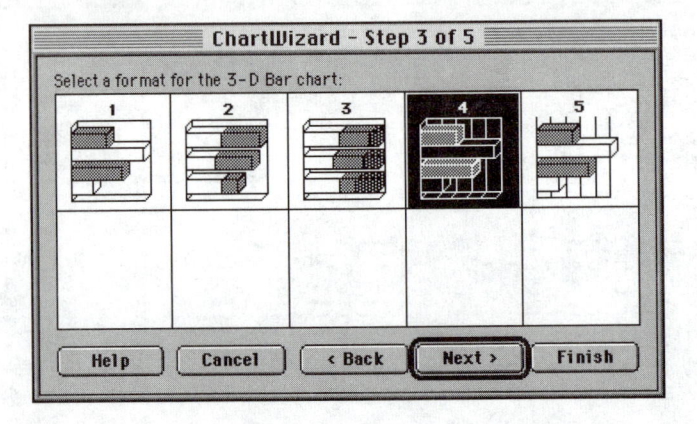

Figure 8.5 *The 3-D Bar chart formats.*

Pie Charts

Pie charts are great for displaying proportional relationships between data, such as the share each bagel flavor contributes to the hole, er, whole. The pie chart's primary limitation is that it can only display one data series.

Figure 8.6 shows the Pie chart formats.

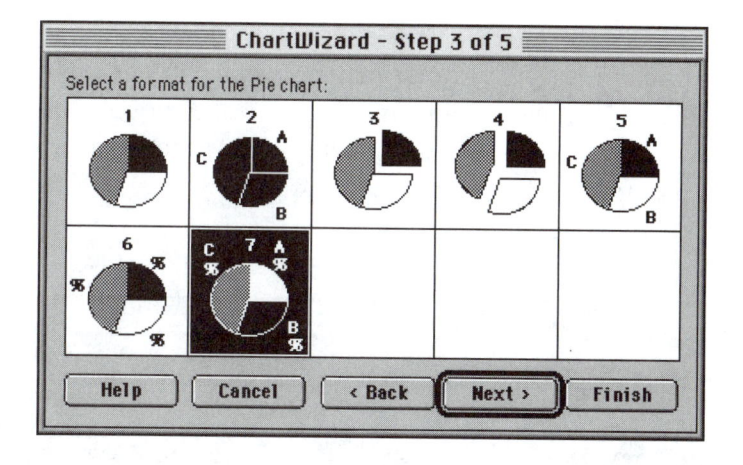

Figure 8.6 *The Pie chart formats.*

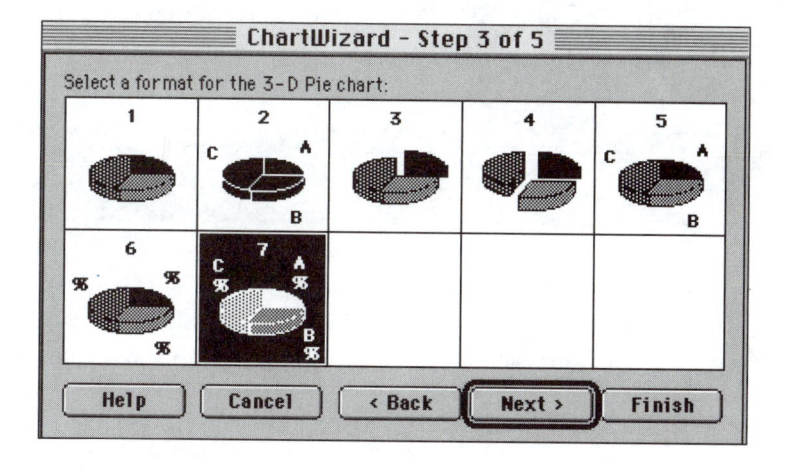

Figure 8.7 *The 3-D pie chart formats.*

Pie charts are also available as 3-D charts. However, unlike 3-D column and bar charts, 3-D pie charts don't gain an additional axis. Their only advantage is their different appearance. Figure 8.7 shows the 3-D pie chart formats.

Doughnut Charts

Doughnut charts are much like pie charts, and are used for the same purpose. However, they have one major advantage over pie charts–they can be used to plot more than one data series. A doughnut chart with more than one data series uses a separate ring for each series.

Figure 8.8 shows the Doughnut chart formats.

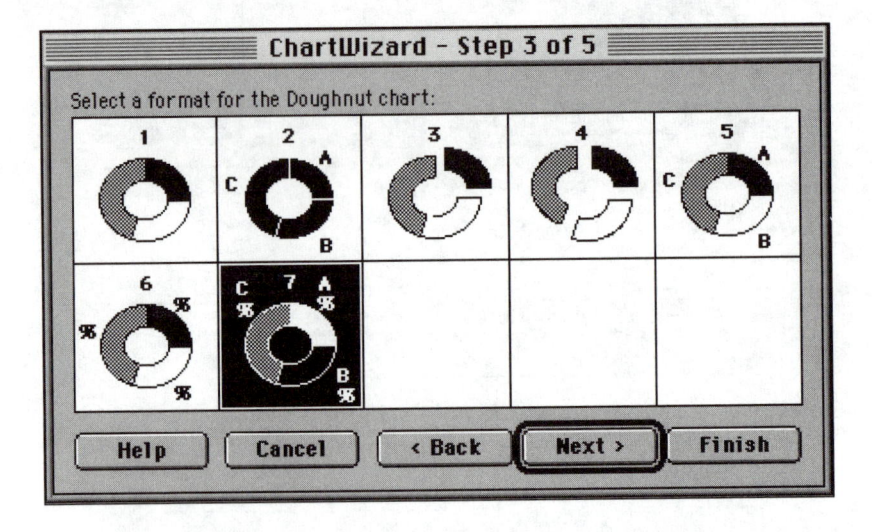

Figure 8.8 The Doughnut chart formats.

Figure 8.9 is an example of a Doughnut chart with three data series.

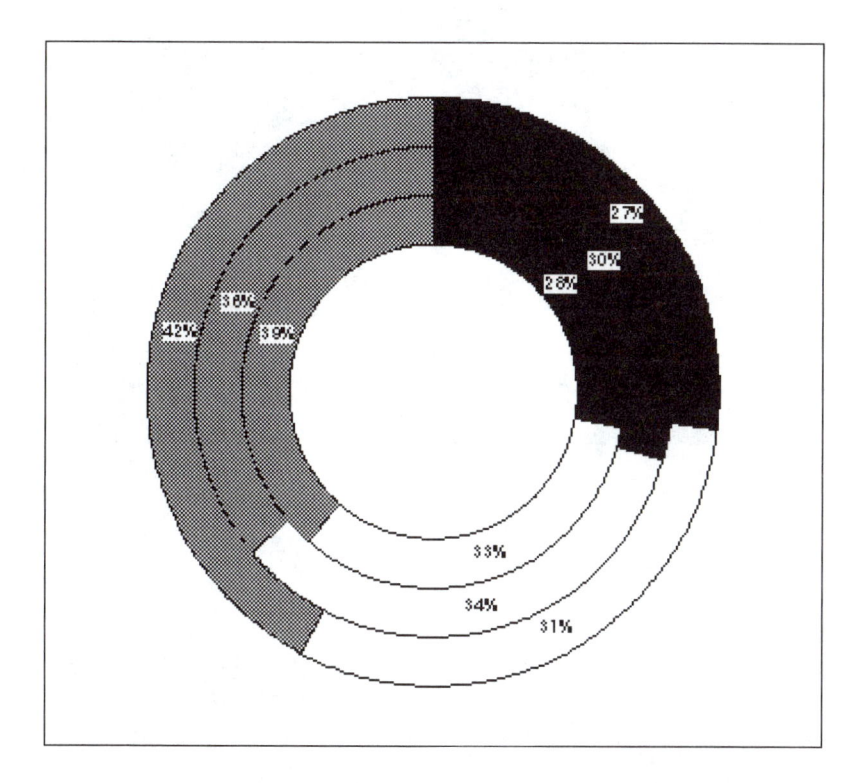

Figure 8.9 *A Doughnut chart with multiple data series.*

Line Charts

Use *line charts* to emphasize the continuity of data over time. They are also a good choice for showing trends. They are especially useful for showing large sets of data, such as the sales of a product over a five-year period. Several of the line chart format options are particularly useful for charting highs and lows, such as snowfall or stocks, and are sometimes referred to as Hi-Lo and Hi-Lo-Close charts. Options 7, 8, and 9 are of the Hi-Lo variety.

Figure 8.10 shows the Line chart formats.

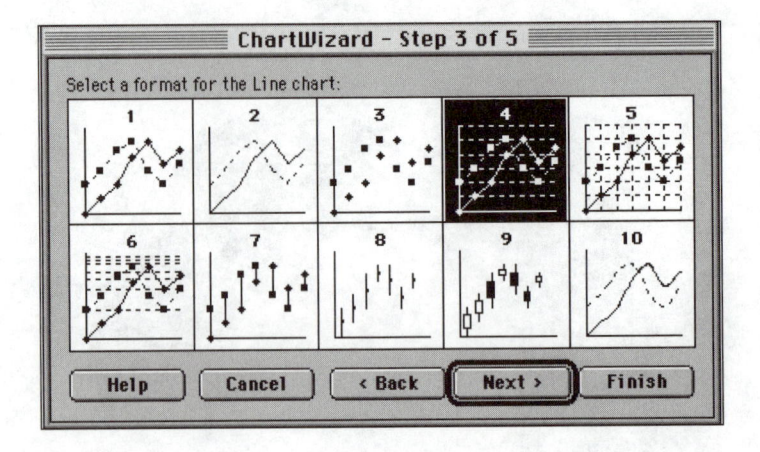

Figure 8.10 *The Line chart formats.*

Figure 8.11 shows the available 3-D line chart formats.

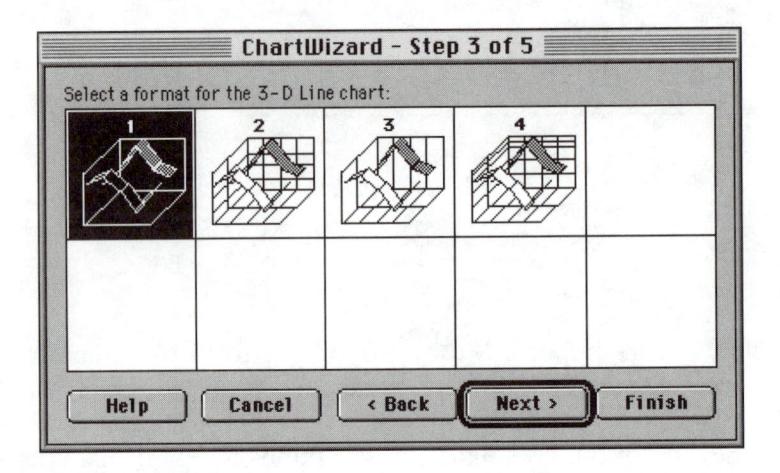

Figure 8.11 *The 3-D line chart formats.*

Area Charts

Area charts are essentially line charts with the space between the lines filled in. Figure 8.12 shows the area chart formats.

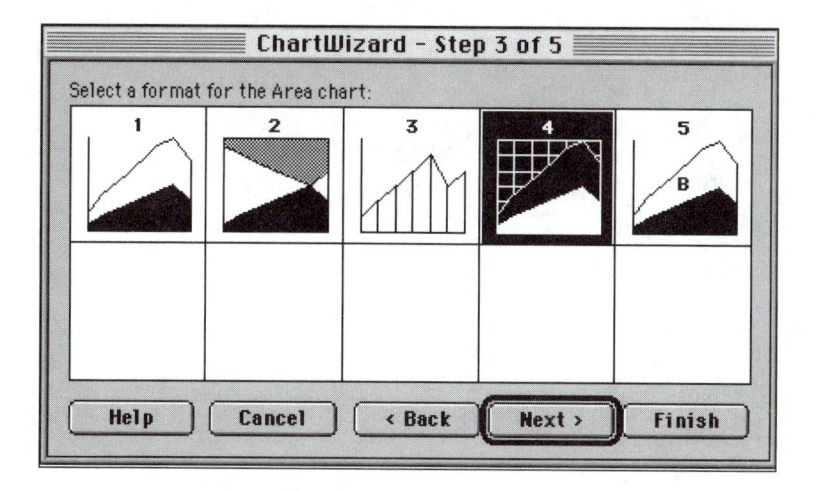

Figure 8.12 The Area chart formats.

Figure 8.13 shows the 3-D area chart formats. Like the 3-D column and bar charts, this gives them an additional axis.

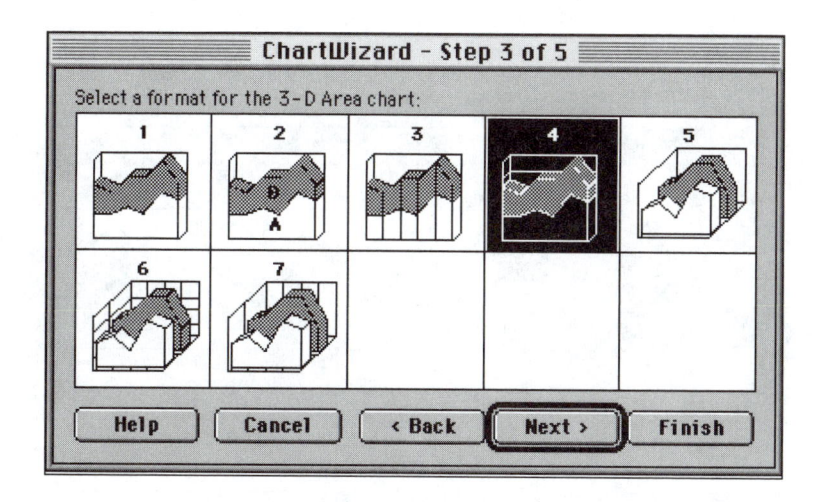

Figure 8.13 The 3-D Area chart formats.

3-D Surface charts are similar to 3-D Area charts. Figure 8.14 shows the 3-D Surface chart formats.

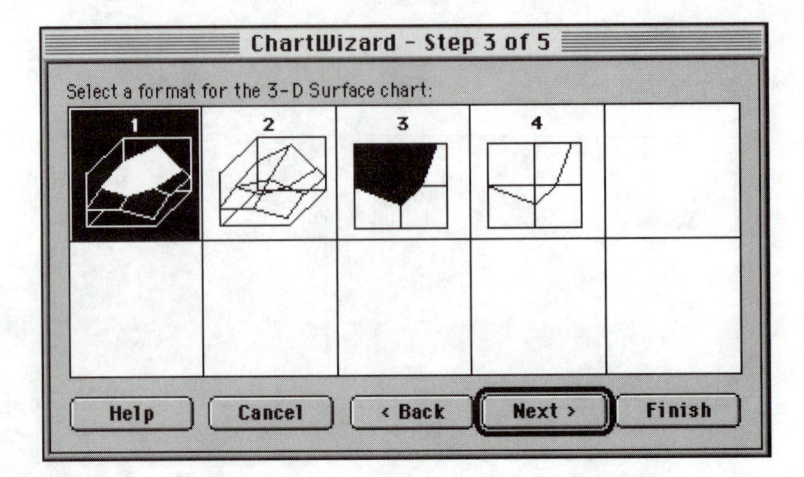

Figure 8.14 *The 3-D Surface chart formats.*

Radar Charts

Radar charts are similar to line charts, but are often used for comparing the whole value of several data series. Figure 8.15 shows the radar chart formats.

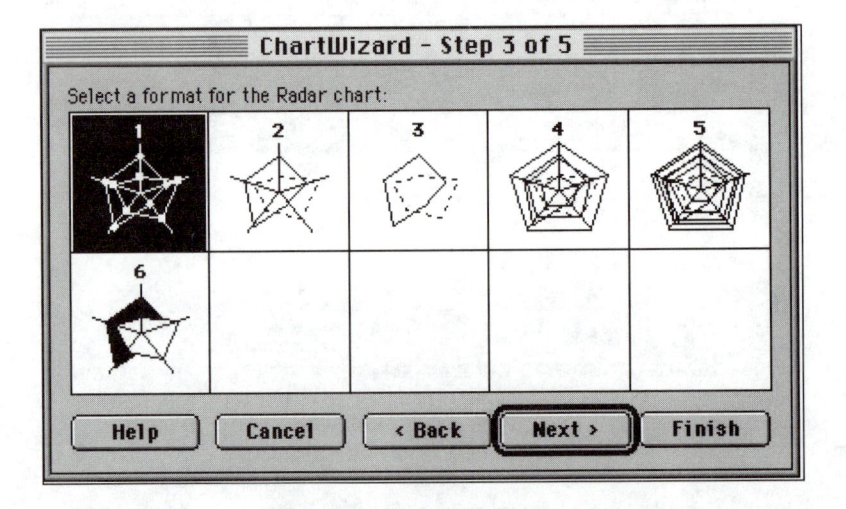

Figure 8.15 *The Radar chart formats.*

XY (Scatter) Charts

Unlike the other chart types discussed so far, *XY charts* use both axes for values. This allows you to plot relationships between two data series, such as the effect of temperature on an electronic component's failure rate.

Figure 8.16 shows the XY (Scatter) chart formats.

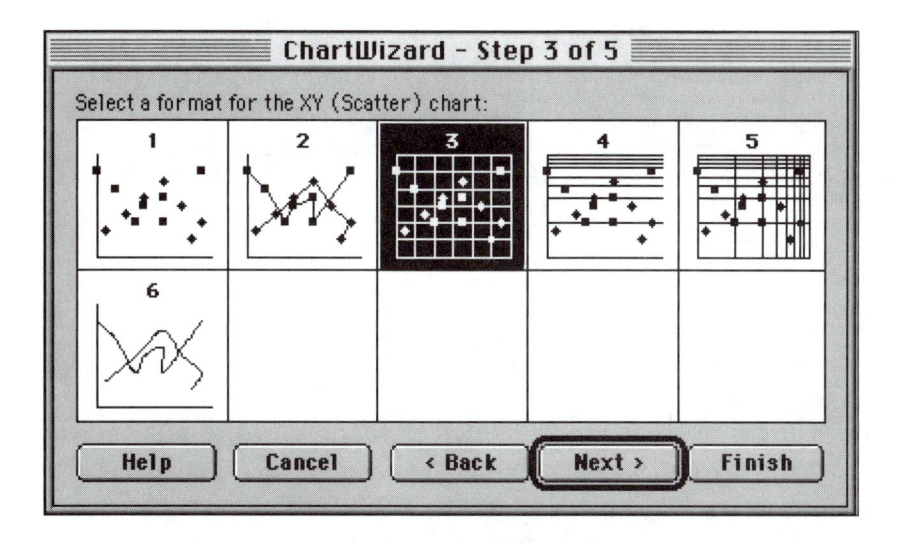

Figure 8.16 *The XY chart formats.*

Combination Charts

Combination charts let you combine two chart types to contrast multiple data series. For example, you might use the column chart portion of a combination chart to plot store sales, and use a line chart to show the store's projected sales.

Figure 8.17 shows the Combination chart formats.

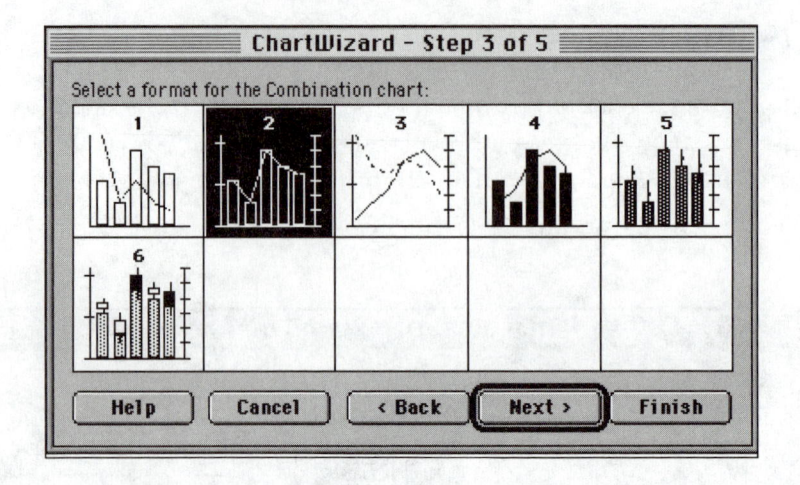

***Figure 8.17** The Combination chart formats.*

Creating Embedded Charts

Let's start by creating an embedded chart next to the numbers in our Spokane Locks and Bagel Corp. First Quarter Budget numbers. We'll start with a chart that plots the first quarter's total income. Later we'll add the total expenses over the three-month period for comparison.

1. Start Excel and open the **lox&bagel** workbook if it isn't already on your screen.

    The first step in the chart creation process is to select the data you want included in the chart.

2. Select the ranges **A3** through **D3** and **A8** through **D8**. Don't forget to hold down the ⌘ key while dragging the mouse to select non-contiguous ranges.

    We included the empty cell A3 in the first range because the ChartWizard understands how to deal with selections if each spans the same number of columns.

3. Click on the **ChartWizard** button on the toolbar and then, without clicking, position the mouse pointer (which is now a crosshair with a chart icon attached) in the upper-left corner of cell F3 as shown in Figure 8.18.

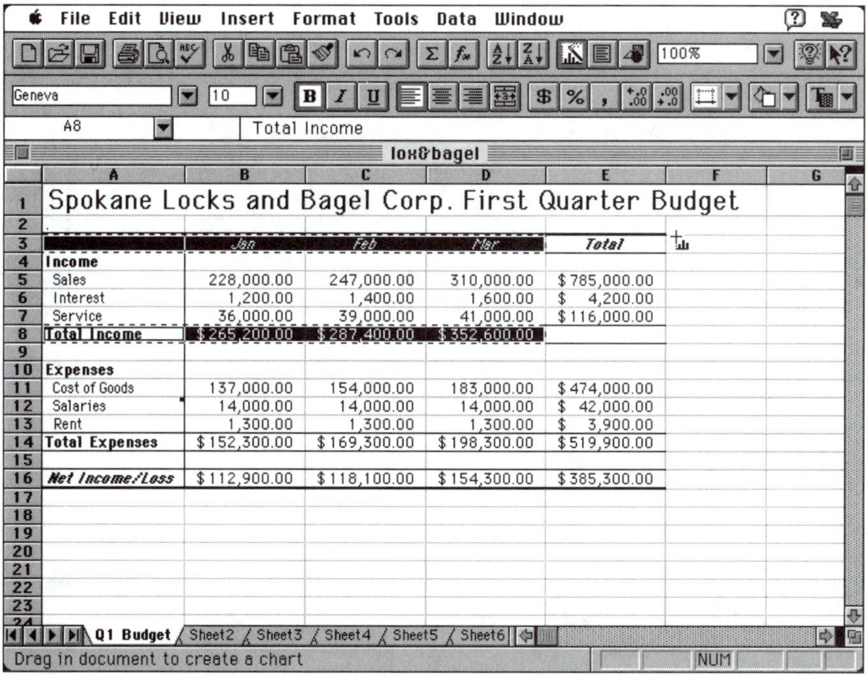

Figure 8.18 *The selected ranges for the chart and the ChartWizard mouse pointer.*

You could just click the mouse and let Excel choose the size of the chart for you, but we'll drag the mouse pointer to the lower-right corner of our desired chart size to create a larger chart that will be easier to work with. You can, of course, change the size of a chart after it's created, and you'll learn how to do that later.

4. Drag down to row 16 and over to column L, as shown in Figure 8.19. The screen will automatically scroll as you drag the mouse pointer to the right edge of the screen.

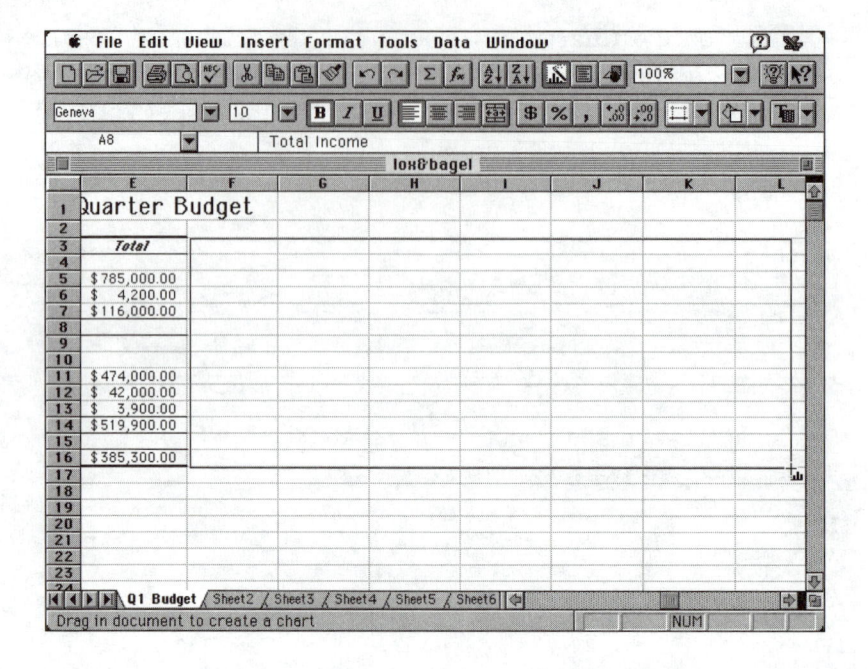

Figure 8.19 *The outline of the chart we are about to create.*

5. Release the mouse button.

   The first ChartWizard dialog box appears, as displayed in Figure 8.20.

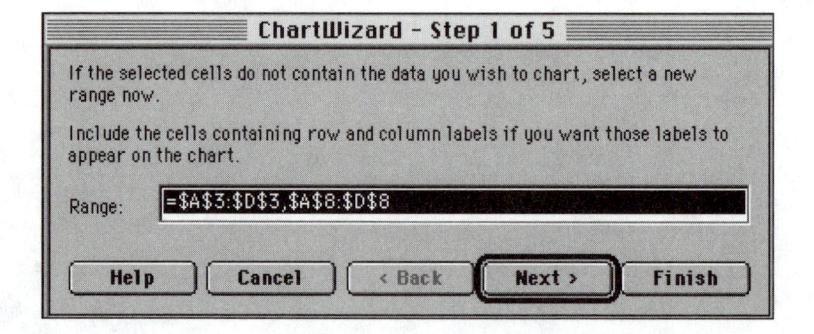

Figure 8.20 *The first of five ChartWizard dialog boxes.*

The Range text box displays the ranges you selected in step two. The dollar sign ($) in front of each column letter and row number indicates that these are absolute references. These references won't change if the data is moved or copied.

Since the ranges are correct, we'll move on to the next dialog box.

6. Click on the **Next** button to move to the next ChartWizard dialog box, as displayed in Figure 8.21.

N O T E

If you want to go back to the previous ChartWizard dialog box to make different choices, you can click on the **Back** button. Click on the **Finish** button to have the ChartWizard complete your chart based on the defaults for the following ChartWizard dialog boxes.

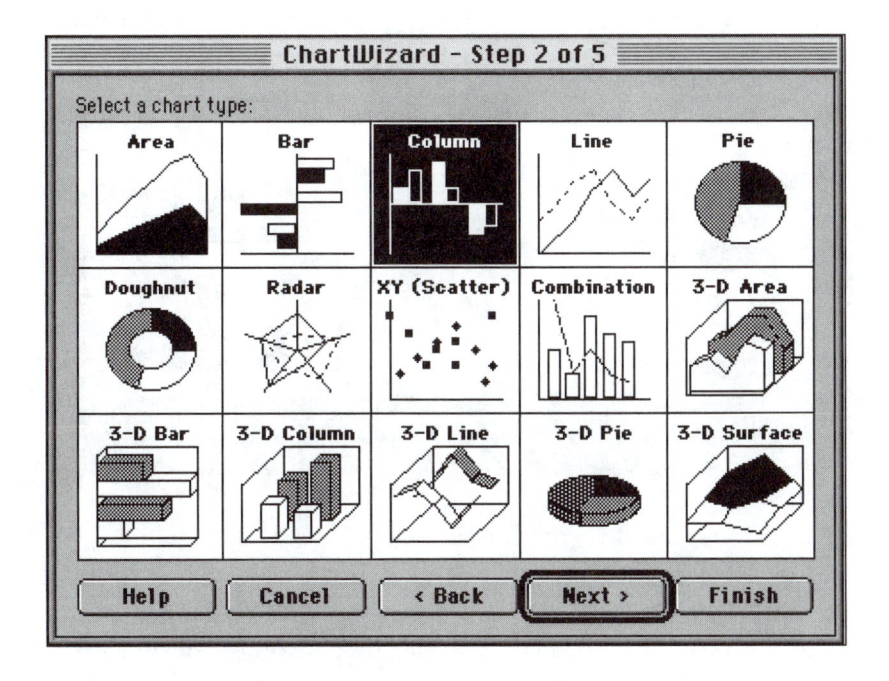

Figure 8.21 *The second ChartWizard dialog box.*

This dialog box lets you choose from among fifteen available categories. The default is the Column chart, which is a fine choice for the type of data we are charting. To choose a different chart type, you would simply click on the chart type of your choice.

N O T E

As discussed earlier in the chapter, there is no one correct choice when choosing chart types. Fortunately, Excel makes it easy to experiment with various chart types–even after you've created the chart–to see how your data will be best presented. You may choose to present the same data with more than one chart type to draw attention to different aspects of the data.

7. Click on the **Next** button to move to the third ChartWizard dialog box, as shown in Figure 8.22.

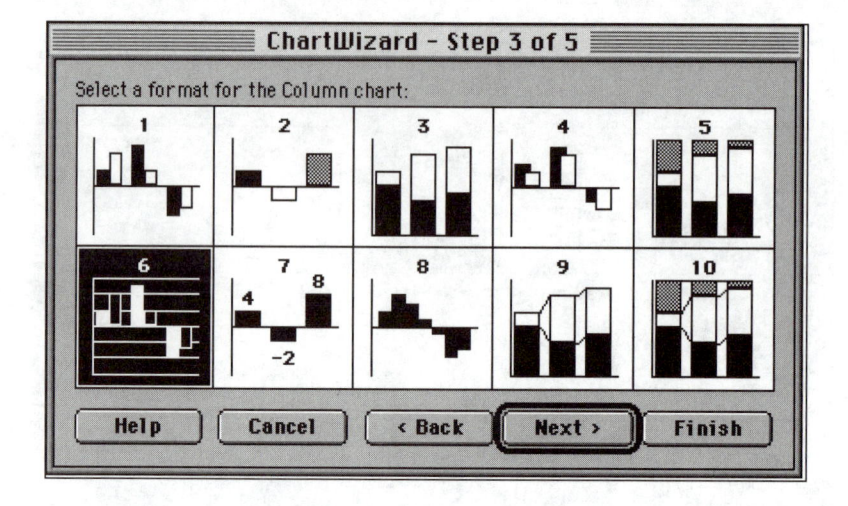

Figure 8.22 *The third ChartWizard dialog box.*

This dialog box lets you choose from a variety of sub-categories of the chart type you've chosen. Once again, we'll stick with the default, although many of the other choices would do nicely too.

8. Click on the **Next** button to display the fourth ChartWizard dialog box, as portrayed in Figure 8.23.

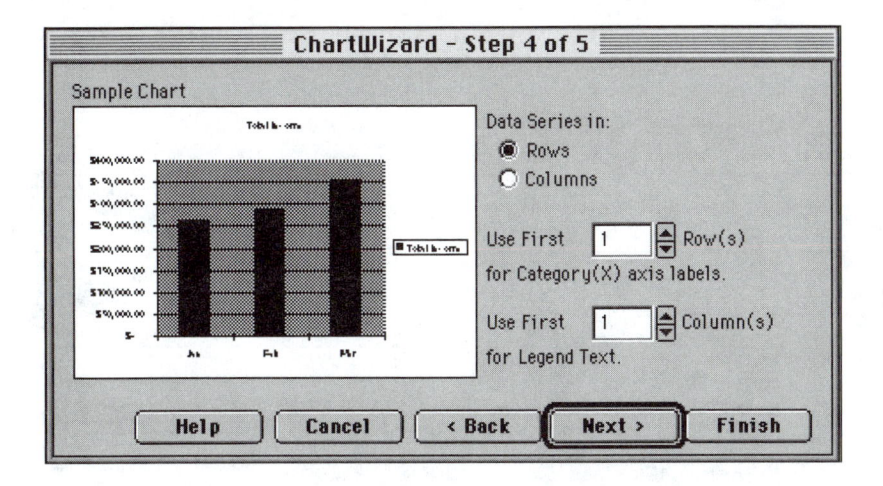

Figure 8.23 *The fourth ChartWizard dialog box.*

This is where we get to see a preview of the chart we are creating and to make sure Excel is charting the data the way we intend. On the right side of the dialog box, the first thing the ChartWizard wants to know is whether the data series are in rows (the default) or columns. Our data series are indeed in rows, so we don't need to change this option.

The next piece of information the ChartWizard wants to know is which row or rows to use for the Category axis (the horizontal, or x-axis) labels.

The first row we selected to chart was row 3, which included the column headings Jan, Feb and Mar–our category labels–so we don't have to change anything here. If you squint, you can see Jan, Feb and Mar under the columns in the sample chart.

Finally, the ChartWizard wants to be sure that the first column contains the text for the legend. The label for our data series, Total Income, is in column A, which is the first column we selected, so we're all set here as well. The legend (on the right side of the sample chart) displays the text and the color/pattern keys for our chart.

There's nothing in this dialog box to change, so let's move on.

9. Click on the **Next** button to move to the fifth and final ChartWizard dialog box, as shown in Figure 8.24.

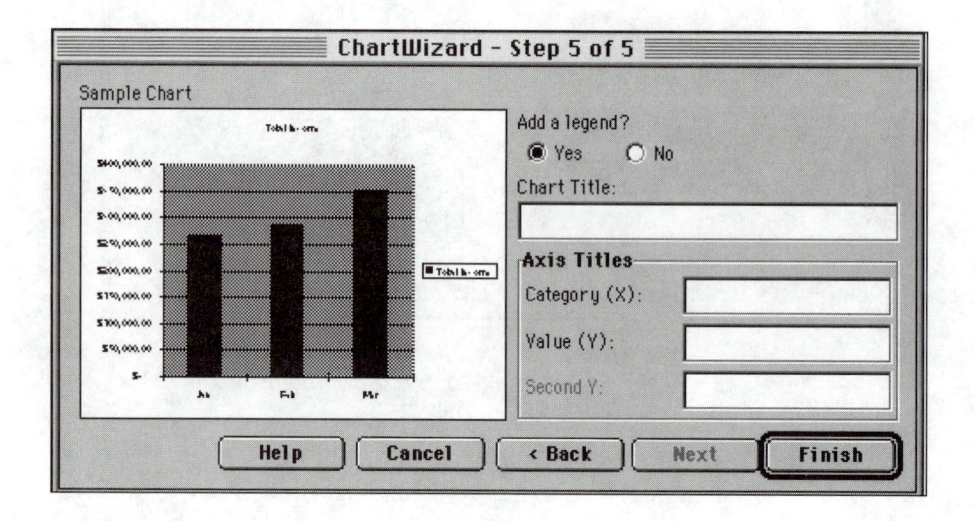

Figure 8.24 The fifth ChartWizard dialog box.

The first option in this dialog box is to add a legend. Without a legend, it would be difficult to tell which columns belong to which data series, so we'll leave the **Yes** option button selected. Next, we have the option of adding a chart title. Let's add one.

10. Click in the **Chart Title** text box and type: **1st Quarter Income vs. Expenses**.

As you type the title, the Sample Chart portion of the dialog box is updated to display the title. We can also add titles to the category (x) axis and the value (y) axis. Let's add a value axis title to show that the numbers indicate dollars, which will be helpful when we remove those distracting dollar signs later.

11. Click in the **Value (Y)** text box and type: **Dollars**.

Before we finish, be sure your dialog box looks like Figure 8.25.

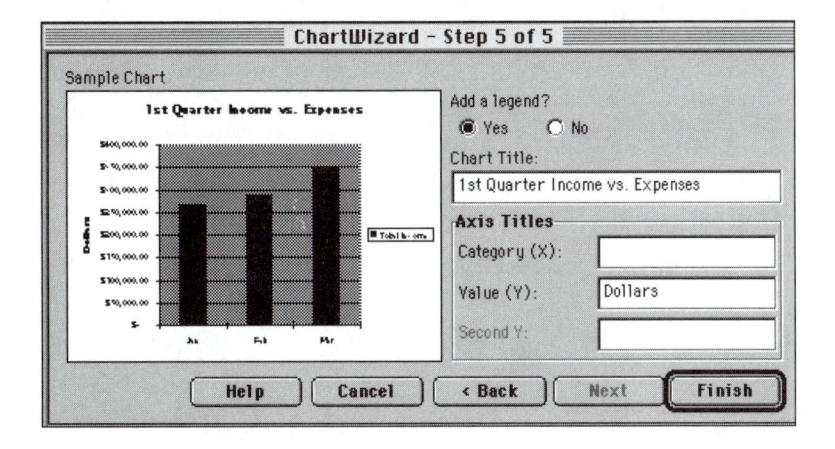

Figure 8.25 *The filled-in final dialog box.*

12. Click on the **Finish** button and then scroll right until the entire chart is visible, as shown in Figure 8.26.

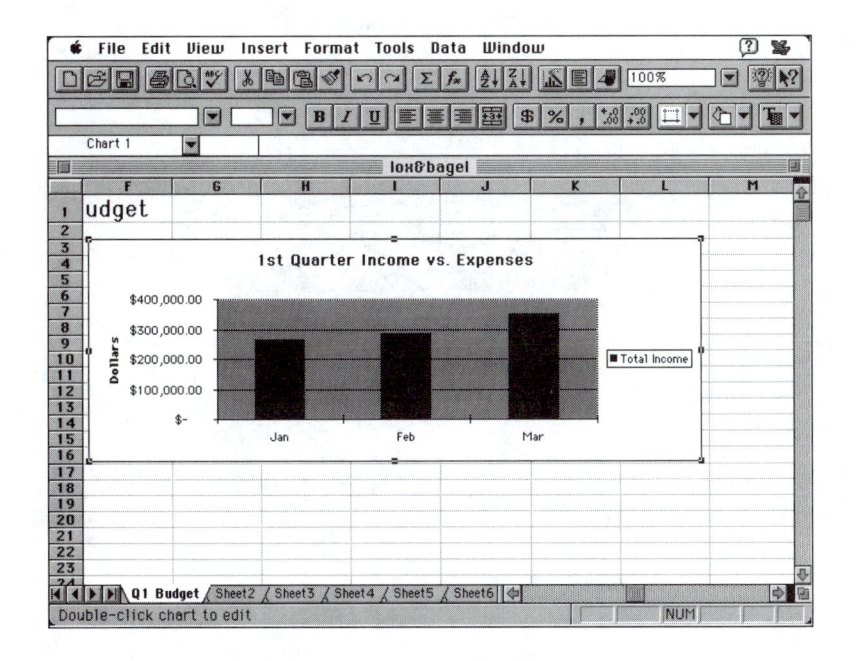

Figure 8.26 *The embedded chart.*

The embedded chart is now part of the worksheet. Notice the handles on each corner and the sides of the chart. These handles indicate that the chart is selected, which means it can be sized and moved, and that the overall chart properties can be manipulated. But the individual chart elements can't be directly manipulated unless the chart is active.

To make an embedded chart active, double-click on it. Note that the status bar in Figure 8.26 displays the message "Double-click chart to edit." Let's activate the chart and examine some of the ways we can customize the chart.

13. Double-click anywhere in the chart to activate it.

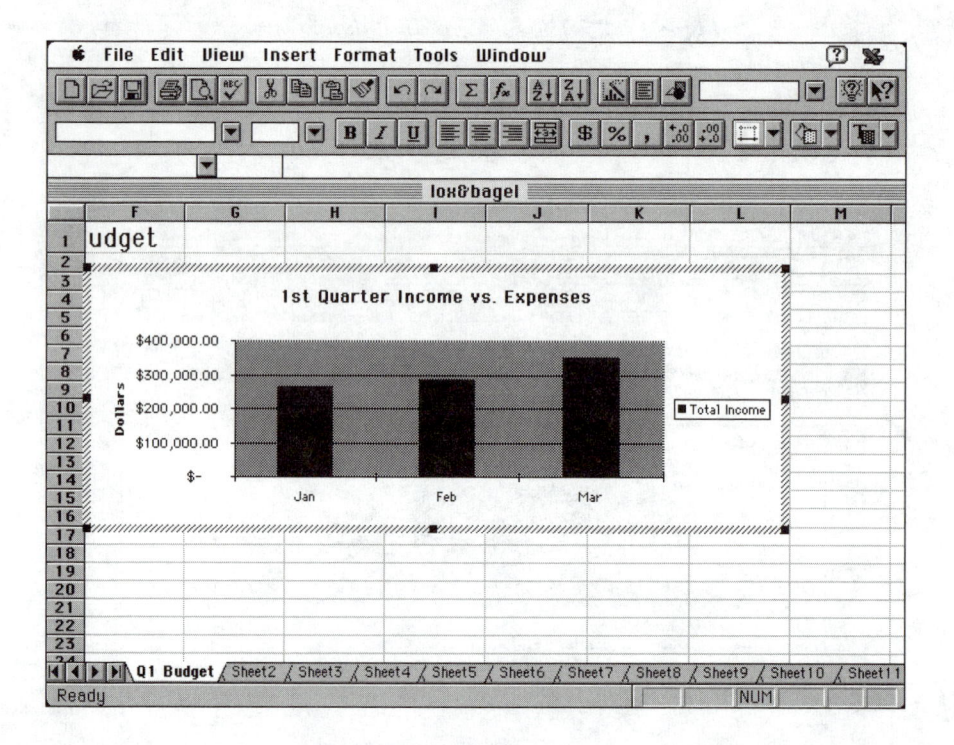

Figure 8.27 *The activated chart.*

The chart's border changes to indicate that it is active. With the chart active, you can point to a chart element and hold down the

⌘ key while pressing the mouse button to use its shortcut menu, or you can double-click on it to display a dialog box to format that element. You can also click on a chart element to select it so you can move or resize it.

We added the value (y) axis title because we knew we wanted to get rid of the dollar signs on the numbers along the y-axis. Let's take care of that detail now.

14. Double-click on one of the numbers along the y-axis to display the Format Axis dialog box as shown in Figure 8.28. Click on the **Number** tab if it isn't highlighted.

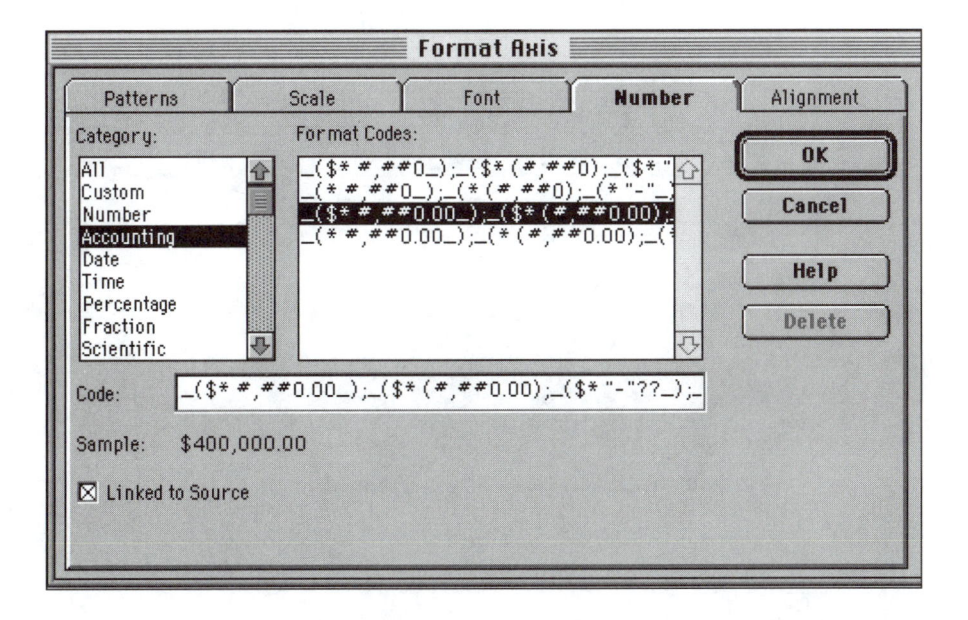

Figure 8.28 *The Number portion of the Format Axis dialog box.*

This dialog box should look familiar to you. It's almost the same as the number portion of the Format Cells dialog box we used earlier in the book. The check box in the lower-left corner of the dialog box tells you that the formatting for the numbers along the value axis are linked to the source.

This means that whatever formatting was applied to the data series being represented is being used here. While this is often a good assumption, we want to make a change here. We don't need to uncheck the Linked to Source check box because, as soon as we choose another number format, Excel will understand that the formatting is no longer linked to the source and remove the check mark.

15. Click on **Number** in the Category list.

16. In the Format Codes list, click on the third code from the top **(#,##0)** and then click on the **OK** button to change the format of the y-axis numbers, as displayed in Figure 8.29.

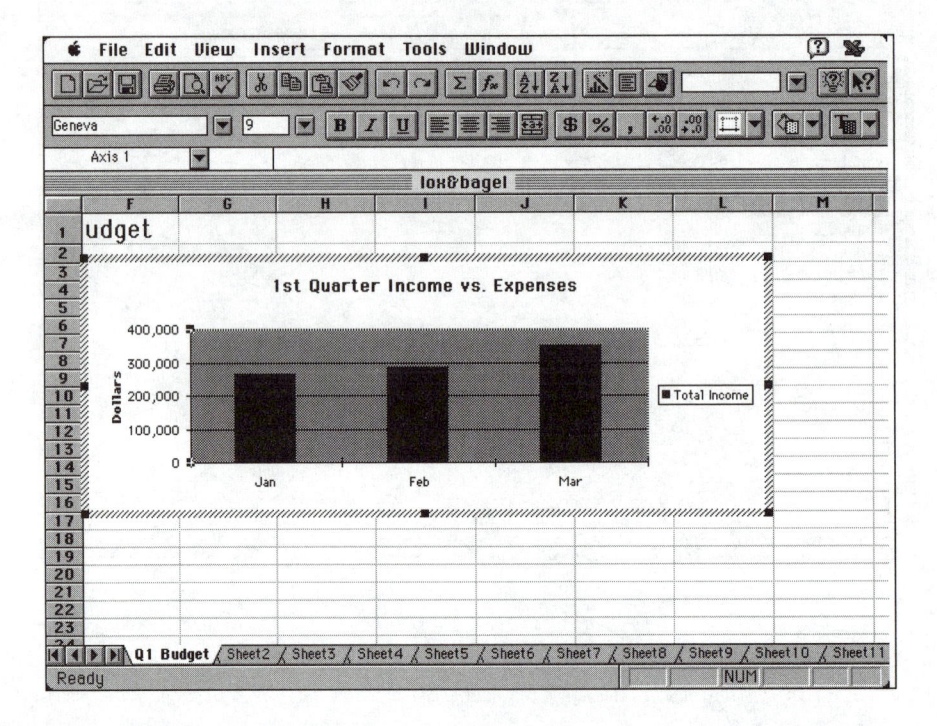

Figure 8.29 *The chart with the reformatted y-axis numbers.*

Next let's change the chart title's font.

17. Double-click on the chart title, **1st Quarter Income vs. Expenses**, to display the Format Title dialog box, as shown in Figure 8.30. Click on the **Font** tab if it isn't highlighted.

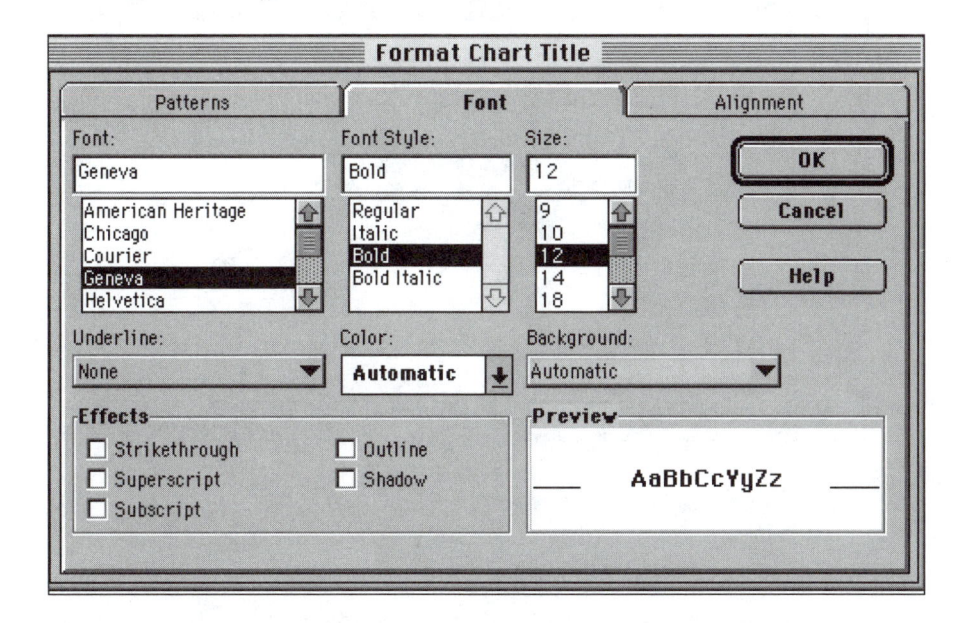

Figure 8.30 *The Font portion of the Format Title dialog box.*

This is the same as the Font portion of the Format Cells dialog box we used in Chapter 6, so its options should be familiar. My system's default font is Geneva, its style is bold and its size is 12-point. Let's change to Times, Bold Italic, 18-point.

18. Scroll down the Font list and click on **Times**. Click on **Bold Italic** in the Font Style list, and then click on **18** in the Size list.

    The Preview portion of the dialog box shows you what your new font choice will look like when applied.

19. Finally, click on the **OK** button the change the title as seen in Figure 8.31.

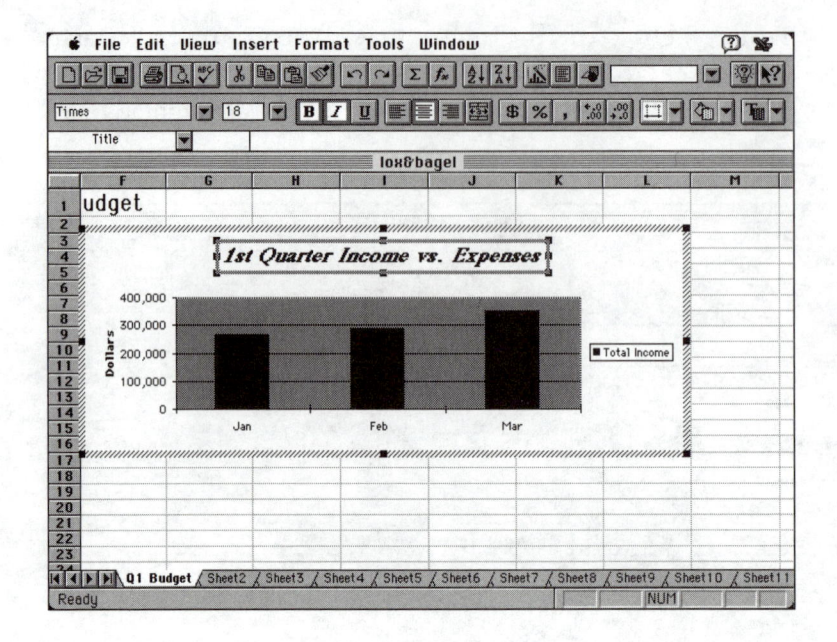

Figure 8.31 *The chart with its newly-formatted title.*

Let's see how easy it is to change chart types.

20. Pull down the Format menu and select **Chart Type** to display the type dialog box, as shown in Figure 8.32.

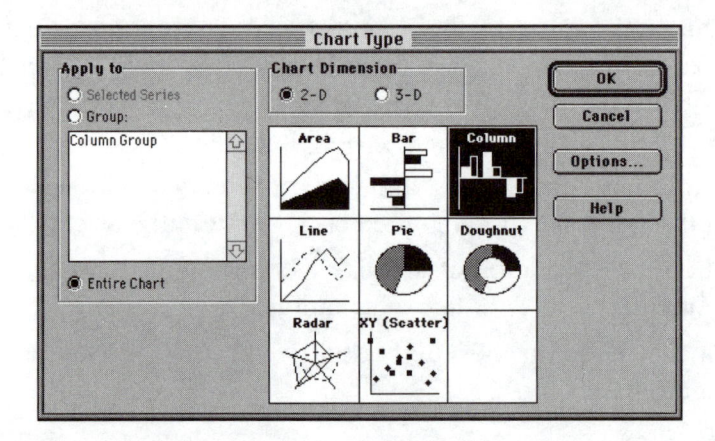

Figure 8.32 *The Chart Type dialog box.*

21. Click on the **Line** chart image in the dialog box and then click on the **OK** button.

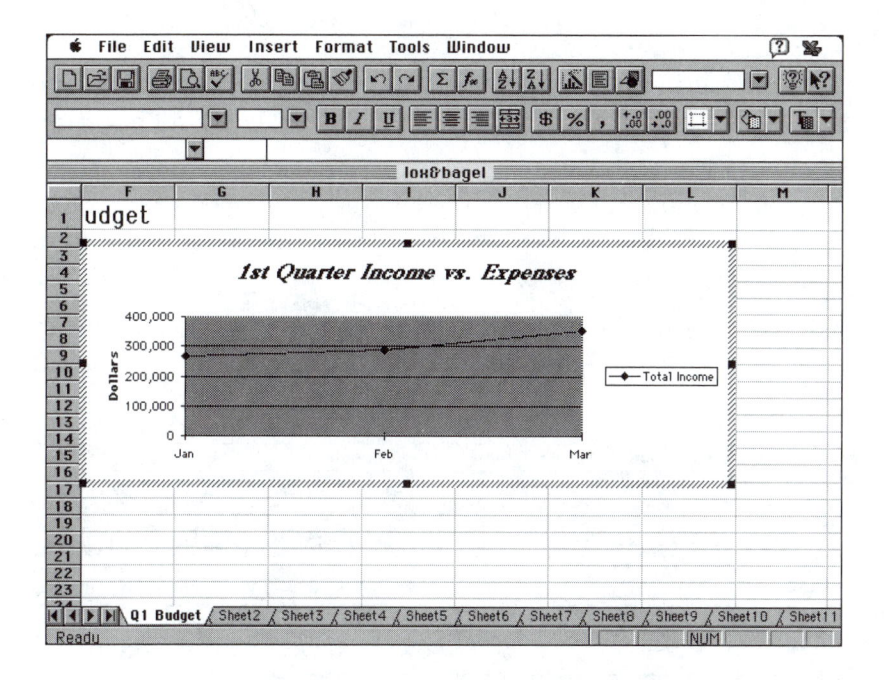

Figure 8.33 *The chart has been changed to a line chart.*

We'll add another data series later in the chapter so the chart will show the comparison between income and expenses. Because this line chart won't show the comparison as clearly as the column chart, let's change it back.

22. Pull down the Edit menu and select **Undo Chart Type**, or click on the **Undo** button on the Standard toolbar to reverse the chart type change you just made.

To prove that the chart really is linked to the worksheet data, let's change some of the worksheet data and see how the chart is affected.

22. Click on any of the worksheet cells outside the chart area to deactivate it and scroll left until column A is visible.

N O T E

While the chart is active, the scroll bars are hidden. They reappear when the chart is deactivated.

The Chart toolbar usually disappears from the screen when the chart isn't selected. Let's change the Sales figure in cell D5 to reflect a more optimistic forecast.

23. Enter **500000** in cell D5 (the March sales figure). Don't forget to click on the **Enter** box on the Formula bar or press the **Return** key to confirm the entry.

24. Scroll right until the chart is visible again and observe the change in the March Total Income column, as displayed in Figure 8.34.

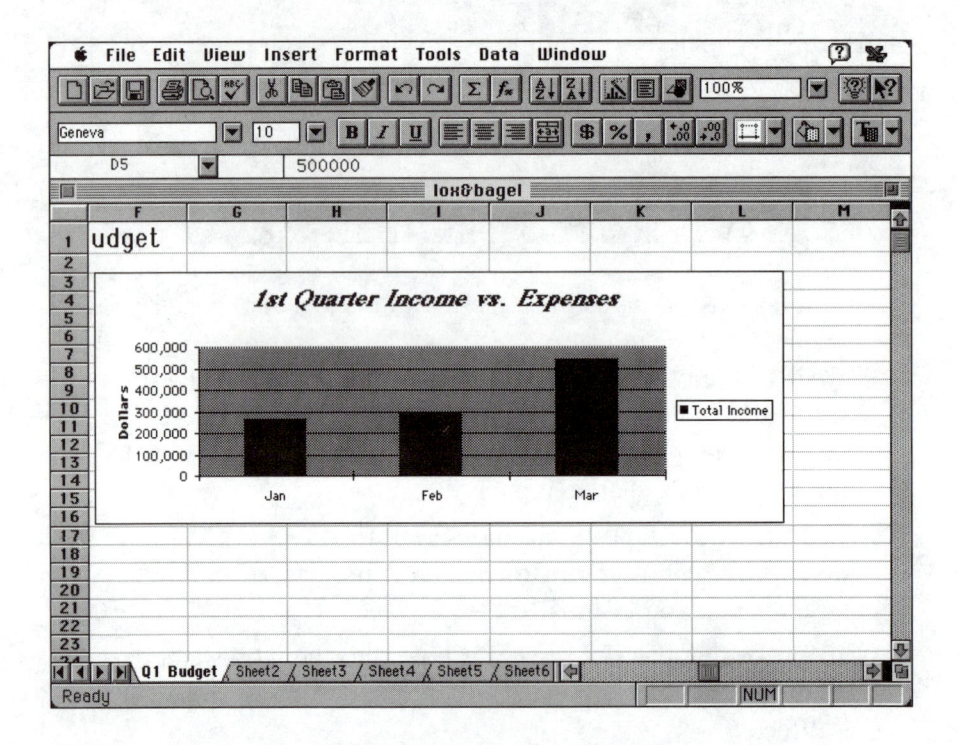

Figure 8.34 *The chart reflecting the new data.*

Adding a New Data Series

If you want to add a new data series to a chart, you can take advantage of an interesting new feature called *drag and plot*. Simply select the new data series in your worksheet, drag it onto the chart, and release the mouse button. The new series is automatically added to the chart. Even the data series label is added to the legend if you include the label in the selection.

Keep in mind that Excel makes a best guess as to how you want the data series applied to the chart. If it guesses incorrectly, you may need to make some modifications manually.

1. Scroll to the left so column A is visible and select cells **A14** through **D14** (the Total Expenses for the quarter).

2. Position the mouse pointer just below the selection so it is in the shape of an arrow pointer, as shown in Figure 8.35.

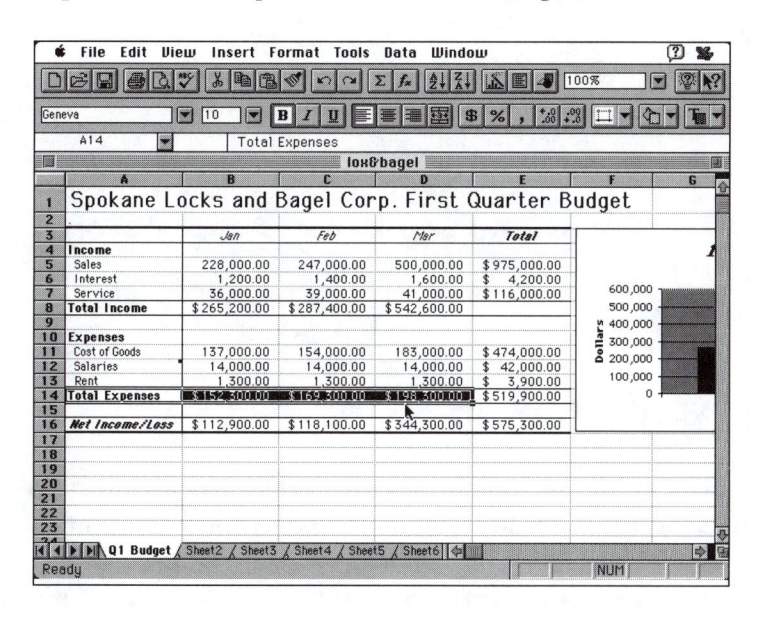

Figure 8.35 *A new data series ready to be added to the chart.*

3. Hold down the mouse button and drag to the right until the mouse pointer is within the visible chart boundaries, then release the mouse button.

4. Scroll to the right so the entire chart is visible, as shown in Figure 8.36.

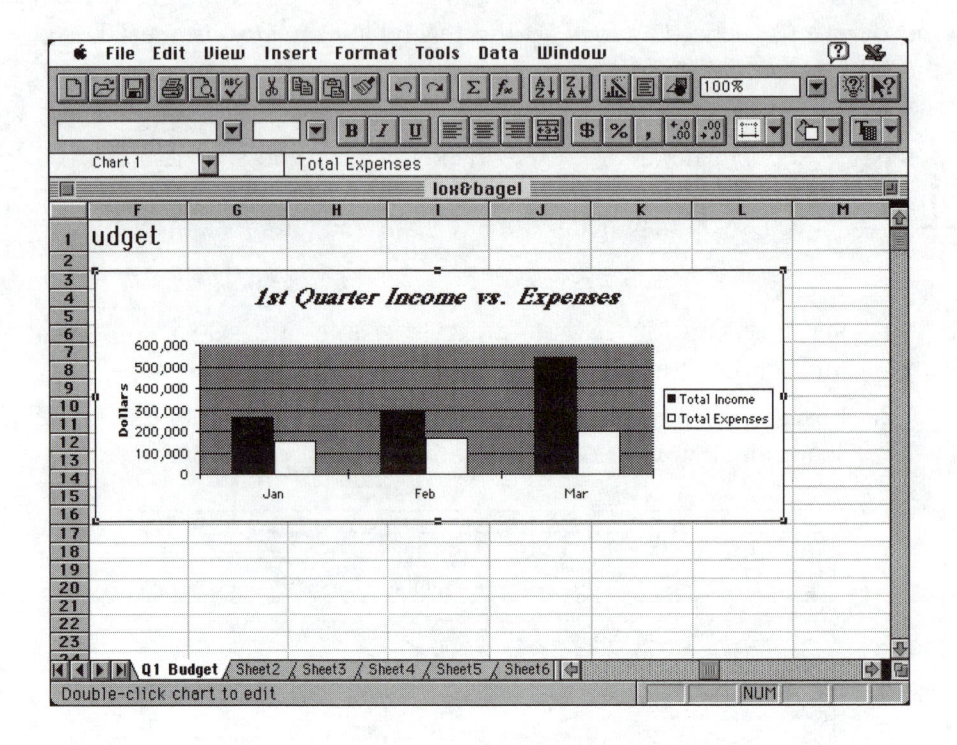

Figure 8.36 *The chart with a new data series added.*

Using Excel's Drawing Tools

Before we're through with this chart, let's add a few more touches with Excel's drawing tools. In addition to the standard chart elements we've discussed, Excel provides a wide variety of drawing tools for adding lines, arrows, circles, and even additional text that isn't one of the normal chart title elements.

The drawing tools aren't just for use with charts. You can add any of these graphic elements to any part of the worksheet. For example, you might want to draw an arrow pointing to a portion of the worksheet you want the reader to notice, and perhaps draw a circle around that portion as well. These graphic elements are used the same way whether you are adding them to a chart or the worksheet.

To use the drawing tools, you must display the Drawing toolbar, so let's do that now.

1. Click on the **Drawing** button on the Standard toolbar to display the Drawing toolbar, as shown in Figure 8.37.

   If the Drawing toolbar obscures part of the chart, you can move it to a more convenient location by pointing to its title bar and dragging it.

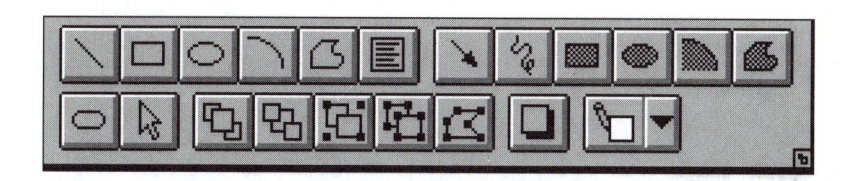

Figure 8.37 *The Drawing toolbar.*

To use one of the drawing tools to create a graphic element, just click on the button and then drag to where you want the shape. Let's add an arrow pointing to the March income column.

SHORTCUT

If you want to use a drawing tool several times in succession, just double-click on it and you won't have to re-select it the next time. When you're through using that tool, just click on it again.

2. Click on the **Arrow** button on the Drawing toolbar and then position the mouse pointer, which is now a crosshair, above and to the left of the March income column, as portrayed in Figure 8.38.

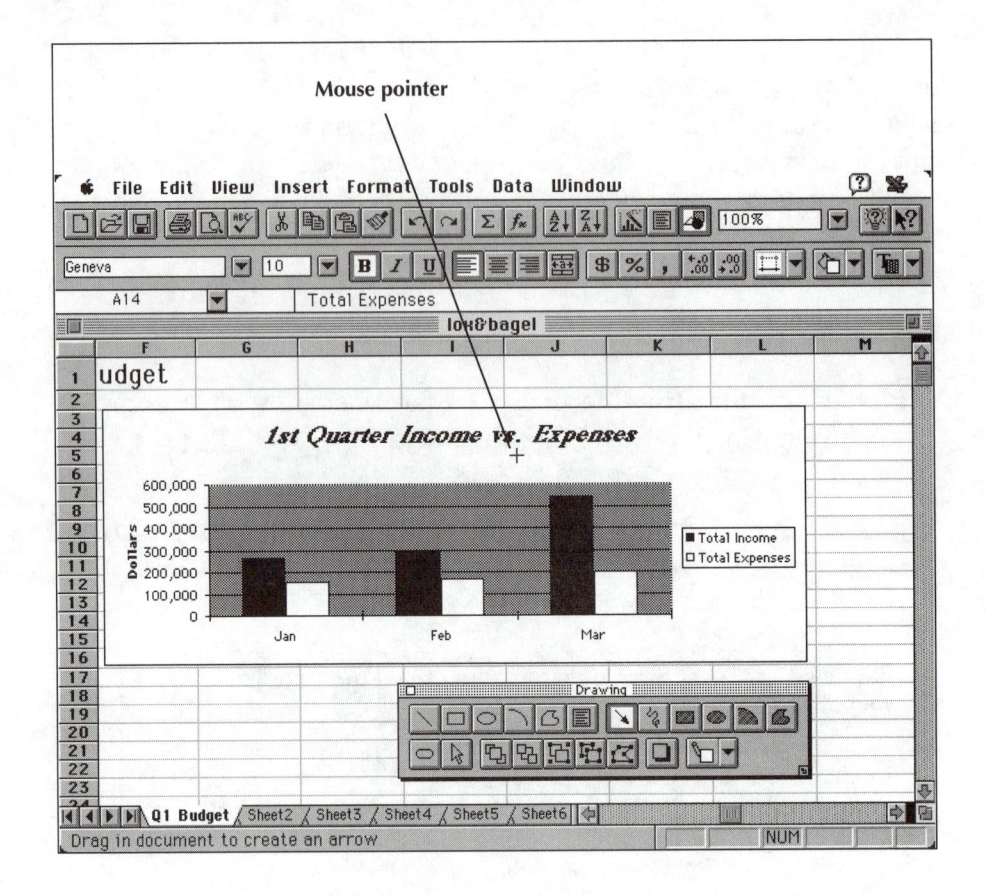

Figure 8.38 *The crosshair mouse pointer ready to draw an arrow.*

Drag the crosshair down and toward the right and release the mouse button to create the arrow, as seen in Figure 8.39.

The handles on the ends of the arrow indicate that it is selected and can be moved or sized. You can also format the arrow, or any other graphic object, by double-clicking on it. Sound familiar? Let's take a look at how we can change the format of the arrow.

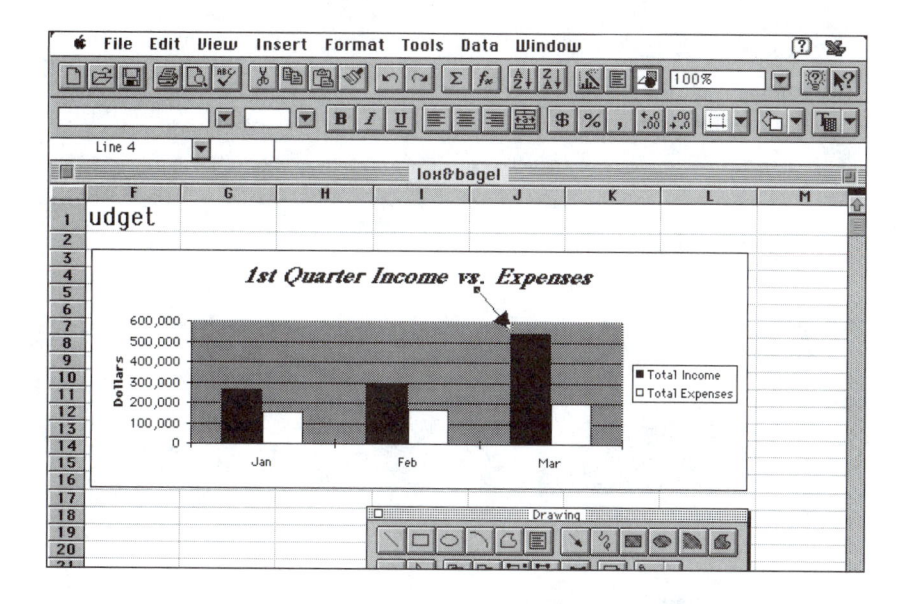

Figure 8.39 *The completed arrow.*

3. Double-click on the **Arrow** to summon the Format Object dialog box, as displayed in Figure 8.40. Click on the **Patterns** tab if it isn't already highlighted.

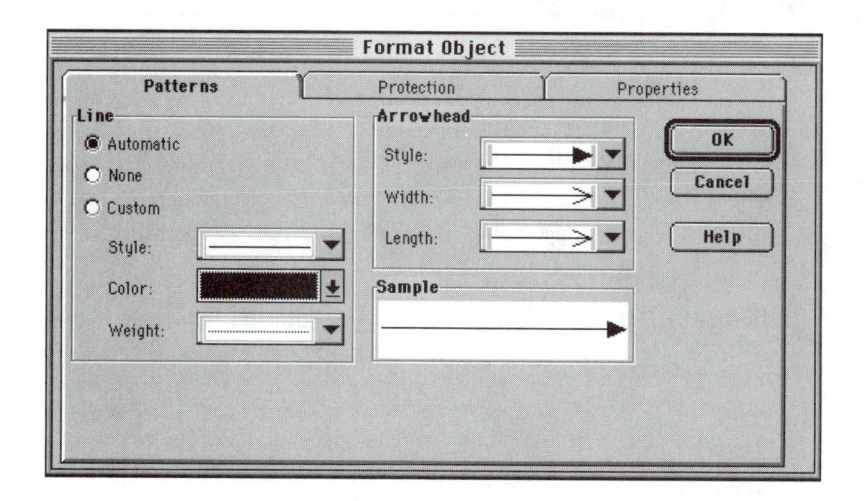

Figure 8.40 *The Patterns portion of the Format Object dialog box.*

The dialog box is specific to the type of object you are formatting. In this case, you can change the type of arrowhead or its line. Let's make the line a bit thicker by changing its weight.

4. Point to the arrow next to the Weight drop-down list and press the mouse button to display the available options, as pictured in Figure 8.41.

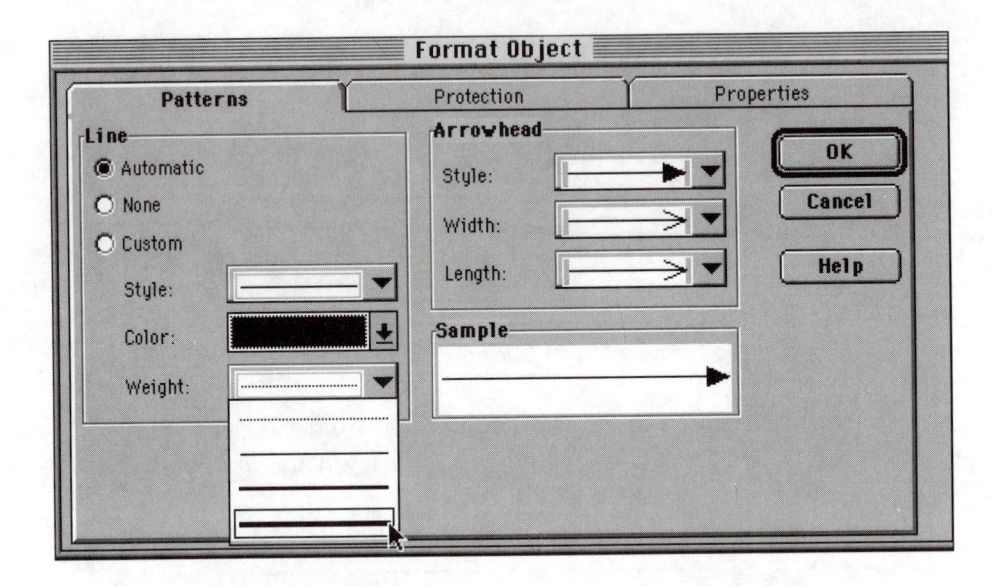

Figure 8.41 *The available line weight choices.*

5. Click on the thickest line at the bottom. (The mouse pointer is pointing to it.)

   The Sample area of the dialog box displays a sample arrow with the selected line weight.

6. Click on the **OK** button to accept the changes.

   Let's draw an ellipse around Mar to further highlight it.

7. Click on the **Ellipse** button on the Drawing toolbar, drag the crosshair around Mar and release the mouse button to create an ellipse similar to the one in Figure 8.42.

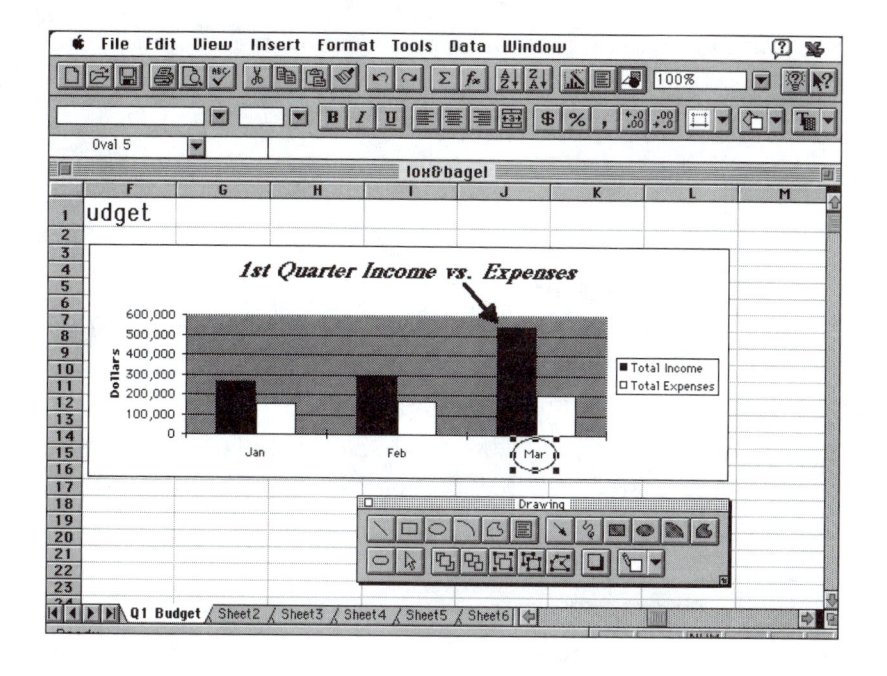

Figure 8.42 *The selected ellipse around Mar.*

NOTE

If you want to draw a perfectly round circle instead of an ellipse, hold down the **Shift** key while using the ellipse tool. The same trick works with the Rectangle tool to create perfect squares.

8. Click on the **Drawing** button on the Standard toolbar (or click on the Drawing toolbar's close box) to remove the Drawing toolbar from the screen.

9. Save your work by clicking on the **Save** button on the Standard toolbar.

Creating Charts in Chart Sheets

The steps for creating a chart in a chart sheet are essentially the same as for creating an embedded chart. The first difference is that you need to start from the Insert menu and not the ChartWizard button on the toolbar.

You can perform the same manipulations on a chart in a chart sheet as in an embedded chart. The only difference is that you can't see the data the chart is based on while the chart is on screen.

Let's create a chart comparing the company's Net Income/Loss for the quarter.

1. Scroll left so column A is visible.

2. Select the ranges **A3** through **D3** and **A16** through **D16**. Don't forget to hold down the ⌘ key while pressing the mouse button to select non-contiguous ranges.

3. Pull down the Insert menu and select **Chart, As New Sheet** to begin the chart sheet creation process.

    The first ChartWizard dialog box appears, just as it did when creating an embedded chart.

4. Click on the **Next** button to accept the selected ranges and move to the second ChartWizard dialog box.

    Since this chart will only have one data series and we are comparing how much each month contributes to the quarter, a pie chart would work well here.

5. Click on the **Pie** which is the last one on the top row of choices in the dialog box, and then click on the **Next** button to proceed.

6. In the third and fourth ChartWizard dialog boxes, click on the **Next** buttons to accept the default options.

7. In the fifth ChartWizard dialog box, click the **No** radio button under Add a Legend, unless that option is already chosen.

    We don't need a legend here because the pie format the ChartWizard selected places the month labels next to each wedge of the pie.

8. In the Title text box, type: **Pie in the Sky Projection** and click on the **Finish** button.

The finished pie chart appears in a chart sheet, as shown in Figure 8.43. The chart sheet is inserted in front of the worksheet containing the data it's based on. If you look at the sheet tabs above the status bar you'll see the highlighted Chart1 tab to the left of the Q1 Budget tab. Of course you can rename chart sheets the same way you rename worksheets.

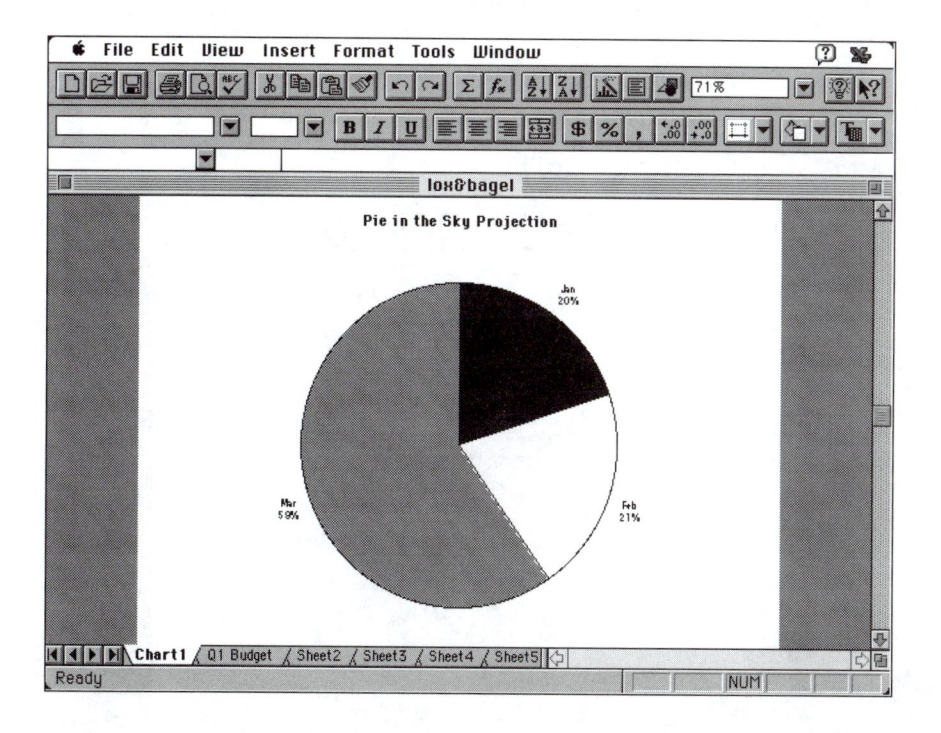

Figure 8.43 *The pie chart in its chart sheet.*

Use exactly the same techniques to format any of the chart elements in a chart sheet that you'd use with an embedded chart. The only step you can omit is double-clicking on the chart to activate it. When a chart sheet is visible, the chart is active and you can manipulate the chart elements.

Printing Charts

You print embedded charts in exactly the same way as the other portions of the worksheet. Just include the embedded chart in the print range and you're all set to go.

Printing a chart on a chart sheet is even easier than printing an embedded chart, since there is no range to select. It is, of course, still a good idea to use **Print Preview** before printing to be sure you'll be printing what you think you'll be printing.

1. Click on the **Print Preview** toolbar button to display a preview of the printed page, as displayed in Figure 8.44.

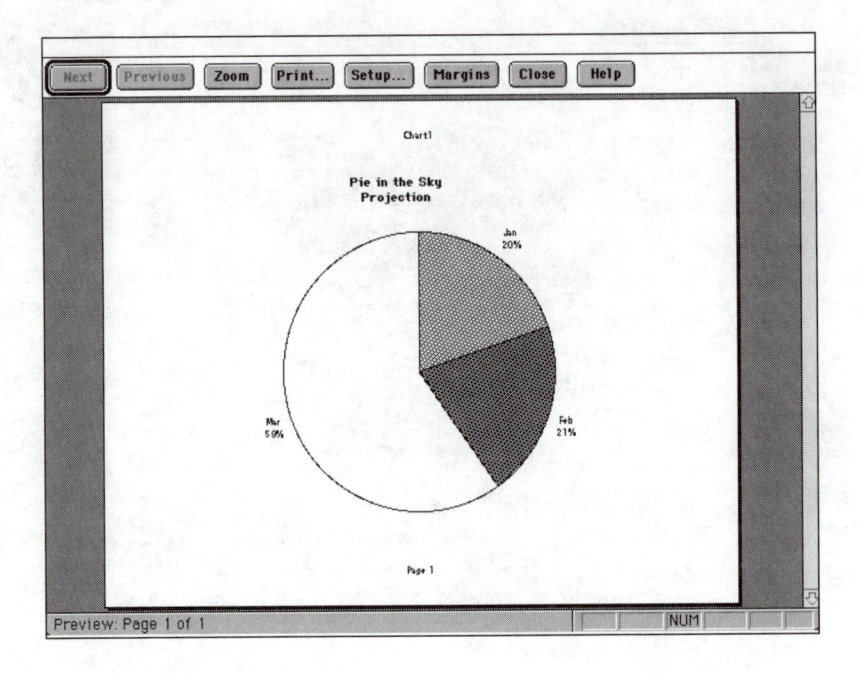

Figure 8.44 *The Print Preview screen for the chart sheet.*

2. When you're ready to print the chart, check to make sure your printer is turned on, is on line and has paper loaded. Then click on the **Print** button.

3. Click on the **Q1 Budget** tab to move back to the worksheet containing your data.

4. Save your work and exit Excel if you're not continuing on to the next chapter now.

When you save your work, you are saving the entire work-book, so you don't need to save the chart sheet separately from the worksheet.

NOTE

A Final Thought

You've learned to turn numbers into dazzling charts that are sure to add punch to your presentations and help you persuade the most skeptical. In the next chapter you'll learn to put Excel's database capabilities to work.

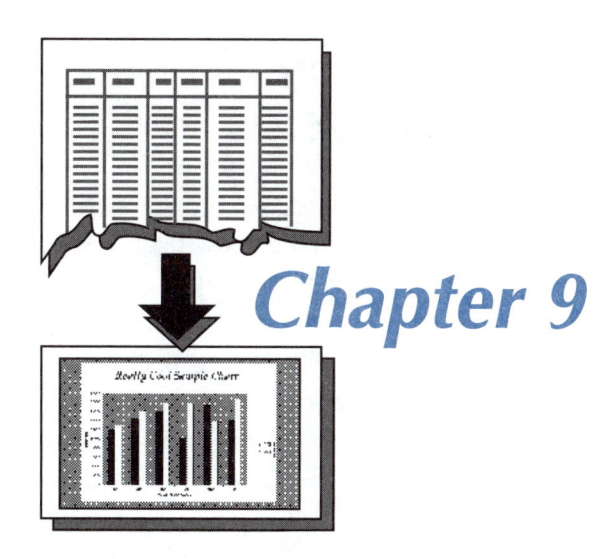

Managing Data

- Database Basics
- Setting Up a Database
- Entering Data
- Searching the Database
- Deleting and Editing Records
- Sorting the Database
- Filtering the Database
- A Final Thought

Database Basics

In addition to the worksheet and charting capabilities we've worked with in the beginning chapters of this book, Excel provides a powerful facility for creating and manipulating databases.

So what is a database? A database is a collection of information (data) organized to make it easy to find and use the data you are looking for. An example of a database you use every day is the phone book. The white pages of the phone book contain several categories of data; Last Name, First Name, Address and Phone Number.

In database terms, each of these categories is called a *field*. All the field entries for one person makes up a *record*. So, on one page of the phone book, there are four fields and perhaps several hundred records. The phone book makes it easy to find the data you want by sorting the records into alphabetical order. With Excel databases, you can sort and search the data in a wide variety of ways. You can even perform calculations on the data, just as you can with any worksheet data.

Setting Up a Database

To create an Excel database, you first enter *field names* in the first row you want to use for your list. Each row below the field name or *header row* is a record. There can't be any blank rows between records, and all the cells in a field should be formatted the same way to facilitate sorting and other database manipulation.

There are a few rules to follow when choosing a field name. Every field name must be unique. For example, if you were creating a name and address list in which you needed two fields for the address to accommodate suite and apartment numbers, they couldn't both be called ADDRESS. You could solve this situation by calling the first field ADDRESS1 and the second field ADDRESS2.

It's best to keep field names as short as possible, yet descriptive enough so that you know what should be entered in the field. If you need to use a field name that is much longer than the column width, consider formatting the text to wrap so it will occupy multiple lines instead of requiring an inordinately wide column. To wrap text, select **Format Cells** from the cell's shortcut menu, and click in the **Wrap Text** check box in the Alignment portion of the Format Cells dialog box..

The field names don't need to be capitalized or formatted in any special way, but using all uppercase letters (assuming the data you enter is in lower or mixed case) tells Excel that the first row is the header, or field name row.

Let's start creating a partial inventory list database for the Spokane Locks and Bagel Corp.

1. Start Excel and open the **lox&bagel** workbook if it isn't already on your screen.

2. Click on the **Sheet2** tab at the bottom of the worksheet to move to a clean worksheet in the same workbook.

Keeping related worksheets in the same workbook is one of the reasons Excel uses workbooks in the first place. We could put the inventory list in a new workbook, but then when we want to work with our various data from Spokane Locks and Bagel, we'd have to open two workbooks instead of one.

3. Enter the field names and data for the first record in the appropriate cells, as shown in Table 9.1.

The formula in E2 multiplies the item's cost by the quantity.

Table 9.1 *The field names and the data for the first record of our inventory database.*

	A	B	C	D	E
1	ITEM	TYPE	COST	QTY	TOTAL
2	Small	Padlock	Hardware	4.33	42	=C2*D2

NOTE
One of the fastest ways to enter the data in this range is to select the entire range first (**A1** through **E2**) and press the **Return** key after each cell entry to move to the next cell in the selection.

Next we'll format the cells containing the field names as center-aligned and first record cells to display the numbers properly.

4. Select the range **A1** through **E1** and format the cells as center-aligned. Position the mouse pointer in the selection and hold down the **Ctrl** key while pressing the mouse button to display the shortcut menu. Then select **Format Cells**, click on the **Alignment** tab, and choose the **Center** option button in the Horizontal portion of the dialog box.

5. Format cell C2 with the number format **#,##0.00**. The number formats are found in the Number portion of the Format Cells dialog box.

6. Format cell E2 with the currency format **$#,##0.00_)**: **($#,##0.00)**; Your screen should now look like Figure 9.1.

Next, let's rename the worksheet.

7. Point to the Sheet2 tab and hold down the **Ctrl** key while pressing the mouse button and select **Rename**.

8. Type: **Inventory** in the Name text box of the Rename Sheet dialog box and click **OK**.

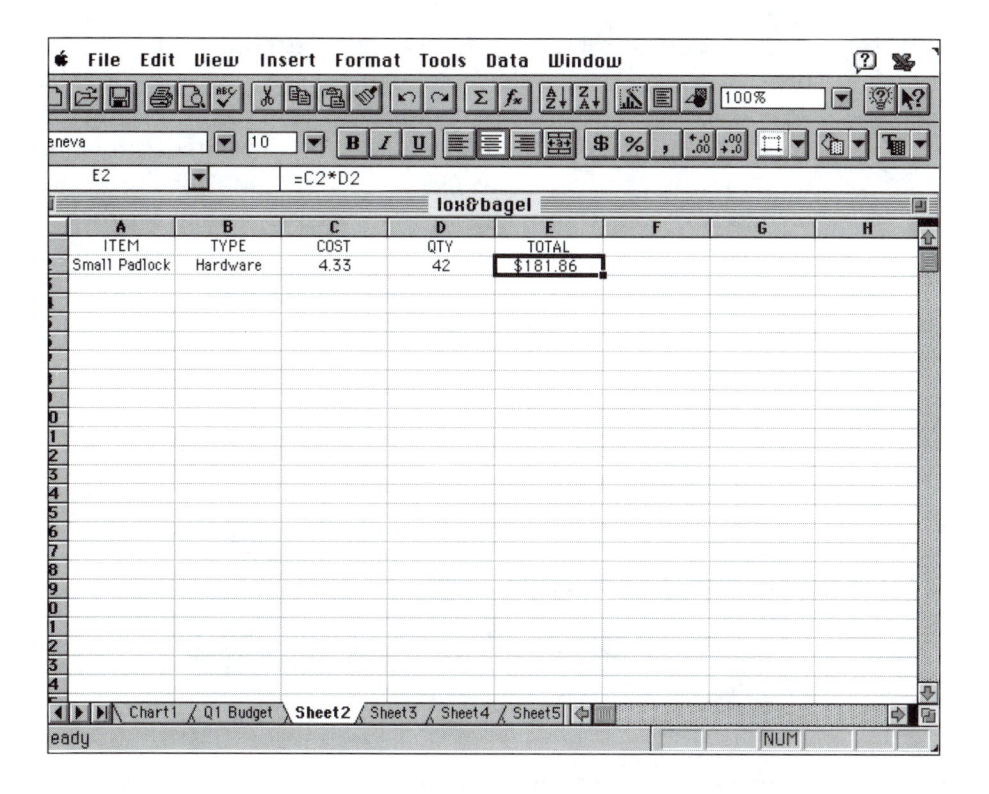

Figure 9.1 *The field names and first record of the database.*

Entering Data

You already entered data in a database when you entered the first record. You can enter data directly into the database in the same way to add as many records as needed. However, Excel provides an even slicker method for entering data in a database–the *data form*.

Once you've started the database, you can use the data form, which includes text boxes for the fields requiring data entry and displays the results of calculated fields.

NOTE There's no right or wrong way to enter data in an Excel database. You may decide that entering data directly into the database and bypassing the data form is the easiest method for you. One advantage of using the data form to enter data is that the cell formatting for the previous record automatically applies to the next record, eliminating the need to format more than one record.

Let's enter the next record using the data form.

1. Be sure one of the cells in the database is active. Pull down the Data menu and select **Form**. The data form dialog box is displayed, as shown in Figure 9.2.

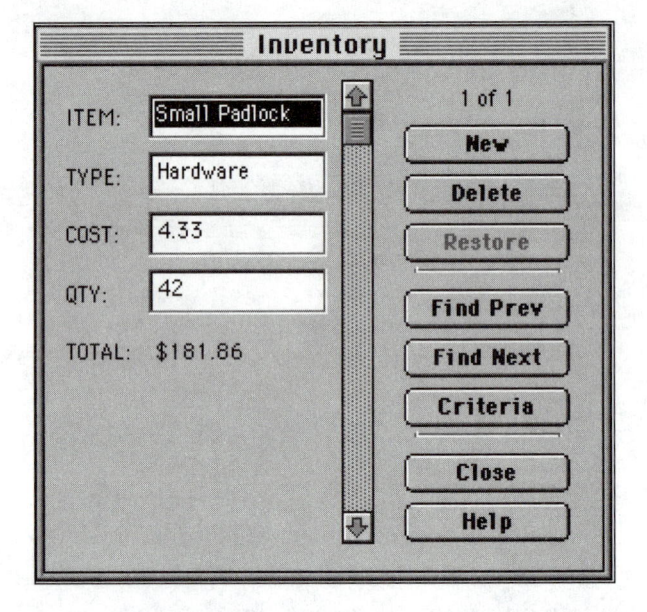

Figure 9.2 *The data form dialog box.*

The title bar in the dialog box displays the name of the sheet where the database is, in this case, Inventory.

The data for the first record is displayed in the text boxes for each field. Notice that the data for the TOTAL field isn't in a text box since, being a calculated field, it can't be edited. The scroll bar to the right of the text boxes is used if you have more fields than can be displayed in the dialog box at one time. In its upper-right corner, the dialog box also displays the number of the record you are currently viewing and the total number of records in the database in the upper-right corner of the dialog box.

Let's add the next record in the data form now.

2. Click on the **New** button to clear the text boxes for the new record entry.

   As you enter new records, the dialog box displays the text *New Record* in the upper-right corner.

3. Type: **Bagel Dogs, Food, 1.27, 375** in the ITEM, TYPE, COST, and QTY text boxes. You can press the **Tab** key to move the insertion point from one text box to the next.

N O T E   If you need to correct a typo in a text box you've already done, you can click in the text box you need to edit, or press **Shift+Tab** until the field you need to edit is highlighted and then type the correct data.

4. Click on the **New** button to add this record to the bottom of the database and clear the text boxes for the next record.

   The new record is added, and you'll notice that the cell formatting was copied from the first record. If the dialog box is obscuring too much of the database, drag it out of the way by its title bar.

   Next, we'll enter the remaining records for the inventory database.

5. Enter the data for the records, as displayed in Table 9.2.

6. Click on the **Close** button to clear the dialog box from the screen.

7. Double click on Column A's column border to accommodate the width of the new entries.

Table 8.2 *The field names and records for the rest of the inventory database.*

ITEM	TYPE	COST	QTY
Plain bagels	Food	.22	456
8 oz. Cream Cheese	Food	1.33	78
BMW keys	Hardware	.87	26
Mercedes keys	Hardware	.47	73
Ferrari keys	Hardware	.56	37
Garlic bagels	Food	.25	133
Jalapeno bagels	Food	.27	277
Chocolate bagels	Food	.32	76
Large padlock	Hardware	5.06	44

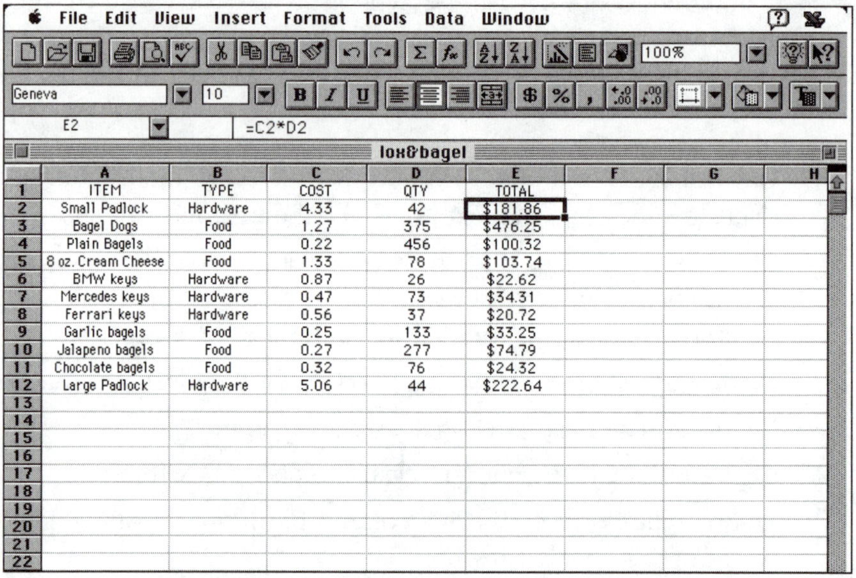

	A	B	C	D	E
1	ITEM	TYPE	COST	QTY	TOTAL
2	Small Padlock	Hardware	4.33	42	$181.86
3	Bagel Dogs	Food	1.27	375	$476.25
4	Plain Bagels	Food	0.22	456	$100.32
5	8 oz. Cream Cheese	Food	1.33	78	$103.74
6	BMW keys	Hardware	0.87	26	$22.62
7	Mercedes keys	Hardware	0.47	73	$34.31
8	Ferrari keys	Hardware	0.56	37	$20.72
9	Garlic bagels	Food	0.25	133	$33.25
10	Jalapeno bagels	Food	0.27	277	$74.79
11	Chocolate bagels	Food	0.32	76	$24.32
12	Large Padlock	Hardware	5.06	44	$222.64

Figure 9.3 *All the records in the database.*

Your screen should now look like Figure 9.3.

8. Click on the **Save** button on the Standard toolbar to save your work before proceeding.

Searching the Database

In the database we've created, there wouldn't be a need to use any fancy searching techniques because there are so few entries, all of which are visible at the same time. However, as the number of records increases to hundreds or thousands, it can be difficult—if not impossible—to find the records you want by visually scanning the list.

Excel provides a couple of ways to find records that meet certain criteria. Later in the chapter you'll learn to use Excel's filtering system to display the records that meet your specifications. But the most straightforward way to find records you're looking for is to use the data form dialog box.

Using the data form dialog box doesn't change the database in any way. As you perform the search, the dialog box displays the records in the database that meet the search criteria, one at a time. Let's use the data form dialog box to search for some records.

1. Be sure one of the cells in the database is still active, pull down the Data menu, and select **Form**.

   The data form dialog box displays *1 of 11* in the upper-right corner, indicating that the data for the first of eleven records is presented.

   The three dialog box buttons used for searching the database are **Find Prev**, **Find Next**, and **Criteria**. If you don't specify any criteria, the Find Prev and Find Next buttons display the data for the previous or next record in the list. Using the Criteria button, you can tell Excel which records to search for; then the Find Prev and Find Next buttons display the previous or next records that meet your criteria.

Let's use the Criteria button to provide Excel with search specifications.

2. Click on the **Criteria** button.

The upper-right corner of the dialog box now displays *Criteria* indicating that you can enter search conditions called *comparison criteria*, in the text boxes. When you perform the search, Excel compares the comparison criteria with the records in the list and displays the first one that matches.

The other difference between this and the normal data form dialog box is that even the calculated TOTAL field has a text box. This is because you can specify search criteria on any field, including calculated fields.

Let's enter criteria to search for the BMW keys.

3. In the ITEM text box, type: **bmw** and then click on the **Find Next** button.

N O T E

The comparison criteria are not case-sensitive, which means that you can type your conditions in upper or lower case–it won't affect the outcome of the search.

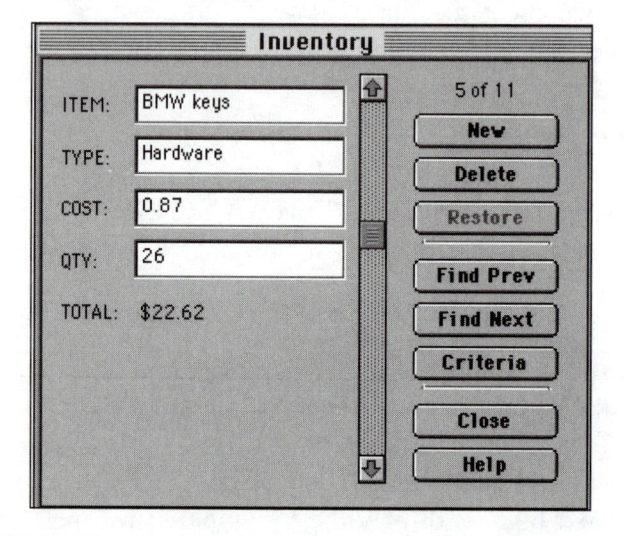

Figure 9.4 *The Data Form dialog box with the BMW keys data.*

The data form now displays the data for the BMW keys record and, in the upper-right corner, displays *5 of 11* indicating that this is the fifth record in the list of eleven records as shown in Figure 9.4. Now let's try finding records that match multiple criteria.

4. Click on the **Criteria** button again so you can enter new criteria.

    The insertion point is at the end of **BMW** in the ITEM text box. We'll delete **BMW** since we won't be using the ITEM field as part of our next search.

5. Press the **Delete** key three times.

    The first comparison criterion we'll use is HARDWARE to locate only records that have HARDWARE entered in the TYPE field.

6. Press the **Tab** key to move the insertion point into the TYPE text box and type: **Hardware**.

    If you enter comparison criteria in more than one text box, the record must meet both conditions. We'll search for records that fall into the Hardware category and also have a total value more than $100.00.

7. Click in the **TOTAL** text box and type: **>100**.

    The > (greater than) symbol is one of Excel's *comparison operators* that can be used to compare values. The other comparison operators are.

    *   = (equal to)
    *   < (less than)
    *   >= (greater than or equal to)
    *   <= (less than or equal to)
    *   <> (not equal to).

    These operators can only be used with numeric values, not text data.

8. Click on the **Find Next** button to display the first record that meets both of the comparison criteria.

    Only two records match both criteria. You can click on **Find Prev** to display the other match.

Deleting and Editing Records

As with any other data in a worksheet, you can delete and edit records directly. If you wanted to delete a record directly, you could select a cell in its row, pull down the Edit menu and select **Delete**, click in the **Entire Row** option button, and then click **OK**. Editing a record's data directly is simply a matter of moving to the cell you want to edit and making the change, just as you would in any cell.

Another way to edit and delete records is with the data form dialog box. An advantage of the dialog box is that you can combine editing and deleting with the search capabilities covered in the previous section. For example, if you wanted to edit all the records that matched certain comparison criteria, you could specify the criteria, click on the **Find Next** button, perform the edits in the text boxes, and click on **Find Next** to display the next record you want to edit.

Let's delete one of the records using the data form dialog box now.

1. Click on **Find Next** or **Find Prev** until the Small Padlock record is displayed in the data form dialog box.

2. Click on the **Delete** button.

    The message box displayed in Figure 9.5 lets you know that what you are about to do can't be undone.

Figure 9.5 *The warning message box.*

N O T E

Excel isn't kidding. When you click on the **Delete** button, the record is removed permanently. There's no way to get it back. Don't let the grayed-out Restore button in the data form dialog box fool you either. That only works for restoring an *edited* record to its original state prior to confirming the edit. So be careful before deleting a record in this way.

There is one safety measure you can take before doing something dangerous like deleting a record—save your work. If you save your work just before deleting the record, you can always close the workbook without saving changes, and then open the saved version to get back to where you were before the deletion.

3. Click **OK** to proceed with the deletion.

   The Small Padlock record is deleted and the other records are moved up to fill in the void left by the deleted record.

4. Click on the **Close** button to clear the data form dialog box.

Sorting the Database

At the beginning of the chapter, I discussed how the phone book makes it easy to find a particular entry. The records are sorted in alphabetical order. When you add records to an Excel database list, you don't need to worry about entering them in the correct order. Excel makes it easy to sort the list in a variety of ways.

N O T E

Your list doesn't even have to be a database for Excel to sort it. Any rectangular area consisting of rows and columns of related data can be sorted in the same manner as database data.

One sorting concept that is important to understand is the *sort key*. The key is the basis for the sort, and you can sort by up to three keys. In the phone book example, the first sort key is the last name. A second sort key, the first name, is used as a tie breaker. If there is more than one entry of a particular last name, those last names are sorted by first names.

Let's perform a simple sort on the inventory database. First we'll sort the list in alphabetical order by the ITEM field. This is so easy you won't believe it.

1. Make any cell in the database in column A (the ITEM field) the active cell.

2. Click on the **Sort Ascending** button on the Standard toolbar.

    Voila! The list is instantly sorted, as displayed in Figure 9.6.

	A	B	C	D	E	F	G	H
1	ITEM	TYPE	COST	QTY	TOTAL			
2	8 oz. Cream Cheese	Food	1.33	78	$103.74			
3	Bagel Dogs	Food	1.27	375	$476.25			
4	BMW keys	Hardware	0.87	26	$22.62			
5	Chocolate bagels	Food	0.32	76	$24.32			
6	Ferrari keys	Hardware	0.56	37	$20.72			
7	Garlic bagels	Food	0.25	133	$33.25			
8	Jalapeno bagels	Food	0.27	277	$74.79			
9	Large Padlock	Hardware	5.06	44	$222.64			
10	Mercedes keys	Hardware	0.47	73	$34.31			
11	Plain Bagels	Food	0.22	456	$100.32			

Figure 9.6 *The sorted database.*

The *Ascending* in *Sort Ascending* means from lower to higher. For an alphabetical sort such as this, it means A through Z. For a numerical sort, ascending would be 1 through 100. The toolbar button to the right of the Sort Ascending button is the *Sort Descending* button, which performs a sort from higher to lower.

In an ascending sort, items that start with numbers move to the top of the list.

N O T E It's a good idea to save your work before performing a sort so you can get back to the original sort order later if you need to.

If you perform a sort and want to return the list to its original order, you can choose **Edit, Undo Sort** before taking any other actions in Excel.

A trick you can use if you think you'll need to return to the original sort order more than once is to add a field for record numbers. In one column in the database, type **1**, and then use the fill handle with the **Option** key to increment the numbers in ascending order down the column. With the records numbered, you can get back to the original order any time you want by performing a sort by the column containing the record numbers.

Let's sort the list in descending order by the COST field.

3. Move to any cell in the database range in column C and click on the **Sort Descending** toolbar button.

   Finally, we'll sort the database by two sort keys. Sorting by two fields isn't quite as easy as clicking on a toolbar button, but it's still pretty darned easy.

   We'll use the TYPE field as the first sort key, which groups the food and hardware items separately. Because there are several records for each of the two types of items, we'll have Excel use the ITEM field as the second sort key.

4. Be sure that any cell in the database is the active cell. Pull down the Data menu and select **Sort** to display the Sort dialog box, as shown in Figure 9.7.

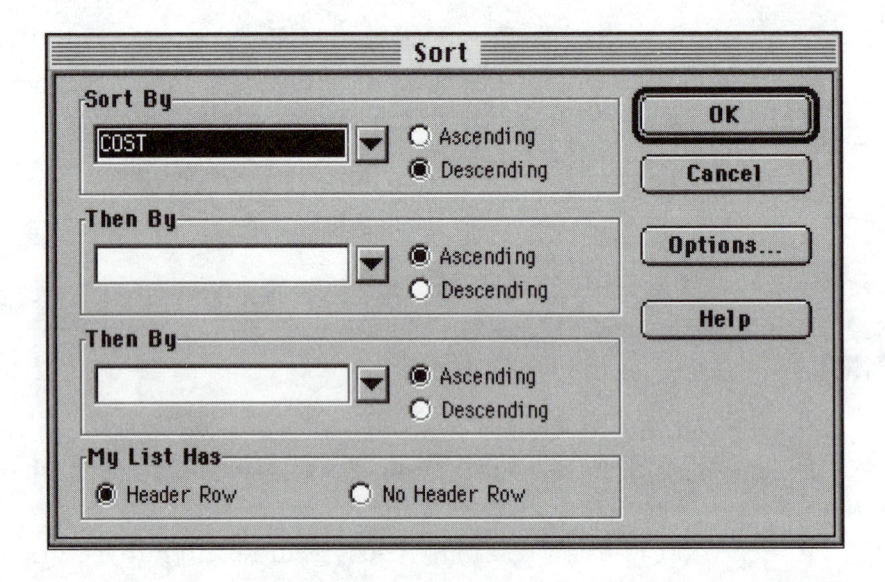

Figure 9.7 The Sort dialog box.

Notice that the entire list is selected, excluding the column headings.

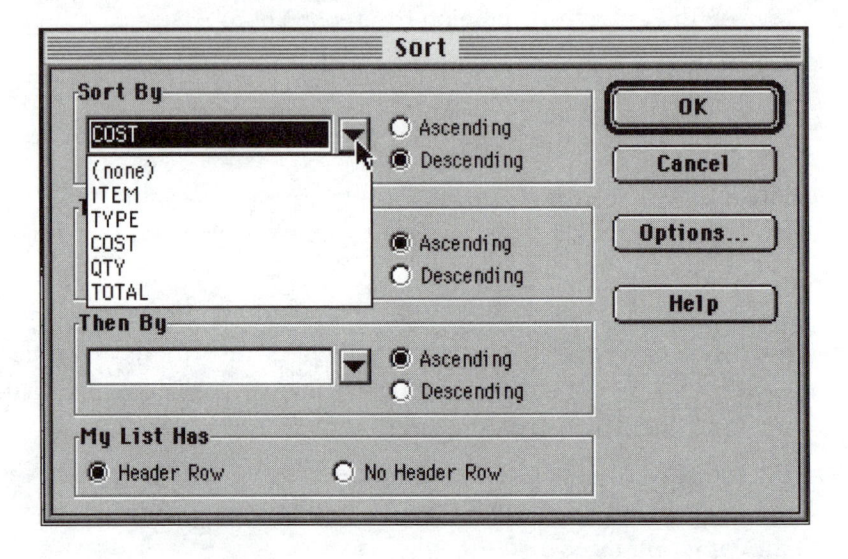

Figure 9.8 The Sort dialog box displaying the drop-down list of field names.

5. Click on the **Arrow** next to the Sort By drop-down list and press and hold down the mouse button to display all the field names in the database, as shown in Figure 9.8.

6. Drag down to highlight **TYPE** in the drop-down list and release the mouse button.

   Each field we choose to sort by can be sorted in ascending or descending order. We'll choose ascending for both of our sort keys.

7. Click on the **Ascending** radio button in the Sort by portion of the dialog box.

8. Click on the **Arrow** next to the Then By drop-down list, highlight **ITEM**, and release the mouse button.

9. Click on the **Ascending** radio button in the Then By portion of the dialog box.

   Since there are no duplicate item names, there is no need for a third sort key. We'll leave the bottom Then By list blank.

10. Click **OK** to perform the sort.

The list is sorted with all the food items at the top, and the item names alphabetized within the food group. Next, the hardware item names are alphabetized within the hardware group, as portrayed in Figure 9.9.

N O T E   Excel can only use three sort keys, which could be a serious limitation for some complex lists. However, as with most limitations in Excel, there is a way around it. If your sort requires more than three sort keys, simply sort multiple times. Specify the first three keys for the first sort, and then choose up to three more and perform a second sort.

	A	B	C	D	E	F	G	H
1	ITEM	TYPE	COST	QTY	TOTAL			
2	8 oz. Cream Cheese	Food	1.33	78	$103.74			
3	Bagel Dogs	Food	1.27	375	$476.25			
4	Chocolate bagels	Food	0.32	76	$24.32			
5	Garlic bagels	Food	0.25	133	$33.25			
6	Jalapeno bagels	Food	0.27	277	$74.79			
7	Plain Bagels	Food	0.22	456	$100.32			
8	BMW keys	Hardware	0.87	26	$22.62			
9	Ferrari keys	Hardware	0.56	37	$20.72			
10	Large Padlock	Hardware	5.06	44	$222.64			
11	Mercedes keys	Hardware	0.47	73	$34.31			

Figure 9.9 *The list sorted by two sort keys.*

Filtering the Database

The major limitation to using the data form to find records that meet certain criteria is that you can only display one record at a time. There will be many times when you'll want to be able to view and manipulate a subset of the list. Excel's filter capability permits you to do just that.

By filtering the database, Excel automatically hides all the records that don't meet your specifications, leaving only the records you want to see displayed on your screen. Just as with sorting, you can have multiple criteria for filtering the database.

Let's use Excel's AutoFilter feature to display only the food records.

1. With any of the cells in the database as the active cell, pull down the Data menu and select **Filter**, **AutoFilter**.

   Drop-down arrows appear next to each field name at the top of each column, as shown in Figure 9.10.

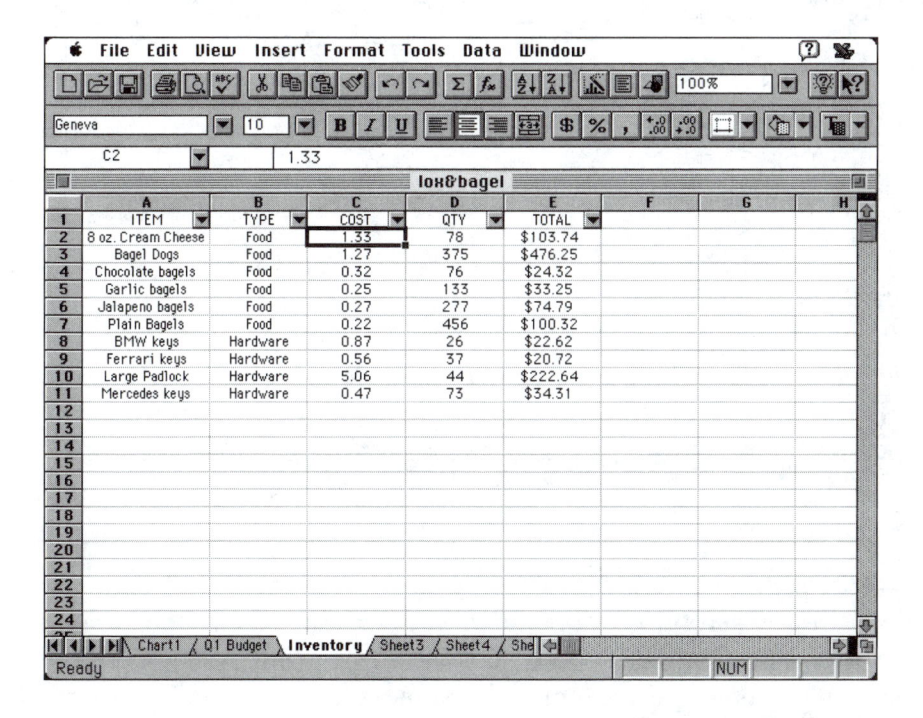

Figure 9.10 *The list with the AutoFilter drop-down arrows displayed.*

2. Click on the drop-down **Arrow** next to the TYPE field.

   The drop-down list provided by the AutoFilter arrows display all the unique entries for that field, as shown in Figure 9.11.

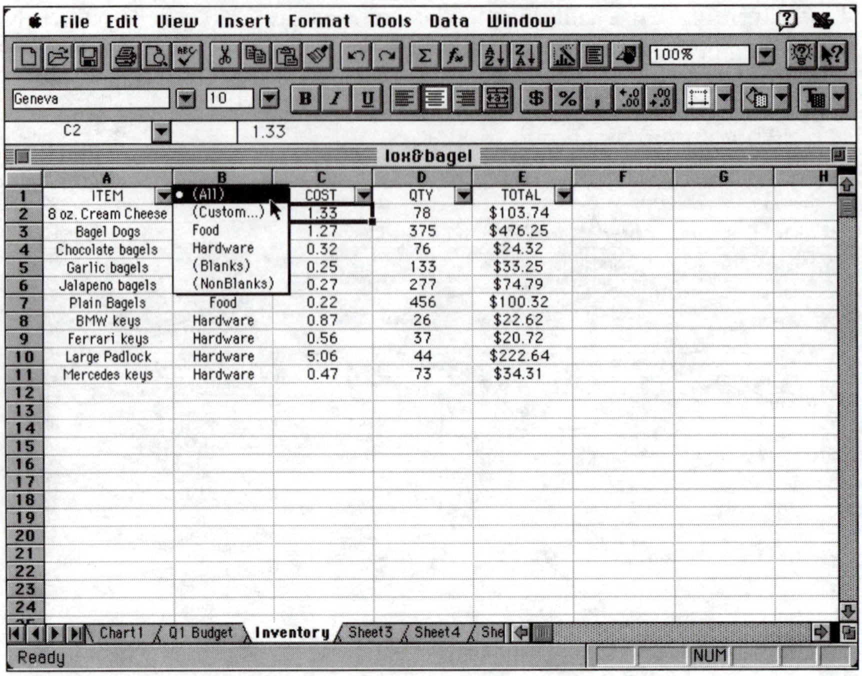

Figure 9.11 *An AutoFilter drop-down list.*

You would select **All** in the drop-down list to cancel a filter selection for that field. Choosing **Custom** lets you specify more complex filter specifications, including the use of the comparison operators used in the data form dialog box. The **Blanks** choice tells Excel you want to display all records that have no entry in that field. **NonBlanks** excludes records with no entry in that field.

3. Drag down to **Food** in the drop-down list and release the mouse button.

Instantly, all the records that don't meet the food criterion are hidden, as shown in Figure 9.12.

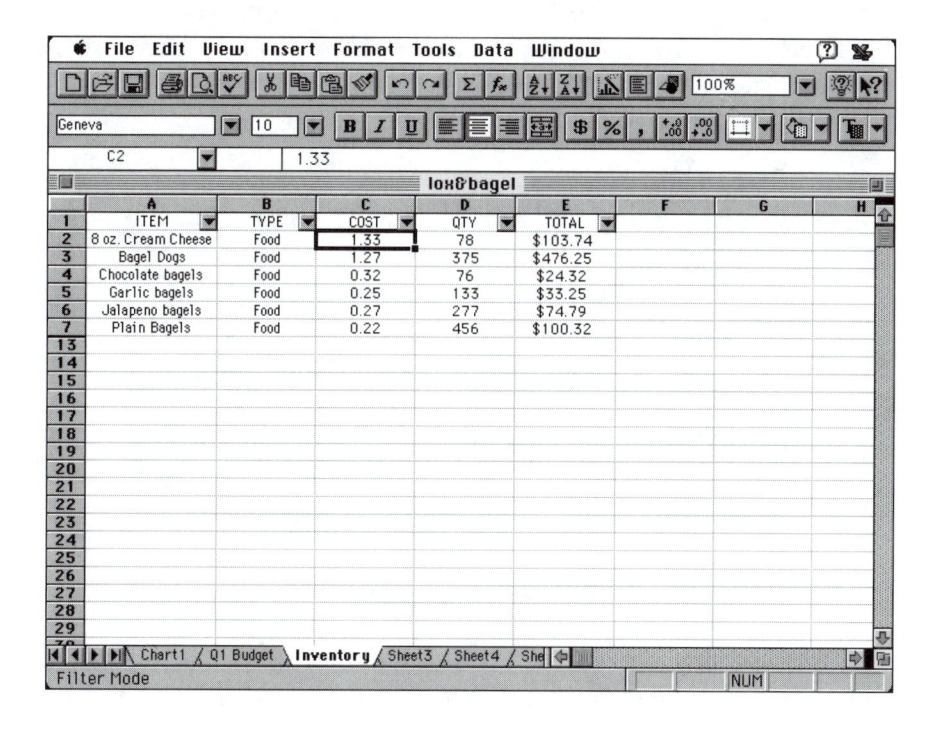

Figure 9.12 *The list with just the food items.*

If you display the list again and choose **All**, the hidden records will reappear.

If you have a very long list of field entries from which to choose, you can move to the desired field quickly by typing the first few letters of that field's name.

Let's filter the list again by specifying a filter criterion for another field. This time we'll only allow Excel to display records from the filtered list that have quantities of greater than 100 and less than 400.

4. Click on the drop-down **Arrow** next to the QTY column heading.

    We'll need to create a custom filter for this field to specify the range of acceptable values.

5. Drag down to highlight **Custom**. This displays the Custom AutoFilter dialog box, as shown in Figure 9.13.

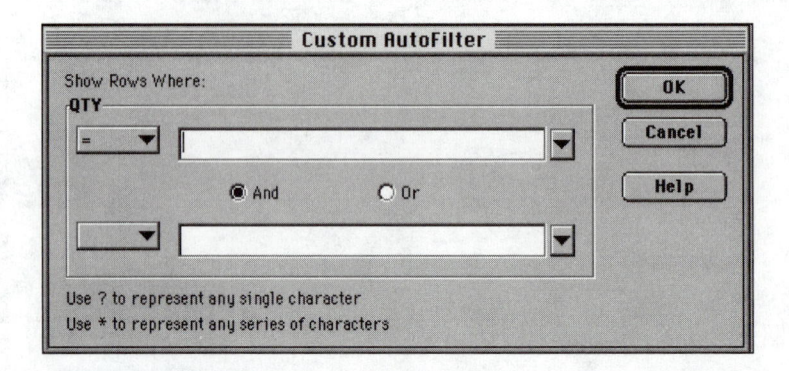

Figure 9.13 *The Custom AutoFilter dialog box.*

The comparison operators must be chosen from their own drop-down list in the dialog box, instead of being typed in the text box as we did in the data form dialog box.

6. Click on the drop-down **Arrow** next to the box with = in it (just below QTY) in the dialog box to display the list of comparison operators, as shown in Figure 9.14.

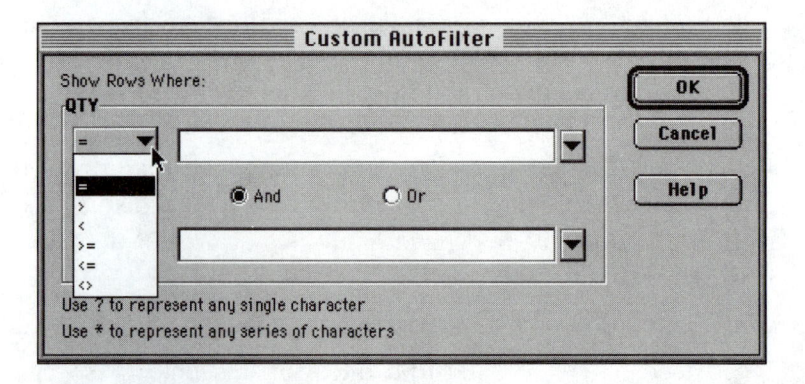

Figure 9.14 *The drop-down list of comparison operators.*

7. Drag down to highlight the > (greater than symbol) in the drop down list and release the mouse button.

8. Click in the text box to the right of the comparison operator list and type: **100**.

9. Leave the And option button selected. Then choose the < (less than symbol) from the bottom drop-down list of comparison operators and type: **400** in the bottom text box.

10. When the Custom AutoFilter dialog box looks like the one in Figure 9.15, click **OK**.

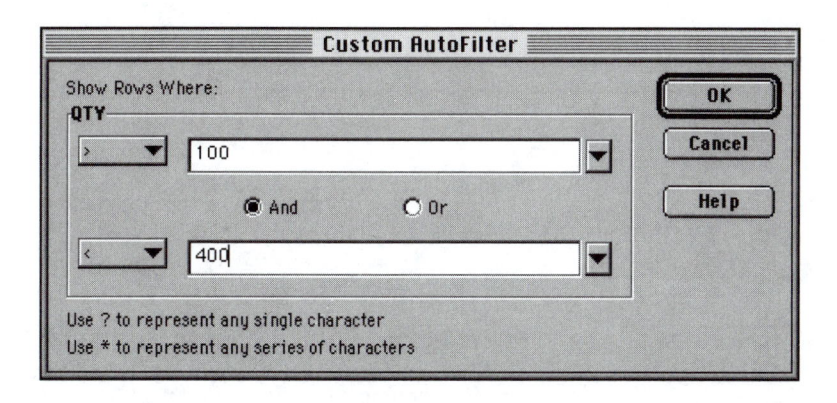

Figure 9.15 *The Custom AutoFilter with the filter specifications entered.*

Your screen should now look like Figure 9.16, with just three records matching the two filter criteria. Oops, 9.16 has 4 records matching. You need to delete Row 4 (Plain bagels).

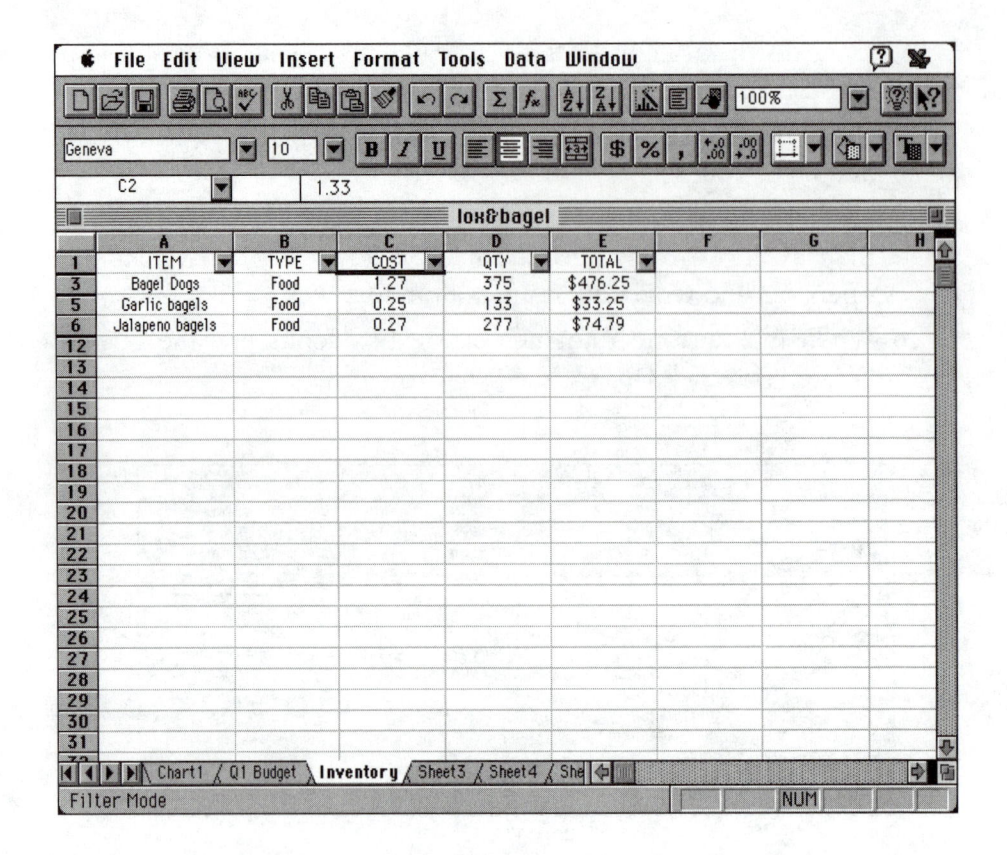

Figure 9.16 *The list after entering the two filter criteria.*

We're finished with the filtered list, so let's turn off **AutoFilter** and redisplay all the records.

11. Pull down the Data menu and select **Filter**, **AutoFilter** to remove the check mark in front of the AutoFilter and reveal the hidden records.

12. Save your work and exit Excel if you aren't moving on to the next chapter now.

A Final Thought

As you work with Excel, you'll find yourself using the database creation and manipulation techniques you've learned in this chapter more frequently than you can imagine. You'll also discover that many of these database concepts also apply to the full-featured database programs used for larger database applications.

In the next chapter you'll learn to use some of Excel's worksheet, data proofing, and analysis tools.

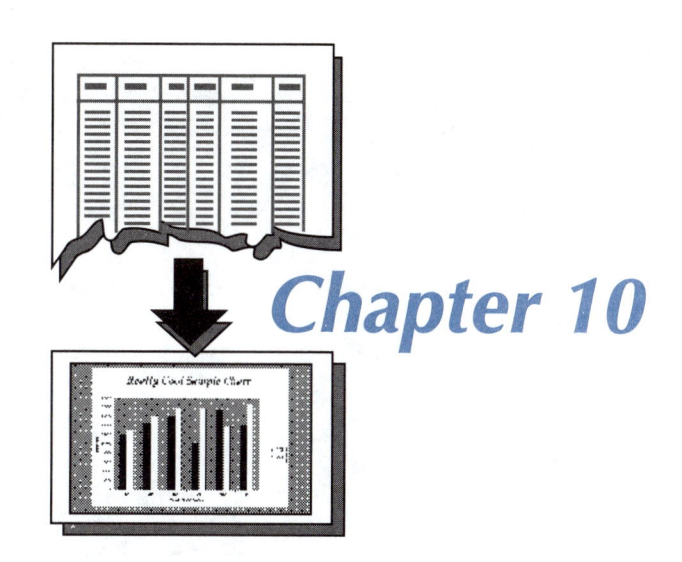

Proofing and Analyzing Worksheet Data

- Using the Spell Checker
- Working with PivotTable Wizard
- Using Scenario Manager
- Using Goal Seek
- A Final Thought

Before finishing the final version of any sort of document, whether from a spreadsheet program, a word processor, or a database, you want to be sure it is as error-free as possible and presents the data you want to present.

Excel provides several tools for making sure your worksheet is accurate, and for looking at the data in various ways to find the best one for your purpose.

Using the Spell Checker

The most obvious place to start ensuring accuracy is with Excel's spell checker. Spelling errors can contribute to a perception that your entire worksheet, and even the logic you used to prepare it, is sloppy. If you want to convince your readers that the data in your worksheet is accurate and that your conclusions are correct, you need to be absolutely sure any spelling errors are corrected.

Many cells in a worksheet contain only values or formulas and you may be wondering how the spell checker deals with these cells. That's easy. Excel ignores the contents of these cells.

So far, we've been entering only correctly-spelled data into our worksheets, so we shouldn't have to worry about checking the spelling. Of course, it's still a good idea to check the spelling just in case there are some typos. Just to be sure we have something to correct, let's edit one of the cell entries so that it is misspelled.

1. Start Excel and open the **lox&bagel** workbook if it isn't already on your screen, and make sure Inventory (the database sheet) is active. If it isn't, click on the **Inventory** tab.

2. Change the contents of cell B2 from Food to **Foood**.

3. Click on the **Spelling** button on the toolbar to start the spell check process.

The Spelling dialog box appears, as shown in Figure 10.1. The cell value of the first misspelled word found is displayed in the lower-left portion of the dialog box (above the two check boxes).

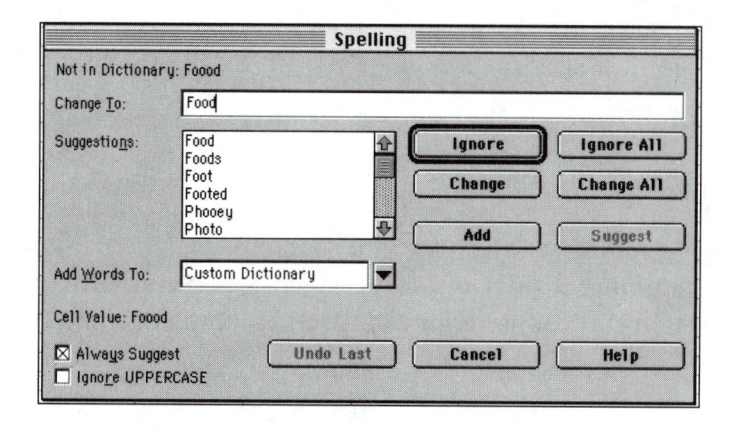

Figure 10.1 *The Spelling dialog box.*

Because the **Always Suggest** check box is checked, the dialog box offers suggestions for correcting the misspelled word. The word in the Change To box is the suggestion Excel thinks is most likely the correct spelling of the word you had in mind. In this case, the Change To box does, in fact, contain the correct spelling. If the spelling of the misspelled word had been too badly mangled, Excel might not have been able to make a correct guess. In that case, you could click on one of the other suggestions in the Suggestion list, or edit the word directly in the Change To box.

NOTE

Having Excel make suggestions every time it stops at a misspelled word can slow down the process, so you might consider clicking in the **Always Suggest** check box to remove the check mark. If Excel stops on a particular word and you want suggestions, you can click on the **Suggest** button.

If you find that eliminating suggestions doesn't improve the speed noticeably, it might be more convenient to have Excel always provide you with suggestions.

You may also want to use the **Ignore UPPERCASE** check box to have the spell checker ignore any word that is in all uppercase letters. This option might be useful if, for example, you had a list of names or other words that wouldn't be in the dictionary, all uppercase.

The Add Words To box displays the name of the custom dictionary where you can add the word if it is correctly spelled, but isn't found in the normal dictionary. The default dictionary for adding words is CUSTOM.DIC, but you can create other dictionaries for use with various types of documents.

If you add a word to the dictionary, the spell checker won't flag that as a misspelled word in other documents. Examples of the kinds of names you might want to add to the dictionary are your name, your company's name, and other special names or terms used in your business.

4. Click on the **Change** button to replace the cell contents with the word in the Change To box.

Excel stops next on *Jalapeno*, which is spelled correctly but isn't in the regular dictionary. We have several appropriate choices. The **Add** button would add the word to the custom dictionary. If you're sure the word is correctly spelled, this might be the best choice. The **Ignore** button would leave the word as it is. **Ignore All** would leave the word as it is and also ignore any other occurrences of the word in this document.

5. Click on the **Ignore** button.

6. Click on the **Ignore** button for any other words Excel stops at.

Excel continues checking the spelling until it reaches the bottom of the worksheet. It then displays the message dialog box shown in Figure 10.2, asking if you want to continue checking from the beginning of the sheet.

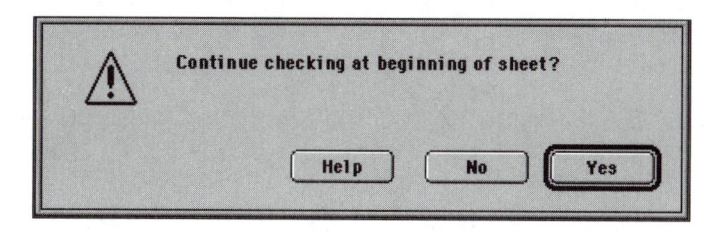

Figure 10.2 *A spelling message dialog box.*

7. Click on the **Yes** button.

When Excel finishes spell checking, it displays the message dialog box shown in Figure 10.3.

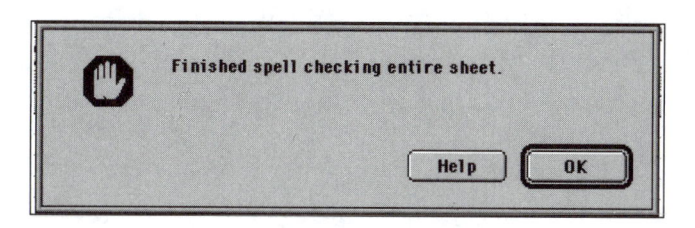

Figure 10.3 *The end of spell check message.*

8. Click on the **OK** button of the message box to end the spell check session.

A common error is to assume that if the spell checker doesn't find any errors, everything is spelled correctly. Wrong! All the spell checker does is to make sure each word in your worksheet matches a word in its regular or custom dictionary.

If there is a word in your document that is a correctly spelled-word, but just not the word you mean, the spell checker won't catch it. For example, if you typed the word *pane* but you meant *pain*, the spell checker won't catch your error.

The moral of this warning is that even when you use the spellchecker, you still need to proofread your document. Better yet, have someone else do it. It's hard to spot your own errors.

Working with PivotTable Wizard

The PivotTable command lets you analyze the data in a list or database. Let's say we want a quick summary of the total of the food items and the total of the hardware items in our list. PivotTable makes this a snap. We'll create this simple PivotTable now.

1. With one of the cells in the list as the active cell, pull down the Data menu and select **PivotTable** to display the first of the PivotTable Wizard dialog boxes, as shown in Figure 10.4.

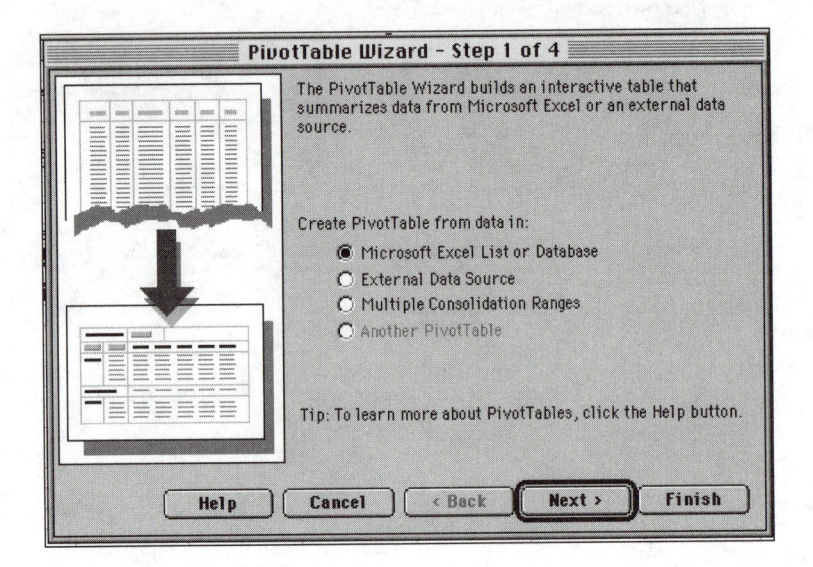

Figure 10.4 *The first PivotTable Wizard dialog box.*

The **Create PivotTable from data in: Microsoft Excel List or Database** is selected, and that's exactly what we want to do, so we'll move on to the next step.

2. Click the **Next** button to display the next dialog box.

The PivotTable Wizard places a dashed line around the data it thinks you want to use for the PivotTable and asks you to confirm (or modify) the range here.

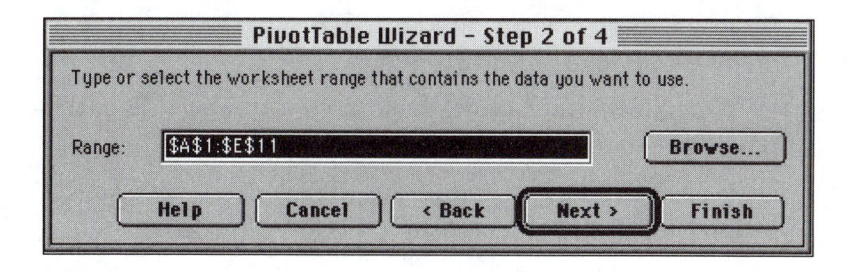

Figure 10.5 *The second PivotTable Wizard dialog box.*

3. Click on the **Next** button to confirm the range and display the third dialog box, as shown in Figure 10.6.

Figure 10.6 *The third PivotTable Wizard dialog box.*

You can place field names in the ROW or COLUMN portion of the dialog box to determine *which* data will be summarized, and place a field name in the DATA portion to determine *how* the data will be summarized. This is accomplished by dragging the field name buttons to the position you want.

We want to summarize the data by type, and have the totals of the types of fields summarized.

4. Drag the **TYPE field name** button (on the right side of the dialog box) into the ROW portion of the dialog box.

5. Drag the **TOTAL field name** button into the DATA portion of the dialog box. (It becomes a **Sum of TOTAL** button).

6. When your dialog box looks like Figure 10.7, click the **Next** button.

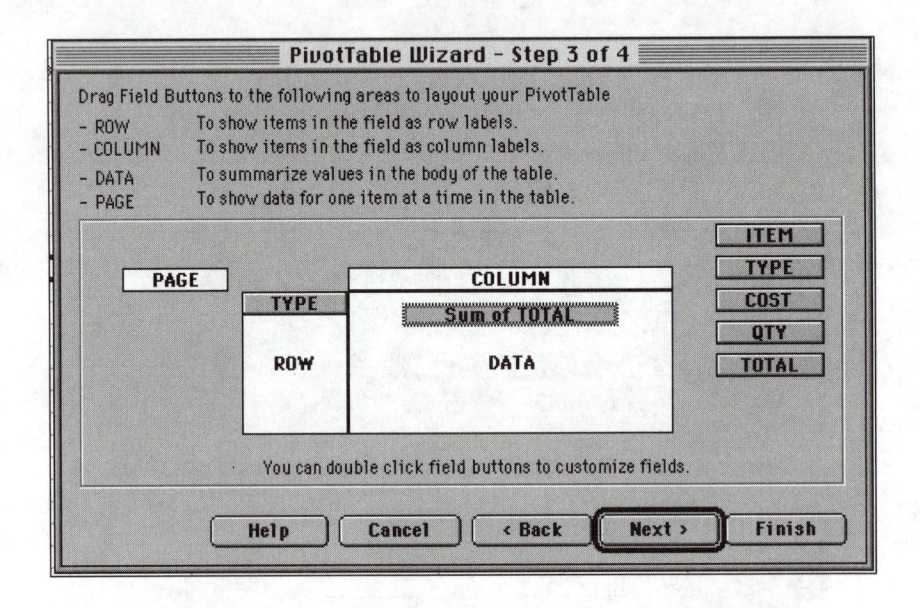

Figure 10.7 *The dialog box with the field buttons in place for the PivotTable Wizard.*

7. In the PivotTable Starting Cell text box, type: **A14** to have the PivotTable placed a couple of rows below our list.

If you don't specify a starting cell in this dialog box, the PivotTable replaces the database, which may not be what you have in mind.

N O T E

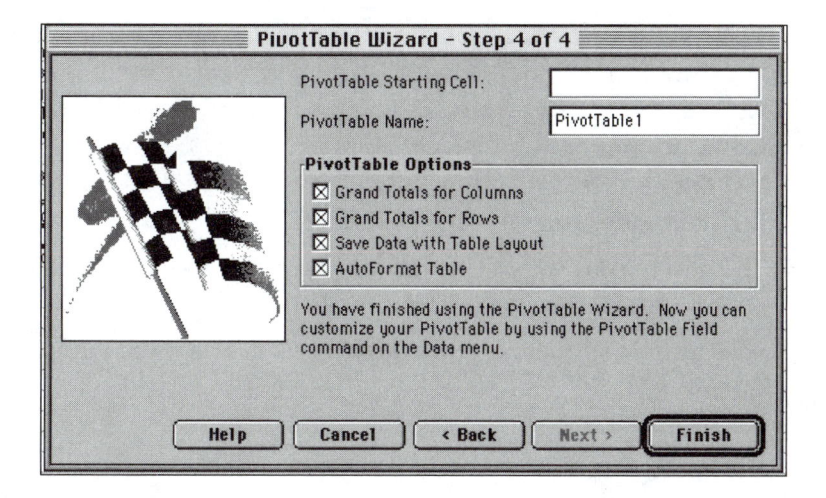

Figure 10.8 *The final PivotTable Wizard dialog box.*

8. Click on the **Finish** button to accept the PivotTable specifications
    and have it placed on the worksheet, as shown in Figure 10.9.

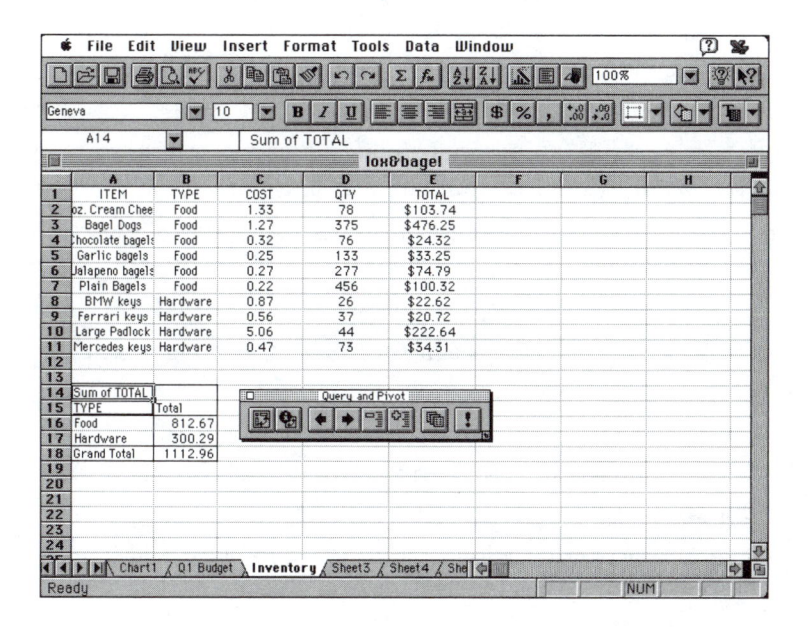

Figure 10.9 *The PivotTable displayed below the list.*

The Query and Pivot toolbar also appears with the PivotTable so you can work with the PivotTable more conveniently. You may want to drag the Query and Pivot toolbar to a new location if it obscures part of the PivotTable or is too far away from the PivotTable. You can remove the Query and Pivot toolbar by clicking in its close box.

The PivotTable we've created displays the food total, the hardware total and the grand total for both.

9. Save your work before proceeding with the next section.

Using Scenario Manager

Playing *what if* is one of the spreadsheet's most useful facilities. You can change values in various cells of the worksheet to see the effect the changes will have. For example, what would happen if January sales increased by $100,000? You could just enter the new value in the Jan sales cell. But then you'd have to re-enter the original value, then the new value, to switch between the scenarios.

Excel's Scenario Manager makes switching between various what-if scenarios a breeze by letting you name the scenarios and then choosing the one you want to see from a list in a dialog box.

Let's create scenarios for our budget worksheet to allow us to switch among several sales possibilities.

1. Click on the **Q1 Budget** tab to make the budget worksheet data visible. Pull down the Tools menu and select **Scenarios** to display the Scenario Manager dialog box, as shown in Figure 10.10.

2. We don't have any scenarios defined yet, so click on the **Add** button to add a scenario.

The Add Scenario dialog box appears, as shown in Figure 10.11.

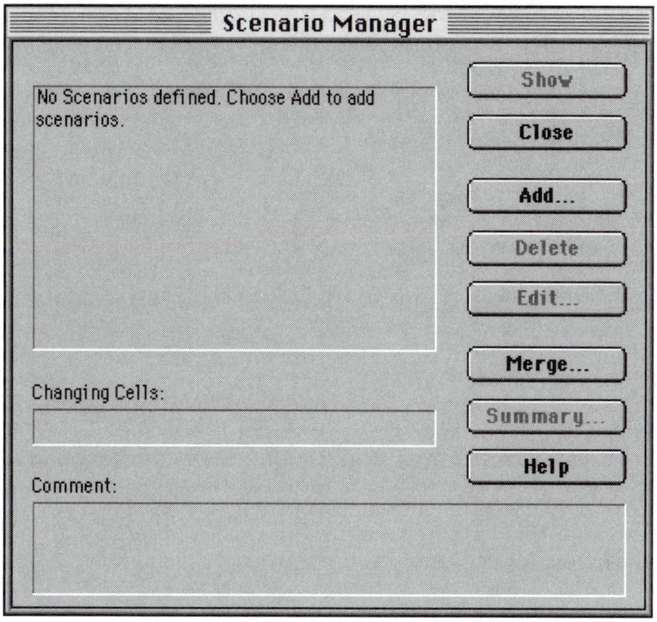

Figure 10.10 *The Scenario Manager dialog box.*

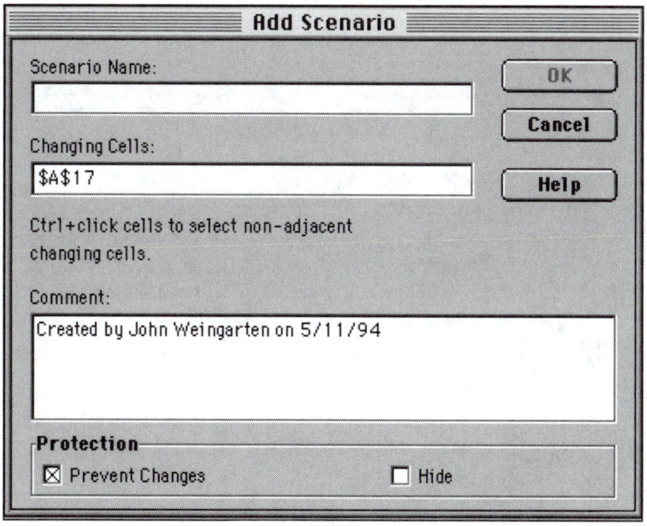

Figure 10.11 *The Add Scenario dialog box.*

3. In the Scenario Name text box, type: **Best Guess**.

4. Drag the I-beam mouse pointer across the entire comment that says *Created by Your Name on MM/DD/YY* and type: **This is what I expect sales to be.**

5. Drag the dialog box by its title bar down far enough so cells B5, C5 and D5 are visible, then drag over the contents in the **Changing Cells** text box to select it.

   This is where we define which cells will have different values for the scenario.

N O T E

The cells you specify as the Changing Cells should not contain formulas, but rather contain values that formulas depend on. For example, B5 is the cell containing the January sales value, but several formulas in the worksheet depend on this value for their results. Therefore, B5 is a good choice for a Changing Cell.

6. Click on cell **B5**, then hold down the ⌘ key while you click on **C5** and then **D5**.

7. When your dialog box looks like Figure 10.12, click **OK**.

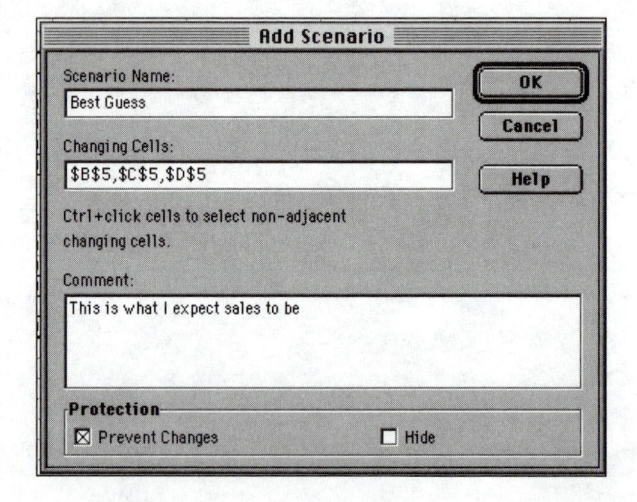

Figure 10.12 The completed Add Scenario dialog box.

The Scenario Values dialog box appears, as shown in Figure 10.13, where you can enter the values for this scenario. For our Best Guess scenario, we'll leave the values as they are.

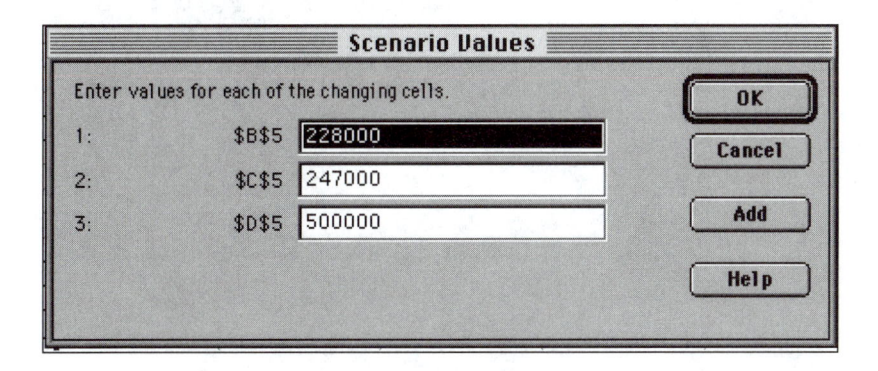

Figure 10.13 *The Scenario Values dialog box.*

8. Click on the **Add** button to display the Add Scenario dialog box and try another scenario.

9. In the Scenario Name text box, type: **Wishful Thinking**. Then edit the Comment box so the comment is **Not a chance**, and click **OK**.

10. Edit the values in the Scenario Values dialog box so the values are **328,000** for B5, **347,000** for C5 and **410,000** for D5, then click the **Add** button again so we can add one more scenario.

11. In the Scenario Name text box, type: **The Sky Is Falling!** Then edit the Comment box so the comment is **We're in big trouble**, and click **OK**.

12. Edit the values in the Scenario Values dialog box so the values are **128,000** for $B#5, **147,000** for C5 and **210,000** for D5, then click **OK** .

The Scenario Manager dialog box appears once again, as shown in Figure 10.14, with the three scenarios listed.

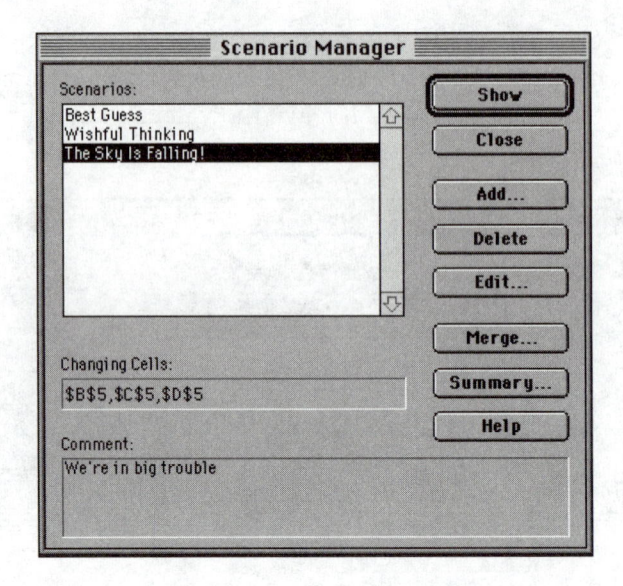

Figure 10.14 The Scenario Manager dialog box with the three scenarios shown.

You can now click on any of the scenario names in the Scenarios list. When you click on the **Show** button, the worksheet changes to the values for that scenario. You can switch among the scenarios while still in the dialog box and view the changes on the worksheet. When you close the dialog box the worksheet displays the values from the last chosen scenario.

As you switch among the three scenarios, notice that the numbers in cells E5, B13 through E13, and B16 through E16 change. You may have to move the Scenario Manager dialog box out of the way to see the changes.

13. When you're finished experimenting with the scenarios, switch to the Best Guess scenario to return to our original numbers. Then click on the **Close** button to clear the Scenario Manager dialog box.

When you save your workbook, your scenarios are also saved. They are available whenever you work with this worksheet in the workbook.

Using Goal Seek

Goal Seek is another weapon in Excel's vast arsenal you can use for determining answers to your questions. What Goal Seek does is almost magical. It can change the value in an argument cell to reach a specified result in the formula cell.

Let's try using Goal Seek to find out how expensive a piece of equipment can be purchased if the maximum monthly payment the company can afford is $500.

1. Scroll down the Q1 Budget worksheet so cells A26 through B29 are visible, and click on cell **B29** (the cell containing the **PMT** function) to make it active.

2. Pull down the Tools menu and select **Goal Seek**.

   The Goal Seek dialog box appears, as shown in Figure 10.15.

Figure 10.15 *The Goal Seek dialog box.*

The *Set Cell* is the cell containing the formula. Because our formula cell was the active cell when we called up the Goal Seek dialog box, it's already entered in the Set Cell text box.

The *To Value* text box is where you specify what you want the result in the formula cell to be.

3. Click in the **To Value** text box and type: **-500**.

   Remember, you need the minus sign because this payment represents an outflow.

The *By Changing Cell* text box lets you specify which cell's value you want to change to produce the desired result. We want to change the loan amount.

4. Click in the **By Changing Cell** text box and type: **B28** (or you can simply click on cell **B28**).

5. Click **OK** to have goal seek perform its magic.

The Goal Seek Status dialog box appears, as shown in Figure 10.16.

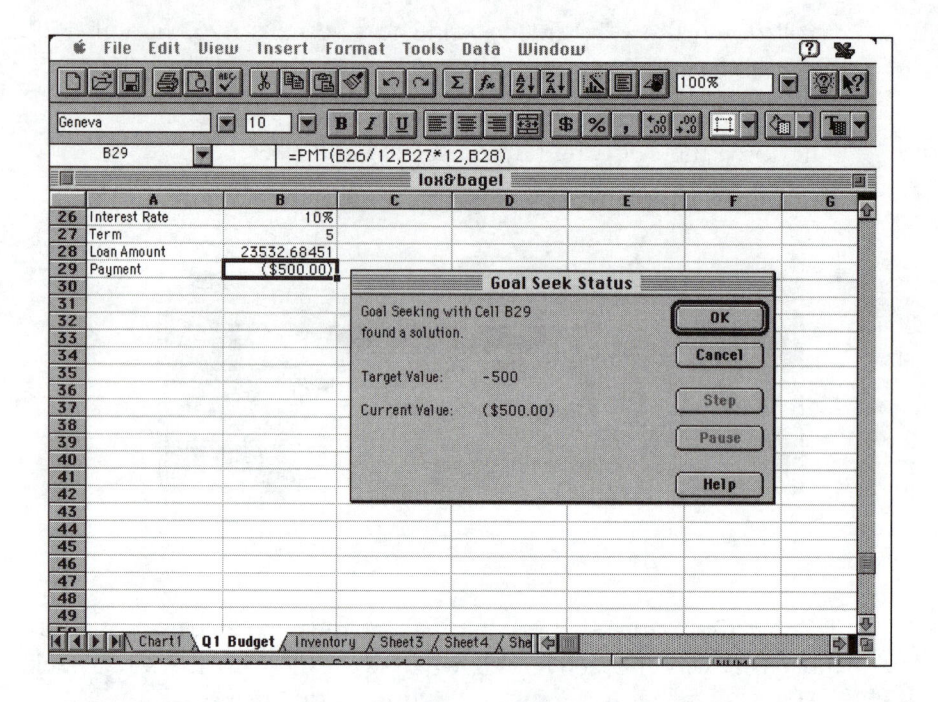

Figure 10.16 *The Goal Seek Status dialog box and the new loan amount required to achieve the goal.*

If you click **OK** the changes remain entered in the cells. Clicking **Cancel** returns the values to what they were before goal seeking. If you click **OK** by mistake and want to return to the original values, immediately click on the **Undo** button.

6. Click **Cancel** to return to the original values.

7. Save your work and exit Excel if you're not continuing on to the next chapter now.

A Final Thought

In this chapter, you've learned to use just a few of Excel's tools for proofing and analyzing your worksheet data. You now know how to ensure that your data is free of spelling errors. You also learned how to view the data in a variety of ways using PivotTable and Scenario Manager.

In the next chapter you'll learn about one of the biggest time savers in Excel—Macros.

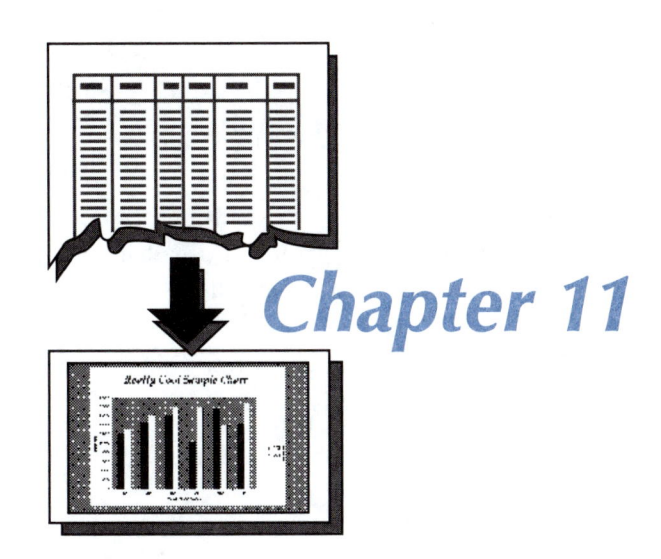

Chapter 11

Automating Your Work with Macros

- Understanding Macros
- Recording a Macro
- Running a Macro
- Assigning Macros to Menus, Shortcut Keys and Buttons
- A Final Thought

225

Understanding Macros

Without a program, your computer is nothing more than a big, expensive paperweight. A *program* is a set of instructions, in a language your computer can understand, that allows it to perform useful (or so one would hope) tasks. Excel is a big computer program that tells your computer what to do. A *macro* is nothing more than a little program (in this case, inside Excel) that tells Excel what to do.

Don't let the word *program* scare you. You can use Excel macros to cut time-consuming, repetitive tasks down to size without knowing the first thing about programming. Excel lets you record any series of Excel actions for later use, just as you would record a series of sounds on a tape recorder for playback.

Suppose you routinely format groups of selected cells in some particular way. Perhaps you center their contents, surround them with a border, and adjust the column width to accommodate the longest entry. To do this manually, you'd have to perform three separate tasks requiring many mouse actions or keystrokes. However, if you record these tasks as a macro, you can perform them all at once with a couple of mouse clicks or keystrokes to run (play) the macro. You'll even learn a few tricks for assigning macros to menus, buttons, and shortcut keys so they are even easier to use.

Another common use for a macro is to automate the typing of frequently-entered text, such as your name and address or company name. Recording frequently-entered text as macros saves time and eliminates typos—assuming you typed it correctly while recording the macro.

This cell formatting example is a very simple example of what you can do with macros. Literally any series of tasks can be consolidated into a single macro. No series of tasks is too simple or too complex to be turned into a macro. Consider the toolbar buttons. You've likely noticed by now that the toolbar buttons are shortcuts for performing tasks with just the click of a mouse.

Some buttons, such as the Open button, don't save you much time. Instead of clicking on the **Open** button, you could simply choose **File**,

Open. It may hardly seem worth the effort to have a button to save one keystroke or mouse click. However, since opening files is something that you repeat many times during a typical Excel session, the amount of time you save by using the button is truly worthwhile.

Let's discuss the issue of programming a bit. As I said, you don't need to know anything about programming to make good use of macros, and that's true. However, if you take the time to learn a little bit about Excel's programming language, you can extend your macros' potential flexibility and complexity enormously.

Even if you don't do any programming and just use Excel's macro recorder, you are actually programming. Huh? Let me explain. When you turn on the macro recorder and perform the tasks you want included in the macro, Excel creates a computer program for you and runs the program when you play the macro.

The programming language Excel uses to create your macro is called **VBA** (Visual Basic for Applications). This language is an extension of the BASIC programming language. In fact, you may already have some familiarity with BASIC. If you already know a little about any version of BASIC, you won't have any trouble adapting to VBA. If you have no clue about the ins and outs of programming, but have some healthy curiosity, you can quickly learn some simple VBA programming from the documentation included with Excel.

Recording a Macro

To start recording, simply pull down the Tools menu and select **Record Macro**, **Record New Macro**. Then enter a macro name and description and perform the tasks you want included. There are a couple of things to take into account before you start recording. The first is planning.

When you record a macro, everything you do (including mistakes) is recorded in the macro and turned into program code. Let's say you start recording a macro while in one worksheet and then realize that you want the macro to take effect on another worksheet, so you switch to the other worksheet and start performing the tasks you want as part of the macro. The problem is, whenever you run the macro, the first thing it will do is switch to a different worksheet, which probably isn't what you want to do at that point. Recording a macro with a lot of mistakes can also slow down the execution of the macro.

If you want the macro to manipulate some selected cells, as in the cell formatting example discussed earlier, you'll want to perform the macro recording tasks on a single active cell in the worksheet, and then select that cell before starting the recording process. This way, when you run the macro, it performs on the current selection.

You'll also want to consider whether the macro uses *relative* or *absolute referencing*. The concept is the same as the absolute versus relative referencing discussed in copying formulas. If your active cell is A1 when you start recording the macro using absolute referencing, then you click on cell D6, the first thing the macro does when played is move to cell D6. If you were using relative referencing—which is the default—the macro would move three columns to the right and five rows down, which is D6's relative position from A1. As a general rule, relative referencing allows your macros to operate correctly in a variety of situations.

Finally, you'll want to decide where the macro will be stored. If you are creating a macro that is only applicable to the active workbook, you can store the macro there. You can also store macros in a new workbook, but then you have to open that workbook whenever you want to use that macro.

If you want to make your macros are portable (usable in a variety of workbooks and situations) the best approach is usually to store them in the *Personal Macro Workbook*. The Personal Macro Workbook is a hidden workbook that is always available for use with any workbook you have open.

Let's start recording the cell formatting macro now.

1. Start Excel and open the **lox&bagel** workbook if it isn't already on your screen. Then click on the **Sheet3** tab so we can record this macro on a fresh worksheet.

   It isn't necessary to record the macro on an unused sheet, but doing so ensures that you won't mess up any existing worksheet data while recording your macro.

2. Click on cell **B2** to make it the active cell. Then pull down the Tools menu and select **Record Macro**, **Record New Macro**.

   The Record New Macro dialog box appears, as shown in Figure 11.1.

   For this macro, any active cell would work. However, using a cell that is at least one row down and one column over will allow us to see all sides of the border the macro adds.

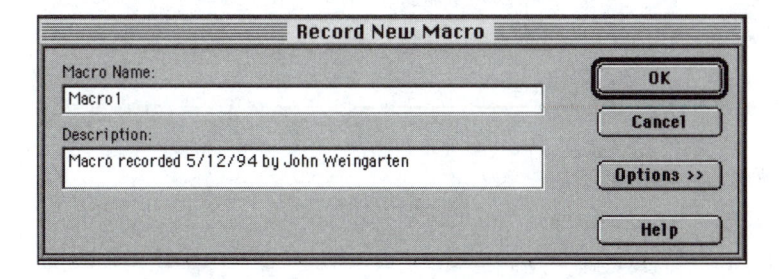

Figure 11.1 *The Record New Macro dialog box.*

You could allow Excel to name the macro for you (in this case Macro1) but that's not very descriptive, so let's give it a new name.

3. Drag the mouse to select the text in the Macro Name text box, type: **CellFmt** and press the **Tab** key to highlight the contents of the Description box.

4. In the Description box, type: **Formats selection center aligned, places border and AutoFits column width.**

   This macro will work on any group of selected cells, so we want to make sure it's available whenever we need it.

5. Click on the **Options** button to expand the dialog box so the Record New Macro options are visible, as shown in Figure 11.2.

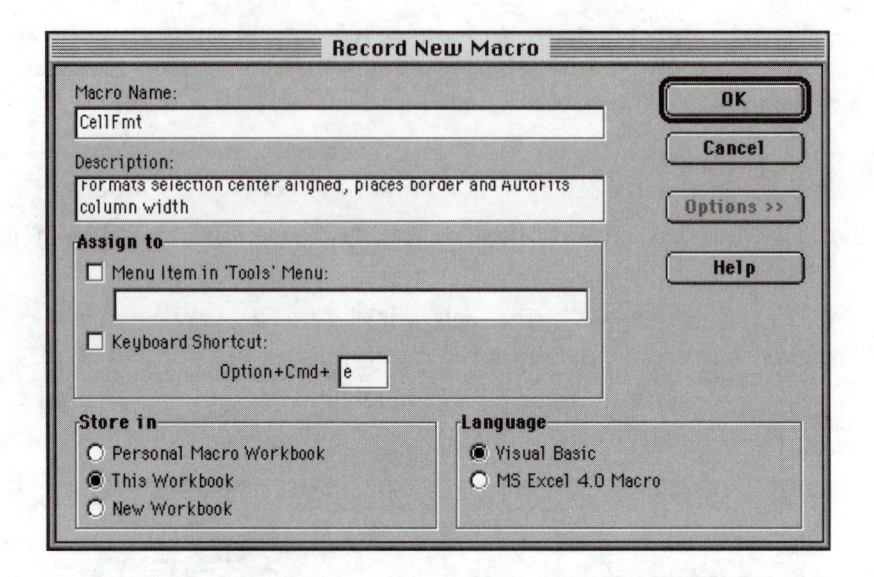

Figure 11.2 *The expanded Record New Macro dialog box.*

We'll cover the Assign To portion of the dialog box later in the chapter. For now, let's make sure we store the macro in the Personal Workbook.

The Language section of the dialog box lets you choose whether you want to record the macro in Visual Basic or the MS Excel 4.0 Macro language. Unless you are sharing macros with users who haven't yet upgraded to version 5, you should always use Visual Basic. Not only is Visual Basic a more powerful language, but it is also the language that will the standard for all future Microsoft applications. You might as well get used to it.

6. Click on the **Personal Macro Workbook** option button and then click **OK** to begin the macro recording session.

You can tell you are recording a macro because the status bar displays the message *Recording*. There is also a little toolbar floating on the screen with a Stop Macro button, as displayed in Figure 11.3.

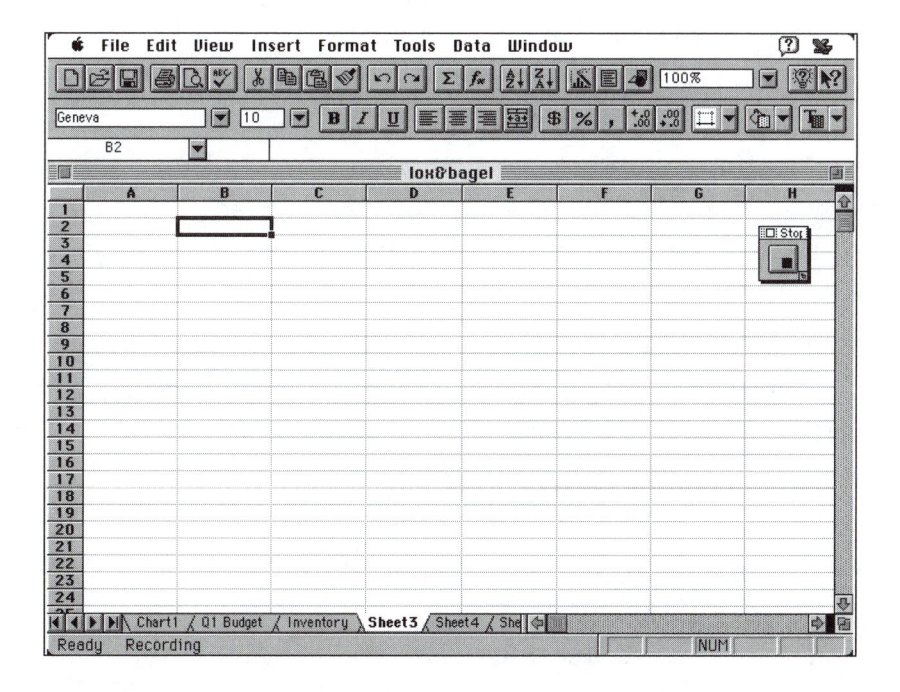

Figure 11.3 *Ready to record with the Stop toolbar and the status bar displaying Recording.*

Before we perform our macro tasks, we need to make sure we are using Relative References so the macro will work on any group of selected cells and not just B2.

7. Pull down the Tools menu and select **Record Macro**, **Use Relative References**, unless there is already a check mark in front of Use Relative References. If there is already a check mark, drag the mouse pointer out of the menu to remove the menu without selecting any commands.

Now, we'll proceed to format the active cell for center alignment, place a single-line border around it, and AutoFit the selection.

8. Display the shortcut menu for the active cell by pointing to it and holding down the **Ctrl** key while pressing the mouse button.

9. Select **Format Cells**, click on the **Alignment** tab, and choose **Center** in the Horizontal area of the dialog box.

10. Click on the **Border** tab, then click on **Outline** in the Border section of the dialog box and click **OK**.

11. Pull down the Format menu and select **Column**, **AutoFit Selection**.

12. Click on the **Stop Recording Macro** button in the floating Stop toolbar, and then click on another cell so you can see the border around the cell.

You can't tell that the type in the cell is centered or the width adjusted to accommodate it, since the cell is empty. You'll see the complete results of the macro when you run it on a real selection.

Running a Macro

Now that we've recorded a macro, let's select some cells in the sheet containing our database and try it out.

1. Click on the **Inventory** tab (the database sheet) to display it. If you already adjusted the width of column A and B to accommodate the largest entries, reduce their widths now so at least some of the text in each is obscured. Finally, if the Query and Pivot toolbar is still on your worksheet, remove it by clicking on the **Close box** in its upper-left corner.

2. Select cells **A2** through **A11** and choose **Tools**, **Macro**. Then click on **'Personal Macro Workbook'!CellFmt** so that it is highlighted, as shown in Figure 11.4.

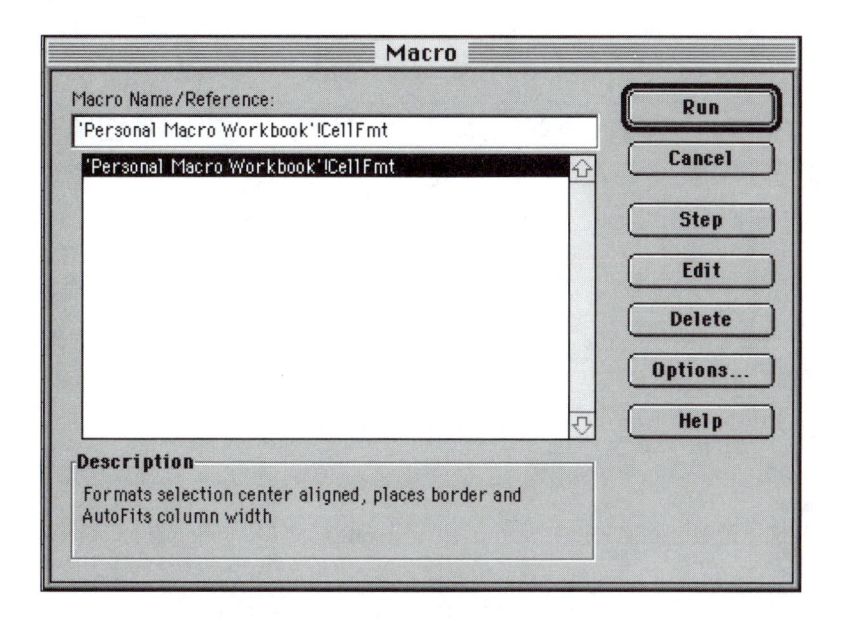

Figure 11.4 *The Macro dialog box.*

 Your Macro dialog box may contain the names of other macros if there are any others stored in the Personal Macro Workbook, or on any other open workbook.

3. Click on the **Run** button to execute the macro.

4. Click on a cell outside the selection so you can see the results of the macro.

The list of items in column A is now center-aligned, with a border around it and the column width adjusted to fit the largest entry, as shown in Figure 11.5.

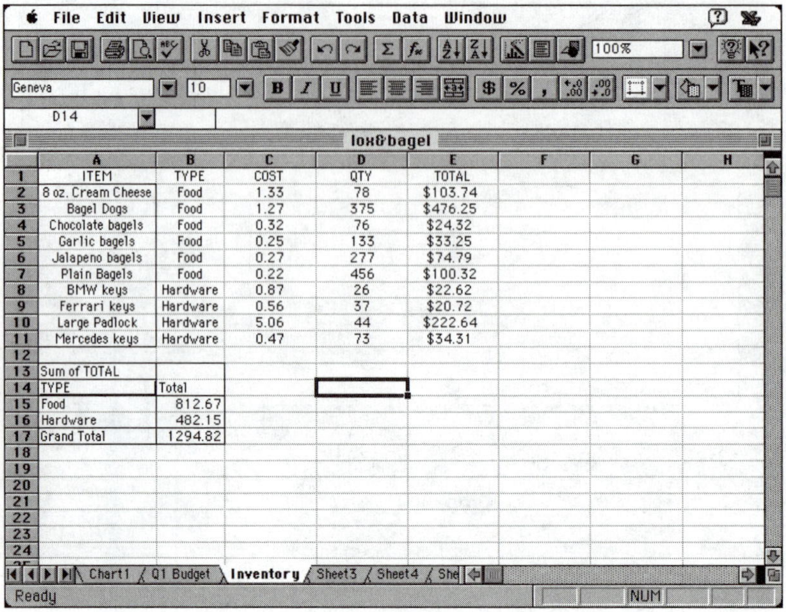

Figure 11.5 *The Inventory worksheet after running the macro.*

That's all there is to running a macro from the Macro dialog box. Next we'll take a look at ways to make it even easier to run a macro.

Assigning Macros to Menus, Shortcut Keys, and Buttons

The whole point of using macros is to save time. That being the case, pulling down the Tools menu, selecting **Macro**, clicking on the macro name, and then the **Run** button is a far too tedious a process for executing a simple macro.

In the expanded Record New Macro dialog box, you may have noticed that there was an *Assign To* area. This area lets you assign the macro to a menu option, a shortcut key, or both.

We'll change the options for the CellFmt macro in the Personal Macro workbook. The Personal Macro workbook is hidden, so before we can make any changes to the CellFmt macro, we must unhide the Personal Macro workbook.

1. Pull down the Window menu and select **Unhide** to display the Unhide dialog box, as shown in Figure 11.6.

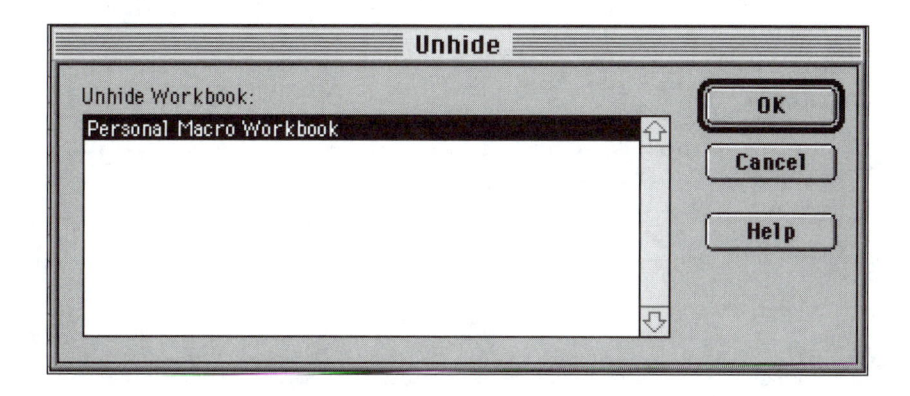

Figure 11.6 *The Unhide dialog box.*

If there are any other open but hidden workbooks, these will be listed along with Personal Macro Workbook.

2. Click on **Personal Macro Workbook** if it isn't already highlighted, and then click **OK**.

The Personal Macro Workbook with one tab (Module1) and the Visual Basic toolbar are displayed, as shown in Figure 11.7.

If other macros have been recorded and stored on the Personal Macro Workbook, they may be displayed on your screen. You may need to scroll down to view the CellFmt macro.

With the macro displayed, you could edit it to correct mistakes or add functionality. Even if you don't know the first thing about programming, you may find it interesting to look over the macro. You'll be surprised at how easily you'll understand what's going on.

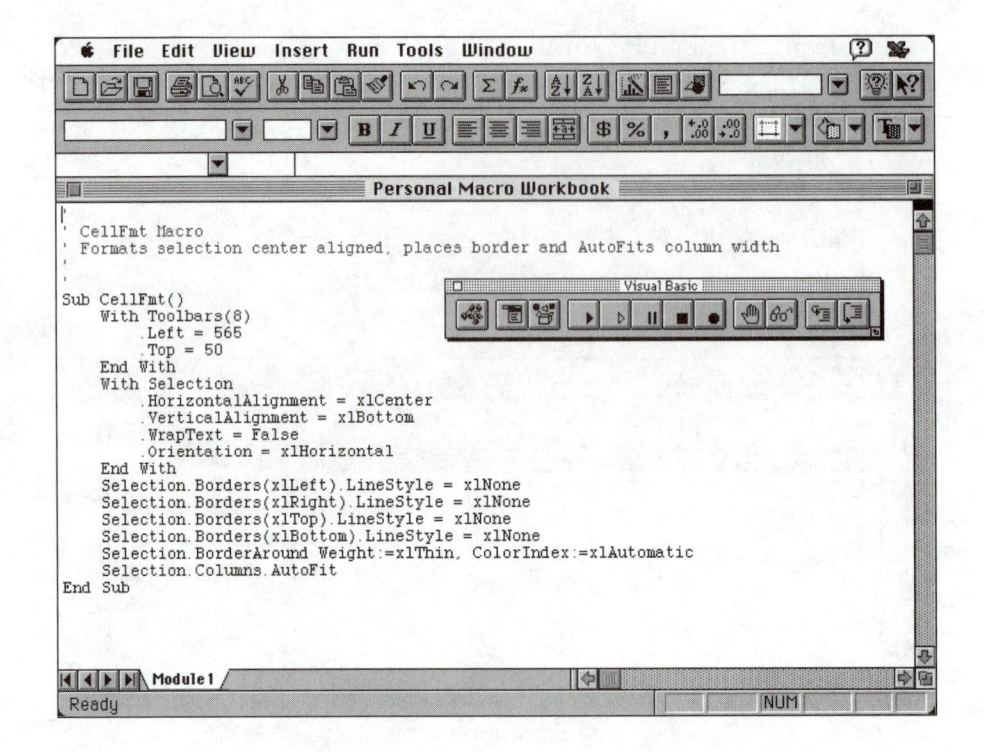

Figure 11.7 *The Personal Macro Workbook.*

 Unless you know what you're doing and have a reasonable understanding of Visual Basic, don't edit the macro in any way. Even making some seemingly innocuous changes could render the macro completely useless.

WARNING

Now that the workbook containing our macro is unhidden, we can switch back to the Budget workbook and change the macro's options.

3. Pull down the Window menu and select **lox&bagel** in the bottom portion of the menu.

4. Pull down the Tools menu and select **Macro**. Click on '**Personal Macro Workbook'!CellFmt**, then click on the **Options** button to display the Macro Option dialog box, as shown in Figure 11.8.

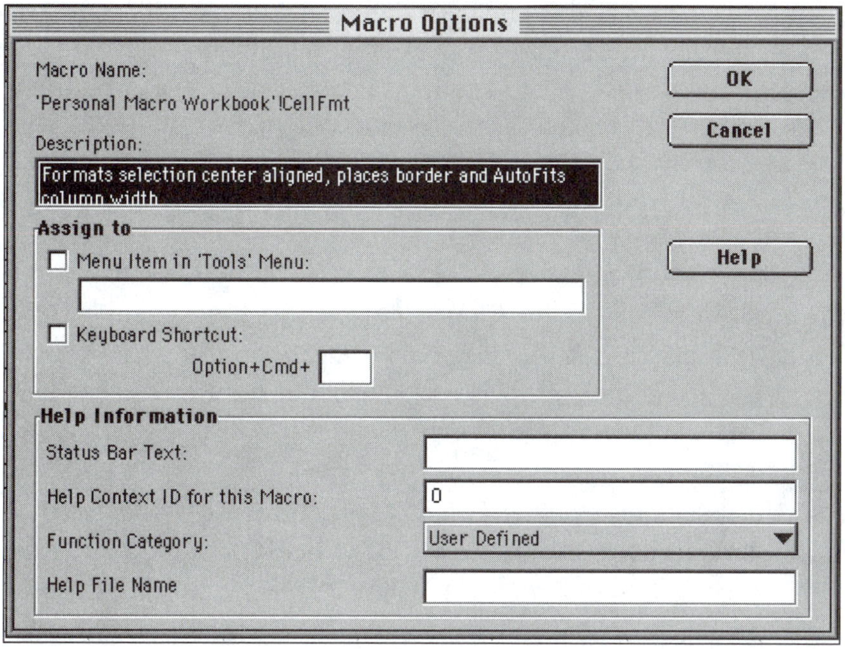

Figure 11.8 *The Macro Options dialog box.*

The Assign To portion of the Macro Options dialog box is the same as the Assign To portion of the expanded Record New Macro dialog box. You can do everything before you start the recording process in exactly the same manner as you do after the macro is recorded.

By default, the **Shortcut Key** check box is unchecked. You can use any of the 26 alphabet letters in either uppercase or lower-case, giving you 52 possible shortcut key combinations. The keys you press to run a macro are **Option+⌘+** a specified letter key. To change the shortcut key, click in the text box next to **Option+Cmd+** and type the letter you want. If you want to use the letter in uppercase, press **Shift** plus the letter.

For no particular reason, other than the fact that it's not normally assigned to another task, we'll use the letter *e*.

5. Click in the text box to the right of **Option+Cmd+** and type: **e**.

If you choose to assign a different shortcut key to this macro, that's OK, but make a note of it so you'll be able to remember how to invoke the macro later. In fact, it's not a bad idea to keep a complete listing of all your macros and their shortcut keys handy. You could create the list in an Excel database or in your word processing program.

The Keyboard Shortcut check box is checked when you enter a shortcut key in the text box.

We'll also assign this macro to a menu item on the Tools menu. In real life, you probably wouldn't use both a shortcut key and assign the macro to a menu item—you'd most likely choose one or the other.

6. Click in the text box below **Menu Item in 'Tools' menu** and type: **Center/Border/AutoFit**. Click **OK** and then click the **Close** button of the Macro dialog box.

The check box in front of Menu Item in 'Tools' menu is checked as soon as you start entering the text in the text box.

The text you typed—Center/Border/AutoFit—is the text that will appear in the Tools menu. The menu width will adjust to accommodate as much text as will fit on one line across the screen. However, it's best to keep the menu text reasonably short so it won't obscure too much of the screen.

We now have two new ways to run the macro: from the Tools menu and the shortcut key. Let's use them both.

7. Select cells **B2** through **B11** (the category column) and pull down the Tools menu, as shown in Figure 11.9.

8. Drag down to highlight **Center/Border/AutoFit** in the bottom portion of the menu and release the mouse button.

There now, wasn't that easier? In order to use the shortcut key on a column that needs reformatting, close the **lox&bagel** workbook without saving it, then open it again.

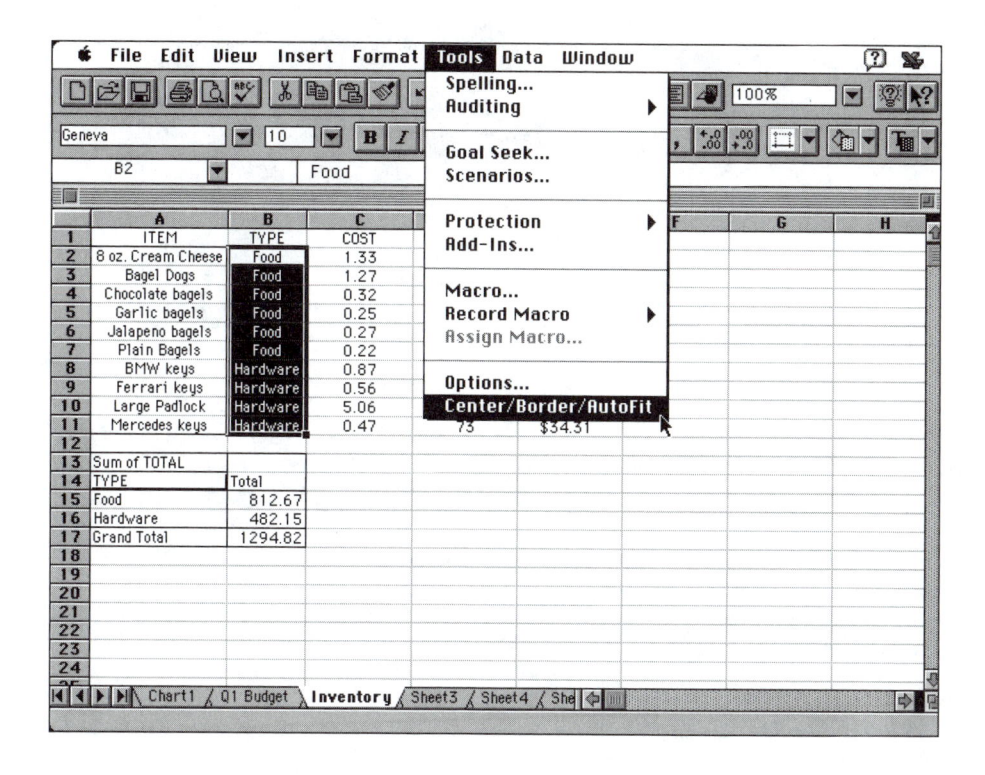

Figure 11.9 *The Tools menu with its new choice at the bottom of the menu.*

9. Close the **lox&bagel** workbook by clicking in its **Close box** on the left side of its title bar. Click on the **NO** button when asked if you want to save changes to **lox&bagel**. Then reopen the **lox&bagel** workbook and click on the **Inventory** sheet tab.

10. Once again, select cells **B2** through **B11** and press the shortcut key combination, **Ctrl+e** (or whatever your shortcut key is).

    This is getting just a bit too easy, don't you think? Well, we're still not finished making life easier with macros. Next, we'll assign the macro to a button, which we'll then add to the Formatting toolbar.

11. Close the **lox&bagel** workbook again without saving and reopen it, as before.

12. Pull down the View menu and select **Toolbars** to display the Toolbars dialog box, as shown in Figure 11.10.

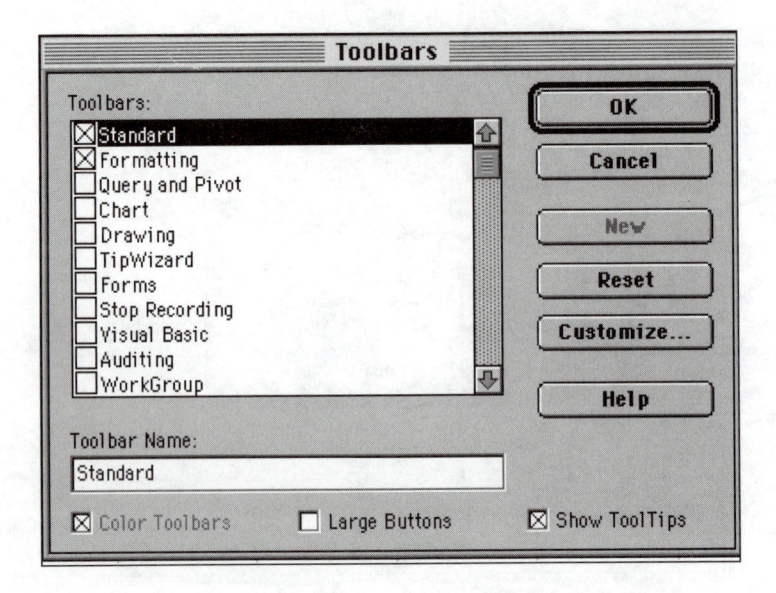

Figure 11.10 *The Toolbars dialog box.*

N O T E

From this dialog box, you can add or remove any toolbars you want displayed on the screen by clicking in the check box next to the toolbar name. Remember, the more toolbars you display, the less screen *real estate* you'll be able to see.

13. Click on the **Customize** button to display the Customize dialog box, as shown in Figure 11.11.

    You can use the Customize dialog box to assign macros to any of the button icons used in any of the toolbars. Instead of using a button that is already used in another toolbar, it makes more sense to choose a button from the group of custom buttons that Excel supplies.

14. Scroll down to the bottom of the Categories list and click **Custom** to display the group of buttons shown in Figure 11.12.

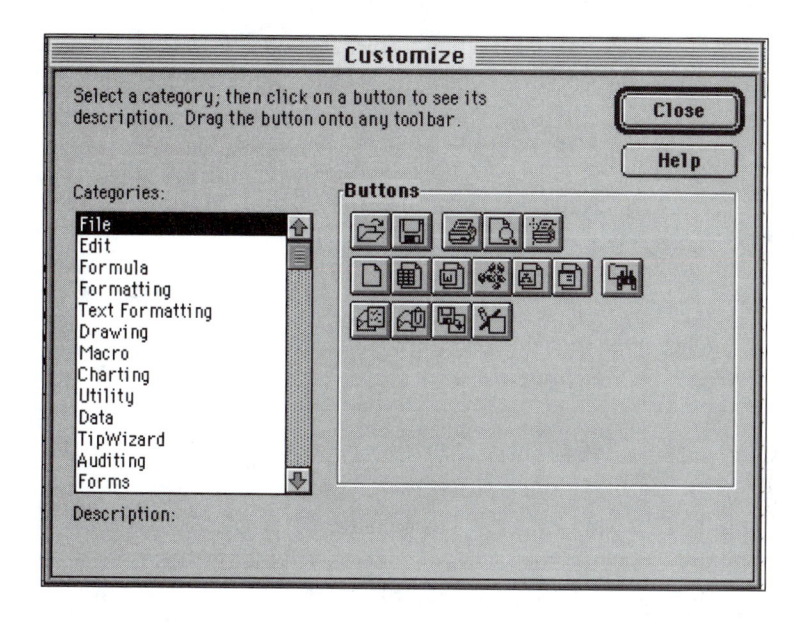

Figure 11.11 *The Customize dialog box.*

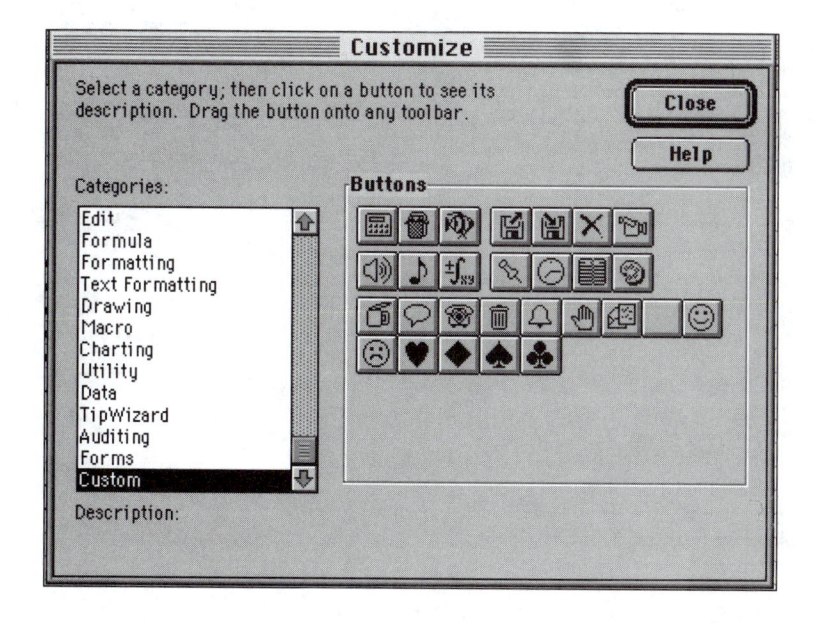

Figure 11.12 *The Custom buttons.*

You can add any button to any visible toolbar by dragging it to the position you want on the toolbar. We'll drag a button onto the Formatting toolbar.

NOTE You can create some space on a toolbar for your new macro buttons (or just remove some clutter) by simply dragging the button you want to remove down onto the worksheet and releasing the mouse button. We have enough room to add another button to the Formatting toolbar, so we don't need to remove any buttons.

15. Drag the button you want to add–let's use the *smiley face* that's on the right side of the third row of buttons–to the Formatting toolbar, between the Underline and the Align Left buttons. Release the mouse button to accept the new button position and display the Assign Macro dialog box, as shown in Figure 11.13.

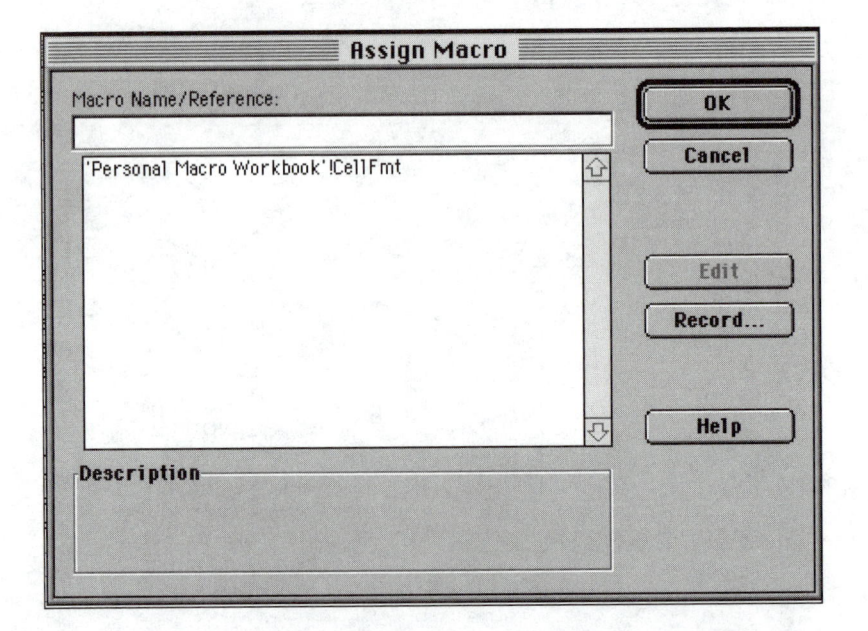

Figure 11.13 *The new button on the Formatting toolbar and the Assign Macro dialog box.*

You can assign any available macro in the Macro Name/Reference list to the button.

16. Click on **'Personal Macro Workbook'!CellFmt** and then click.

17. Click on the **Close** button of the Customize dialog box to complete the toolbar button assignment.

18. Select **B2** through **B11** again and then click on your new **smiley-face** macro button.

That's all there is to making macros easier to execute. You should have no excuses for avoiding them anymore, even though they involve that nasty programming stuff.

19. Pull down the Window menu and select **Personal Macro Workbook** to switch to display the Personal Macro Workbook.

20. Pull down the Window menu and select **Hide** to conceal the Personal Macro Workbook.

21. Save your work and exit Excel if you aren't proceeding to the next chapter now. Click on the **Yes** button when asked if you want to save the changes to the Personal Macro Workbook.

A Final Thought

This chapter covered the basics of planning, recording and executing macros. I strongly encourage you to invest more time and energy exploring the vast power of macros and macro programming. It will be time well spent.

The next chapter looks at the process of linking worksheets.

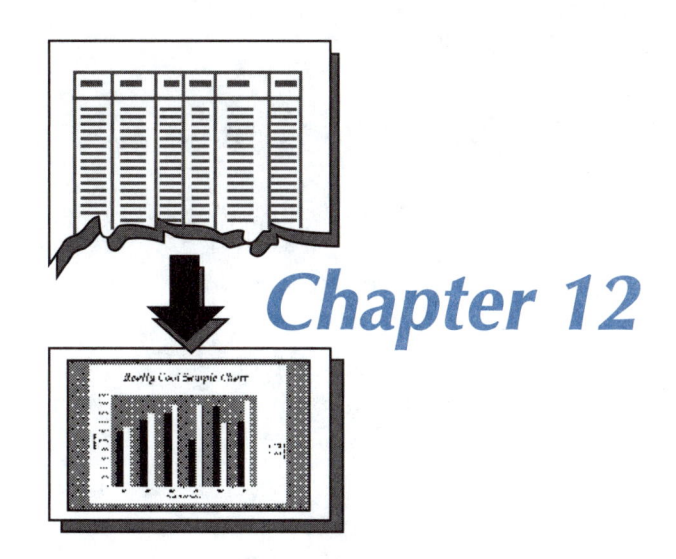

Chapter 12

Linking Worksheets

- Understanding Linking Concepts
- Creating Links
- Updating Links
- A Final Thought

Understanding Linking Concepts

So far, we've been working in only one workbook, and the separate worksheets we've created within that workbook have no special relationship to each other, except that they contain information about a single company.

There are many situations that call for tying data from two or more workbooks together. This process of tying data together is called *linking*. You can also link data between worksheets in the same workbook.

There is nothing mysterious about linking. When you link data from one worksheet to another, you are simply using the referencing concepts we've been discussing since we first started creating formulas. However, when you create links to other worksheets—whether they are in the same workbook or a different one—the reference includes the workbook name (if it's a different workbook), the sheet name, and then the cell address or range.

Linking is commonly used for several different purposes. First, you can use linking to break a large, complex worksheet into smaller, more manageable chunks. You might want to keep some confidential data in a separate worksheet to keep prying eyes away, or you may want to segregate your worksheet by company, department, or activity.

A very good reason for linking worksheets in different workbooks is to summarize data from several company divisions. Suppose your company has offices in three cities; each creates a worksheet detailing weekly sales activity. By linking, the manager at each location you could send the data via a disk or over a *WAN* (wide area network) containing the workbook to company headquarters, where the new numbers could be brought into the summary, or master, worksheet.

Of course, you don't have to place confidential information in a separate sheet. You can hide any portion of a worksheet that you don't want in plain sight. However, it can be less cumbersome to place the data in another worksheet so it is available to you by switching to that sheet, rather than having to unhide and rehide it every time you want to see the data.

When you create links, you are dealing with at least two worksheets, a *source worksheet* and a *dependent worksheet*. The source worksheet contains the data that you want to bring into the dependent worksheet. After a link is created, the linked data in the dependent worksheet is automatically updated when the linked data in the source worksheet is updated.

Linking worksheets is different from a simple copy-and-paste operation. If you copy a value from one worksheet and then paste it into another, you are simply copying the value and not establishing a link. If the value in the source worksheet (the one you copied from) changes, the value in the dependent worksheet won't change.

If you try to use copy-and-paste to copy a formula from one worksheet to another, it won't work at all. The requisite workbook and worksheet portions of the reference won't be copied, so you'll end up with an invalid formula.

Creating Links

If the worksheets you want to link are already created, you can simply open them and create the link references from the source worksheets to the dependent worksheet.

We'll create three simple worksheets in separate workbooks to track sales data for Spokane Locks and Bagel's three locations. These will be the source worksheets. We'll then create a dependent worksheet to let us summarize the data from the source worksheet.

1. Start Excel and, if the **lox&bagel** workbook or any other workbooks containing data are on your screen, close them. Then click on the **New Workbook** toolbar button to open a fresh workbook.

2. In cell A1, type: **SALES**.

3. In cell A3, type: **Total Sales** and press **Return** to confirm the entry.

We'll copy the worksheet to two other sheets in two new work-books. This worksheet is simple enough that we may as well enter the data manually into the other worksheets. But copying the worksheet can be a real time saver when you want to create multiple worksheets with identical structures.

4. Pull down the Edit menu and select **Move** or **Copy Sheet** to display the Move or Copy dialog box, as shown in Figure 12.1.

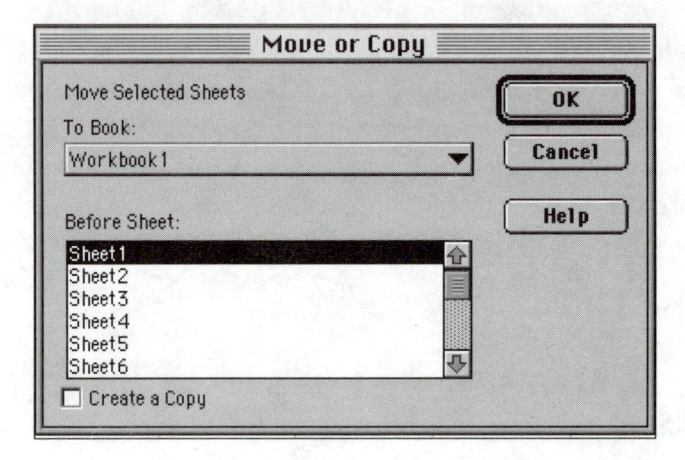

Figure 12.1 *The Move or Copy dialog box.*

5. Click on the **drop-down Arrow** under To Book: to display the list of books to which you can move or copy the worksheet, as shown in Figure 12.2.

6. Drag down to highlight **(new book)** and release the mouse button.

7. Click on the **Create a Copy** check box and then click **OK** to make the copy.

8. Repeat steps 4 through 7 to make another copy of the worksheet.

9. Click on the **New Workbook** toolbar button to display a new empty workbook, so we can enter the structure for our summary sheet.

10. In cell A1, type: **MASTER SALES SHEET**.

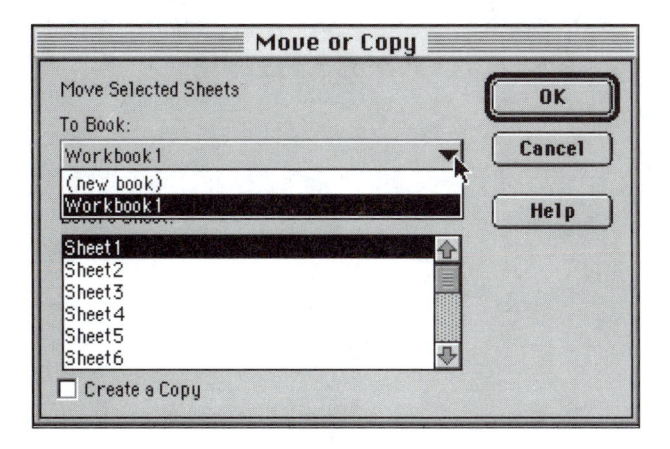

Figure 12.2 *The drop-down list of available workbooks.*

11. In cell A3, type: **Downtown**; in A4, type: **Valley**; and in A5, type: **Northside**. Press the **Return** key to confirm the entry.

    Now we'll enter the sales figures into our source worksheets and then create the links. We could switch to each of them one at a time, but it's often easier to be able to see a portion of all of the worksheets at once. To do this we'll use the Macintosh's ability to organize the four workbook windows into four equal-sized tiles on the screen.

12. Pull down the Window menu and select **Arrange** to display the Arrange Windows dialog box, as shown in Figure 12.3.

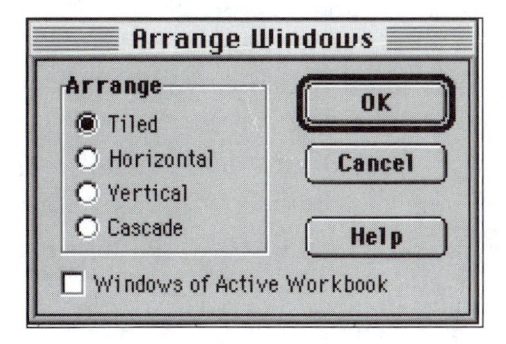

Figure 12.3 *The Arrange Windows dialog box.*

13. The Tiled option is the default, so just click the **OK** button to tile the four windows, as shown in Figure 12.4.

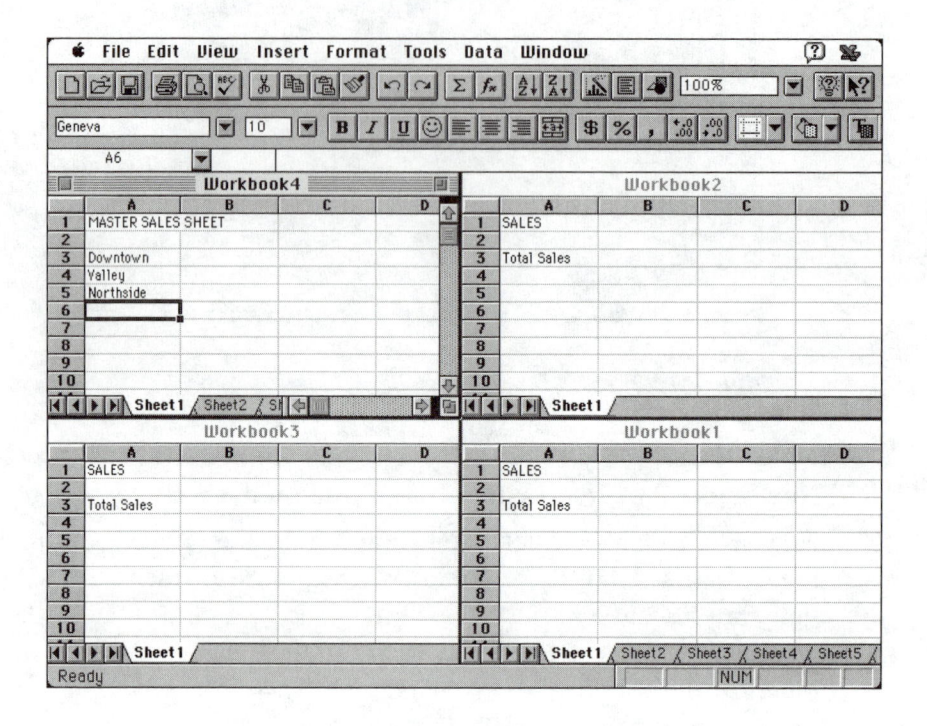

Figure 12.4 *The tiled windows.*

You can easily tell which window is active—it's the one with the highlighted title bar and the Scroll bars. You can change active windows by choosing **Window** and then the name of the window you want, but the easiest way to change active windows is to simply click on the one you want.

Let's add location and sales information in cells B1 and B3 in each of the source windows.

14. Click anywhere in the window in the upper-right portion of the screen. In the figure it's Workbook2.

15. In cell B1, type: **DOWNTOWN**; in B3, type: **$31,000** and then click anywhere in the window below—Workbook1 in the figure—to make it the active window.

16. In cell B1, type: **VALLEY**; in B3, type: **$27,500** and then click in the window on the lower left—Workbook3 in the figure—to make it the active window.

17. In cell B1, type: **NORTHSIDE**; in B3, type: **$58,000** and then click in the Master Sales window in the upper left.

    With the windows tiled, creating the links is a snap. All we need to do is start the formula as we would when creating any other formula—with an equal sign—and then point and click.

18. Click in cell **B3**, where the Downtown sales figure will be in the Master Sales sheet, and type: **=**. Make the Downtown sheet active by clicking in it, then click in cell **B3** and then in the **Enter** box on the formula bar to accept the entry.

NOTE

When creating a link reference, clicking on another worksheet doesn't *really* make it the active window. It just allows you to include references from the window and use scroll bars to find the portion of the sheet you want.

The formula in the formula bar is "**=[Workbook2]Sheet1!B3**" Next we'll add the other links.

19. Press the **down arrow** key to make B4 (the Valley sales cell) active and type: **=** then click in the Valley window and then on cell **B3** of the Valley window, and press **Return**.

20. With cell **B5** in the Master Sales sheet selected, type: **=** and then click in the Northside window, then on cell **B3**, and click on the **Enter** box to accept the entry.

    The sales numbers for each location are now linked to the master sheet, as shown in Figure 12.5.

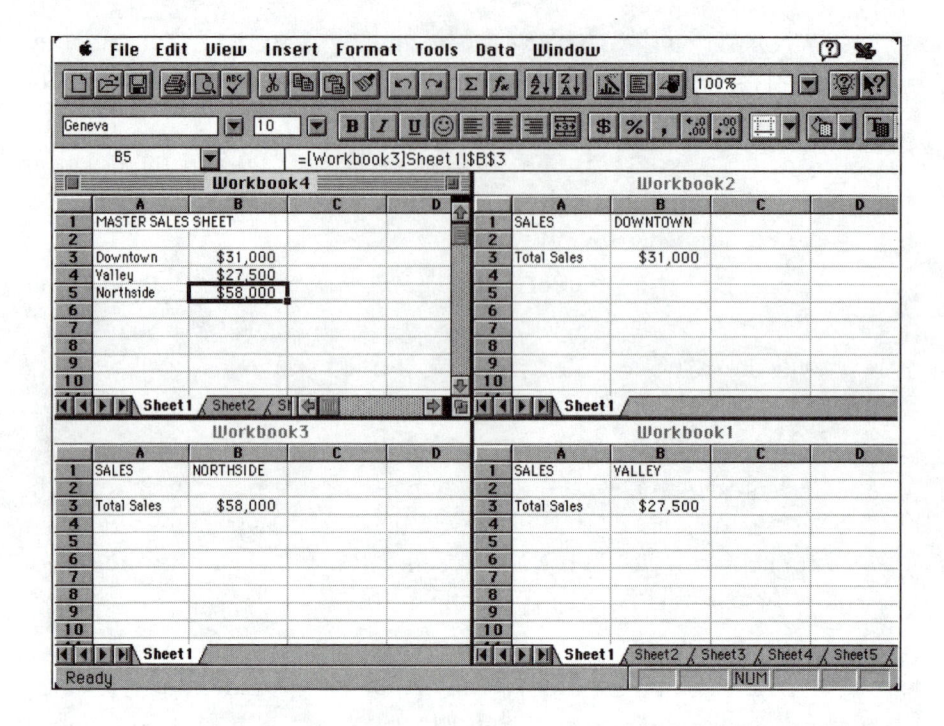

Figure 12.5 *The Master Sales Sheet with sales numbers.*

If any of the sales numbers in the source sheets change, the numbers in the dependent Master Sales sheet will also change. Let's try changing one of the numbers to see if it works.

21. Change the sales number in the Downtown sheet to **$41,000** and notice the number in the Master Sales window change.

Maintaining Links

You'll often make changes in your linked worksheets that will require them to be updated. For example, if you save these workbooks and name them something other than Book1 through Book4, the link references will no longer be correct. However, when you open the dependent document later, you'll be given an opportunity to have Excel automatically update the links.

Let's save and close the workbooks now.

1. Close the Downtown workbook, saving it with the name **Downtown**.

2. Close the Northside workbook and save it with the name **Northside**.

3. Close the Valley workbook and save it with the name **Valley**.

4. Close the Master Sales workbook and save it with the name **Master Sales**.

   We'll just open the Master and Valley workbooks to see how Excel updates the links.

5. Open the **Master Sales** workbook.

   Excel prompts you with a message dialog box asking if you want to update the automatic links, as shown in Figure 12.6.

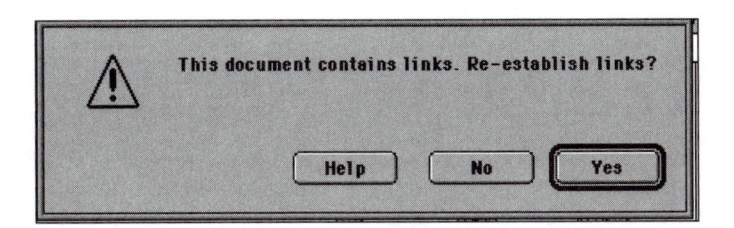

> This document contains links. Re-establish links?
>
> [Help]   [No]   [Yes]

Figure 12.6 *The message dialog box to update links.*

6. Click on the **Yes** button to update the links and open the workbook.

7. Click on cell **B4** and notice that the reference now indicates the Valley workbook.

8. Open the **Valley** workbook and try changing the sales number to assure yourself that the link has been maintained.

9. Close all open workbooks and exit Excel if you're not moving on to the next chapter now.

A Final Thought

In this chapter, you learned to take advantage of some of Excel's powerful features for working with multiple workbooks. In the next chapter, you'll learn about some of the ways you can customize Excel to make your working environment suit your requirements.

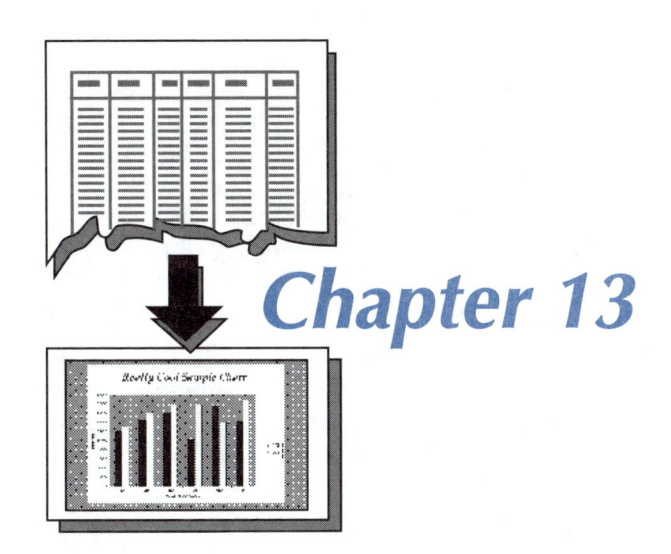

Customizing Excel

- Setting Excel's Options
- Using AutoSave
- Changing Views
- A Final Thought

This chapter covers various ways of customizing your Excel environment. It's also something of a potpourri of Excel information that didn't have a clearly logical location in any of the other chapters.

Some of the sections in this chapter, such as using AutoSave, allow you to work in Excel with greater confidence knowing your data will be automatically protected, even if you forget to save. Other sections show you how to specify such options as how Excel calculates formulas, whether you will be prompted for summary information when saving workbooks, and how many sheets there are in a workbook by default.

You'll also learn to alter your perspective of the worksheet by changing view options.

Setting Excel's Options

Excel's Options dialog box provides tremendous flexibility, allowing you to change most of the ways you interact with the program. Let's take a look at some of these options now.

1. Start Excel, if it isn't already running, and make sure there is a worksheet—any worksheet will do—on your screen.

    Since we won't be stepping through the procedures discussed in this chapter, it doesn't matter which worksheet is on the screen.

2. Pull down the Tools menu and select **Options**. Then click on the **General** tab to display the General portion of the Options dialog box, as shown in Figure 13.1.

    We'll examine some of the more interesting options in the dialog box without changing them. However, I will offer some of my recommendations for these options.

    The *Reference Style* choices—A1 or R1C1—determine how you refer to cells in the worksheet. You'll want to leave this as the default, A1, unless you are more comfortable with a fairly old spreadsheet program from Microsoft called *Multiplan*. On second thought, even if you *are* more familiar with Multiplan, you're still better off sticking with the default, since that is the way all modern spreadsheet programs refer to cells.

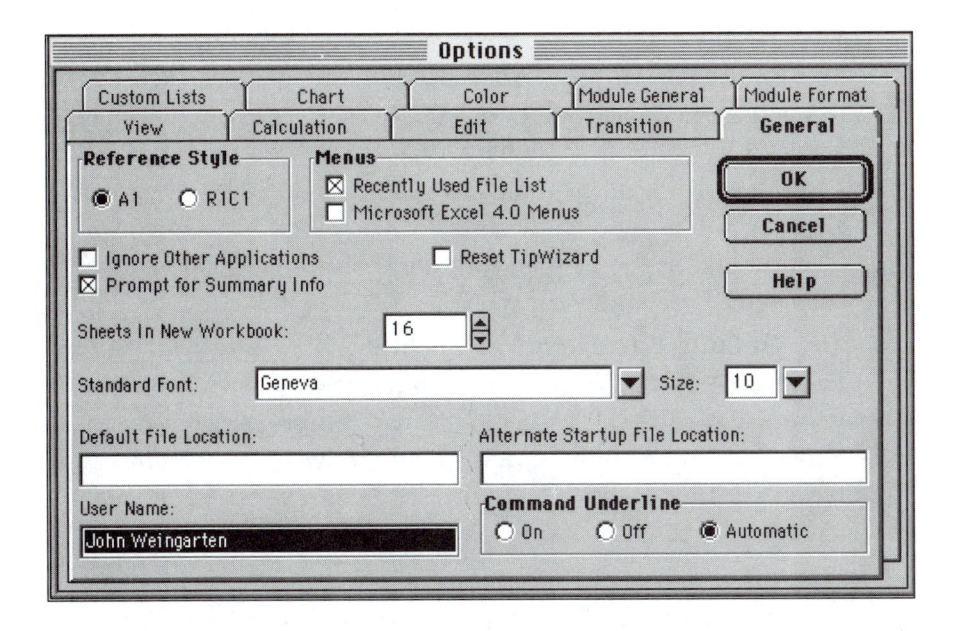

Figure 13.1 *The General portion of the Options dialog box.*

The *Menus* area of the dialog box provides two check boxes. The first lets you turn off the display of the last four recently used files at the bottom of the File menu. I can't think of any reason to turn this option off. The other option lets you use the menus from the previous version of Excel, version 4.0. Again, I can't think of a good reason to use this option. You may as well get used to the 5.0 menus, since this book and all the documentation that comes with Excel 5.0 refers to them.

- **Prompt for Summary Info** may be turned off if you aren't entering any information into the Summary dialog box and aren't having trouble locating your files from their file names.

- **Sheets in New Workbook** default is 16. You can always add or delete worksheets from a workbook, so the value in this option doesn't matter much. However, if you consistently use more or fewer worksheets in a workbook, you may want to increase or decrease the value to save you the trouble of doing it later.

- The **Standard Font** and **Size** lists let you specify which of your available fonts and font sizes you want to use for future worksheets. Changing the defaults won't change the fonts or sizes on existing worksheets. You might consider changing the font and/or size if you find the default difficult to read on your screen. Keep in mind that if you change to a larger size, you won't be able to see as much data on your worksheet at one time.

- The **Default File Location** and the **Alternate Startup File Location** let you specify which directories you want to use for your Excel files. The files in each of these directories appear when you choose **File**, **Open** or **File**, **Save**. I recommend specifying a folder for the Default File Location so your files will always be where you expect them to be.

  To enter a Default File Location, click in the text box and type the complete path to where your files are stored. For example, if your files are stored in a folder called *documents* inside the *Microsoft Excel* folder, you would enter Microsoft Excel:Documents in the text box.

- **User Name** is the name that was entered when Excel was first installed on the computer. If you aren't the person who installed the software, you can simply delete the name in the text box and enter yours. They can always change it back when they return from vacation.

  Next, let's take a look at a couple of the options you might want to change in the Edit portion of the dialog box.

3. Click on the **Edit** tab to display the Edit portion of the Options dialog box, as shown in Figure 13.2.

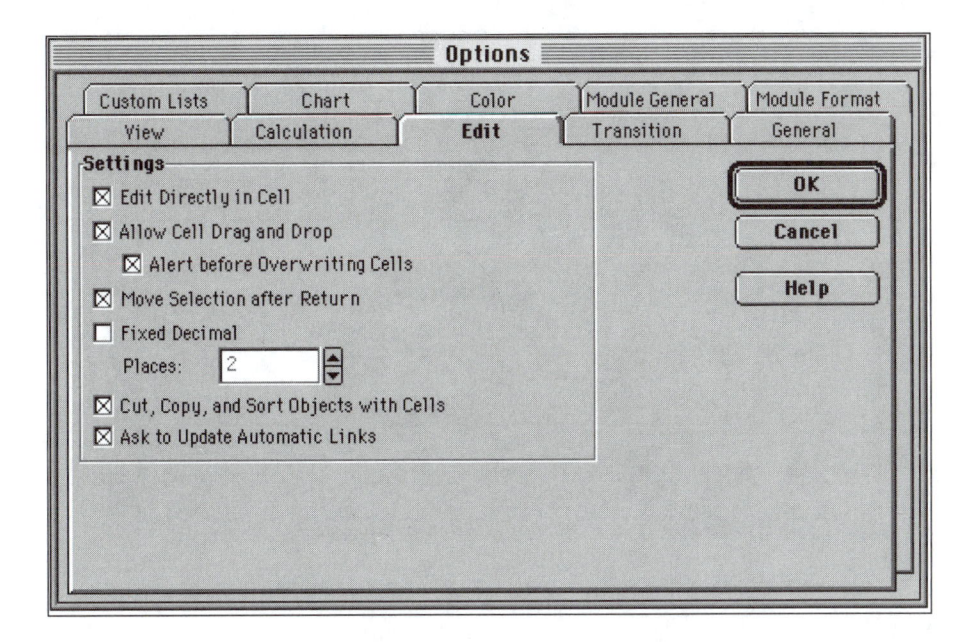

Figure 13.2 *The Edit portion of the Options dialog box.*

- **Move Selection after Return** (the default) causes the active cell to move one row down after you accept an entry by pressing **Return**. If you want to be able to press the **Return** key without changing the selected cell, click in the check box to remove the check.

  If you almost always enter numbers with a certain number of decimal places, it can save you time if you don't have to enter the decimal point. If you specify a certain number of decimal places (2 is the default) and click in the **Fixed Decimal** check box, Excel will enter your decimal point for you. You can always override this option by manually entering a decimal point.

  Next, let's take a look at how Excel calculates.

4. Click on the **Calculation** tab to display the Calculation portion of the Options dialog box, as shown in Figure 13.3.

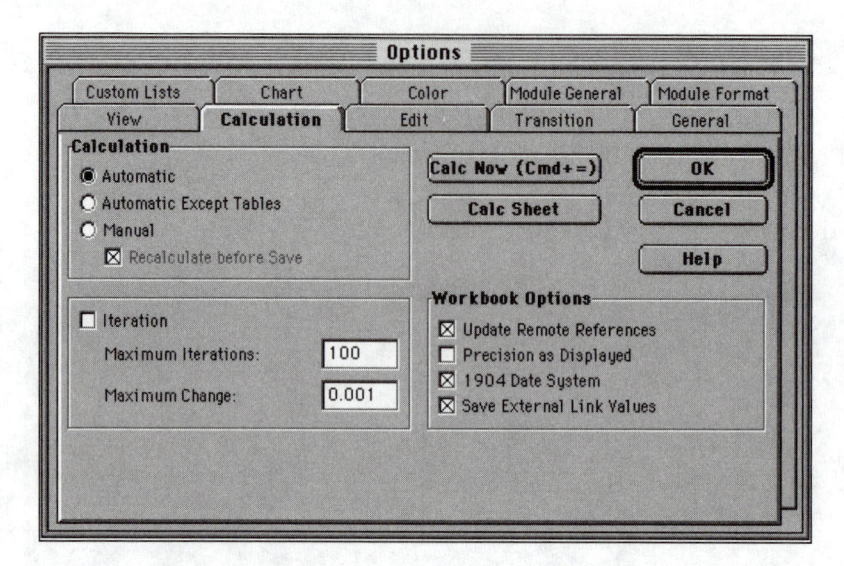

Figure 13.3 *The Calculation portion of the Options dialog box.*

The options in the Calculation area of this portion of the dialog box let you choose whether Excel calculates automatically (the default) or manually. You can also choose to have Excel calculate automatically except for tables (such as PivotTables).

As you've worked through the steps in this book, you probably noticed that when you changed numbers referred to by formulas, the recalculations occurred almost instantly. This is because the examples in the book are very simple and very small. However, if you are working with larger, more complex worksheets containing many formulas and functions requiring recalculation when numbers are changed, there can be quite a long delay while Excel performs the calculations.

The actual length of time required for calculations depends on the size and complexity of the worksheet, as well as the speed of your computer. If your computer is fast enough, even very large worksheets may recalculate fast enough to satisfy you. However, when you find that the delays become burdensome as you are entering or editing worksheet data, consider switching to manual recalculation by clicking in the **Manual** radio button.

Be sure to keep the **Recalculate Before Save** check box checked so the numbers will be brought up to date when you save the workbook. Whenever you want to perform a calculation to see the current state of your worksheet, you can use the keyboard shortcut, ⌘+=.

The 1904 Date System check box in the lower-right portion of the dialog box is of particular interest if you share files with others who are using Excel for Windows. The Windows version of the program tracks dates based on the year 1900 instead of 1904. So, if you are sharing files with Windows folks, click on **1904 Date System** check box to remove the check mark and switch to the 1900 Date System.

Next, let's take a look at the View portion of the Options dialog box.

5. Click on the **View** tab to display the View portion of the Options dialog box, as shown in Figure 13.4.

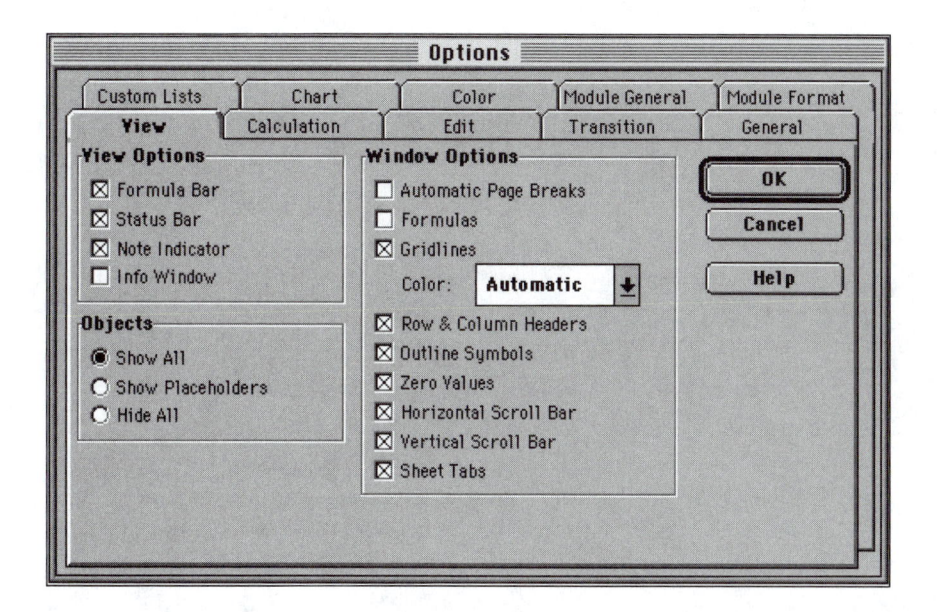

Figure 13.4 *The View portion of the Options dialog box.*

The View portion of the dialog box is a bit different than the other portions of the Options dialog box we've looked at. Any changes to the settings in the other portions of the dialog box become the new default settings for new workbooks. This is also true of the changes made in the Show area of the View portion of the dialog box. However, changes made in the other areas of the View portion of the dialog box only affect the current worksheet.

For example, if you turn off the gridlines by clicking in the **Gridlines** check box, the gridlines will be removed from the active worksheet, but not from other worksheets, even in the same workbook.

This dialog box lets you turn on or off various screen elements that can make it easier to navigate in Excel, but can also add clutter to your screen. A good rule of thumb is to remove any elements that you don't use. For example, in the Show area, you can uncheck the Formula Bar, the Status Bar and Note indicators. These are all very useful elements and I recommend that you keep all of them on your screen.

You can also add the Info Window, which isn't checked by default. The Info Window displays the current active cell reference, any formula it contains, and any attached note. The Info Window doesn't take up any screen real estate since you have to switch to it to see it, which you do from the Window menu.

All the options in the Show area of the View portion of the dialog box, except the Info Window option, can be turned on and off from the View menu. Since you may want to turn these elements off and on while working in a particular worksheet, the View menu is the fastest way to make these changes.

The Objects area of the dialog box lets you choose whether to show all objects, show placeholders (gray rectangles), or hide objects. The objects in question here are graphic elements such as charts and pictures. Showing all of them (the default) presents you with the most accurate representation of what your printed page will look like. Not surprisingly, though, it can slow down your navigation through the worksheet, especially on a slower computer or a large worksheet. Showing the placeholder can speed things up and won't affect the printout. Hiding these objects causes them not to print at all.

A couple of the options in the Window Options area of the dialog box bear discussion. The Automatic Page Breaks check box allows you to choose whether Excel displays horizontal and vertical lines where your printed pages end. This can be a very useful option for determining where portions of your worksheets will fall on the printed pages as you enter and edit data, without having to use Print Preview.

The Formulas option can be especially useful for finding and displaying all the formulas on a worksheet without selecting one cell at a time. It's easy to forget where you placed your formulas, particularly in larger worksheets, and this can shed some light on the situation. Figure 13.5 shows a portion of the budget worksheet in the **lox&bagel** workbook with the formulas displayed.

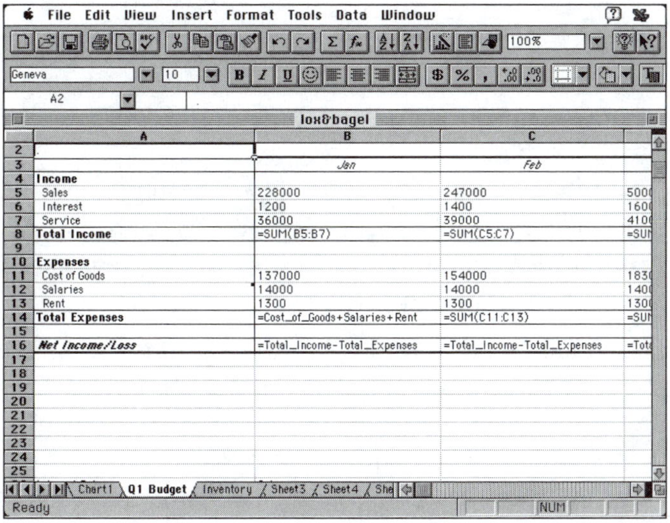

Figure 13.5 *Part of the Q1 Budget worksheet with formulas displayed.*

Finally, before moving on to the next section, let's take a look at the Color portion of the Options dialog box.

6. Click on the **Color** tab of the Options dialog box.

The Color portion of the Options dialog box appears, as shown in Figure 13.6.

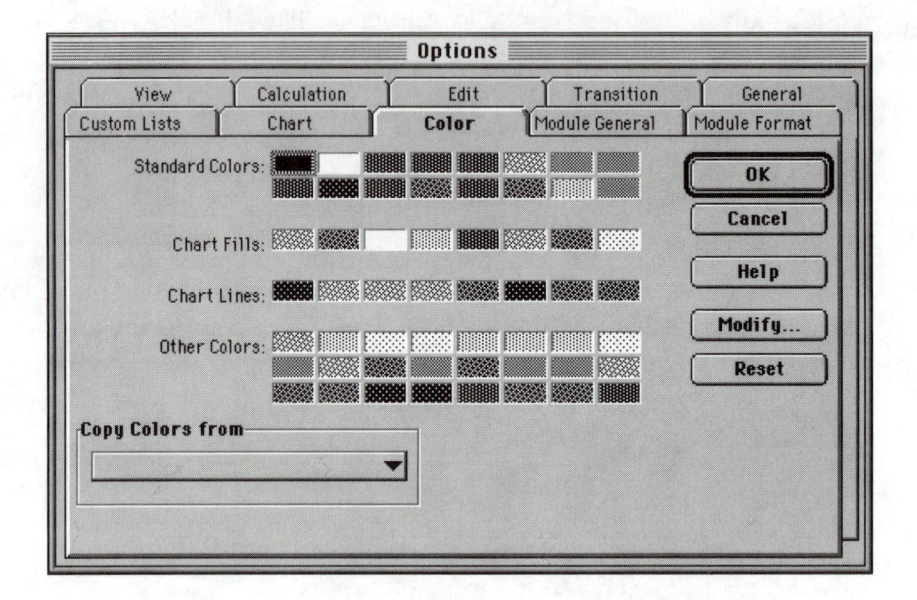

Figure 13.6 The Color portion of the Options dialog box.

This portion of the dialog box lets you specify colors or shades as defaults. The colors or shades with the borders around them are the current defaults. You can change the defaults by clicking on the colors or shades of your choice.

There are many other options in the Options dialog box for customizing your environment. In each portion of the dialog box, as in most other dialog boxes, you can click on the **Help** button to get explanations of the various options.

7. Click on the **Cancel** button to clear the Options dialog box from your screen without making any changes.

Using Autosave

Excel provides a host of extra little programs, designed for enhancing Excel. Included in the group of add-in programs is a program for creating slide shows from Excel screens, which you can use for presentations. There is a program for querying external databases, which can be quite useful when data is kept in files created by other programs, such as dBASE.

The add-in we're going to discuss here is AutoSave. There is no more important procedure in Excel, or any other computer program for that matter, than saving your work. It doesn't matter which other skills you master or what sort of fancy-schmancy worksheets you create, if you lose them to a power failure or some other computer mishap.

Of course you can save your work manually, but anything that can be done to automate the process and relieve you of that burden is welcome. AutoSave does just that. With AutoSave you can instruct Excel to save your work automatically at specified intervals.

Let's take a look at AutoSave now. Skip the first two steps if AutoSave is already one of the choices on your Tools menu.

1. Pull down the Tools menu and select **Add-Ins** to display the Add-Ins dialog box, shown in Figure 13.7.

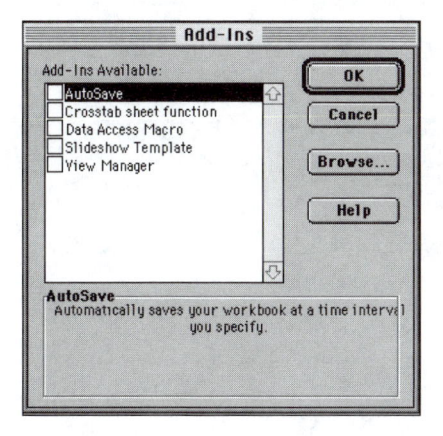

Figure 13.7 *The Add-Ins dialog box.*

This dialog box displays the add-in programs on your computer's hard disk. The ones with checks in their check boxes are currently available to Excel.

2. Click in the **AutoSave** check box (if it is unchecked) and then click **OK** to make AutoSave available.

NOTE

Browse through the other add-ins to familiarize yourself with their functions. You can also use the **Help** button to learn more about each of them.

In addition to the add-ins included with Excel, several companies offer other add-in programs for performing many specialized tasks. You'll see ads for and reviews of these in some of the popular computer magazines. You may also receive offers for some of these through the mail after you send in your registration form.

3. Pull down the Tools menu and select **AutoSave**, which should now appear as one of the commands in the Tools menu. This displays the AutoSave dialog box, as shown in Figure 13.8.

Figure 13.8 The AutoSave dialog box.

By default, the check box in the upper-left portion of the AutoSave dialog box is checked, and the default save interval is ten minutes. The rule of thumb for how often you should

AutoSave is the same as for how often you should save manually. Save often enough that, if you lose your work just before the next save, you won't be too upset. For most folks, that's between 10 and 20 minutes.

The Save Options area of the dialog box lets you choose whether AutoSave saves only your active workbook (the default), or all open workbooks. Since saving all open workbooks could cause each save to take a few extra precious seconds, it's usually best to have AutoSave just save the active workbook.

The final check box tells Excel to prompt you before proceeding with a save. I strongly recommend that you use this option. This way, if you've made some changes to the worksheet that you don't want saved, you can prevent the save.

If you choose to be prompted before the save, Excel displays the AutoSave confirmation dialog box shown in Figure 13.9 after the specified number of minutes.

Figure 13.9 *The AutoSave confirmation dialog box.*

If you want to proceed with the save, click on the **Save** button. If you don't want to save, click **Cancel**. The Skip button also works, but its primary purpose is to allow you to skip saving certain workbooks and save others when you've chosen to have AutoSave save all open workbooks.

Just because your work is saved to your computer's hard disk often enough, you shouldn't feel too secure about the safety of your data. If you have important data stored on your computer, you must also back it up to floppy disks or tape (if you have a tape back-up system. This is critical, because things can go wrong that are more serious than a power failure.

If your computer breaks altogether or is stolen or burned in a fire, you can at least restore your important data to another computer from your backups.

Changing Views

There are a number of options for changing the view of your worksheet that aren't part of the Options dialog box we discussed earlier. The first of these is another add-in called View Manager.

As you work with larger worksheets, you'll find yourself jumping back and forth between the far reaches of the worksheet to view and edit different portions. You can use the Go To method we discussed earlier, but even that method can become confusing. An easier way to move around the worksheet is to assign names to the various views you want to move to in the View Manager.

To add a named view, move to the portion of the worksheet you want to be able to return to and then use View Manager to assign it a name. Let's install and then take a look at View Manager now. (If View Manager already appears on the View menu, you can skip the next two steps).

1. Pull down the **Tools** menu and select **Add Ins** to display the Add Ins dialog box.

2. Click in the **View Manager** check box (if it is unchecked) and then click **OK** to make the View Manager add-in available.

3. Pull down the View menu and select **View Manager** to display the View Manager dialog box, as shown in Figure 13.10.

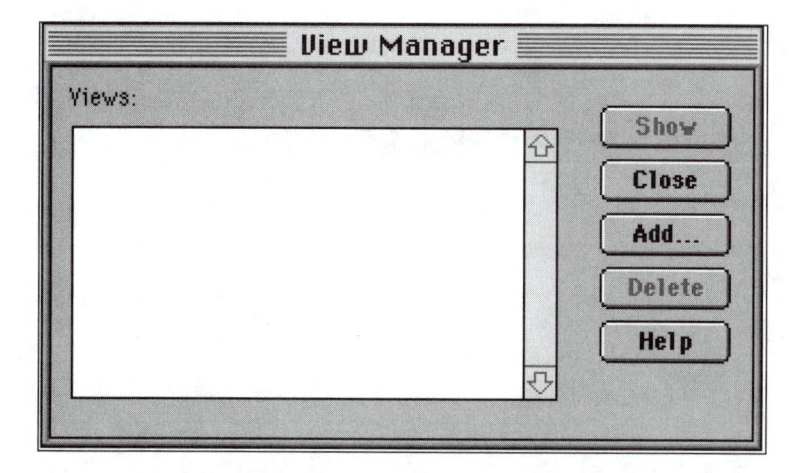

Figure 13.10 *The View Manager dialog box.*

4. Click on the **Add** button to display the Add View dialog box, as shown in Figure 13.11.

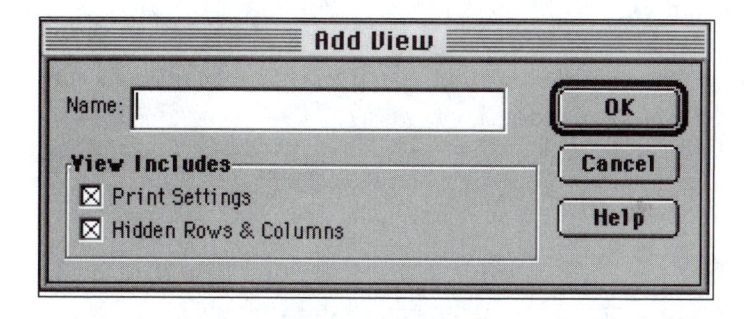

Figure 13.11 *The Add View dialog box.*

5. Enter a name for the view and click **OK**.

You'll usually want to keep the print settings and hidden rows and columns with your views, so keep these check boxes checked.

Figure 13.12 displays an example of the View Manager dialog box with several views from which to choose.

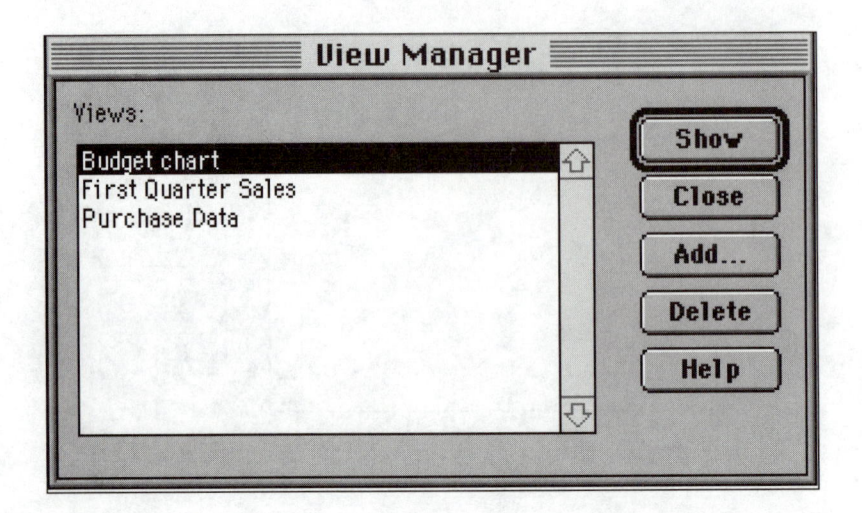

Figure 13.12 *The View Manager dialog box with several named views.*

The views you name in the View Manager only relate to the active worksheet. You can use View Manager to switch among workbooks, or even among worksheets in the active workbook.

After you've added views, you can move to them by pulling down the View menu and selecting **View Manager**, then highlighting the desired view and clicking on the **Show** button.

Let's take a look at another useful feature for changing the view of your worksheet, the Zoom feature. Until now, we've been looking at our worksheets at the default (100%) zoom. If you want to step back from your worksheet to get a bigger picture, you can zoom out to a smaller percentage. You can also zoom in to see more detail in a smaller portion of the worksheet.

You can use the zoom control drop-down list on the Standard toolbar (the one that has 100% in it now), as shown in Figure 13.13, or the Zoom dialog box from the View menu to change your view. Take a look at the Zoom dialog box.

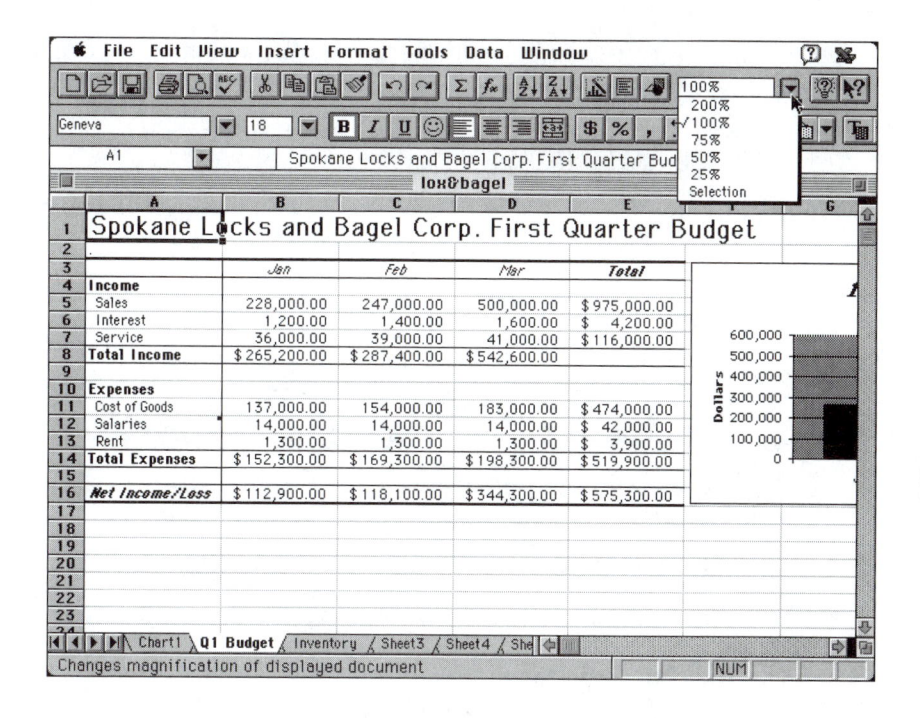

Figure 13.13 *The zoom control drop-down list.*

6. Pull down the View menu and select **Zoom** to display the Zoom dialog box, as shown in Figure 13.14.

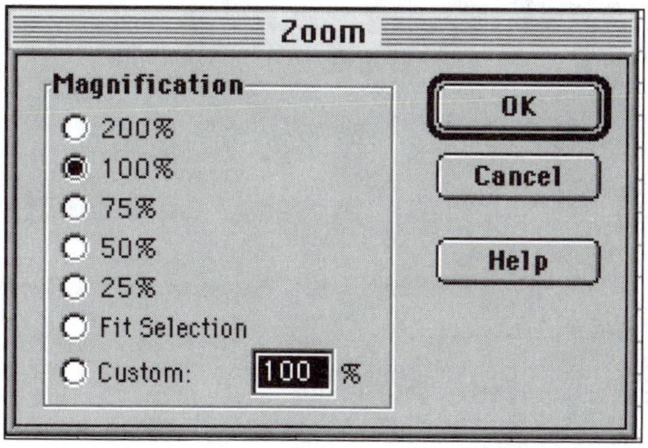

Figure 13.14 *The Zoom dialog box.*

7. Click in any of the radio buttons next to the zoom sizes, or click in **Custom** and enter a number from 10 to 400. Then click **OK**.

The larger the number, the less worksheet area you'll be able to see. The Fit Selection option adjusts the selected cells to fit in the window. Figure 13.15 shows a portion of the budget worksheet zoomed to 200%.

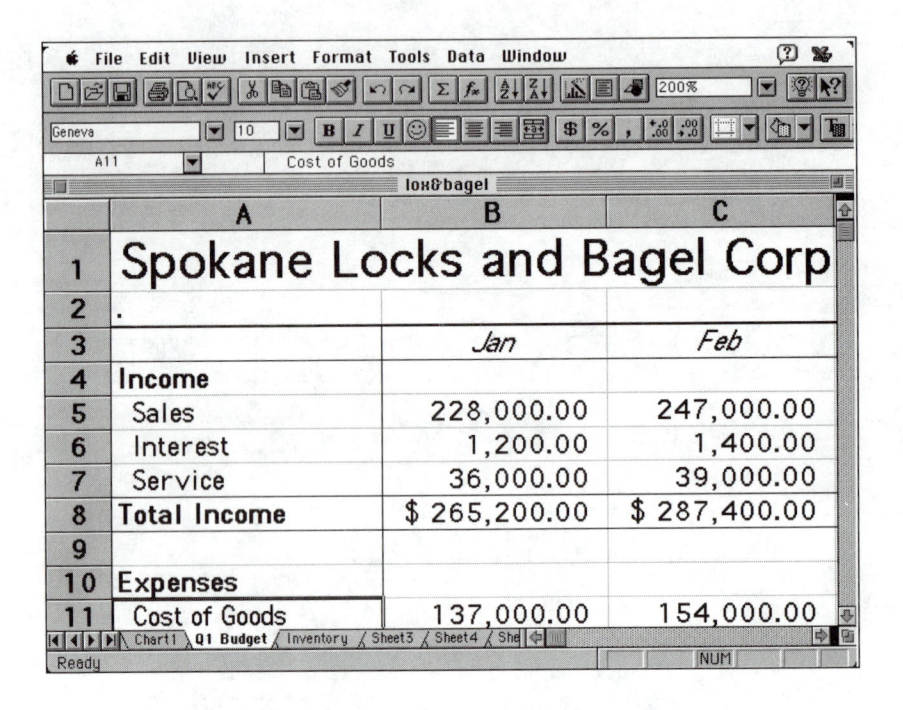

Figure 13.15 *An example of a 200% zoom*

Figure 13.16 shows the budget worksheet at a 75% zoom.

SHORTCUT

The zoom percentage you choose only affects the appearance of your screen. It has no effect on what will be printed. Also, zoom percentages are saved as a part of your named views in View Manager.

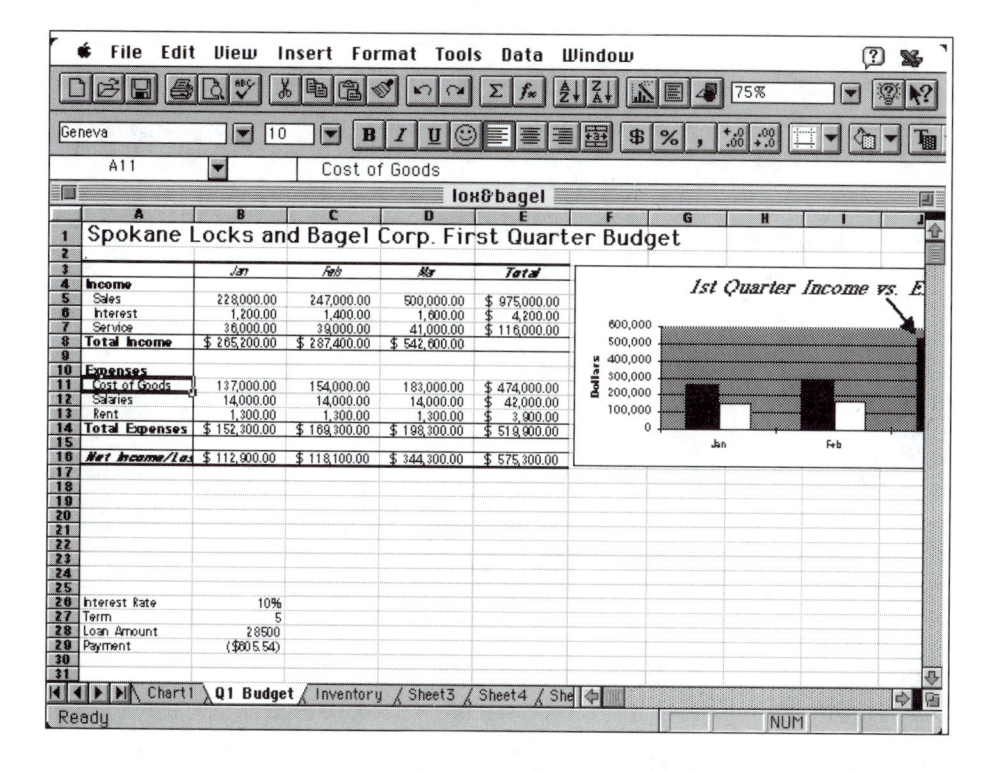

Figure 13.16 *The budget worksheet at 75% zoom.*

In addition to changing views with the View Manager and zooming, you can split windows vertically, horizontally, or both. You can also freeze the window panes to keep titles or other data in view.

The easiest way to split windows is by dragging the vertical or horizontal split box. Let's try it.

8. Position the mouse pointer over the horizontal split box (just above the up arrow of the vertical scroll bar) so it assumes the shape of a double-headed arrow, as shown in Figure 13.17.

9. Press the mouse button and drag down until the split bar is between rows 18 and 19, and then release the mouse button.

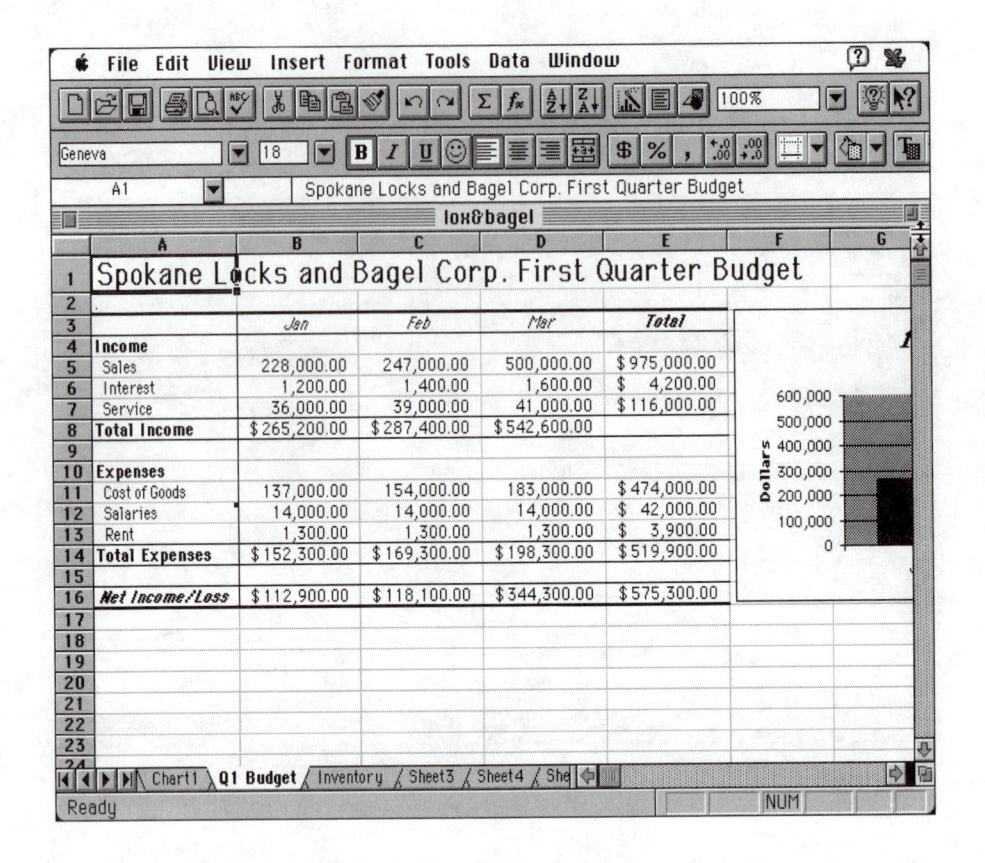

Figure 13.17 *The mouse pointer on the vertical split box.*

If the mouse pointer is in the worksheet area as you drag the split bar, the split bar jumps to each gridline as you drag. If you want to position the split bar between gridlines, drag the mouse pointer *inside* the scroll bar.

A split bar appears on the worksheet, along with a second vertical scroll bar, as shown in Figure 13.18.

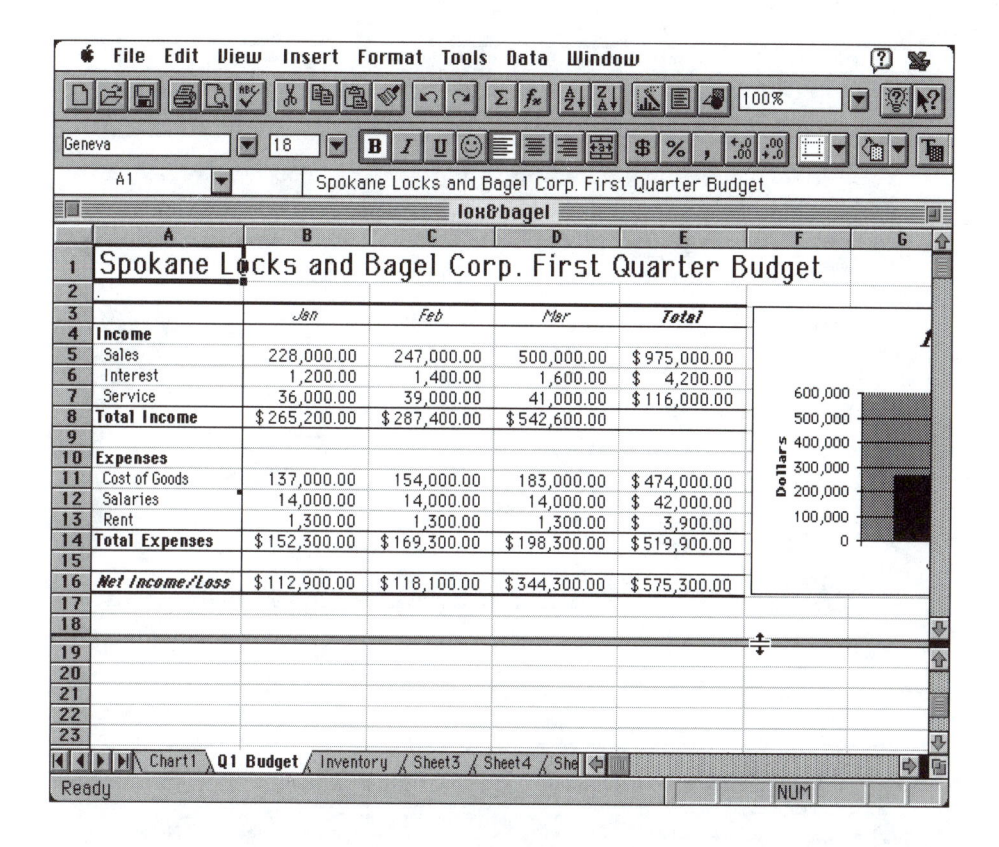

Figure 13.18 *The split bar splitting the worksheet.*

10. Click in the bottom pane and scroll down, using the bottom vertical scroll bar, until the payment data is visible, as shown in Figure 13.19.

    Let's remove the horizontal split and try using the vertical split.

11. Pull down the Window menu and select **Remove Split**, or just double-click on the **split bar**.

12. Position the mouse pointer over the vertical split box (just to the right of the horizontal scroll bar's right arrow) so it assumes the shape of a double-headed arrow.

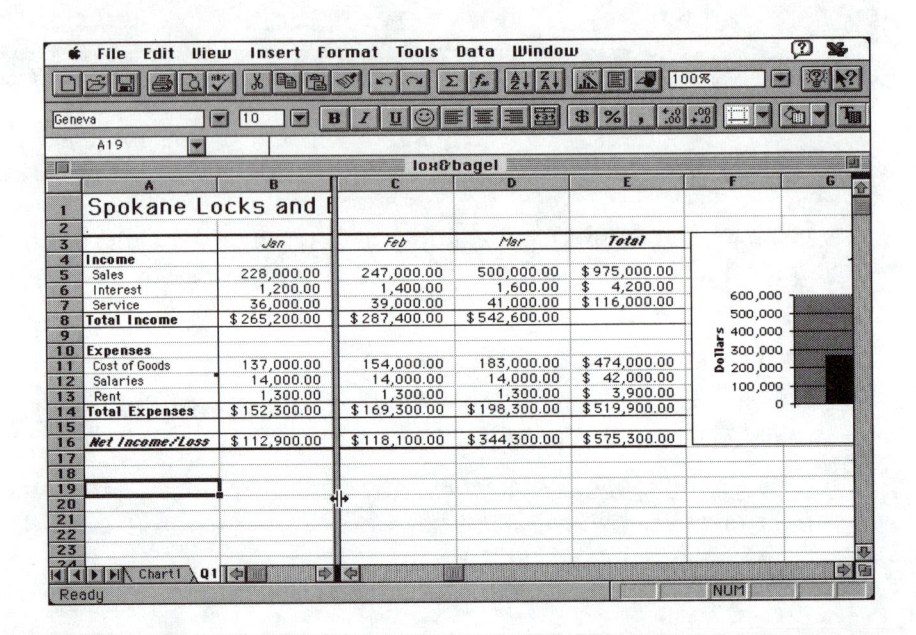

Figure 13.19 *The two panes scrolled to different positions.*

Figure 13.20 *A vertical split bar between columns B and C.*

14. Click on any cell on the right pane and use the horizontal scroll bar under that pane to scroll the chart into view, as shown in Figure 13.21.

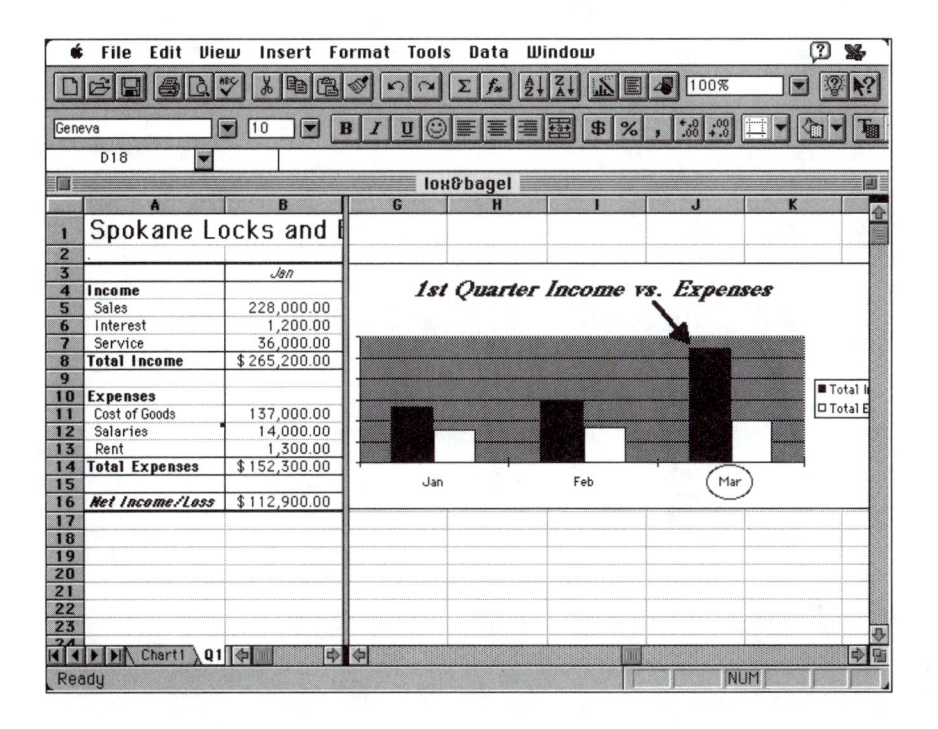

Figure 13.21 *The right pane scrolled so the chart is visible.*

15. Double-click on the **split bar** to remove the split.

A Final Thought

In this chapter, you learned to customize Excel in a variety of ways. You also learned to use View Manager, Zoom, and the split boxes to alter views of the worksheets.

In the next chapter, you'll learn about switching and customizing toolbars.

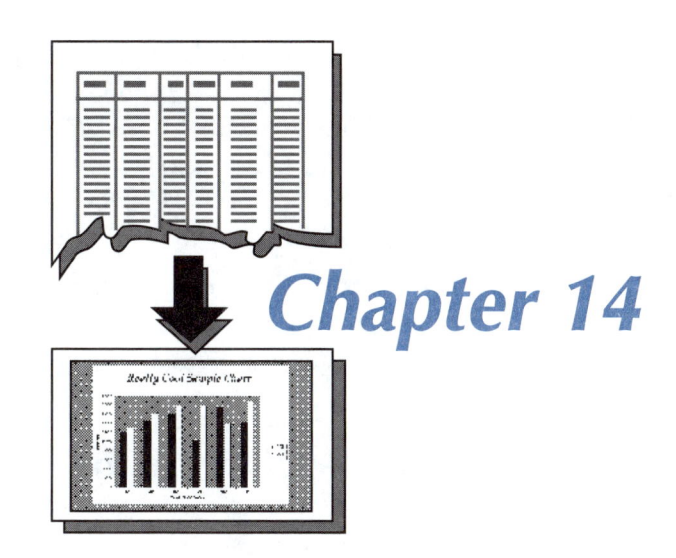

Chapter 14

Switching and Customizing Toolbars

- Display and Position Toolbars
- Create Custom Toolbars
- Design Custom Toolbar Buttons
- A Final Thought

As you've seen throughout this book, toolbars are often the fastest and easiest way to initiate Excel tasks. With a click of the mouse, you're off and running with an operation that might otherwise take several mouse clicks or keystrokes.

You can make toolbars even more useful by customizing them to include just the buttons you use most often for a particular type of operation, or by creating custom buttons.

Display and Position Toolbars

Excel automatically displays the Standard and Formatting toolbars and positions them at the top of the screen. You've also seen Excel display other toolbars such as the Query and Pivot toolbar when working with PivotTables, and you've displayed the Drawing toolbar by clicking on the **Drawing** button on the Standard toolbar.

Let's see how you can choose other toolbars and position them wherever you want them on the screen.

1. Start Excel if it isn't already running, and make sure there is a worksheet on your screen.

   You don't need to have any particular workbook open since we'll be displaying and moving toolbars without actually using the buttons.

   The shortcut menu is the fastest way to choose which toolbars are displayed on your screen. There is also a Toolbars dialog box which makes additional toolbars available, as well as a few extra options. We'll start with the shortcut menu.

2. Point to any toolbar button and press the **Ctrl** key while pressing the mouse button to display the toolbar shortcut menu, as shown in Figure 14.1.

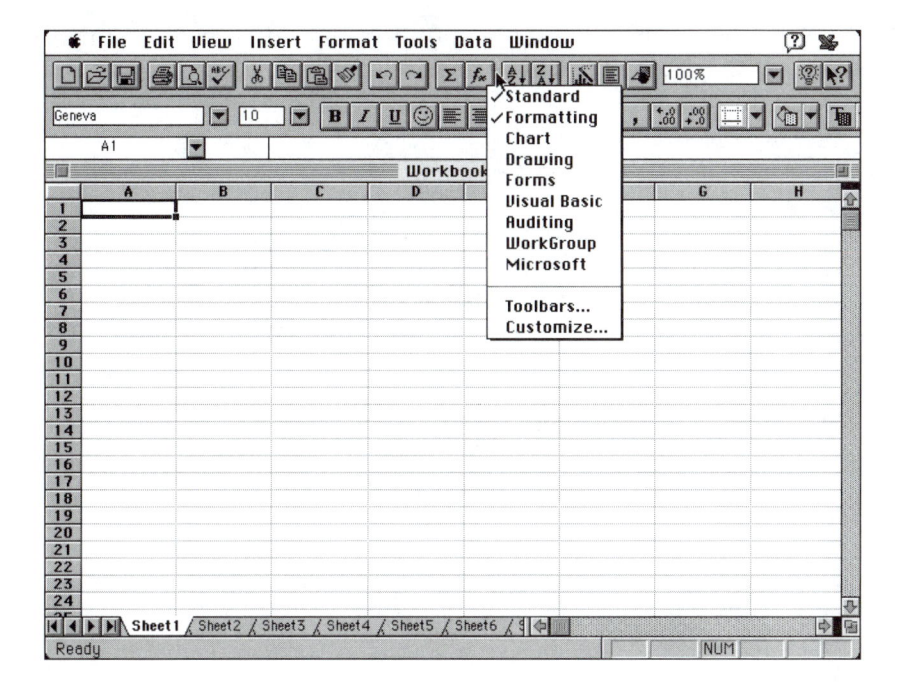

Figure 14.1 *The toolbar shortcut menu.*

The toolbars that are currently displayed have a check mark in front of their names on the shortcut menu. You can remove a toolbar from the screen by dragging down the shortcut menu to highlight its name and releasing the mouse button. If the toolbar name you drag to doesn't have a check mark, the toolbar will be displayed.

If you frequently switch to other Microsoft applications, you'll find that the Microsoft toolbar is one of the most useful and time saving toolbars included with Excel. Using this toolbar, you can instantly switch to any of your other Microsoft programs at the click of a button. Most newer Microsoft applications also have Microsoft toolbars available so you can easily switch from them back to Excel or another program.

We'll display the Microsoft toolbar now.

3. With the toolbar shortcut menu displayed, drag down to highlight **Microsoft** and release the mouse button to display the Microsoft toolbar shown in Figure 14.2.

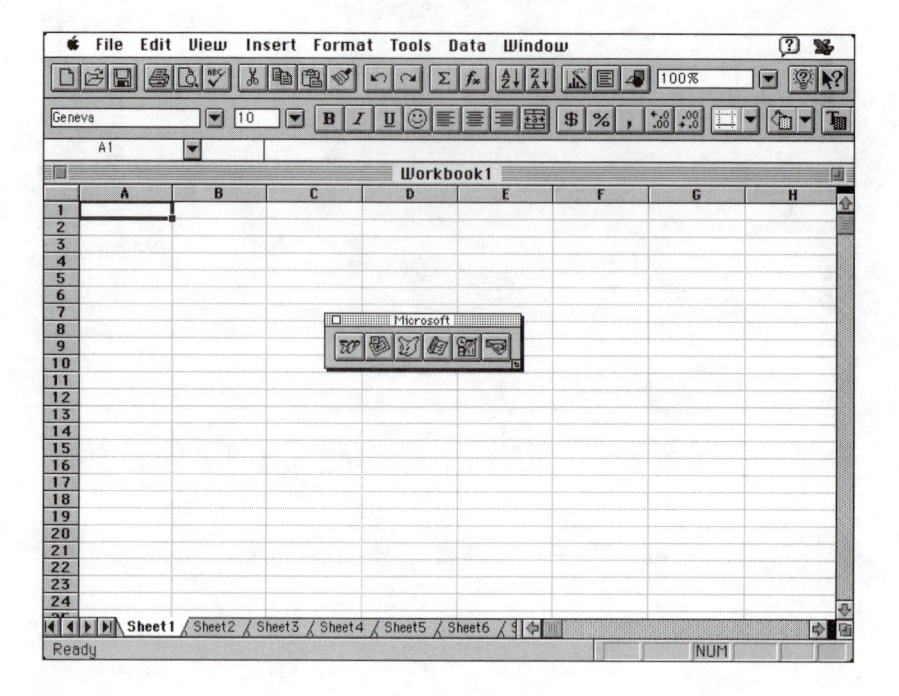

Figure 14.2 *The Microsoft toolbar.*

N O T E All the available toolbars with the functions for each of their buttons are listed in Appendix D. You can mix and match buttons to create your own custom toolbars, or create your own custom buttons.

As with other toolbars, you can see what the function of each of these buttons is by simply moving the mouse over a button and reading the ToolTip. The lower-left portion of the status bar displays a longer description of the button.

Toolbars can be moved by placing the mouse pointer on one of the areas between a toolbar border and the buttons and then dragging. However, if the toolbar is floating, it's easier to move it the same way you move other windows—dragging it by the title bar. You can remove a toolbar by clicking on its name in the shortcut menu or by simply clicking on a floating toolbar's close box in its upper-left corner.

Often, having a toolbar floating on the screen obscures important information or is distracting, even if you move it out of the way. One solution to this problem is to *dock* it in one of the docking positions.

There are four docking locations: the top, bottom, and both sides of the screen. In fact, the Standard and Formatting toolbars are docked at the top of the screen now. You can dock a toolbar by moving it to one of the docking areas. The exception is that you can't dock a toolbar to the left or right side of the screen if it has buttons with drop-down lists (such as the Zoom Control button on the Standard toolbar) or buttons with tear-off palettes (such as the Borders button on the Formatting toolbar).

The Microsoft toolbar doesn't have any drop-down lists or tear-off palettes, so let's dock it to the left side of the screen.

4. Drag the Microsoft toolbar by its title bar to the left side of the screen until you see a vertically-oriented outline of the toolbar. Then release the mouse button.

The Microsoft toolbar is now docked on the left side of the screen, as shown in Figure 14.3.

The vertical position depends on where the outline was when you released the mouse button. You can move the toolbar up or down by positioning the mouse over any space between the buttons and the edges of the toolbar.

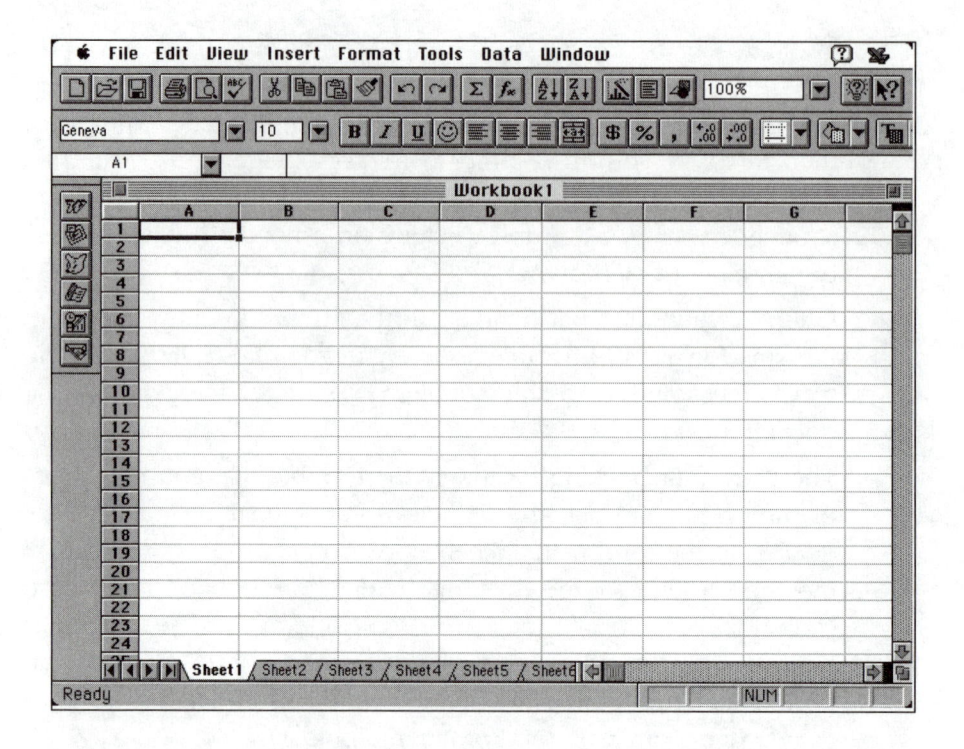

Figure 14.3 *The Microsoft toolbar docked on the left side of the screen.*

N O T E

For a toolbar with very few buttons such as this one, it's a good idea to position it at the top or bottom of the docking area to leave room for another toolbar, should you decide to add one.

The Standard and Formatting toolbars, which are docked, can be undocked or docked in another position by dragging them to where you want them. Let's undock the Formatting toolbar and position it as a floating toolbar near the top of the worksheet.

5. Move the mouse pointer into the Formatting toolbar (but not on top of a button) and drag it down so the top edge of its outline is just below the column headings. Now release the mouse button.

The Formatting toolbar should be positioned approximately like the one in Figure 14.4.

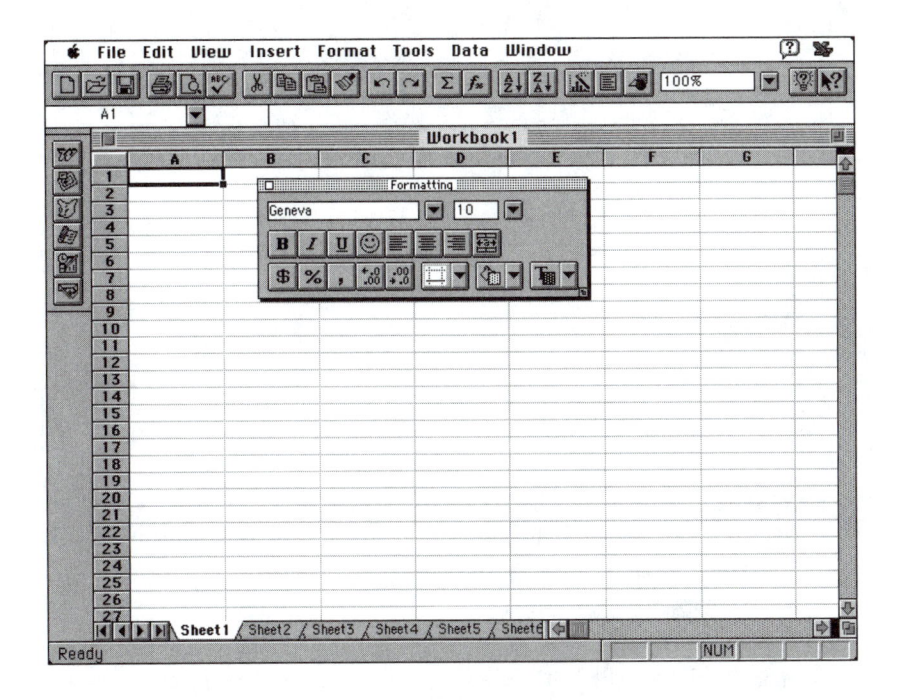

Figure 14.4 *The undocked Formatting toolbar positioned near the top of the worksheet.*

Now the problem is that the Formatting toolbar is taking up a large chunk of worksheet real estate, because it isn't as wide and short as it was in the docked position. There is a solution. Excel allows us to change the shape of the toolbar. Instead of three rows of buttons we'll change it so there are only two rows of buttons. Then the toolbar can fit more comfortably on the screen.

6. Position the mouse pointer over the size box in the lower-right corner of the toolbar and drag to the right about a quarter of an inch.

The Formatting toolbar should look approximately like the one in Figure 14.5.

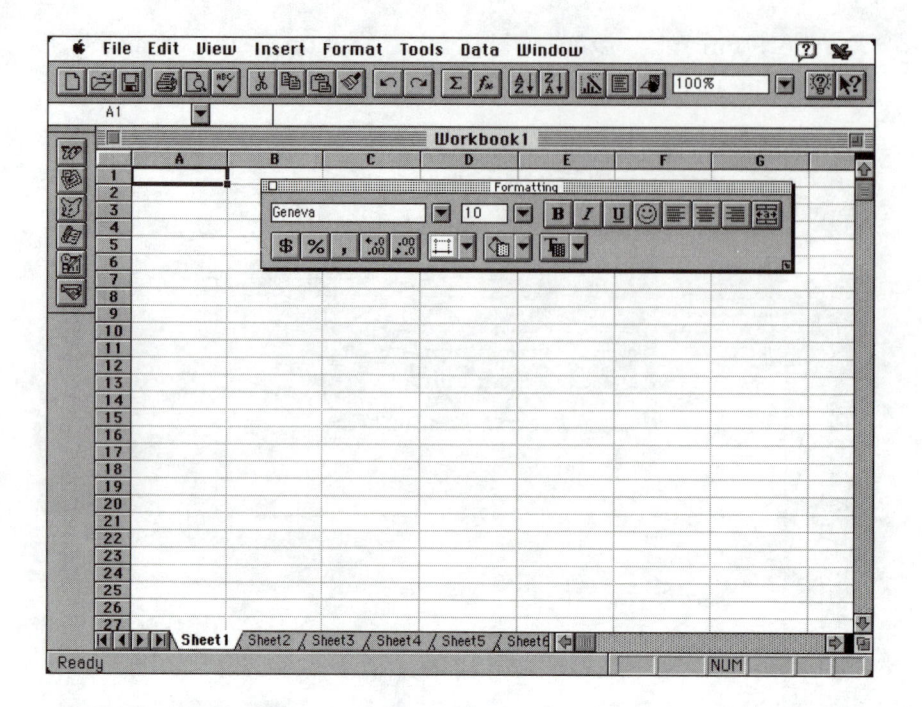

Figure 14.5 The resized Formatting toolbar.

Before moving on, let's dock the Formatting toolbar so it will be in its normal position the next time you use Excel.

7. Move the Formatting toolbar up to the top of its outline in the Formula bar, and release the mouse button to dock it below the Standard toolbar.

SHORTCUT

You can quickly dock a floating toolbar by double-clicking on its title bar or any area that isn't occupied by one of its buttons. You can undock a docked toolbar by double-clicking on any area that isn't occupied by a button.

Now let's check out the Toolbars dialog box, which is used to choose toolbars and change some of their options.

8. Pull down the View menu and select **Toolbars** to display the Toolbars dialog box, as shown in Figure 14.6.

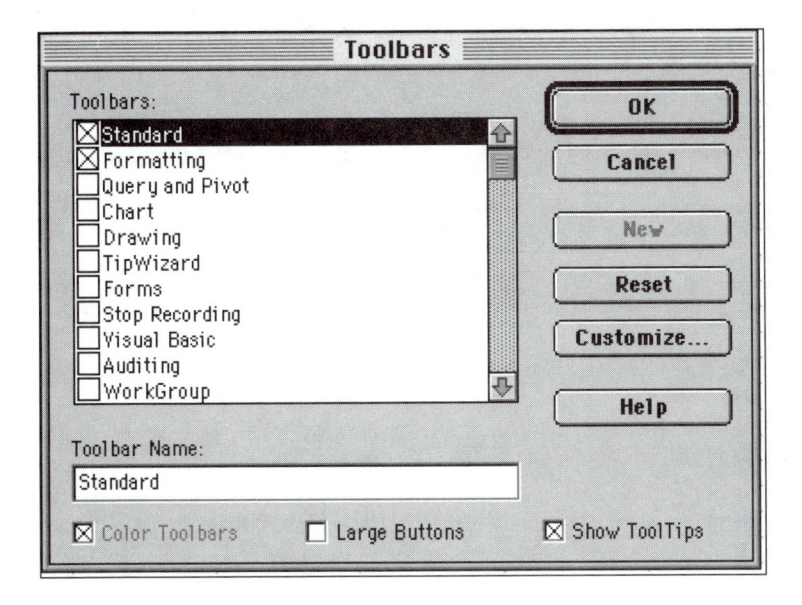

Figure 14.6 *The Toolbars dialog box.*

You can use the check boxes in the Toolbars dialog box to choose which toolbars to display. Notice that, if you use the scroll bar to scroll down the list of toolbars, there are more toolbars to choose from in the dialog box than are available from the shortcut menu.

The check boxes across the bottom of the Toolbars dialog box allow you to change several toolbar options.

The Color Toolbars check box lets you choose whether the toolbar button faces are displayed in color or black and white. If your Macintosh has a monochrome screen, this option is unavailable.

The Large Buttons option lets you display extra-large toolbar buttons. If you have difficulty discerning the detail of the buttons, choose **Large Buttons**. Try it now to see its effect.

9. Click on the **Large Buttons** check box and then click **OK** to enlarge all the toolbar buttons, as shown in Figure 14.7.

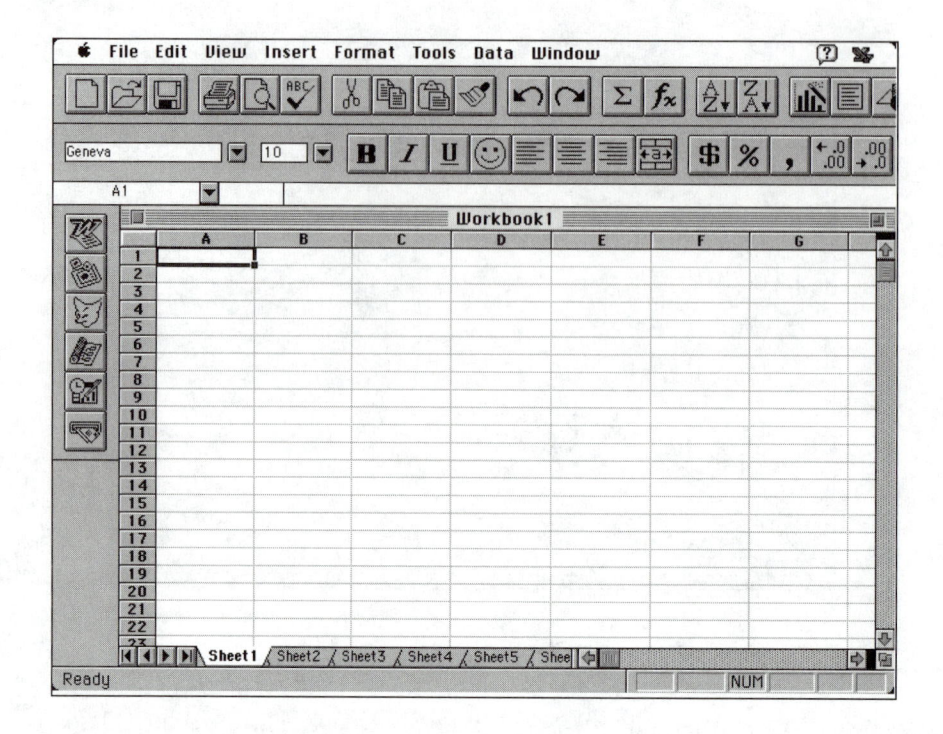

Figure 14.7 Large toolbar buttons.

N O T E

With large buttons, some of the buttons on some toolbars (such as the docked Standard and Formatting toolbars) aren't visible. If you want to display large buttons and have all of the buttons visible, just undock the toolbars. Of course that would create another problem—a great deal of your worksheet would be obscured by toolbars.

One way to solve this problem is to remove a few buttons so that all the remaining buttons are visible in their docked position. You'll learn how to do this in the next section—*Creating Custom Toolbars*.

Before we move on, let's return to normal-sized toolbar buttons.

10. Pull down the View menu and select **Toolbars**, or choose **Toolbars** from the toolbar shortcut menu to display the Toolbars dialog box.

11. Click on the **Large Buttons** check box to remove the check mark.

    Before closing the dialog box, let's talk about the last check box in the dialog box. The Show ToolTips check box lets you turn off the tooltips feature, which shows what a button does when the mouse pointer is positioned over it. My advice is to leave this option checked. I can't think of any reason why you'd want to turn this feature off.

12. Click **OK** to remove the dialog box and return the toolbars to their normal size.

Create Custom Toolbars

Now that you know how to display and position the toolbars supplied by Excel, let's look at how to customize toolbars. There are several ways to modify toolbars to suit the way you work. You can alter existing toolbars by adding, removing, or changing the position of buttons. You can also start from scratch with a new toolbar equipped with your choice of buttons.

With the Toolbars or Customize dialog box on the screen, you can remove or reposition any button on a toolbar that is currently displayed by simply dragging it:

- Off the toolbar
- To a new position on its toolbar
- To any other visible toolbar.

Let's try removing and repositioning some buttons. We'll use the Customize dialog box to perform some additional customization. Open the Customize dialog box by clicking the **Customize** button on the Toolbars dialog box, or from the toolbar shortcut button.

1. Position the mouse pointer over any toolbar and hold down the **Ctrl** key while pressing the mouse button to display the toolbar shortcut menu. Then drag down to **Customize** and release the mouse button to display the Customize the dialog box, as shown in Figure 14.8.

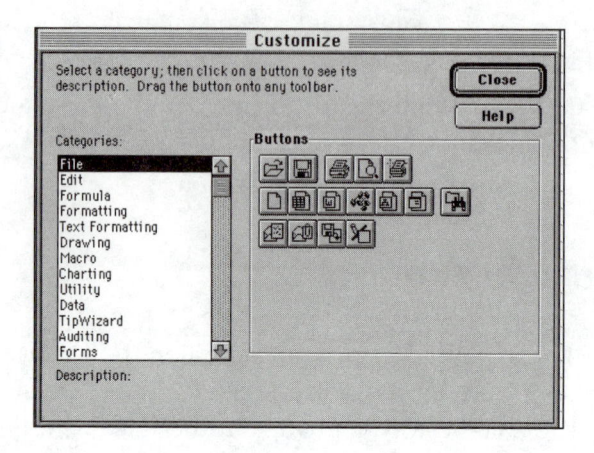

Figure 14.8 *The Customize dialog box.*

The Customize dialog box contains all the existing buttons you can use to add to a toolbar. The buttons are separated into logical categories to make it easy to find the button you want.

Before we add any buttons, let's make some room on the Formatting toolbar so we won't obscure any buttons when we add some new one to it.

Let's say you've decided that you don't need the Bold, Italic, and Underline buttons because you've memorized the keyboard shortcuts for these. (Okay, I'll tell you: ⌘+**Shift+B** for bold, ⌘+**Shift+I** for italic, and ⌘+**Shift+U** for underline.) We'll remove these buttons from the Formatting toolbar now. Let's also get rid of the Smiley Face button we added in the Macro chapter, if it's still on your Formatting toolbar.

2. Drag the **Bold** button from the Formatting toolbar onto the worksheet and then release the mouse button. Repeat the process for the Italic, Underline, and Smiley Face buttons so the toolbar looks like the one in Figure 14.9.

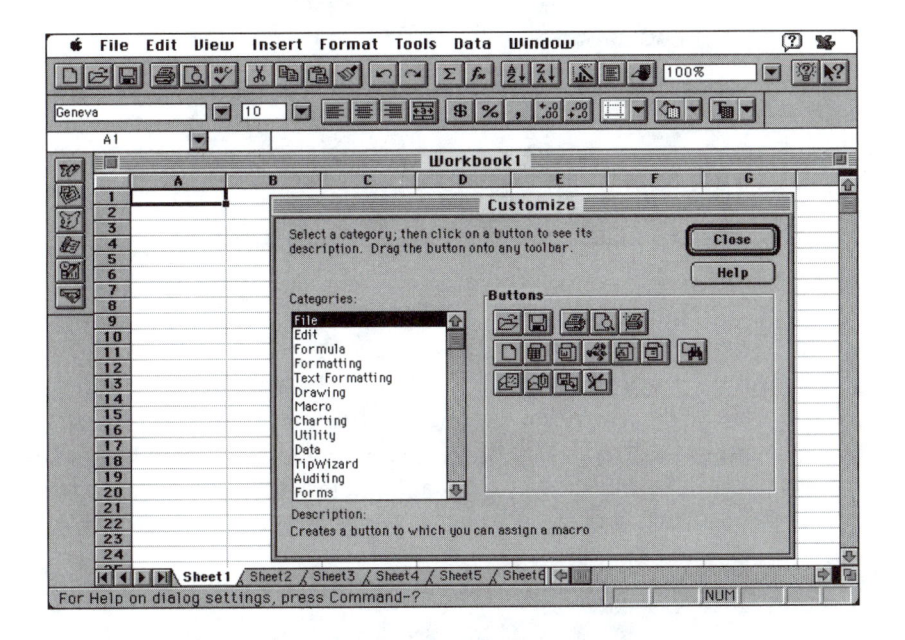

Figure 14.9 *The Formatting toolbar without the Bold, Italic, and Underline buttons.*

We'll add buttons for Double Underline, Strikethrough, and Rotate Text Down. All these buttons are in the Text Formatting category but you could, of course, add buttons from different categories.

3. Click **Text Formatting** in the Categories list to display the Text Formatting buttons, as shown in Figure 14.10.

NOTE

You can't see the ToolTips when you move the mouse pointer over a button in the Customize dialog box, but you can see a description of the button's function by clicking on it. The description appears in the Description area at the bottom of the dialog box.

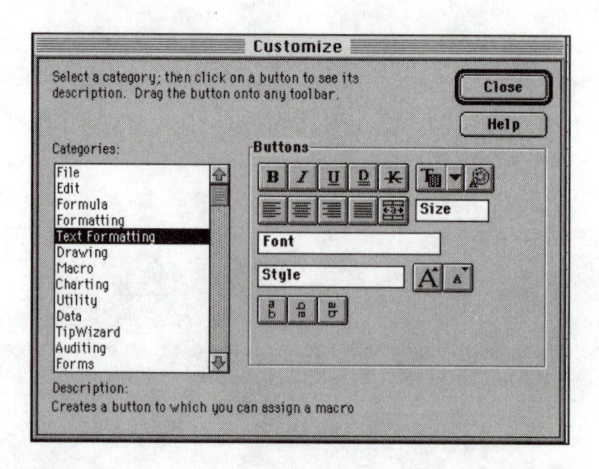

Figure 14.10 *The Text Formatting buttons.*

4. Drag the **Double Underline** button (a D with two lines under it; the description is *Double underlines selected text*) up to the Formatting toolbar, so its outline is between the Font Size and the Align Left buttons, as shown in Figure 14.11.

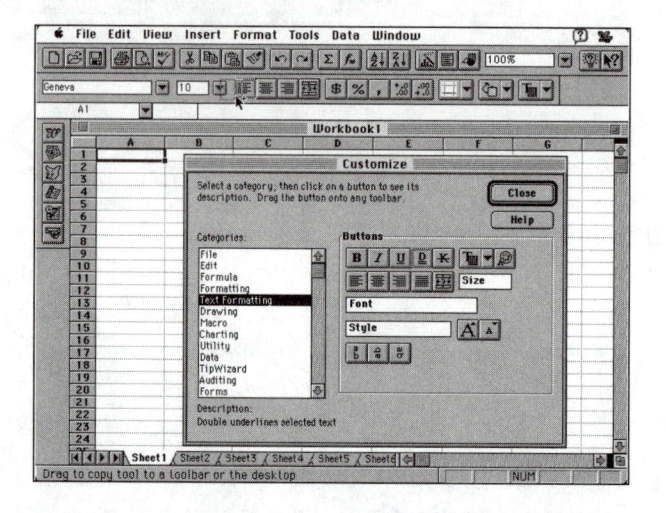

Figure 14.11 *The outline of the Double Underline button ready to be placed on the Formatting toolbar.*

5. Release the mouse button to accept the placement of the new button.

   If the button ended up to the left or right of its intended position, you can simply drag it left or right to reposition it where you want it.

6. Drag the **Strikethrough** button (a K with a line through it; the description is *Draws a line through selected text*) to the position just to the right of the Double Underline button and release the mouse button.

7. Drag the **Rotate Text Down** button (the button with *a b* on its side; the description is *Rotates text sideways, reading top to bottom*) to the position just to the right of the Strikethrough button and release the mouse button.

   The Formatting toolbar should now look something like the one in Figure 14.12.

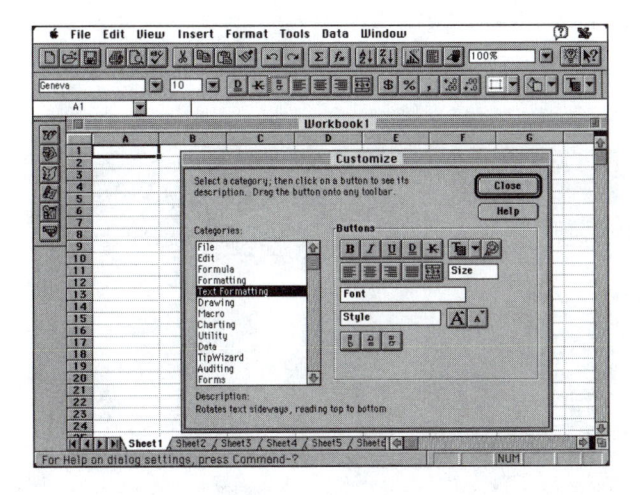

Figure 14.12 *The Formatting toolbar with its three new buttons.*

Now let's create a custom toolbar with just the buttons we want. We could just drag a button from the Customize dialog box onto the worksheet to create a new toolbar named Toolbar 1, Toolbar

2, etc. However, it usually makes more sense to enter a name for the new toolbar before creating it, which is done from the Toolbars dialog box.

8. Click on the **Close** button to remove the Customize dialog box from the screen.

9. Pull down the View menu and select **Toolbars**, or select **Toolbars** from the toolbar shortcut menu to display the Toolbars dialog box.

When you create a new toolbar, you'll want to choose a name that denotes the group or category of buttons you plan to add to it. If you are creating a toolbar with a conglomeration of buttons that don't relate to each other except for the fact that you want them on a toolbar, a name such as *My Toolbar* might be a good way to designate your toolbar. In fact, that's exactly what we'll do right now.

10. Select the text in the Toolbar Name text box by dragging the mouse over it and type: **My Toolbar**.

The Toolbars dialog box should look like the one in Figure 14.13.

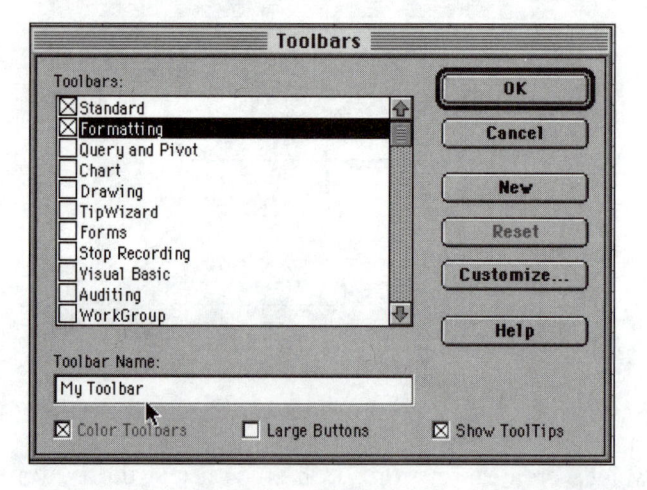

Figure 14.13 *The Toolbars dialog box with the name of our new toolbar entered in the Toolbar Name text box.*

Notice that as soon as you enter a name in the text box, the New button becomes available.

11. Click on the **New** button.

The blank new toolbar appears and the Toolbars dialog box switches to the Customize dialog box, as shown in Figure 14.14.

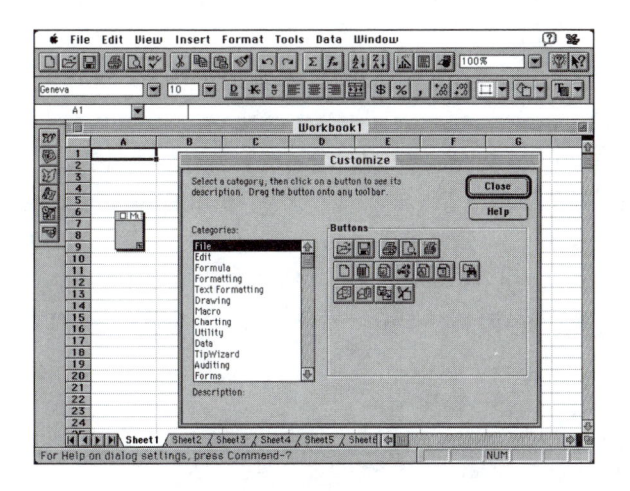

Figure 14.14 *The beginning of the new toolbar next to the Customize dialog box.*

N O T E

The toolbar will widen and lengthen as you add buttons to it. The way you see it now, it isn't wide enough to fit the entire title *My Toolbar*. If you only plan to add one or two buttons to a toolbar, use a very short name.

Let's add several buttons from different categories to the new toolbar. As you add them, don't worry too much about getting them positioned just right since you can always reposition them. Also, we are going to position the buttons in a single row, but if some of them end up stacked vertically, you can resize the toolbar by dragging a border.

12. From the File category of buttons, drag the **Open** button onto the new toolbar, and release the mouse button.

I know what you're thinking. The Open button is already on the Standard toolbar so why are we putting it on the new toolbar? Just because a button is already in use on one toolbar doesn't mean you wouldn't want it on another. If you are equipping *My Toolbar* with your most frequently used buttons so you won't need to display any other toolbars, you will very likely want to have several of the buttons from the Standard and Formatting toolbars on it.

13. Click on **Drawing** in the Categories list and drag the **Arrow** button (the description is *adds an arrow*) to the right of the Open button on the new toolbar, then release the mouse button.

14. From the Charting category, drag the **ChartWizard** button (the description is *Creates embedded chart or modifies active chart*) to the right of the Arrow button, then release the mouse button.

The new toolbar should now look something like the one in Figure 14.15

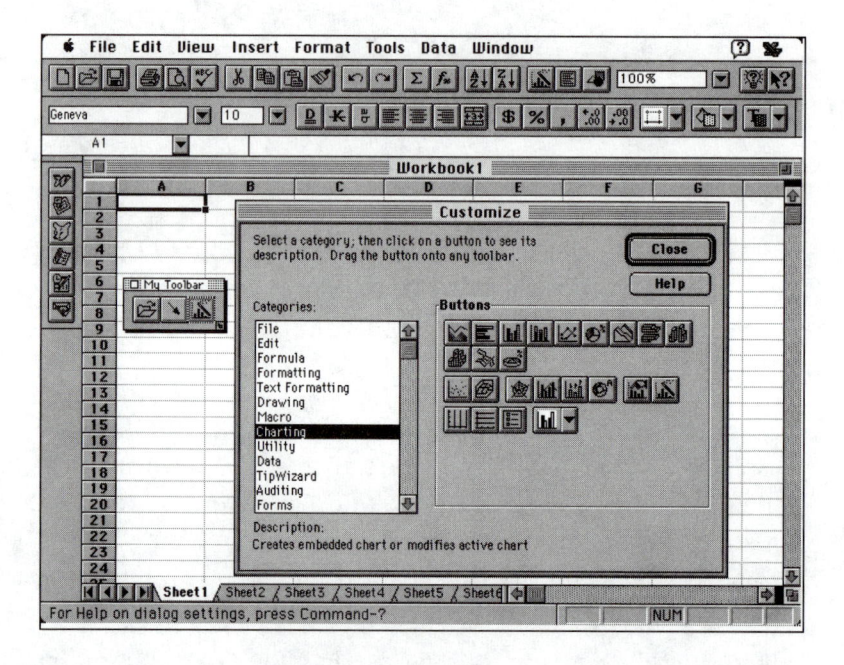

Figure 14.15 *My Toolbar with the three buttons added.*

The new toolbar is listed on the toolbar shortcut menu and in the Toolbars dialog box, so you can display and remove this toolbar from your screen as you would any other toolbar.

Let's leave the Customize dialog box on screen since we'll be using it in the next section.

Design Custom Toolbar Buttons

If putting together your own collection of buttons isn't enough customization for you, you can change the image of any button on any toolbar. The simplest approach, if you can find an existing image you like, is to copy the image to the button you want to change.

If you need an even more custom image than that, you can edit a button's image or design your own using the Button Editor or just about any other paint-type graphics program.

I'm not very creative when it comes to graphic design. On second thought, "not very creative" is an overstatement. Drawing stick figures is about as far as I got in art class. So don't expect any great-looking (or even good-looking) button images from these examples.

The first thing we'll do is replace the image of one of the buttons on *My Toolbar* with one from the Customize dialog box. To do this, click on the button you want to use in the dialog box and copy its image to the Clipboard, click on the button with the image you want to replace, then paste the image from the Clipboard. It's actually easier than it sounds.

Let's replace the image on the Open button with an image from the Custom category. The Custom category buttons are normally used to attach macros, as you learned in Chapter 11, *Automating Your Work with Macros*. However, we can copy any image we want. Since these don't already have functions assigned to them, they are a natural choice.

1. Scroll down the Categories list until the **Custom** category is visible, then click on it to display the Custom category buttons, as shown in Figure 14.16.

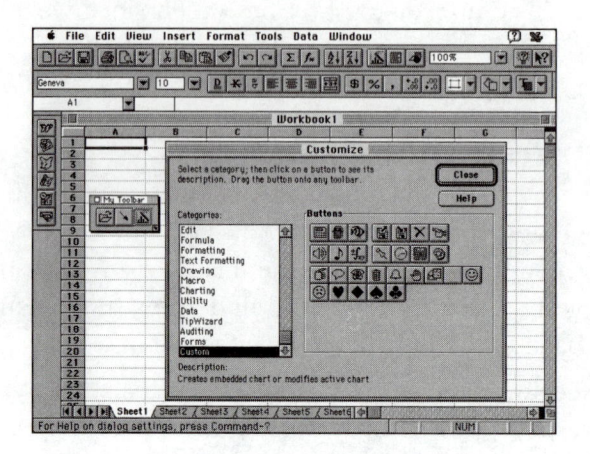

Figure 14.16 *The Customize dialog box with the Custom category buttons displayed.*

Let's use the heart image on the bottom row of buttons for our new image.

2. Click on the **heart** button just to the right of the frowning face button on the bottom row.

3. Pull down the Edit menu and select **Copy Button Image**.

   The heart image is now stored on the Clipboard, ready to be pasted on top of another button.

4. Click on the **Open** button on *My Toolbar*. Then pull down the Edit menu and select **Paste Button Image**.

   The Open button in *My Toolbar* should now look like the one in Figure 14.17.

   With the Customize or Toolbars dialog box open, pointing to a button, holding down the **Ctrl** key, and pressing the mouse button displays a special shortcut menu for customizing the button. Let's edit the heart button to customize it even further.

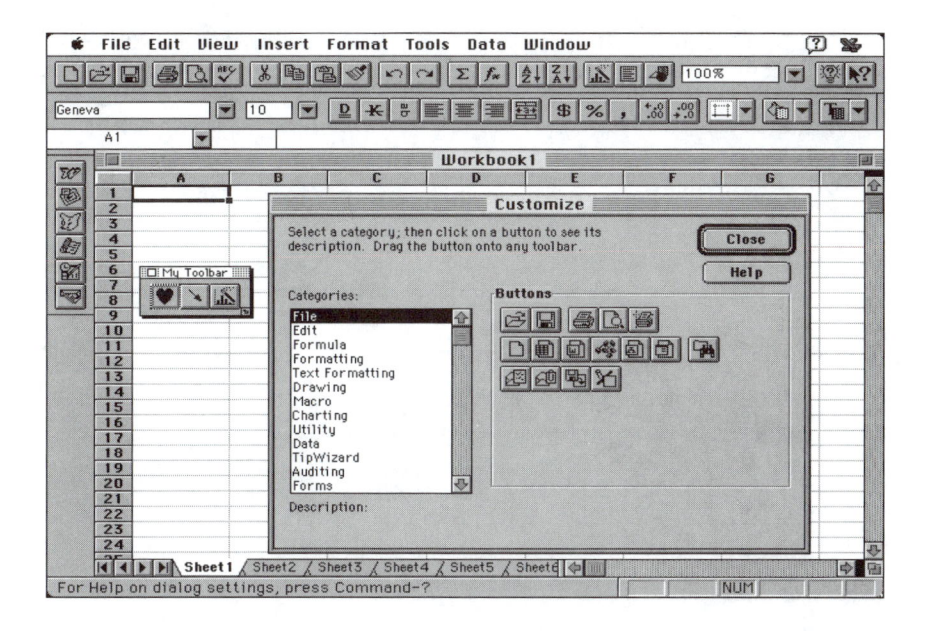

Figure 14.17 *Now My Toolbar has a heart.*

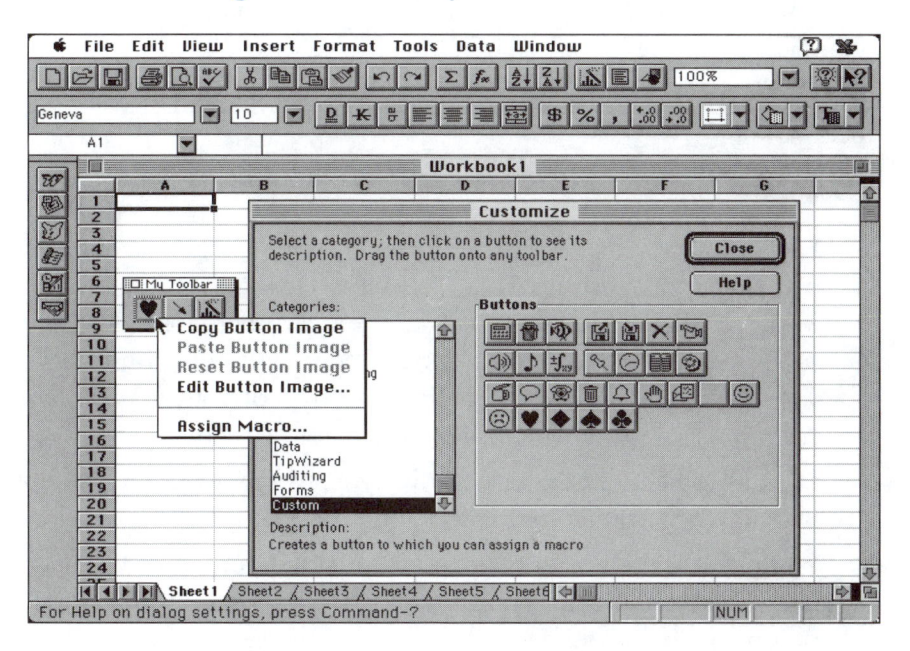

Figure 14.18 *The shortcut menu for customizing a button.*

5. Point to the heart button on *My Toolbar* and hold down the mouse button to right-click to display its shortcut menu, as shown in Figure 14.18.

6. Select **Edit Button Image** from the shortcut menu to display the Button Editor dialog box, as shown in Figure 14.19.

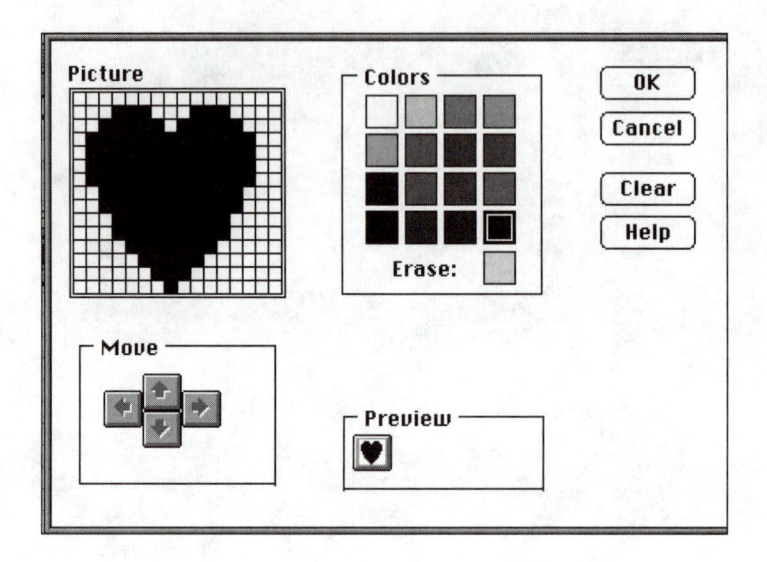

Figure 14.19 The Button Editor dialog box.

Each small box in the Picture portion of the dialog box represents one dot or pixel of the image. You can click on a color or shade in the Colors portion of the dialog box and then apply that color or shade to any dot in the picture simply by clicking on it. If you want to apply the color or shade to a series of dots, you can drag the mouse over the dots to paint the color or shade.

Clicking on the **Erase** box allows you to erase any of the dots that are filled with color by dragging or clicking on them.

You can use the arrow buttons in the Move portion of the dialog box to move the entire image up, down, left or right, if the image doesn't already extend to the edges of the Picture box.

The **Clear** button lets you remove the entire image so you can start fresh and create your own image.

Let's add a black horizontal line on the top and bottom rows and erase a few dots in the middle of the heart to create an open heart. Remember, I told you this wouldn't be too creative.

7. Click on the black box in the Colors portion of the dialog box and drag across the top and bottom rows of the Picture portion of the dialog box.

The Preview portion of the Image Editor dialog box shows, in actual size, what your button will look like as you edit it.

N O T E

8. Click on the **Erase** box and erase about nine dots in the middle of the heart so the Picture portion looks like Figure 14.20.

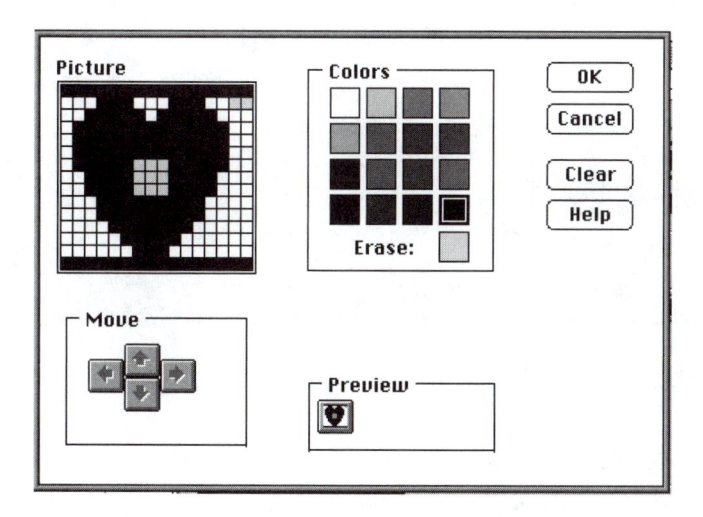

Figure 14.20 *The open heart with top and bottom borders.*

9. Click **OK** to close the Image Editor dialog box and accept the modifications.

10. Click on the **Close** button to remove the Customize dialog box.

The Image Editor doesn't offer a wide variety of graphics tools to create complex images. For me that's a good thing. However, if you want more design flexibility, consider using a more sophisticated paint-type program, such as MacPaint, to create an image. You can then copy your design to the clipboard and paste the image onto the button of your choice using the technique just described.

Before we finish this chapter, let's get the screen back to normal. We'll remove the Microsoft toolbar, delete *My Toolbar*, and reset the Formatting toolbar back to its original configuration.

11. Pull down the View menu and select **Toolbars** to display the Toolbars dialog box.

12. Scroll down the Toolbars list until you can see the Microsoft and My Toolbar check boxes.

13. Click on **My Toolbar** in the Toolbars list to remove the check mark and, if you want to delete the toolbar, click on the **Delete** button to display the message dialog box shown in Figure 14.21.

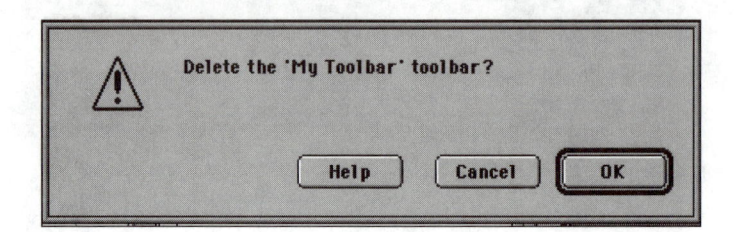

Figure 14.21 *The message dialog box to confirm the toolbar deletion.*

14. Click **OK** to confirm the deletion of *My Toolbar.*

15. Click on **Microsoft** in the Toolbars list to remove the check mark, so the toolbar won't be displayed when the Toolbars dialog box is closed.

16. Finally, scroll back up the Toolbars list and click on **Formatting** twice so it is still checked and highlighted. Then click on the **Reset button** to return it to it default setup.

17. Click **OK** to remove the Toolbars dialog box.

Your screen should be back to the way it looked before you started this chapter.

A Final Thought

In this chapter, you learned to display, position, and customize your toolbars to make them work as efficiently as possible for you. Don't forget to check out Appendix D for a complete listing of Excel's toolbars and their button functions.

In the next chapter, you'll learn about using other programs with Excel and why you might want to do so. You'll also learn the concepts and terminology of sharing data with other programs.

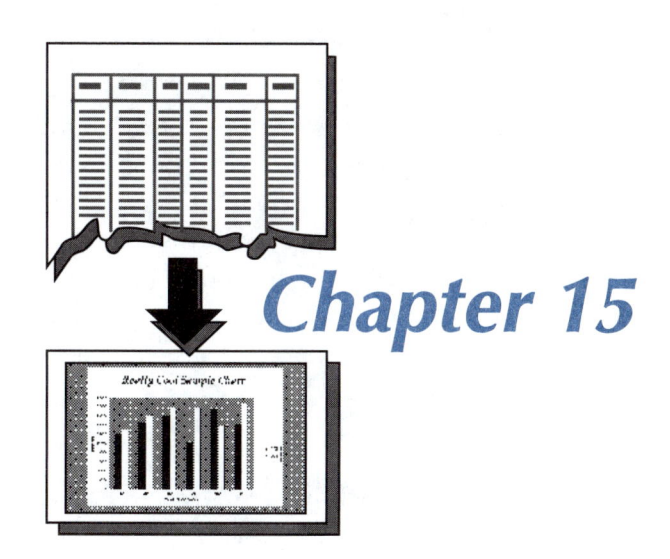

Chapter 15

Using Excel with Other Programs

- Why Use Other Programs with Excel?
- An Office Overview
- Choosing Which Office Program to Use
- What is OLE and Why Should I Care?
- Publishing and Subscribing
- A Final Thought

No program is an island (Gee, that sounds familiar). But seriously, few computer users rely solely on one program. If you are using Excel—and I think it's safe to assume you are since you're reading this book—chances are you have other programs at your disposal.

If you have Microsoft Office, which includes the Word word-processing program and the PowerPoint presentations program, you have the ability to create compound documents using parts of two or more of the programs.

Why Use Other Programs with Excel?

For as long as people have been creating paper documents, they've been adding bits and pieces of various types of information together—cutting out a picture from one place and pasting it into another, cutting out a chart here and pasting into a report there. In computer jargon, documents that include pieces from several applications are called *compound documents*.

The technology to create computerized compound documents has been like the Holy Grail—very elusive. Finding such a technology would mean far greater computer productivity. The possibilities seemed endless, but the search for a means to accomplish it seemed never-ending.

In several places throughout this book, I've mentioned the value of using other, more specialized, programs for accomplishing certain tasks. For example, you can create and edit toolbar buttons with the Button Editor. However, using a more flexible program, such as MacPaint, allows you greater freedom of expression and control.

Certainly Excel isn't the best tool for every job. It's an incredible spreadsheet program and excels at creating and formatting number-oriented documents. But when it comes to creating text-oriented documents, you'll want to use a word processing program with all the tools for formatting words such as Word.

Use the best tool for the job may just sound like common sense. And it is. Of course you use a word processing program if you are writing a report for your company proposing to hire some new employees for your department. You want to format the report to be as attractive—and persuasive—as possible.

But words alone probably won't make this proposal fly. The words will likely need to be backed up by some numbers demonstrating the various costs and benefits these proposed new employees will bring. I hope you know by now that the best tool for that job is a spreadsheet program such as Excel.

You could create and print the report with your word processing program. Then you could create and print a worksheet, and perhaps a chart for emphasis, from Excel and insert the worksheet and chart pages into the report. But imagine how much more professional-looking and convincing the report would be if the worksheet and chart were integrated into the body of the report.

Right there, smack dab in the middle of a beautifully formatted word-processed page, you place your worksheet and your chart, as if you had used scissors and paste, but without the muss and fuss. And the worksheet and chart can be linked to the report document so that, when the data is changed in the worksheet, the changes are instantly reflected in the report.

An Office Overview

Microsoft Office is a combination, or *suite*, of programs including Excel, Word, and PowerPoint. Word is a word processing program. Word processing is the single activity performed by more computer users than any other. From simple memos to complex reports or even books, word processing programs provide the tools for entering, formatting, and editing text, and printing documents.

PowerPoint is a presentation graphics program that provides all the tools necessary to create dazzling presentations using overhead transparencies, 35mm slides, or your computer screen.

There are some tremendous advantages to using Office instead of a mish-mosh of programs from other companies. First, all the Office programs are arguably the best programs available in their respective categories.

As you work with the Office programs, you'll find that several major consistencies jump out at you. The menus for the programs are almost identical. Of course, the options within the menus are appropriate for the particular program you're working with. Microsoft also ensures that dialog boxes, toolbars, shortcut menus and program help all operate consistently. There's even a consistent shortcut for switching among the Office programs. There are also hundreds of minor consistencies that give the suite a unified feel.

This consistency makes learning the second and third programs much easier than the first. After you've learned any one of the programs, you'll find yourself guessing, often correctly, about how to perform a task in one of the other programs. After a short while it all starts to feel natural and automatic.

The Right Tool for the Job

Deciding which of the Office programs to use for a particular task or project is the first—and often the most difficult—challenge. There is some overlap in capabilities, so many projects could be completed using any of the programs. Choosing the best one for the job, however, makes the job go more smoothly and gives you greater flexibility to do it the way you want.

Picking the correct program might seem to be a matter of common sense—working with words, use Word; manipulating numbers, use Excel; creating a presentation or a chart, use PowerPoint. Well, it's not quite that easy because there's a shared set of capabilities among the members of the office ensemble.

Word, for example, has a table feature for manipulating rows and columns, and can even perform calculations like Excel. Word also has the ability to create charts. Excel, in addition to its extensive number-handling capability, can also create dazzling charts. You may find the need for a specialized database program; however, Word and Excel each have the ability to create databases and to sort and select portions of the database that meet certain criteria. PowerPoint also lets you work with text and create charts.

The path to the best choice becomes even murkier when you take into account the ability to link portions of any of these programs to any other. So how do you decide?

As a general rule, Word is the best choice for primarily text-oriented documents. When you need to work extensively with numbers and calculations, Excel is usually the preferred tool. Excel also makes the most sense for charts, especially those that reflect data in an Excel spreadsheet. PowerPoint is normally the tool you'll turn to for presentations that pull together elements from the other two programs.

Ultimately, the best advice I can give is to learn the capabilities, strengths and weaknesses of all the Office programs. It also helps if you know what elements you'll want to include in your document. If you know what the programs can do and what you want to accomplish, choosing the right one can be as easy as picking socks to go with your shoes.

The following are some more concrete examples of tasks, and which program is best suited to each job.

Word makes putting together almost any written document a breeze. From business and personal letters to book-length manuscripts, simple memos to annual reports to almost any legal document, Word has the tools to make them appear just the way you want.

For number-oriented documents, from simple household budget worksheets to forecasts for multi-national corporations, from a cash flow analysis for a sandwich shop to a portfolio analysis for a multi-million dollar pension fund, Excel provides tools for deftly manipulating the numbers to answer the questions you are posing and find the best solutions when you are wondering *what if....*

Excel is also the first place to turn when you want to transform the numbers from your Excel worksheets into charts. A column chart showing the relationship between income and expenses is a sure way to clarify the numbers. A pie chart to compare the contribution each division is making to the company makes a stronger statement than numbers alone. A line chart showing the ups and downs of the various investments in the pension fund can help make better choices than staring at a bunch of numbers.

The word-oriented documents created in Word, the number-oriented worksheet documents created in Excel, as well as the related charts, can all be used as parts of a presentation. The point of most documents created in Word and Excel is to persuade and enlighten, so it makes sense that by simply putting them together you can create a persuasive presentation. True enough. But if we want to use the right tool for the job (that is the heading after all), PowerPoint is the likely choice.

Let's say you're making a presentation to the board of directors to convince them to recommend the acquisition of another company. You might use Word to create an analysis of the proposed acquisition, but you could also use salient portions of the analysis, as well as Excel charts, to create slides for the presentation. Within PowerPoint itself, you might add slides with bulleted lists of important points, as well as speaker's notes to use during the presentation.

PowerPoint lets you add music, digitized speech, and even video clips to create a multi-media presentation with the kind of production values you would expect to find in a Pepsi commercial. If you can't convince the board with all those tools at your disposal, maybe it's time to move on to the next project.

The next two sections describe some of the nifty new features in the latest versions of Word and PowerPoint.

 As of this writing, the new versions of Word and PowerPoint that have the consistent interface I've referred to have not been released. They should be available shortly.

A Quick Look at Word

When it comes to word processing programs, there are none with more capabilities—combined with incredible ease of use–than Microsoft Word 6.0. This new version includes all the features you expect in a world-class word processing program. However, some of its new features truly set this program apart from the competition.

Almost Unlimited Undo

If you're as prone to mistakes as I am, this feature alone is worth the price of admission. In the last version of Word, you could only undo the last thing you did. If you didn't realize the error of your ways until you did a few more editing steps, you were out of luck.

Version 6.0 keeps track of the last 100 changes you made to your document, and you can undo any individual change or sequence of changes. You can also redo any series of changes you undid.

AutoCorrect

This feature actually corrects your mistakes automatically as you type them. No human intervention is required, which suits me just fine. Suppose you have a nasty habit of typing *teh* instead of *the*, or *recieve* instead of *receive*. AutoCorrect automatically corrects these and many other common mistakes as soon as you press the spacebar.

AutoCorrect can also ensure that the first letter of each sentence and the names or days, such as Monday, Tuesday, etc. are capitalized. You can also add your own mistakes to the list of items so they will be automatically corrected.

AutoText

This feature is similar to the Glossary feature in the previous version of Word. You can use AutoText to store text passages or graphics and then retrieve them with a mouse click or keystroke.

AutoFormat

Wouldn't it be great if you had your own personal design expert to format your documents tastefully? Word does! AutoFormat can analyze your document and apply the formatting it thinks is best suited to the content. Of course, AutoFormat doesn't always make a good guess, so you have the opportunity to choose from several format templates, or reject the changes altogether.

Shortcut Menus

Just as in Excel, holding down the **Ctrl** key and pressing the mouse button while pointing to almost any object on the Word screen displays a shortcut menu of options for manipulating that object. This can be a tremendous time saver. Rather than using a variety of menus to find the appropriate options, they are right there in one place. The other Office applications also make use of shortcut menus.

Wizards

Word's Wizards present you with a series of dialog boxes to aid in creating a variety of types of documents. You can create the structure for several types of letters, memos, newsletters, fax covers, and tables by simply answering questions in the Wizard's dialog boxes. With Wizards, you can create sophisticated documents, even if you don't know how to use most of the features involved in their creation.

A Quick Look at PowerPoint

If you make presentations, whether to small or large groups, you'll wonder how you ever got along without PowerPoint. This program provides all the tools necessary to create dazzling presentations using overhead transparencies, 35mm slides, or your computer screen.

Your presentations can incorporate text, charts, graphics, and even sound and video, if your computer has the equipment to add these niceties. You can print your presentation to hand out to your audience. You can also create speaker's notes to help the presenter remember what to say as the slide show progresses.

Of course, you can also easily incorporate documents and pieces of documents created in your other Office programs into your presentations.

One of PowerPoint's best features is the way it can lead you by the hand through the entire process of creating a presentation. All you need to worry about is what exactly you want to present, and PowerPoint does the rest.

Even if you've never used the previous version of PowerPoint and have no idea where to begin creating presentations, there's no need to panic. PowerPoint makes creating presentations easy, even for novice users. And, as Microsoft points out, if you know how to use Excel 5.0 or Word 6.0, you already know how to perform over 100 tasks in PowerPoint.

In addition to the new features that have been added to Word and Excel—such as shortcut menus for any object on the screen, ToolTips, and Wizards—PowerPoint 4.0 adds a number of unique features.

The AutoContent Wizard

Word and Excel have Wizards, but PowerPoint's AutoContent Wizard is special. This Wizard provides you with a brief interview and then creates your entire presentation for you—almost. Just add your own specific text, add any graphic objects, change the look with the Pick a Look Wizard, and your presentation is complete.

The Pick a Look Wizard

The Pick a Look Wizard guides you through the formatting of your presentation so you'll end up with one that looks professionally designed.

The ClipArt Gallery

The ClipArt Gallery provides a new, easier way to add the expanded collection (over 1,000 pieces) of included graphics to your presentations. Just pick from the groups of thumbnail sketches.

Free Rotate

You can now freely rotate text or other objects 360 degrees. You can also edit rotated text and objects.

Freehand Drawing

As you give electronic presentations on your computer screen, you can use the freehand drawing tool to add temporary annotations to your slides.

Some PowerPoint Terminology

- *Slides* are the heart of every presentation you create in PowerPoint and can be presented as overheads, 35mm slides, or electronically on screen. Slides can contain text, graphics, charts, and even sound and video.

- *Outlines* contain the text of your slide presentation. You can enter text for your slides directly on the slides or in the outline.

- *Speaker's notes* provide the presenter with a page that corresponds to each slide. It contains a small image (thumbnail) of the slide, along with any additional notes.

- *Audience handouts* are printed copies of your presentation. You can have two, three, or six slides per handout page and you can add additional elements, such as other text or graphics. For example, you might want each page of the handout to include your company logo.

- *Placeholders* let you quickly add the type of element you're likely to want in a particular portion of the slide. When you pick a layout for your presentation, placeholders for such elements as text, graphics, and charts are included. Just click or double-click in the placeholder (depending on the type of placeholder) to add or edit the element.

- *Objects* are the individual elements that make up presentations. Text elements—such as titles or bulleted lists, graphics, and charts—are each individual objects and can be moved, sized, rotated, and even overlap other objects in a presentation.

What is OLE and Why Should I Care?

There are four ways to insert information from another program into a document:

- *Paste* from the Clipboard
- *Embed* an object
- *Link* an object, or
- *Subscribe* to a published edition.

NOTE The specific steps for sharing data between programs is beyond the scope of this book. Information about using OLE (Object Linking and Embedding) and Publishing and Subscribing can be found in Excel's help system and Excel's printed documentation.

When you select information in a document and then choose **Edit**, **Cut** or **Edit**, **Copy** (or use a keyboard shortcut or toolbar button to cut or copy), the information is stored on the *Clipboard*. The Clipboard is a temporary holding area that stores information until you cut or copy something else. The Clipboard only holds the last thing you cut or copied, and overwrites it with the next thing you cut or copy.

You can retrieve the Clipboard's contents by positioning your insertion point (or active cell) where you want the information to go—whether in a different location in the same document, a different document in the same program, or even a document in a different program—and then choosing **Edit**, **Paste**.

Cutting or copying and then pasting information is simple and straightforward, but has some limitations. Typically, the information you paste is treated as ordinary text or graphics that either can't be edited at all, or must be edited using the available tools of the program in which you pasted it.

In Chapter 12, *Linking Worksheets*, you learned how to use a simple form of linking to tie several source worksheets to a dependent worksheet. This is a valuable form of linking, but is only the beginning.

OLE—The Answer is Here

OLE, which is supported by all the main Office applications, has every-thing computer users have been searching for—almost. Linking informa-tion between programs is easier and more straightforward than ever before.

Perhaps best of all is the way you can edit embedded objects. Embedded objects can now be edited in place, sometimes called *visual editing*. With in-place editing, you edit the object right in the document where it's embedded, surrounded by the other parts of the document. This way you can see your edits in context, which greatly enhances efficiency.

When you edit an embedded object, the menus and toolbars of the application the object was *created* is replaced with the menus and tool-bars of the application the object is created in. You're able to edit the embedded object without ever leaving the document.

Documents using OLE require more of your computer's resources than simple documents created in one application. If you have a slower Mac with relatively little memory, you may be better off avoiding OLE. Trying to create compound docu-ments with your slower computer may take more time and patience than it's worth.

However, the benefits of OLE are so compelling that you would be wise to upgrade or replace your computer so you have enough muscle to make working with OLE bearable!

Linking or Embedding? That's the Question

When creating a compound document, the first decision you have to make is whether to link the data to or embed the data in the document. Let's take a look at the differences.

Linking places a representation of the data from one document in another. The primary advantage is that the data in the representation is updated when the data in the source document is updated.

Linking would be the right choice if you were putting a portion of an Excel worksheet, such as a budget, into a Word document where you wanted to be certain the Word document always reflected the latest budget numbers.

One disadvantage to linking is that the data isn't quite as easy to edit. You don't have the advantage of in-place editing. When you double-click on the linked data, the source document appears in its original application. It's not a big problem, just a bit less convenient.

Another disadvantage to consider is that the document containing the source data must be available in order to edit the linked data. If you delete the source document, you won't be able to edit the linked data.

Choose *embedding* if you don't need the data updated from a source document. A graphic image, such as clip art, wouldn't usually have to be updated and is a perfect candidate for embedding.

Embedding makes your work easier by allowing in-place editing. The menus and toolbars are replaced with the menus and toolbars of the application in which the embedded document was created. In the example of an Excel worksheet in a Word document, the Word menus and toolbars would be replaced with the Excel menus and toolbars, allowing you to edit the worksheet data in the context of the Word document, but using Excel's tools.

The primary disadvantage of embedding is that it makes the document larger by roughly the size of the source document. For example, if you embed a 15,000-byte Excel worksheet into a 15,000-byte Word document, the result is a Word document of about 30,000 bytes. Linking, on the other hand, adds very little to the size of the document.

Publish or Perish

In addition to using OLE for linking and embedding, all the Office applications and many other Macintosh programs allow you to share data using the *Publish* and *Subscribe* methods. When you *publish* a selected portion of a document you make it available to another program or even another user on a network. The other program or user can then *subscribe* to the edition that has been published.

Publishing and subscribing is similar to linking in OLE. In fact, the published edition can be updated so the subscriber always has the latest data. The primary advantage to publishing and subscribing compared with OLE is that most recent Macintosh programs support this technology. However, very few programs other than the Office programs support OLE. Also, publishing and subscribing is often the best way to share data across a network.

A Final Thought

In this chapter, you learned some of the basic concepts of using Excel with other programs, and using OLE and publishing and subscribing to share data between applications. This just scratches the surface of Excel's ability to work with other programs. You'll find that combining Excel with other programs adds up to more than the sum of the programs and greatly enhances your ability to create complex documents.

Of course, there are no limits to the ways you can work with Excel, and you should now have a good start on that journey of exploration. I hope this book has helped you to gain the skill and confidence to produce usable worksheets that will make your life easier and more enjoyable.

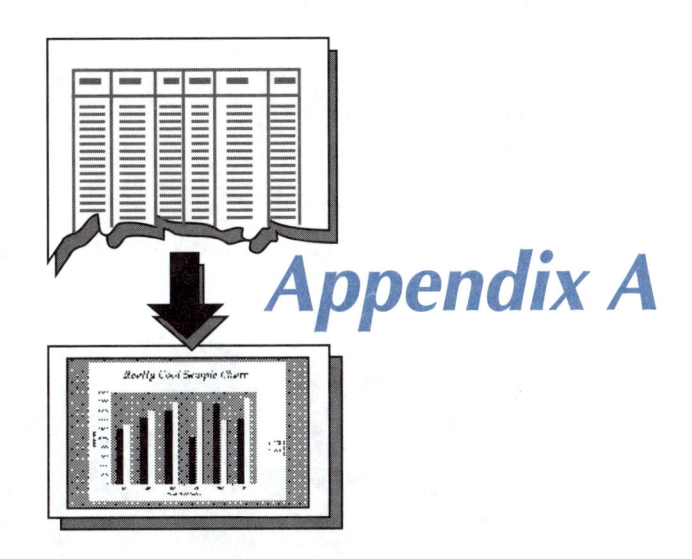

Installing And Optimizing Excel

Installing Excel

Those nice folks at Microsoft have made installing Excel just about automatic. In this appendix, you'll learn to install Excel on your computer.

NOTE These instructions assume you are installing Excel on a stand-alone computer (one not connected to a network). If you are on a network, contact your network administrator for instructions on installing using Excel.

To start the installation process:

- Insert Microsoft Excel Disk 1 into the floppy drive.

  An icon for Install Disk 1 appears, as shown in Figure A.1.

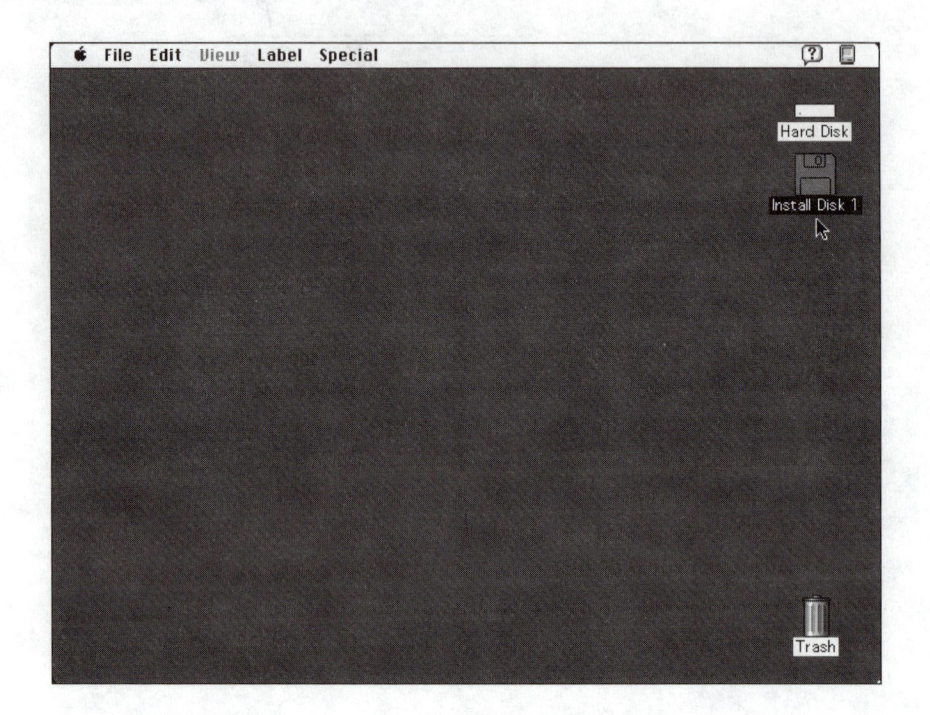

Figure A.1 *The Mac desktop with the icon for Excel Install Disk 1.*

- Double click on the **Install Disk 1** icon to open it, as shown in Figure A.2.

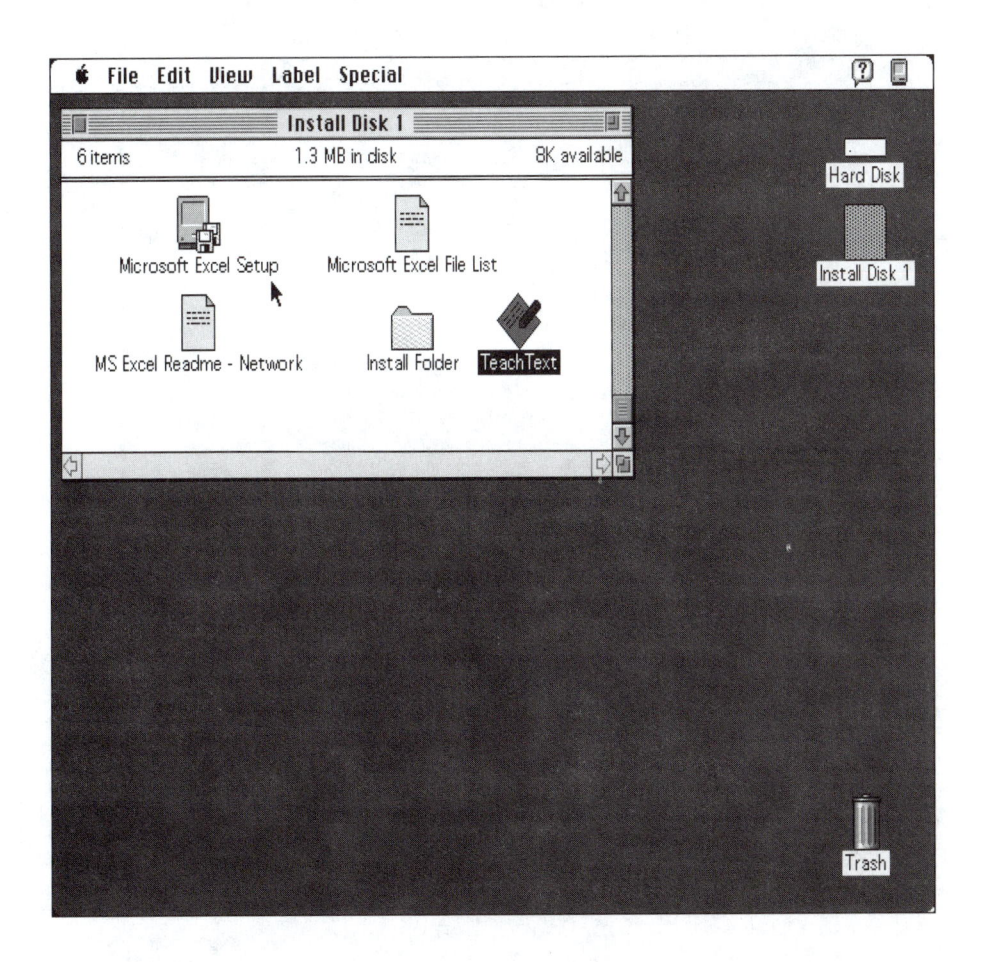

Figure A.2 *The icons for setting up Excel.*

- Double click on the **Microsoft Excel Setup** icon.

  After a short time, Excel displays the Microsoft Excel 5.0 Setup dialog box, as shown in Figure A.3.

Figure A.3 *The Microsoft Excel 5.0 Setup dialog box.*

• Click **OK** to proceed with the installation.

The next dialog box, shown in Figure A.4, asks you to enter your name and the name of your organization. Enter them (the organization name is optional), and then click **OK**.

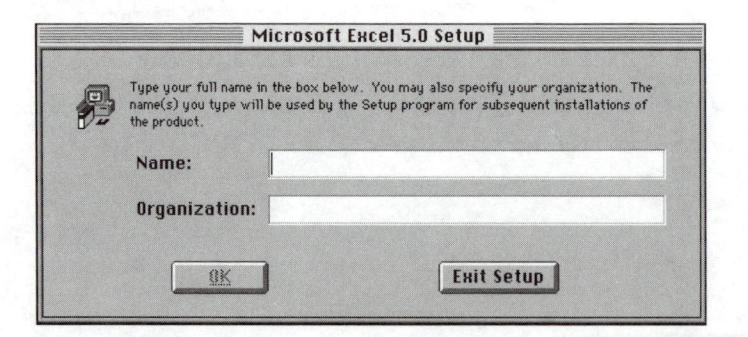

Figure A.4 *The setup dialog for entering your name and company.*

- The next dialog box, shown in Figure A.5, asks you to confirm the data you entered in the previous dialog box. If it is correct, click **OK**. Otherwise, click on the **Change** button and make the corrections.

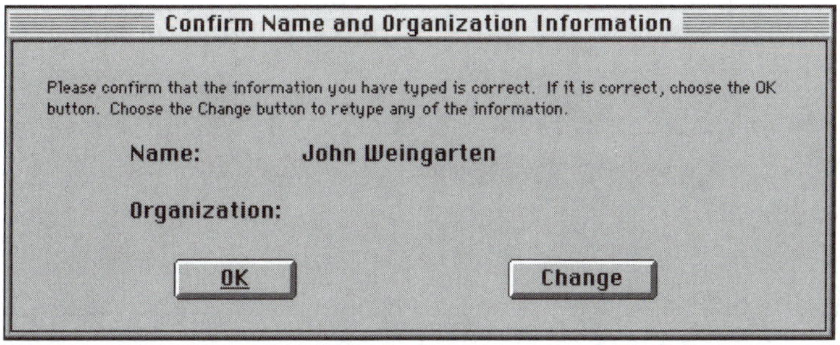

Figure A.5 *The dialog box confirming your name and company.*

Figure A.6 *The setup dialog for selecting the installation folder.*

- The dialog box shown in Figure A.6 asks you to confirm the folder where you want to install Excel. The default is a folder named Microsoft Excel. Unless you have a good reason for choosing another folder, click on the **Setup** button. If you want to change the installation folder, click on the folder name you want to use, or click on the **New Folder** button and specify the name of the new folder.

- You are now presented with a dialog box with three large buttons for specifying the type of installation you want, as shown in Figure A.7.

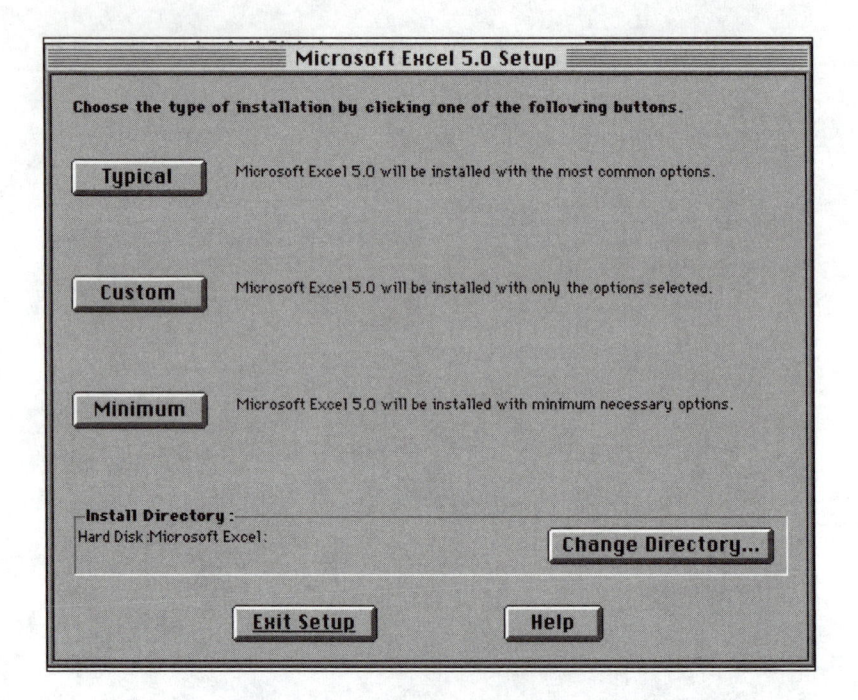

Figure A.7 The Setup dialog box with the three installation choices.

The *Typical* installation option, as the name implies, installs all the essential Excel elements and the most commonly used add-in programs, such as AutoSave and View Manager. If you're not sure what portions of Excel you want to install, this is the choice that makes the most sense.

The *Complete* installation option lets you choose which portions of Excel to install. If you have lots of available hard disk space, you can choose this option. Excel will display the Microsoft Excel 5.0 Custom dialog box, shown in Figure A.8.

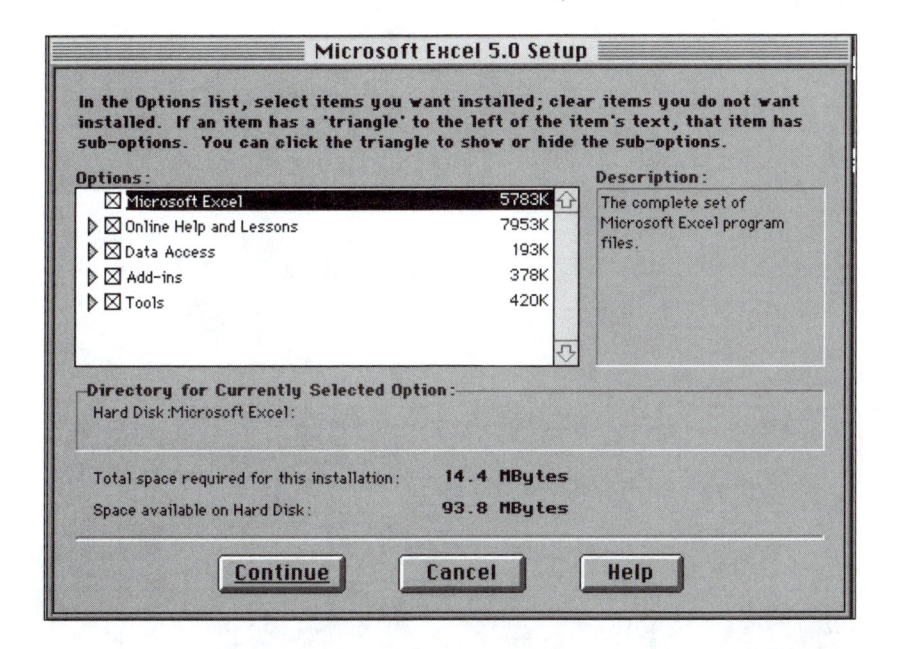

Figure A.8 *The Custom dialog box.*

Notice that the bottom portion of the dialog box tells you how much disk space is required for the portions of Excel you have chosen to install, and how much space is available. If you click on the check box of an option you don't want to install, the number for the amount of space required changes.

You can click on the **Continue** button to install everything, or click in any of the check boxes next to items you don't want to install and then click **Continue**. The one item on the list that you *must* install for Excel to run is Microsoft Excel.

You can also choose which parts of the various programs you want to install. For example, you can click on the triangle next to Add-ins to display a list of available add-ins, and then use their check boxes to specify which add-ins you want installed.

The Minimum option only installs the essential files required for Excel to run. If you are really pressed for disk space, this is the option to choose.

Don't be too concerned about making a mistake when you choose which installation method to use. You can always return to the setup program later and add or remove portions of the program as your requirements change.

Finally, you'll see a dialog box displaying the progress of the installation, as shown in Figure A.9.

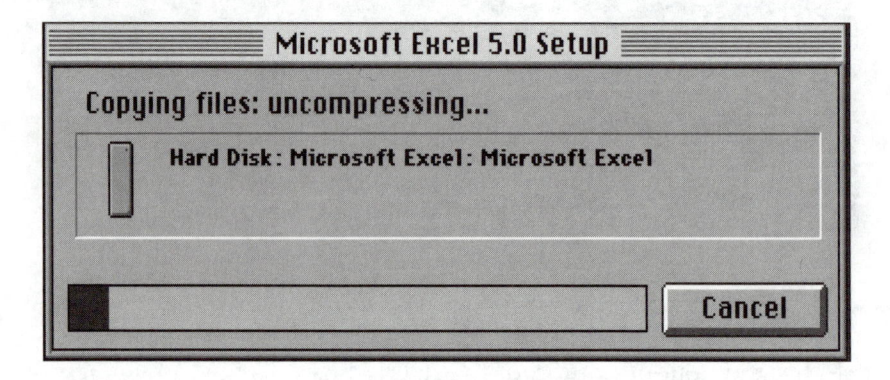

Figure A.9 *The dialog box displaying installation progress.*

Now, just feed the disks into your drive as prompted. When the installation is complete, you'll see the dialog box shown in Figure A.10 telling you that all went well. Just click on the **OK** button to clear the dialog box. That's all there is to it.

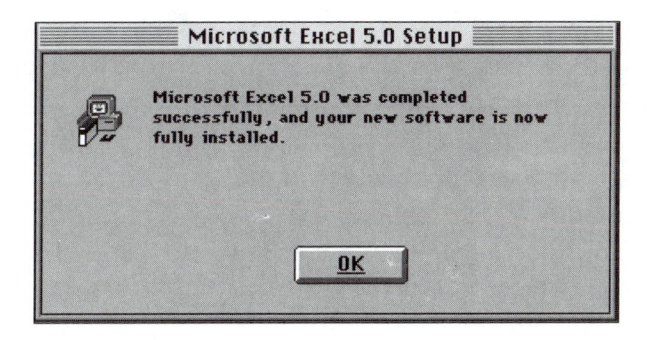

Figure A.10 *The installation is complete.*

Optimizing Excel

The steps you can take to maximize Excel's performance are, for the most part, the same steps that will maximize the performance of most programs. If you have an incredibly fast computer and you are working with relatively small worksheets, you may have no need for optimization. Everything already happens in a flash for you. If, on the other hand, you want any little performance boost you can get, read on.

The first thing to consider how much *RAM* (Random Access Memory) your computer has and how it is configured. Most programs, and Excel is no exception, perform best with lots of memory. While you can get away with 4 MB (megabytes) of RAM, Excel will be much happier with 8. If you don't have enough memory, Excel will be forced to store portions of worksheet data on the hard disk, which, no matter how fast it is, is many times slower than memory.

If your Excel operations are unacceptably slow—and you have the funds—consider upgrading your computer. If you are still working with an older Mac equipped with a 68030 or 68020 processor or older (these numbers refer to the type of main processing chip in the computer), it may be time to upgrade to a fast 68040 machine.

If you can't afford more memory or a faster machine, here are a few tips for making the most of what you have. Don't use large fonts or graphics unless absolutely necessary. These graphic elements will slow you down as you work in Excel. You can always use the Show Placeholder option in the View portion of the Options dialog box to speed up worksheets that require graphics. Also, if calculations are causing you to spend too much time waiting, choose **Manual** from the Calculation portion of the Options dialog box. One more thing to try would be *not* to use wallpaper or screenwalkers or eyes that watch your cursor movement. These use up valuable memory real estate. Also, minimize your desktop.

If you still find the program too slow, just remember how long it took you to perform calculations like these before you had a computer! Don't you feel better now?

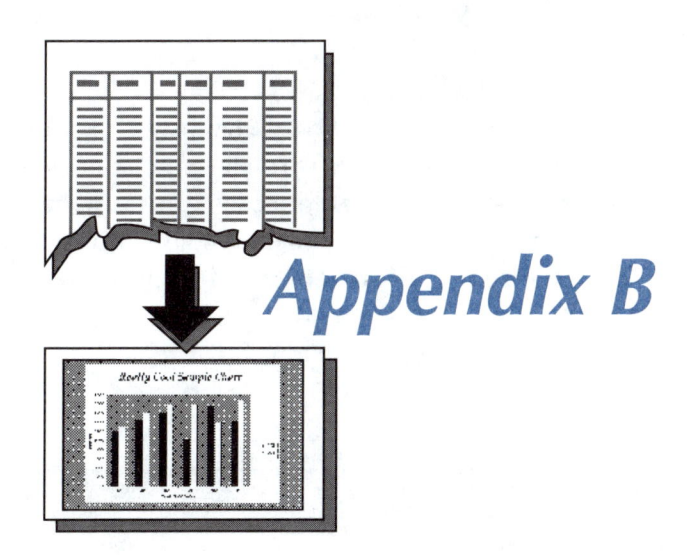

Appendix B

Keyboard Shortcuts

Excel provides keyboard shortcuts for almost everything you can do with the mouse. I concentrated on the mouse actions to accomplish most tasks in the book. However, you'll save time if you use some of the keyboard shortcuts, particularly if you are a touch typist. Some fast typists find that removing their hands from the keyboard to use the mouse slows them down. Using keyboard shortcuts allows you to keep your hands on the keyboard.

This list of keyboard commands is not comprehensive; these are just some of my favorites. You'll find a complete guide to the keyboard commands in Excel's help facility. To view the keyboard commands in help, pull down the Help menu, select **Microsoft Excel Help**, and click on **Reference Information**. Then, in the General Reference portion of the MS Excel Help window, click on **Keyboard Guide** to display the help window shown in Figure B.1.

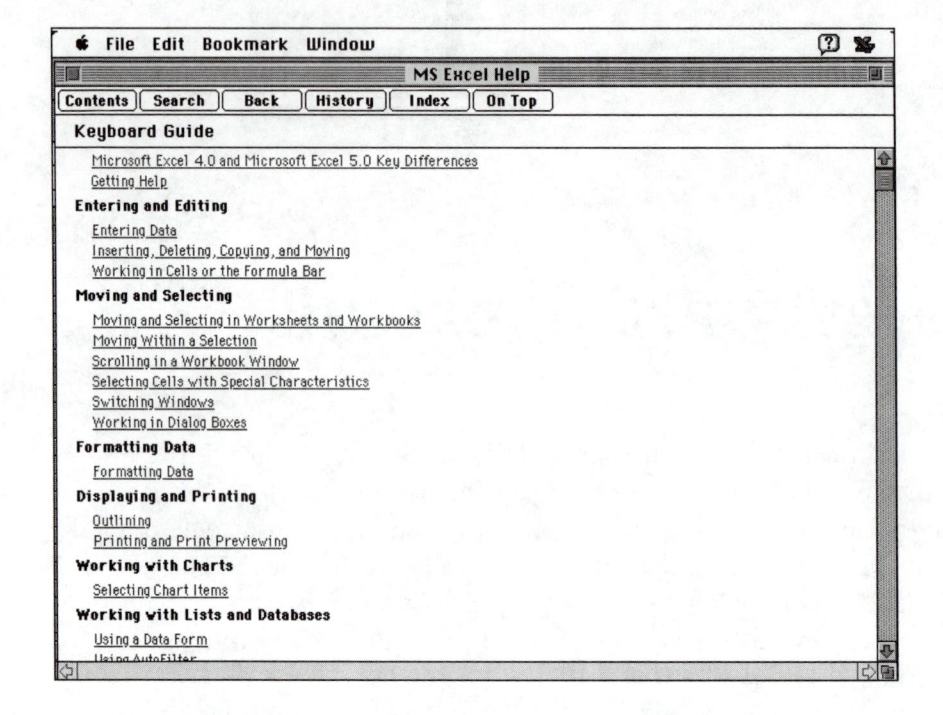

Figure B.1 *The help window for selecting keyboard guides.*

You can click on any of the underlined choices to choose among a variety of keyboard guides in different categories.

Figure B.2 shows Excel's keyboard guide for Inserting, Deleting, Copying, and Moving.

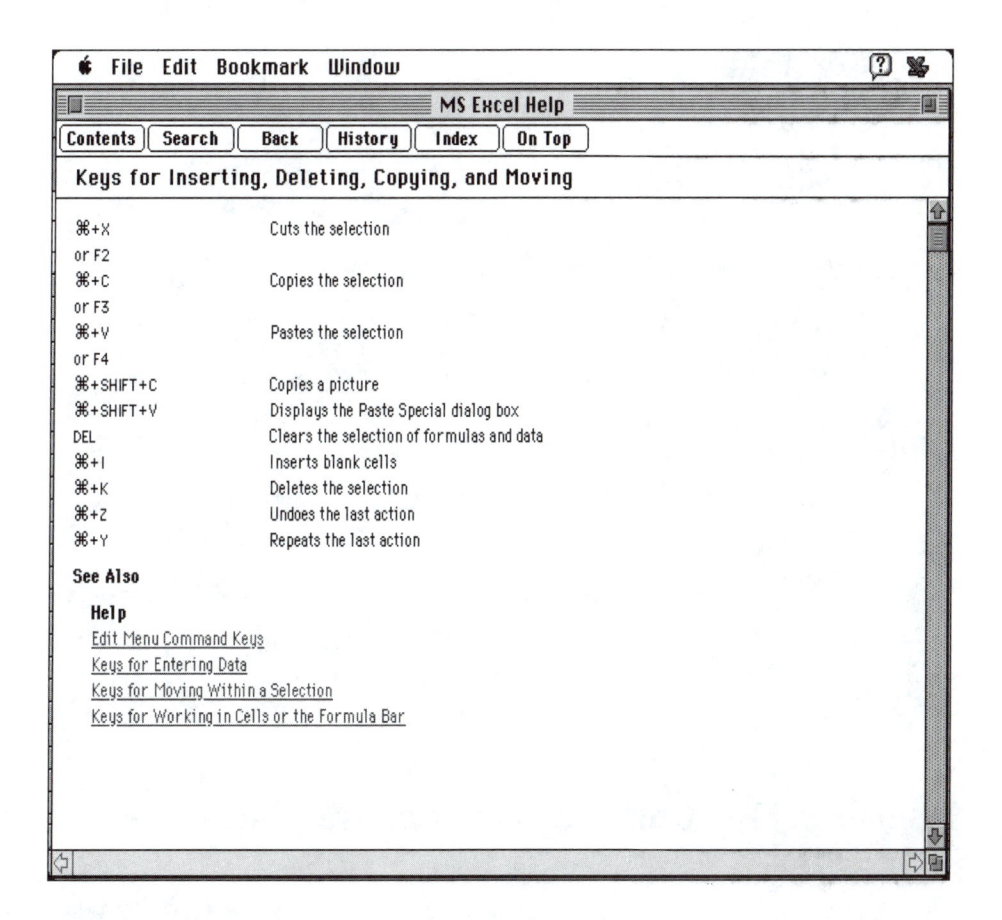

File   Edit   Bookmark   Window

MS Excel Help

Contents | Search | Back | History | Index | On Top

Keys for Inserting, Deleting, Copying, and Moving

⌘+X	Cuts the selection
or F2	
⌘+C	Copies the selection
or F3	
⌘+V	Pastes the selection
or F4	
⌘+SHIFT+C	Copies a picture
⌘+SHIFT+V	Displays the Paste Special dialog box
DEL	Clears the selection of formulas and data
⌘+I	Inserts blank cells
⌘+K	Deletes the selection
⌘+Z	Undoes the last action
⌘+Y	Repeats the last action

See Also

Help
Edit Menu Command Keys
Keys for Entering Data
Keys for Moving Within a Selection
Keys for Working in Cells or the Formula Bar

Figure B.2 *The keyboard guide for Inserting, Deleting, Copying, and Moving.*

Notice that some of the keyboard commands require function keys (F1 through F12) as well as some other special keys not found on the standard keyboard, such as the Home and End keys. These keys are available if you are using an extended keyboard. If you don't have an extended keyboard you'll have to use an alternative keyboard command or perform the task using Excel's menu.

Entering data

TO	PRESS THESE KEYS
Cancel an action	**⌘+Period or Esc**
Repeat an action	**⌘+Y**
Undo an action	**⌘+Z**
Copy selection	**⌘+C**
Edit a cell note	**⌘+Shift+N**
Calculate all sheets in workbook	**⌘+=**
Calculate active sheet	**⌘+Shift+Plus Sign**
Insert AutoSum function	**⌘+Shift+T**
Enter date	**⌘+- (Hyphen)**
Enter time	**⌘+; (Semicolon)**

Inserting, Deleting, Copying and Moving

TO	PRESS THESE KEYS
Cut selection	**⌘+X**
Copy selection	**⌘+C**
Paste selection	**⌘+V**
Clear selection contents	**Delete**
Undo last action	**⌘+Z**

Moving and Selecting

TO	PRESS THESE KEYS
Extend selection one cell	Shift+Arrow key
Extend selection to end of current data region	⌘+Shift+Arrow key
Move up or down to edge of current data region	⌘+Up Arrow key or ⌘+Down Arrow key
Move left or right to edge of current data region	⌘+Left Arrow key or ⌘+Right Arrow key
Select entire column	⌘+Spacebar
Select entire row	Shift+Spacebar
Select entire worksheet	⌘+A

Moving Within a Selection

TO	PRESS THESE KEYS
Move down	Enter
Move up	Shift+Enter
Move left to right	Tab
Move right to left	Shift+Tab
Collapse selection to active cell	Shift+Delete

Formatting Data

TO	PRESS THESE KEYS
Apply General number format	**Ctrl+Shift+~**
Apply Currency format	**Ctrl+Shift+$**
Apply Percent format	**Ctrl+Shift+%**
Apply Date format (Day-Month-Year)	**Ctrl+Shift+#**
Apply two decimal place format with commas	**Ctrl+Shift+!**
Apply plain text	**⌘+Shift+P**
Apply or remove bold	**⌘+Shift+B**
Apply or remove italic	**⌘+Shift+I**
Apply or remove underline	**⌘+Shift+U**
Hide rows	**Ctrl+9**
Unhide rows	**Ctrl+Shift+(**
Hide columns	**Ctrl+0 (zero)**
Unhide columns	**Ctrl+Shift+)**

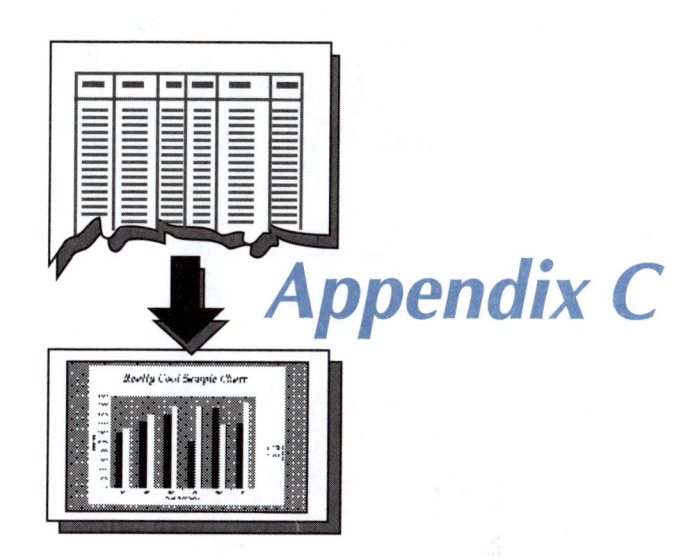

Appendix C

Toolbar Reference

Here are all the toolbars included with Excel. Each button is labeled with its tooltip. Don't forget that you can create your own custom toolbars using these and many other buttons available in the Customize dialog box.

The Standard Toolbar

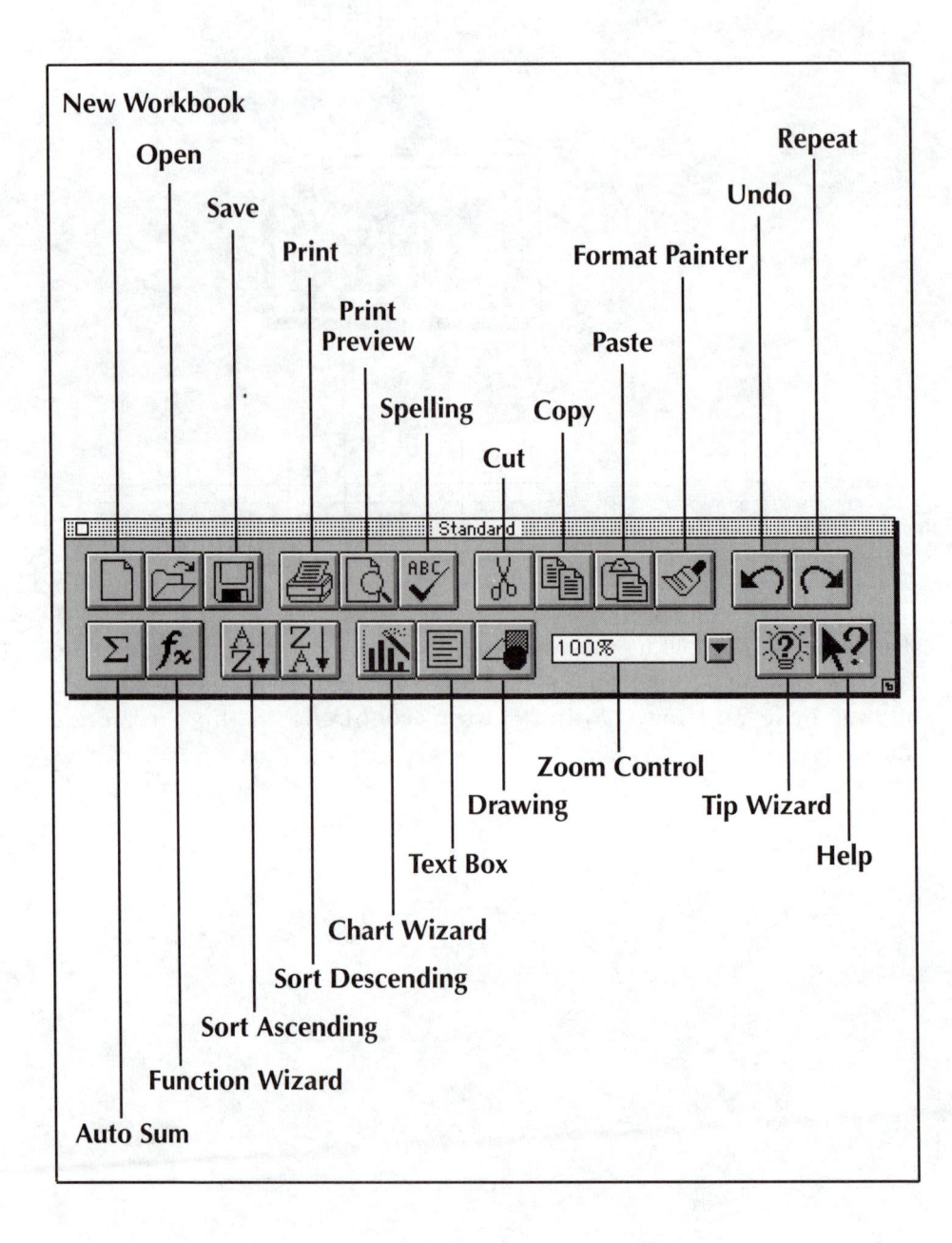

The Formatting Toolbar

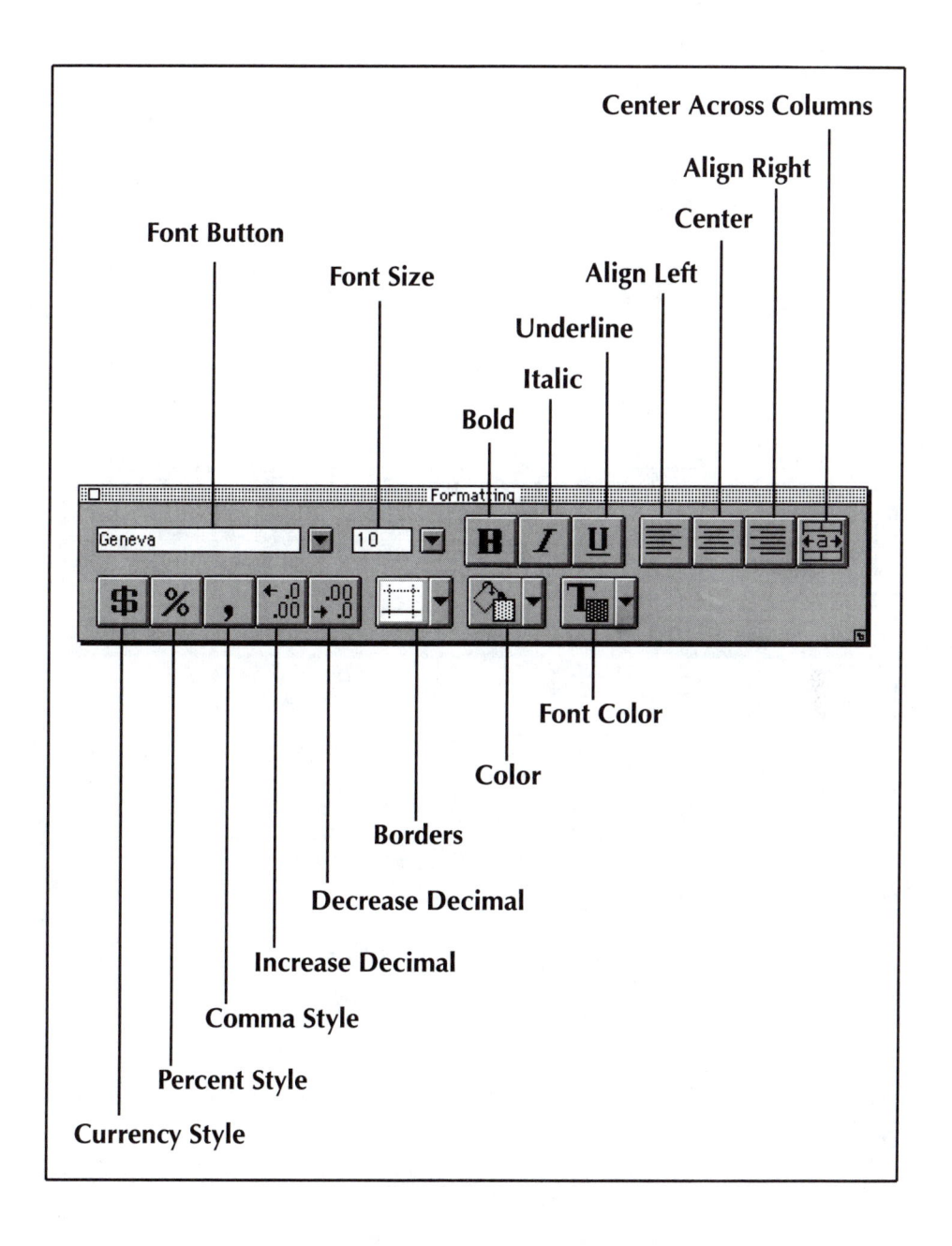

The Drawing Toolbar

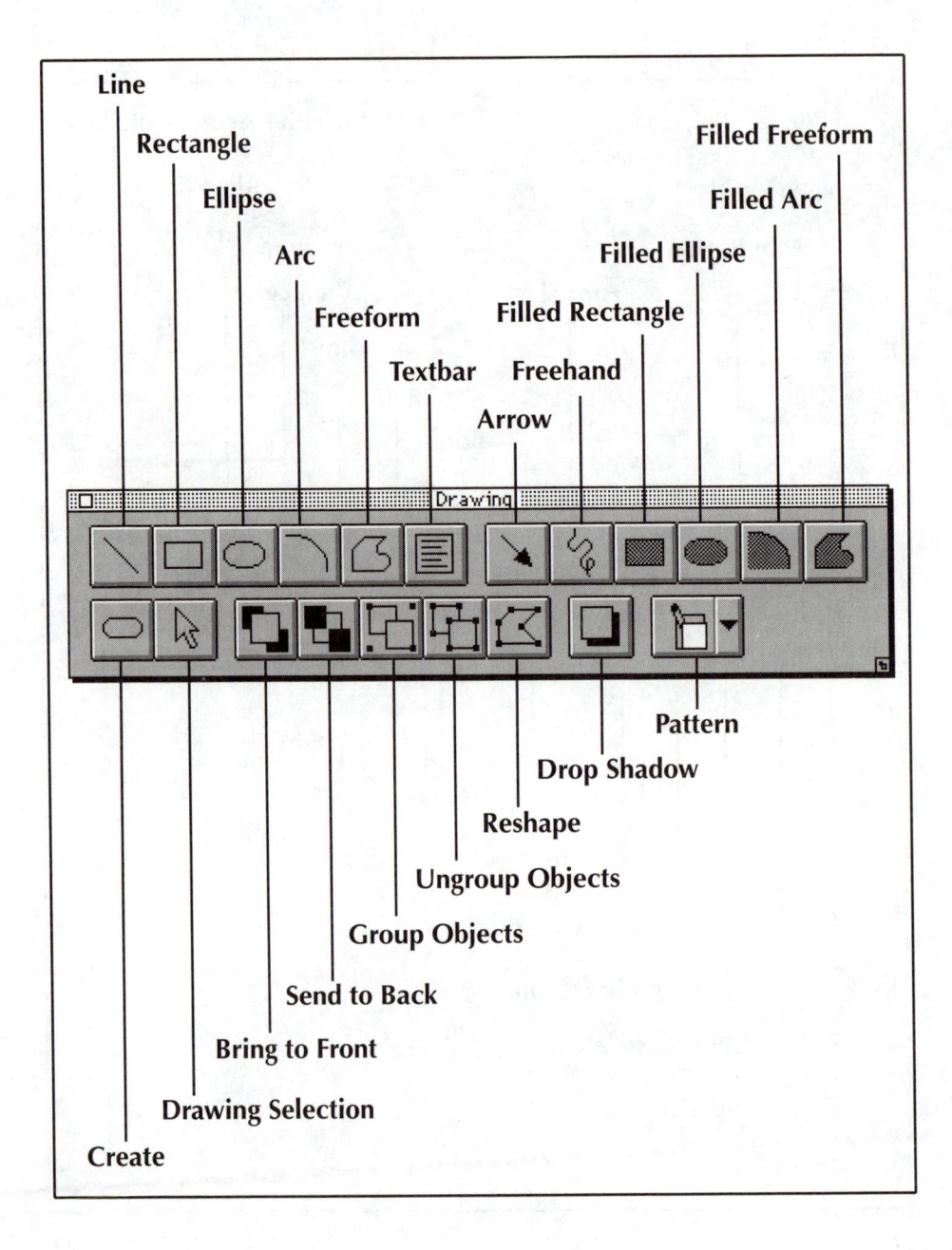

The Forms Toolbar

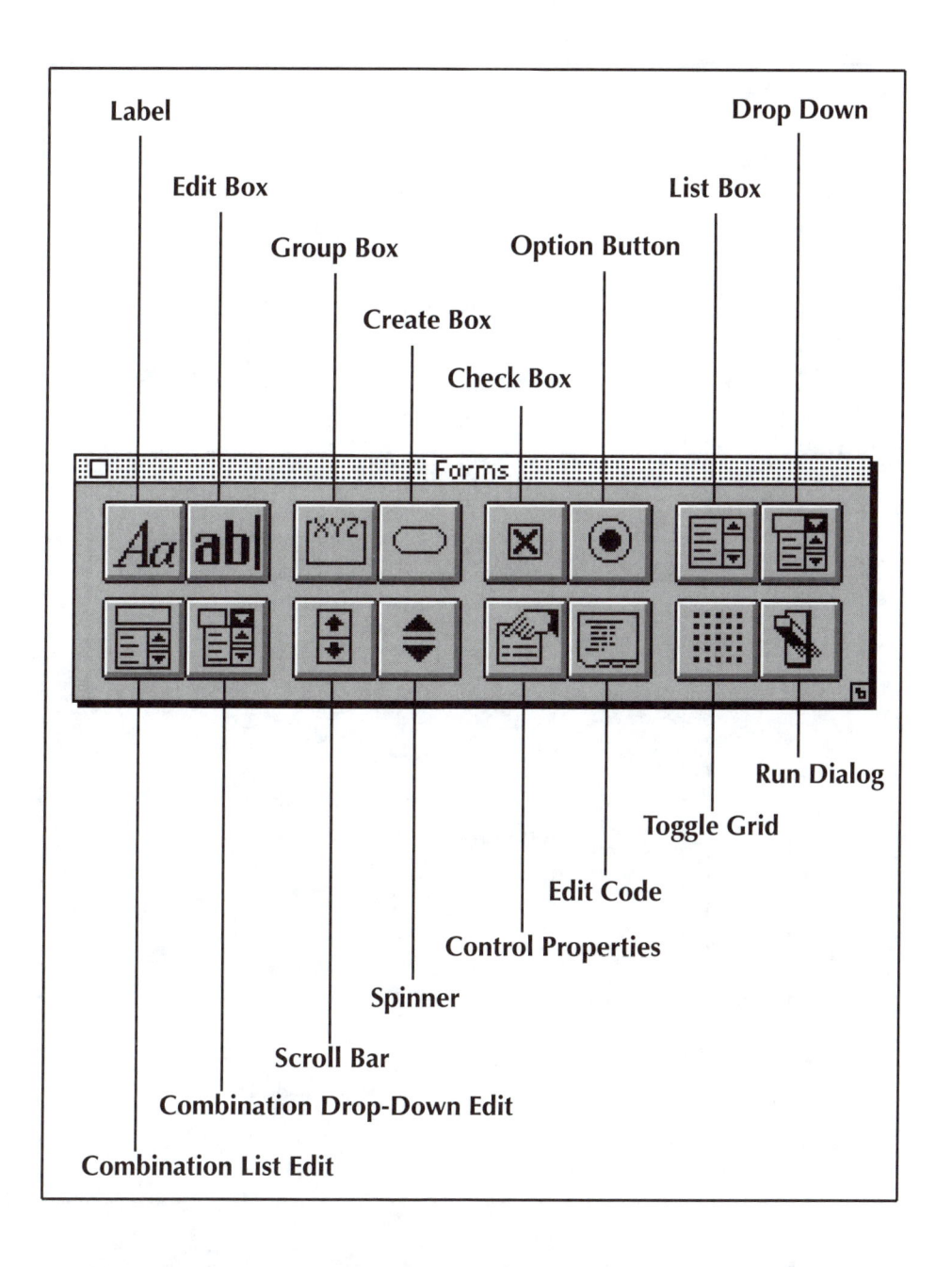

The Visual Basic Toolbar

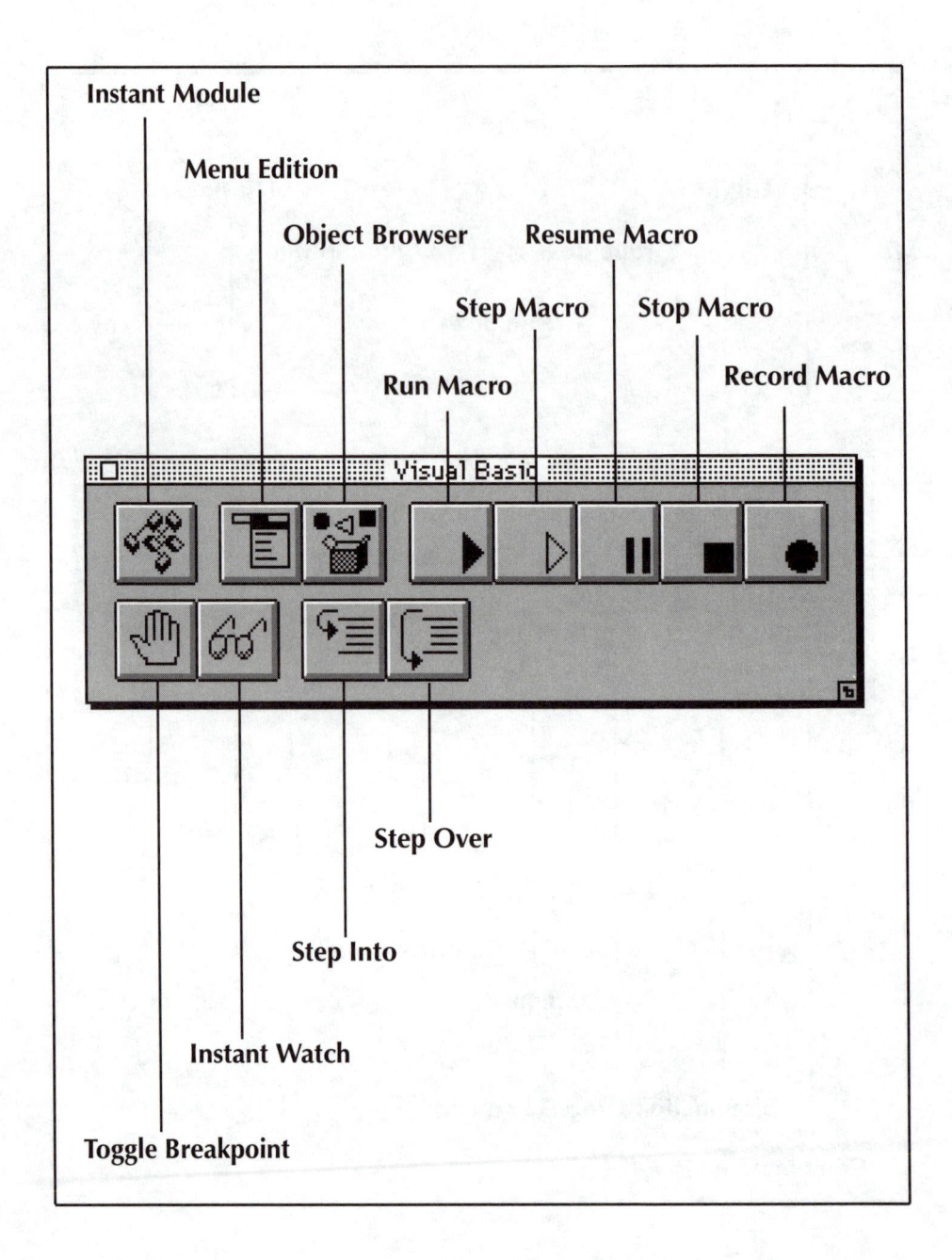

The Auditing Toolbar

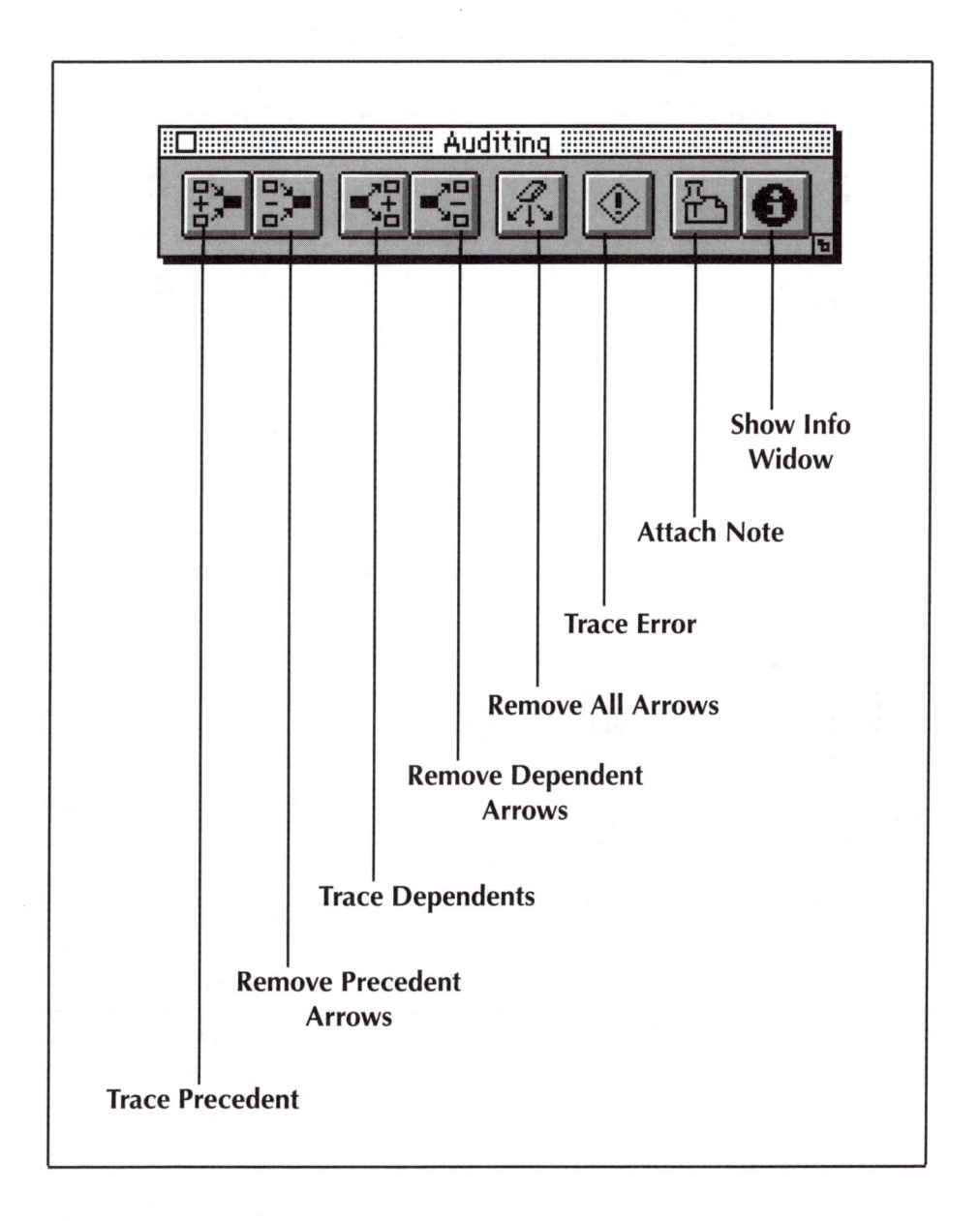

Show Info
Widow

Attach Note

Trace Error

Remove All Arrows

Remove Dependent
Arrows

Trace Dependents

Remove Precedent
Arrows

Trace Precedent

The Query and Pivot Toolbar

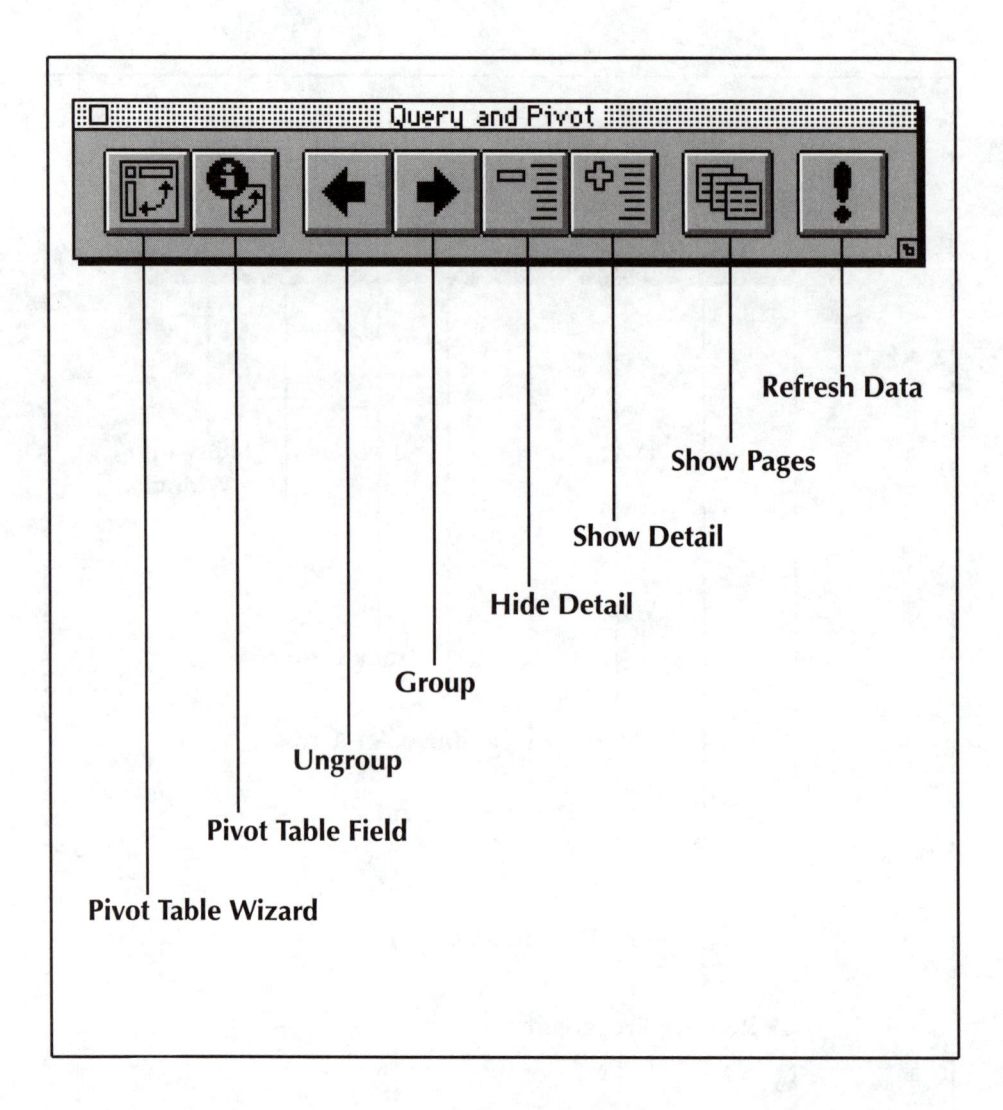

The Chart Toolbar

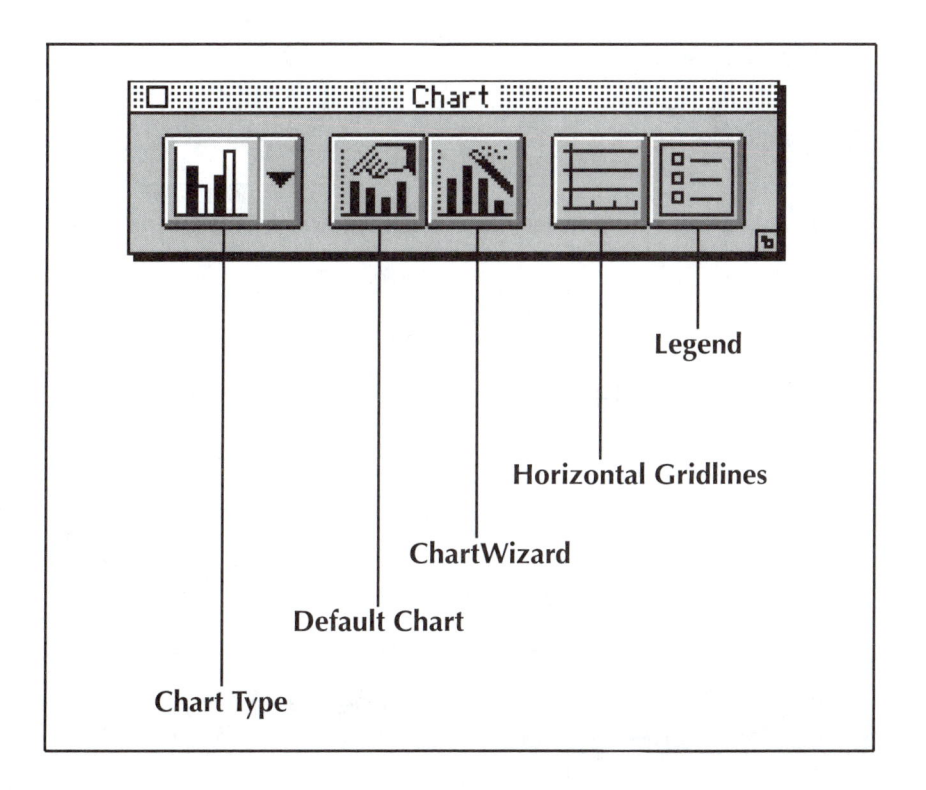

The Stop Recording Toolbar

The WorkGroup Toolbar

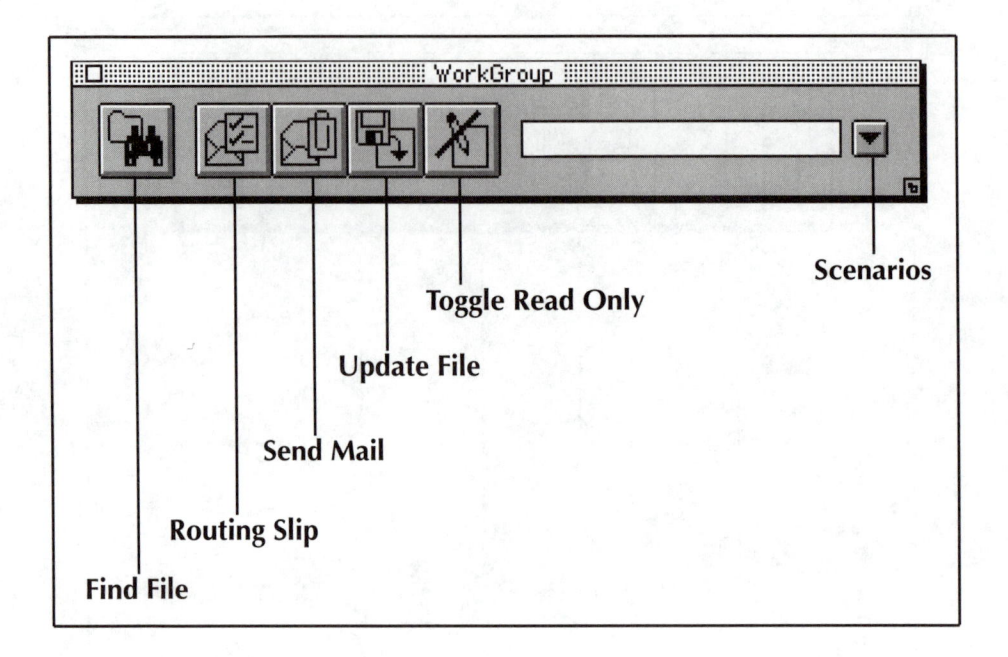

Scenarios

Toggle Read Only

Update File

Send Mail

Routing Slip

Find File

The Full Screen Toolbar

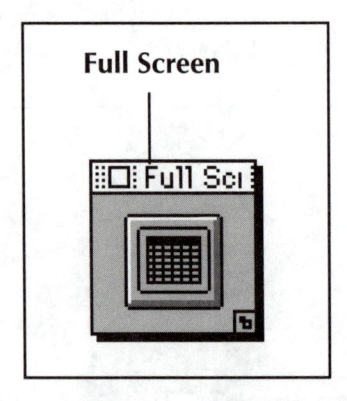

Full Screen

The Microsoft Toolbar

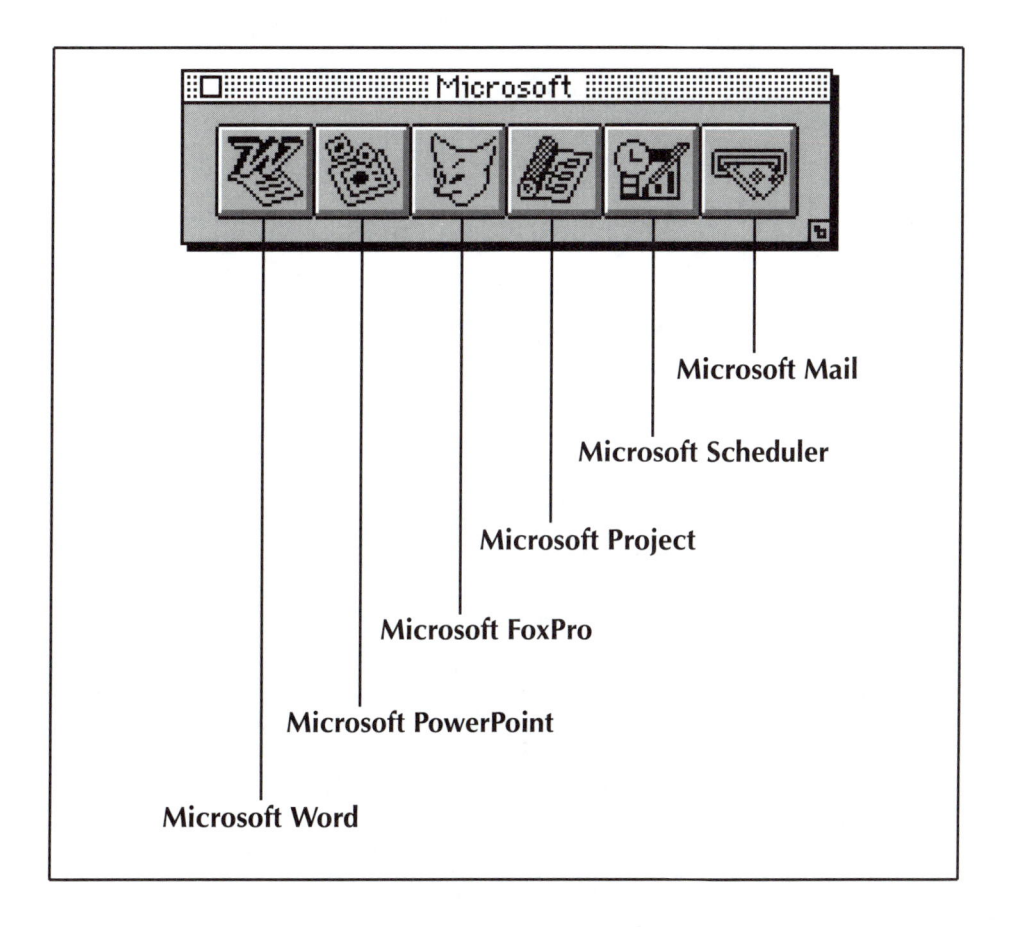

Glossary

active cell

    The worksheet cell that is currently selected.

cell formatting

    Appearance changes applied to cells, such as alignment, fonts, and borders.

cell

    The rectangular area on a worksheet that is the intersection of a column and a row.

close box

    The box in the upper-left corner of a window you can click on to close the window.

comparison operators

Symbols used to compare values, such as > (greater than), = (equal to), etc.

comparison criteria

A set of search conditions used to find the data you're looking for in a list or database.

data series

A group of related data points that are plotted in a chart.

data point

A piece of data that is represented in a chart.

default

Settings that are preset. Excel comes with default settings for many options, such as column width. Most defaults can be changed.

dependent worksheet

A worksheet that uses linked data from one or more source worksheets.

field name

The label in the first row of an Excel database list used to name the fields.

field

A category of information in a database list. A column in an Excel database is a field.

fill handle

The handle in the lower-right corner of the active cell or selection used for moving, copying, and filling data from the cell or selection into other cells.

folder

An icon that looks like a file folder into which you can place other icons representing documents, programs, or even other folders.

function

A predefined formula used to calculate a result for a cell or range of cells.

header row

The first row in an Excel database containing labels for the field names.

hotkeys

The keys used to initiate a command. The sequence of underlined menu letters are hotkeys.

icon

A pictorial representation of an object or element. Excel is started from an icon; the toolbar buttons are icons.

insertion point

The flashing vertical line indicating where text is inserted. The insertion point is sometimes called a cursor.

link

A reference between two worksheets. Useful for summarizing or consolidating data from multiple worksheets or work books.

macro

A series of actions that has been recorded, or programmed, and named, which can be executed by running (playing) the macro. An Excel macro is really a small program within Excel.

mouse

> A hand-held pointing device that you move across your desktop to control the on-screen pointer.

name list

> The list of names assigned to cells or ranges of cells on the worksheet. The name list is opened from the name box on the left side of the formula bar.

Personal Macro Workbook

> A workbook for storing macros that you want to have available all the time. The Personal Macro Workbook is usually hidden, but is always opened when you start Excel.

point

> A size measurement, usually referring to font size. One point is approximately 1/72 of an inch.

program

> A sequence of instructions that can be run by a computer. Excel is a program.

proportional fonts

> Fonts with variable-width characters. Proportional fonts usually look more professional than monospaced fonts, in which each character occupies the same width.

pull-down menus

> A list of commands opened by choosing its name from the menu bar.

record

> A collection of fields pertaining to one database entry.

relative reference

A cell reference that determines its position relative to the starting location. Relative referencing allows formulas to work properly, even when they are copied to other areas of the worksheet.

scroll bars

Devices used for navigating vertically and horizontally in a window. Vertical scroll bars are usually on the right side of the window. Horizontal scroll bars are usually on the bottom.

shortcut menu

A list of commands that is relevant to a particular area of the screen. Shortcut menus are opened by holding down the **Ctrl** key while pressing the mouse button.

size box

The box in the lower-right corner of a window you can drag to resize the window.

sort key

The field used as the basis for a database sort. Up to three sort keys can be used at one time in an Excel sort.

source worksheet

A worksheet with linked cells or ranges that provide variable information to the dependent worksheet.

toolbar

A palette of buttons you can click to perform specific tasks.

tool tip

A short description of a toolbar button that appears just below the mouse pointer when it is on a toolbar button.

user interface

The kind of menus, dialog boxes and other elements used to interact with the program. The Macintosh provides a graphical user interface because it incorporates many graphical elements for your interaction.

VBA

Visual Basic for Applications. This is the primary programming language used for Excel macros.

workbook

A collection of sheets (worksheets, chart sheets, etc.) that is saved with one file name. A workbook can contain up to 255 sheets.

x-axis

The horizontal plane of a chart. Sometimes called the category axis.

y-axis

The vertical plane of a chart. Sometimes called the value axis.

zoom box

A box in the upper-right corner of a window, used to enlarge or shrink the window.

Index